A. H. Winton

The Story of Lackawanna County

AILEEN SALLOM FREEMAN

FOSi
Ltd

CREDITS

Editorial: Richard Freeman
Murray Freeman
Alice McWilliams Sallom

FICTION

This is a fictionalized account of
the erection of Lackawanna County, Pennsylvania.
The people, events and places described in
this story are real and some of the conversations
were transcribed at the time they occurred,
but because not all of them were, this
story must be categorized as fiction.
Originally published in hardcover
form without pictures in 1979.
Excerpts appeared in
The Scranton Times in August 1978
with permission from the author.

FIRST ILLUSTRATED EDITION
August 1997

Library of Congress Card Catalog Number: 97-60452

Published by FOSI, Ltd.
Paupack, Pennsylvania 18451-0184

Manufactured in the United States of America

ISBN 0-9644199-4-7

ACKNOWLEDGMENTS

The Scrapbook - Vol. I and Vol. II of A. H. Winton,
compiled by him;
Lackawanna Historical Society;
Wyoming Historical and Geological Society;
The Pennsylvania Historical Society, at Philadelphia;
Wayne County Historical Society.

ILLUSTRATIONS:

Lackawanna Historical Society;
City Atlas of Scranton, Pennsylvania
C. M. Hopkins, C.E., Philadelphia, 1877;
A Half Century in Scranton
Benjamin H. Throop, M.D., Scranton, 1895;
Memorial of the Erection of Lackawanna County
Robert H. McKune, Scranton, 1882;
Prominent Men
Dwight J. Stoddard, Scranton, 1906;
The Story of Scranton
John Beck, Northridge, CA, 1986;
The Wyoming Valley
J. A. Clark, Scranton, 1875;
Goble Dean;
John T. Whitmore, M.D.;
Author's collection.

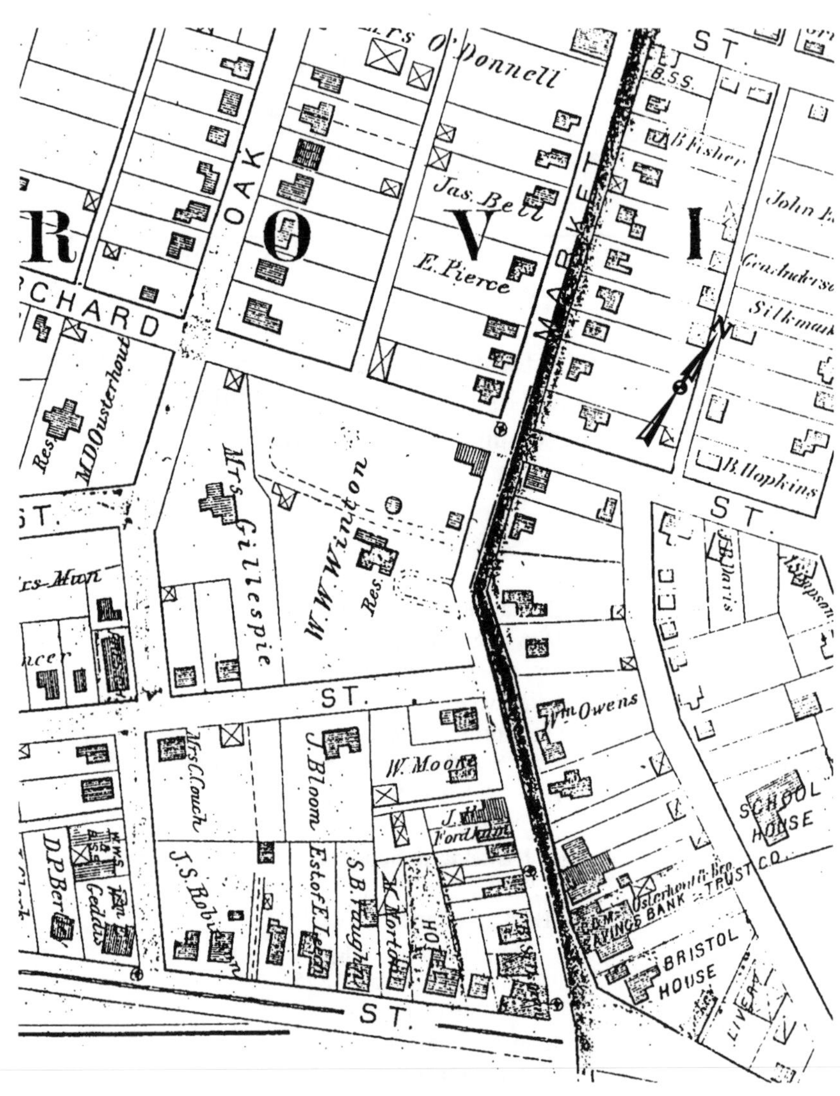

PROVIDENCE SECTION OF
SCRANTON CITY
CIRCA 1878

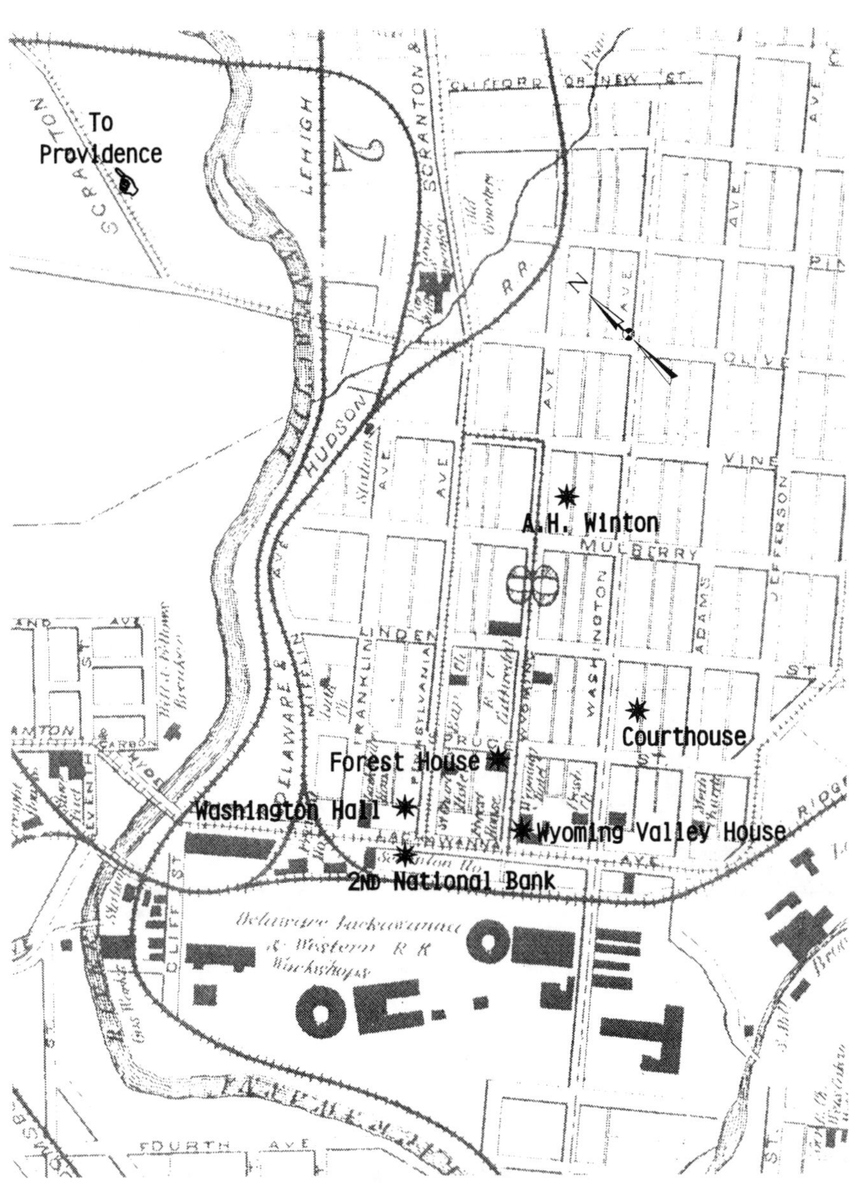

SCRANTON, PENNSYLVANIA CIRCA 1878

LUZERNE COUNTY - erected 1786,
LACKAWANNA COUNTY - erected 1878,
PENNSYLVANIA

1

The year was 1863, and Aretus Heermans Winton was smiling as he emerged from the Luzerne County Court House in Wilkes-Barre, Pennsylvania. His smile broadened into a chuckle on remembering his discussion with Joseph Hand Scranton, county clerk. Joe had been very kind to him and had willingly filled in the license as the twenty-four-year-old lawyer had requested. Never again would he have to hear "Aretus," anywhere; he was "A.H." His father was known as W. W. Winton and, God willing, his would equal the respect his father had earned in the valley. And he would be known as A. H. Winton.

The war was raging some three hundred miles to the south. The broad pleasant valley known as Wyoming would escape the conflict this time, which was unusual because some of the bloodiest fighting of the Revolutionary War had taken place in this very area. In all of northeastern Pennsylvania there was nothing like the Wyoming Valley. A flat broad expanse some five miles wide, running in an east-west direction for almost fifty miles, it was an idyllic earthly paradise, especially when the sun shone down from an afternoon sky. It was surrounded by the strong, tall mountains encircling the valley, not hemming it in, but giving a sense of security, strength, and peace to its inhabitants. The mountains were hard, rugged, and individualistic, but never cruel, to the people they protected.

Just how hard they were, the residents of the valley had been finding out. For almost fifty years before A.H. paid $10.00 to be legally licensed as a lawyer, the mountains had been giving up their treasure of hard anthracite coal. At first, it had been a trickle, slowly drifting toward New York city aboard the canal boats along the Delaware and Hudson Canal towards Rondout, New York. But now, at war, the North needed all the energy and fuel it could get. And northeastern Pennsylvania had that fuel.

The valley had originally been home to the Indian tribes that constituted the Six Nations, the great Iroquois Confederation founded by the legendary Hiawatha: the Senecas, the Mohawks, the Onondagas, the Oneidas, the Cayugas, and later the Tuscaroras. Towards the end of this era, before the area was dominated entirely by the white man, driving the Indians north and west into Canada, the displaced Delawares had also affiliated themselves with the Six Nations. As the white man had spread out from the Atlantic coastline, moving steadily inland, the Indians had retreated, consolidating themselves within isolated areas. Northeastern Pennsylvania had been one such pocket. But even that was eventually lost to the Indians, for slowly, family by family, white settlers with the pioneering spirit said "good-bye" to their families in Connecticut and Rhode Island, and moved west. By 1776, there were over two thousand inhabitants scattered throughout all of the Wyoming Valley.

A.H. was anxious to return home to Providence, some fifteen miles northeast of Wilkes-Barre and adjacent to Scranton. Descending from the County Court House steps, he smiled at young law clerk John B. Collings as he passed him on his way to the train stop. Collings was an apt student, interested in his subject, and had talked with A.H. from time to time in the Court House.

John Collings "hallooed" him, and asked why he was in Wilkes-Barre on such a cold day.

A.H. waved his license for John Collings to see.

"This calls for a celebration," the other replied, and A.H. found himself propelled along the street to the Collings's home. Inside, he was introduced to one of John's sisters, Alice Collings. When she smiled "Hello," A.H. made up his mind then and there; however, it wasn't until 1865, two years later, that he was able to persuade her to say yes.

With their union, the saga of an American family, and its contribution to the growth of America, began.

* * *

Through a land grant of 1620 from Charles I to the Duke of Lenox, the Earl of Warwick and others, reconfirmed forty-two years later by Charles II; and then through a separate land grant in 1681 by the same Charles II to William Penn, a conflict as to the intended ownership of the Wyoming Valley arose among the colonists in the New World. The early settlers of both Connecticut and Pennsylvania felt that they and they alone had the exclusive rights to that northern quarter strip of Pennsylvania.

In actuality, however, far more New Englanders came into the Wyoming Valley to settle than Pennsylvanians. To understand this, one must have a clear picture of the topography of the land and how the arrangement of mountain chains favored east-west travel over any north-south movement.

North of the Blue Ridge (Chestnut Ridge) that travels almost due east and west just above Easton, Bethlehem, and Allentown, the section of the Appalachian Mountains in northeastern Pennsylvania angles gently from north-east to southwest. The young, aggressive fourth generation of New England settlers were anxious to spread their wings. With a whole vast continent beckoning to them, they were quick to answer the challenge. Traveling was easy for them when they stayed in the valleys; and eventually they arrived at the largest and most pleasant of all the valleys, Wyoming, first sighted about fifty miles west of the Delaware River. Today's Interstate 84 highway follows pretty much the same route as the early settlers took. In a little over two hours one can now travel by car from New London, Connecticut, to Scranton.

The Pennsylvanians, on the other hand, had a much harder course to follow to settle the northern lands. The Blue Ridge was a barrier, both physically and psychologically. Access to the north could be gained only through a few peepholes such as Wind Gap, Little Gap, and the much larger Delaware Water Gap. Further west, the Susquehanna River itself provided a path through the mountains, but to follow its twists and turns was time-consuming.

Those who pushed north along the Delaware River through the Delaware Water Gap were prone to settle by the river's bank rather than add another westward leg of almost fifty miles to their journey. The settlements in Wayne and Pike Counties in Pennsylvania, Sussex and Warren Counties in New Jersey, and those in Orange County, New York, were more advanced because of their direct river link with the cities to the south (Easton, Trenton, Philadelphia) than were the communities in the interior of Pennsylvania.

The only other water passage opened to the Pennsylvanians was the Susquehanna River north. This a few followed, mostly Presbyterians of Scottish-Irish and German backgrounds.

The settlers who arrived in the Wyoming Valley in 1769 were forty in number. They had been early subscribers to The Susquehanna Company of Connecticut's 1762 offer of land in the interior. The very first subscribers of The Susquehanna Company, about two hundred in number, had taken possession of their new land at the time of the offer, 1762. Outside of a few Moravian missionaries who had come into the area solely to Christianize the Indians, the settlers of 1762 were the first white people there. The Indians soon made short work of their grand plans. Before any permanent buildings could be erected, the Indians had either killed or driven the newcomers off their land.

So for a period of almost seven years, things were at a standstill, the Iroquois continuing to dominate the Pocono Mountain area. Then, in 1769, this small group of forty gathered courage, and once again the white man reached the banks of the Susquehanna River in the Wyoming Valley, in the Wilkes-Barre area. They, and all that followed them, were young people of solid, middle-class families in Rhode Island and Connecticut. Almost any of them could claim as parent a minister or a church deacon. Among the settlers of the Wyoming Valley, there was no "reject" from the towns and cities along the Atlantic coast; no one a proven misfit, sent by his community to rid itself of an undesirable citizen, nor any "get-rich-quick" opportunist; there were only young eager lives respectful of God, and thankful for the broad pleasant sunlit valley in which to grow their crops of rye and wheat and new delicious-tasting apples.

One such young man, who came in 1772 from Lebanon County, Connecticut, was Elisha Blackman. He was accompanied by his father, also Elisha, his mother Lucy, his brothers Ichabod and Eleazer, and his sisters Lucy and Lovinia. The youngest Blackman child, Eleazer, was seven, and the oldest, Lucy, was seventeen, when they had their first glimpse of the Wyoming Valley. It was a beautiful sight to them after the days of travel from Connecticut; and as with all first loves, the love for this particular land remained stronger in them than all the hardships they would have to endure.

The father and his sons (little Eleazer helping, too) soon staked out a farm close to and south of the area's protecting fort, Forty Fort. Then they quickly set about constructing a log house large enough to accommodate themselves. For a total of six years they were to clear and plough the land, rejoice in the panoramic display of color from the surrounding mountains in the fall, and sing a song of joy in the spring as the cold winter snows were melting away. They were also to celebrate one of the first marriages in the valley, after pretty Lovinia Blackman had caught the eye of Darius Spafford, a blacksmith.

There was also constant danger. Neither the father nor his two older sons would venture out into the fields without a musket, for fear of marauding Indians. The French and Indian War had been over for ten years when Elisha and his family arrived in the Wyoming Valley, but there was still a small remnant of Indians who refused to settle down to a peaceful coexistence. On a less violent scale, nevertheless best described as warfare, the Blackmans had to remain constantly on the alert to protect their property and boundary lines from marauding "Pennsylvanians" as well. Leaving their farm for more than a few hours, since first laying claim to the land, was unthinkable. They had on several occasions surprised their Pennsvlvanian neighbors moving field markers as much as 300 feet.

It was a hot day, this August first of 1775. Elisha Blackman, the father, had just come from the garden with a sackful of tender, tiny, freshly picked ears of corn. His hand was on the door when a deafening rumble and thunder broke the silence of the hot summer day.

"Ma, hand me my gun. They just sounded the cannon at the fort!"

The two older boys, Elisha, Jr. and Ichabod, came bursting out of the house. They joined their father, and together they raced for the fort.

Forty Fort, the fort was called. It had been built five years earlier, in 1770, on the west bank of the Susquehanna River, almost two miles due north of Wilkes-Barre and across the Susquehanna from that growing town. It was the largest and most prominent of all forts in the whole northeast of Pennsylvania; by reputation, Forty Fort could accommodate a thousand inhabitants!

The three Blackmans hurried into the fort, and joined with the other three hundred residents of the area, in wondering what the summons was about. When the fort had been built, only one cannon was available, and it had been decided to use it for warning signals rather than for any actual fighting. On hearing it, everyone was to hasten immediately to the fort. There had been rumors of attacking Indians in the previous weeks of July 1775, and everyone was chattering, excitedly questioning the summons.

A stranger mounted on a horse separated himself from the shadows and called out a greeting. "Men of Forty Fort, I bring you news. Three and a half months ago there was a battle at Lexington, ten miles outside of Boston! It was between us colonists and the soldiers of our King! Then, two months after that, on the nineteenth of June, there was a larger battle at Bunker Hill. As a result, the King's soldiers are occupying the great city of Boston, taking and doing as they please!"

The courier paused to allow full appreciation of his message. His face was tired and drawn. The dust and travel stains on the stranger's outfit were apparent to Blackman as he stood there with his sons, listening. The rider's horse stood silently, as if fearing to so much as twitch a muscle lest it remind the man on his back to give the command to move, they, man and beast, having done so much traveling in the past few days.

The courier continued, "I have been dispatched by the Second Continental Congress meeting now, today, in Philadelphia, as a special courier to bring news to you, to acquaint you with the details and to take your decision back to the delegates at Philadelphia."

There was complete silence now and the courier lowered his voice to a more conversational tone, "On May tenth, the Continental Congress convened its second session at the State House on Chestnut Street in Philadelphia. Its first action was to protest the battle at Lexington and to assess the significance of our losses there. Then they set about creating an army, the Continental Army, and guided mainly by John Adams from Boston, appointed the Virginia delegate George Washington as the army's commander in chief.

"When I left Philadelphia, General Washington had already departed for Massachusetts, and when I passed through [Port Jervis] over a week ago, I heard a rumor that General Washington had taken command of our forces outside of Boston, and had driven the British out!"

Once again he paused, this time waiting for the cheers to subside, and concluded. "My question to you is: will you fight or not?"

The speaker had risen in his saddle and was standing in his stirrups. His voice was ringing out as a challenge, not as a question.

Stunned, in silence, the assembled men stared back at their speaker. His cold eyes roved over the men, daring them, assessing them. As he slowly sank back into his saddle, murmuring began among his audience. Then, in turn, the murmurs swelled to a single cry, "We'll fight!"

"God's blessing on all of you. It's the right thing to do!"

The courier produced his letter of authorization from the Congress. He described his trip to them: how he had ridden north, following the Delaware, then overland [from Port Jervis], stopping at the small fortifications along the way and acquainting everyone with the situation and what must be done. He had selected that route, he said, because he knew the way was almost entirely free of Indians. Congress had not been sure how the Indians would react to the outbreak of hostilities, and his main task had been to alert the settlers.

When he told those assembled before him what was required of them, namely two companies of their most able-bodied fighting men, there was silence within the fort's walls once again. It had been a good life in the valley, for they had been coping with the known dangers; now a break was to come. At last, it was decided that they could raise the two independent companies needed and dispatch them to join the Continental Army.

The messenger, his mission accomplished, was treated to a good, rib-sticking meal and some potent home-brewed whiskey before departing. He was leaving them to follow the Susquehanna River south to Harrisburg, stopping at every fort large and small along the way to deliver his message, saving the easy journey back along the Lancaster Turnpike for his return trip to Philadelphia.

As soon as their visitor had left, a great discussion arose among the settlers; perhaps they had acted too hastily. There were some present who even expressed vague intentions of remaining loyal to the British crown. It was dusk before they broke up. By then, the settlers had formed themselves into a council, agreed that they had acted rightly, set up an administrative committee, appointed captains for their two volunteer companies, and specified the formation of an irregular force that would remain to protect Forty Fort. The most significant outcome of that August day in 1775, besides their decision to separate from England, was the unity of the Pennsylvanians and the New Englanders. Both parties agreed to forget their land squabbles in the face of the greater danger. A victorious outcome for their common cause was all that mattered.

In the days following, plans and proposals flew thick and fast. Elisha Blackman had been a lieutenant in the Connecticut militia, and was appointed to that rank again. Another settler, William Hooker Smith, was given the rank of captain, and Elisha was designated his lieutenant, in a company to be called the twenty-fourth Connecticut Line. Assigned to protect the fort, they were soon nicknamed the "Old Reformandoes." Elisha's oldest son, Elisha Junior, was enlisted in Captain James Bidlack's Company, which was to represent Wilkes-Barre. The other two boys, Ichabod and Eleazer, were still too young to serve on active duty.

The two volunteer companies, which were to be sent from the Wyoming Valley to join the Continental Forces, were quickly completed. They drilled and marched, preparing for their departure. The best rifles and muskets were brought out to equip the departing troops; this proved to be a mistake, because it left a shortage of arms among the settlers that they were to feel for the three years remaining to them. Ichabod, who was thirteen, drilled without arms, together with the other thirteen- to sixteen-year-olds.

After their troops had departed, the council ordered the building of a secondary fort to the north of Forty Fort. Fort Wintermoot was quickly erected about four miles above, also on the west bank of the Susquehanna. Then life fell into a routine. Drills, scouting parties, sowing and harvesting the fields, and the arrival and dispatching of news made up the daily round of activities in the Wyoming Valley. As the years passed from '75 to '76, and then into '77, there were only a few small skirmishes with the British. In every instance, the enemy's numbers would be greatly augmented by the addition of Indians in a two to one ratio; a party of ten British Rangers would be accompanied by eighteen to twenty Indians and three or four Tories.

At Forty Fort the settlers had two concerns. One was a growing suspicion that those in charge of their advance defense at Fort Wintermoot were not as friendly to the American cause as they should be. The other was a desperate need for additional military aid. They had never received the extra arms requested from the Continental Congress; they worried even more about the failure of their two volunteer companies to return to the area for their defense, as had also been promised. They had written several times to Philadelphia, asking the Congress for military support, but none had ever been assigned.

The growing fear about Fort Wintermoot prompted two families, the Jenkins and the Hardings, to erect another, smaller fort above Wintermoot at the Pittston Ferry bridge. It was hoped this added strength would provide sufficient warning to those at Wintermoot, as well as to anyone considering an attack from the north. The generally held opinion was that an enemy would descend the Susquehanna River from southern New York in the north. The new fort was referred to as Jenkins' Fort.

About the same time that Jenkins' Fort was built, the council voted to strengthen their defenses at Forty Fort itself. Everyone pitched in, lending a hand wherever necessary. Little Eleazer Blackman, now twelve, had his fondest dream come true; he was treated as an equal, and work was apportioned to him. It was his duty, after his father and brothers had felled and stripped the trees, to rope the logs and drive the oxen, dragging the timber back to the fort. There, men would be waiting for the fresh supply of building material. Soon, the improvements were finished. This, then, was the state of affairs by the spring of 1778.

In May of '78, scouts returning to Forty Fort reported signs of activity north along the Susquehanna and into New York, saying they had sighted an occasional British soldier. No one was surprised then when word reached the Wyoming Valley of fighting at Tunkhannock, twenty-five miles north, on the twelfth of June. But the report, on June 30, of a large encampment spread out on the southern bank of Bowman's Creek, ten miles to the north of Forty Fort, brought real concern to the settlers. A patrol confirmed their worst fears; between three and four hundred hostile soldiers, British Provincials or Tory Rangers as they were known locally, and almost seven hundred Indians plus a smaller body of Tories, were camped there.

On July 1, the very heart of Forty Fort's defense was turned and used against it. The gates of Fort Wintermoot were thrown open to the British, and their entire forces came down from Bowman's Creek and established headquarters there. Jenkins' Fort was quickly set ablaze. On July 2, the cannon sounded once again at Forty Fort. This time, all settlers, men, women and children, assembled and prepared to defend. It would have cheered those poor people of the Wyoming Valley, had they known that General Washington and his troops had fought the decisive battle at Monmouth one week earlier (even though the British escaped to New York), for they felt they had been pretty much deserted by the rest of their new country. They had received neither the men nor the arms they had so desperately requested. They needed all the encouragement they could get, for their irregular force under Colonel Zebulon Butler was half the size of the enemy.

On the third of July, 1778, a white flag, demanding surrender, was sent to Forty Fort from the British in control at Fort Wintermoot. Inside Forty Fort there was a hasty meeting, and it was decided that there was no alternative but to reject the demand for surrender; instead, they decided to fight. Around two o'clock in the afternoon, Colonel Butler and his six companies marched out of the fort and headed north towards Fort Wintermoot, young Elisha Junior marching with Captain Bidlack on the right.

When the gates were opened and the six companies marched out northward towards the enemy, one company, Captain Smith's, remained behind. Both Smith and his lieutenant, Elisha Blackman, had advocated the retention of at least one company in the fort, as defense in case of an attack there. Also, these early settlers were realistic, practical people and they knew the superior strength was with the enemy. If the battle should go against the settlers, there ought to be a reserve force, to command and protect the survivors.

The six companies were almost to Fort Wintermoot before they saw their enemy. As Wintermoot, in front of them, burst into flames, the enemy suddenly appeared behind them. Turning, Colonel Zebulon Butler's men commenced fighting at once. It was violent and bloody, but it was a battle. As the larger British force gained the advantage and the men of Forty Fort retreated, the Indians took over, seeming to compete among themselves in doing the most savage and vicious killing.

Up to this point, Elisha Junior had been fighting hard. He was aware that his companions were falling, but he was pleased with his fighting prowess, and that he had been lucky enough to repel every advance. He was proud of the way he had been able to hold his position; then he saw an Indian dismember one of the wounded. Screams and yelling were all around him. The battle was no longer a battle; it had become a massacre—Elisha Junior could never recall exactly how he had reached the river. Once there, he saw that it wasn't safe either; he watched a savage reach out for a head, and scalp the man as he was swimming. In the confusion that followed, Elisha Junior was one of the fortunate eight from his company who escaped.

When evening came, those inside Forty Fort realized the seriousness of their situation. Most of the Indians participating in the battle were Delawares, displaced from the Delaware River valley. Still angry over the notorious Walking Purchase forty-one vears earlier, the sons had been well indoctrinated by the fathers, and the fury, rage, frustration, and humiliation of the older generation were repaid in full by the children. All night long, the butchering of Colonel Butler's fallen and captured men continued. Afterwards, the British admitted that they had paid the Indians for two hundred and twenty-five scalps, adding that the number could have been higher, because in their frenzy and haste, the Indians had overlooked many opportunities to obtain these grisly tokens for redemption.

On July 4, Forty Fort surrendered; the terms were that the inhabitants would be allowed to leave the valley unmolested. Elisha Blackman would accompany the women and children, Captain Smith's Company serving as protection and guide on the long journey. It was agreed that the people in the fort have safe passage to Stroudsburg. The occupants of the fort, the women and children, began the long, long trek backwards that would eventually take them to

Connecticut. At the time they quit the valley, the retreating settlers were almost two thousand in number. It was a hard march; the travelers had commenced their journey with absolutely no preparation. Shoes and clothing were soon to wear out, and for food the travelers were dependent on whatever berries and game they could gather along the way.

On the night of the massacre, young Elisha Junior stayed in the valley. He had plunged into the Susquehanna River while an Indian was busily removing the scalp of a nearby swimmer. Keeping himself under the surface of the water as he swam, Elisha prayed that he would escape detection. He headed for an island in the middle of the river. At length, he reached the island and circled to the far side before coming out of the water onto the shore. The sandy beach, not too wide, ended abruptly at a one- to two-foot-high embankment. Thick willow bushes and other vegetation hung down gracefully over the sand.

Elisha sprinted for the hollow formed by the willow branches as they hung over the embankment. Huddling flat, he again prayed to escape capture. Once, he heard the almost silent dip of oars from a canoe as it approached the island. He could hear the Indians as they beached their canoe and climbed out to prowl the island. He could hear them walking on the higher ground above him. They, however, never saw him. Eventually, he heard the paddles gently break the water's surface again, this time carrying the scouting party back to their celebration. All night, Elisha Junior listened to the Indian yells and dances. Once he even thought he had caught a glimpse of their Queen Esther as she presided over the gory celebration.

Towards morning, Elisha decided to take a chance, for sounds from the battlefield had almost ceased. Lowering himself gently into the Susquehanna, he swam towards the shore on a southwesterly course. He hoped to touch ground as close to Forty Fort as possible. He preferred the proven safety of the river to an attempted run along the river road. Luck was still with him, and he reached the fort undetected. His family was overjoyed to see him, and to know that he was alive.

When the fort opened its gates on the morning of July 4, to admit the British negotiating team, Elisha Junior hid. The terms of surrender made reference only to women and children, and he feared that he would be dragged off and killed if discovered. After the terms of the surrender had been agreed upon, Elisha Senior joined his son. The two Blackmans, father and oldest son, decided that it would be safer to separate from the group and not appear in the line of marchers as they evacuated Forty Fort. Once again, fortune was with the younger Elisha and kind enough to include the senior Blackman. He and his father ran from the fort unseen, and headed for the river hank, where they found a deserted canoe. They quickly appropriated the find, and paddled downstream as fast as they could. When they had come abreast of their home, they turned inshore and beached the canoe.

The house had a stillness and a deserted air to it when they entered. Elisha couldn't believe that his wife had been making bread beside the fireplace just twenty-four hours earlier. Elisha Junior ran through the house, grabbing whatever supplies he could lay his hands on; his night alone under the willows had taught him some firsthand lessons on the art of survival. Fearing that this might never be their home again, the two Blackmans gathered up what little portable wealth they had. Then they went out, rounded up their cattle, and headed south, following the Susquehanna River away from the British and the Indians.

It was almost eight miles to Nanticoke, the last community before leaving the Wyoming Valley. There, with darkness approaching, the Blackman father and son halted and built a fire. They were silent as they went about their chores; Elisha Junior baked a poor imitation of his mother's bread from some flour he had gathered and thrown into a pillowcase.

The two men were uncertain and depressed as they ate their scanty meal. They had agreed to rendezvous with the rest of the family at Stroudsburg, but there were so many uncertainties between to be resolved that they could not relax. Elisha and his son weren't even sure where they were, or even where they stood in relation to the Delaware Water Gap and its town of Stroudsburg. The elder Blackman had the added worry of his wife and children; his conscience kept nagging him to be beside them.

The final note of gloom was sounded by their futile attempt to round up their herd of cattle. Every animal was lost in the surrounding swamp of laurel and rhododendron. In the darkness of early night, it was impossible to find them. But "it is always darkest before the dawn"; while searching for the cows, they came upon a lone cabin. Its occupant, a woodsman, welcomed them and took them in for the night. "It's a good thing you found me," he said. "Cause if'en you don't cross this here Nescapeck the right way, you ain't gonna make it."

In the morning he pointed out a trail to them, and cheered them with the parting words, "You're traveling light. Shouldn't take you more'n two days."

Grimly, the two men hastened into the woods.

After the fort had opened its gates on July 4, and the remaining settlers had started their long march back to Connecticut, the trip had turned into a nightmare for the surviving families, almost equal to the massacre itself. Food was in short supply, and they were never sure that the Indians might not break their word and murder them all as they walked. After five days of travel, the band reached the Wallenpaupack (Paupack) River valley, skirting it high up on the south side. Eleazer Blackman, holding his mother's hand to steady her, looked down occasionally towards the river. Although much smaller than the Wyoming Valley, the Wallenpaupack Valley had a similarity to it that brought a jump to his throat.

"Ma, will we ever see our home again?"

His mother turned a weary face to him. "God will do what is fit for us, son."

"I know, ma, but will we ever see home again?"

"Shame on you! What about your father and Elisha? Don't you care what happens to them?"

Eleazer was starting to become a man. He was as tall as his mother, yet he couldn't make her understand. People lived and died. In his short life, he had become accustomed to seeing someone as an intimate visitor in their home, only to learn one day that he had gone canoeing and would never return. Then, in a few days, another would come into the warmth of their family unit. The cycle would repeat again and again. The transience and migration of people was a common experience to Eleazer; it was all a part of frontier life. And always, no matter how sad or how difficult it was to get along after such a departure, those left behind were always able to manage, carrying out their daily chores until buoyed up by the next visitor.

It was the authority of belonging, the feeling of roots that Eleazer was trying to get across to his mother. If they didn't reunite with his father and brother, they would manage, somehow; he knew that. But where would they manage? He didn't want to exist just anywhere; he wanted to send out roots into a specific spot.

Three days later, as they could see, in the distance, the solemn, majestic break in the mountain barrier that was the Delaware Water Gap, Eleazer came to a decision. He didn't want to leave the mountains … his mountains.

"Ma, I don't want to go any farther. I love this land too much to leave. Please, can't we go home?"

His sisters and brother, Ichabod, looked at him oddly. The baby was making a fuss again, they seemed to be saying. Lucy, his mother, pursed her lips and refused to answer. Now that they were approaching the Delaware Water Gap, she dreaded putting one foot ahead of the other. Suppose Elisha and her son were not there? She had already buried one husband; she didn't have the strength to be a widow with children again. What had sustained her, during the long march through the woods to Stroudsburg, had been the thought that her husband would be there waiting for her. Now that the time had come to know whether he was there, she was hesitant, afraid to find he was not.

The two Elishas, father and son, had made good time. Thev were waiting for the tired and weary refugees when they came straggling into Stroudsburg. "Lucy!" "Mother!" they called, running to meet the new arrivals. The pent-up emotions of all concerned found relief in a burst of tears.

The survivors of the Wyoming massacre were at a point where they could travel in almost any direction. They were on safe ground at last: now there was no fear of Indian attacks. Also, Washington had chased the British into New York City. But with most of their men slaughtered, the women were hesitant about tarrying long in Stroudsburg. Many of them waited only long enough for instructions and financial aid from their relatives in Connecticut. The Blackmans were a whole family, and did not have the problems confronting the others; their difficulty lay in another direction. Eleazer wheedled, whined, coaxed, and badgered the rest of his family into staying in Stroudsburg, at least for a while. He found a receptive audience in his father and oldest brother. Lovinia seemed willing too, possibly because she thought it would hold the memory of Darius in her heart longer. Eleazer did all he could to keep her on his side.

Finally, Elisha temporized. When he heard a party was forming to return to the valley to bury the dead, he sent his son, Elisha Junior, to join them. In three months, the son was back viewing the carnage. The volunteers worked quickly, and soon returned to Stroudsburg. Then, a decision could no longer be put off by the Blackmans. On his son's return, Elisha asked him how he would feel about returning to the valley, after having gone back and viewed the destruction? Did he want to see the valley again, enough to live out his life there?

"No doubt about it, Pa. There's a future there for anyone who wants it."

The die was cast. Elisha Blackman moved his family to Orange County, New York, opposite Milford, Pennsylvania, at the beginning of one of the main trails that led into the Wyoming Valley. Elisha Junior joined the Continental Army and fought throughout New York State until 1782, when he was honorably discharged. In the meantime, the rest of the family settled down to "making do", waiting for the day when they could return to the Wyoming Valley and home.

1782 was a milestone year. The Blackman family was eagerly awaiting Elisha Junior's arrival after his release from the army, when the news reached them that the Second Continental Congress, the same congress that had sent a messenger so long ago to find out if those in the Wyoming Valley were going to join the fight for Independence from England or not, had ruled in favor of the Pennsylvanians as the only ones legally entitled to settle in the Wyoming Valley. Thus was resolved, once and for all, the question of land ownership in northeastern Pennsylvania.

When news had come, a year earlier, that the actual fighting had stopped and the war was over, Elisha and his son Eleazer, now age seventeen, had joined with everyone else in celebrating and shouting with joy over the war's end, but it hadn't really meant anything to them. The same had been true in 1779, when they had first heard of General John Sullivan's campaign against the Indians who had participated in the Wyoming massacre. When word had come back that Sullivan and his men had reached Newtown (Elmira), New York, and had burned every Indian village in sight, and that Colonel John Butler of the British forces and his infamous Tory Rangers had been crushed (the very same Butler—not Zebulon Butler of the American forces—who had directed the attack against them at Forty Fort), Elisha and his youngest son Eleazer said not a word. That was not what they were most interested in hearing. The knowledge, that the members of the Indians' Six Nations would never live again in their homelands, had not brought a smile of relief to Elisha and Eleazer.

It was the news of 1782 that affected them, the early act of Congress that the Wyoming Valley belonged to those with Pennsylvania claims, and not the Connecticut claimants. It moved Elisha and Eleazer in a way that the cessation of hostilities with England never had. Not to see the beautiful Wyoming again! ... they couldn't believe it. Elisha stormed about the house, railing at Congress. He was even sorry they had won their independence from England if this was the kind of decision the new government was going to make. He sent a letter to Philadelphia expressing his opinion of the whole matter.

Time marched inevitably onward. There was an uncertainty, a purposelessness, to the Blackman household now. Where was home? After all these years, should they try to rejoin their relatives in Lebanon County, Connecticut? If not, where should they go? Where was home to be now?

To remove himself from the family's silently accusing eyes, Eleazer found relief from their inertness in working for Mrs. Hyde, a neighbor. She lived not too far from the Blackmans, with her children. Eleazer liked the woman and enjoyed working for her, even though she was quiet; or was it reserve—he wasn't quite sure which. It took him almost a year of lending a helping hand before he learned that her husband, John Hyde, had been killed fighting for General Clinton in the French and Indian War. And it wasn't until her daughter Corinda had explained that her mother had come from France, that he understood why the woman spoke with a strange accent. Eleazer liked Corinda very much, also. She was almost five years younger than he; she was tall and attractive like her mother, with thick, luxurious black hair, and she had an aristocratic air about her that never ceased to fascinate him. Eleazer often spoke to Corinda about the home he had left so hurriedly. He described the valley to her over and over again. The softness in his face, when he spoke of it, told Corinda how much he loved it.

Everyone took it for granted that Eleazer was courting Corinda; that is, everyone but Corinda herself. A frown would cross her face each time Eleazer came to call. It hadn't taken her long to observe that which perturbed her. Eleazer, she knew, came willingly to see her, but she knew that just as surely he would turn and stare intently to the west for a moment before knocking on the door, as if by the look westward he was assuring himself that his ties with the past were not broken as he contemplated the future.

Then, in 1787, news came. Congress would force Pennsylvania to recognize the rights of those who had come from New England to settle in northern Pennsylvania after all. This time, all the Blackmans, especially Eleazer and his father, celebrated as if the war had just ended.

"Get packing, my dear," Elisha shouted to his wife. "We're leaving for Wilkes-Barre tomorrow!"

Everyone was laughing and shouting and dancing; Eleazer rushed over to tell Corinda and Mrs. Hyde the good news.

"What will happen to us, Eleazer?" Corinda asked.

Eleazer stopped short. He had no answer; he hadn't thought.

Corinda saw his hesitation and turned away. She was remembering the softness to his voice, the dreaminess to his eyes whenever he had mentioned the Wyoming Valley to her. She was very hurt that he hadn't thought of sharing his valley with her.

Eleazer left and returned home, a greatly subdued young man. He was twenty-two now. What about Corinda? That was a very good question. Had he intended to say good-by to her when he had dashed over? No, he reasoned with himself. It had been the joy of an innocent, wanting to share his most cherished dream coming true with someone dear, that had sent him racing over to Widow Hyde's. Someone dear? Yes, that was how he, Eleazer Blackman, thought about Corinda Hyde.

Eleazer broke the news to his mother and father that evening. "Ma, Pa, when we return, Corinda will be going with us."

"Have you asked her?" his mother inquired calmly, having seen this moment coming for some time.

"You'd better do that, son, before making any plans," instructed his father.

After Eleazer had left the room, the senior Blackmans looked at each other. Elisha and Lucy smiled reassuringly, each comforting the other. Their baby was leaving them.

Eleazer savored the next two days. His last hours of freedom; this was how he referred to them privately. He stayed pretty much to himself. Then on the third day, shortly after noon, when he knew Mrs. Hyde would be at home, he knocked at her door.

"I've come for your daughter's hand in marriage," he blurted out through the open doorway.

Mrs. Hyde thought of the subtle nuances so dear to every French woman's heart, as she extended her hand to Eleazer, saying, "Come in, son. I'll tell Corinda you're here."

No time was lost preparing for the wedding. This was because no time could be lost in preparing for the Blackmans' return trip to the grand and majestic Wyoming Valley. At last the great days came: first the wedding, and then the departure; Eleazer's cup was filled and overflowing.

The trip was made quickly and without mishap. And on returning, it seemed as if God had personally answered all their prayers. As they sought to reestablish their original farm, they learned of Anderson Dana's widow, and how, on that memorable day when the cannon had sounded at the fort almost ten years earlier, she had grabbed her husband's record books and taken them with her on her flight. There was no question: the farm that Elisha Blackman and his family had staked out was to be restored to them.

2

The Strong family was slaughtered in its own private massacre in 1778, the same summer as the massacre at Wyoming Valley.

The great Indian Trail, leading from the Wyoming Valley to the upper end of the Delaware River, crossed through the Moosic mountains at Cobb's Gap, passed through the swampland with its laurel and rhododendron (the Great Swamp was so dark and forbidding as to appear black), to cross another well-traveled trail that came down from the uppermost end of the Wyoming Valley. This latter north-south trail led one down past beautiful little Lake Ariel, over the Wallenpaupack (Paupack) River at a point where the river appeared not to flow at all, then curved around on the south ridge of the Wallenpaupack Valley until it disappeared into the woods once again. leading the traveler to the Delaware River at the Delaware Water Gap.

The original east-west trail, from its junction with the north-south trail, followed the same Wallenpaupack Valley, but on the north ridge, crossing the river at the Wilsonville rapids, and hurrying due east towards the Delaware River at Milford, and then to Port Jervis.

One day, the Strong family appeared in the Wallenpaupack River area; they had been following the east-west trail. When they reached the crossroads of the two trails, they hesitated, then finally turned left, pursuing the southern branch of the north-south trail for about three miles. There they stopped; they had found their new home. The year was 1770, and the new settlers named the area Little Meadows.

Accompanying the Strongs was a second, slightly younger family; these were the Jacob Stantons. The Stantons were full of eager enthusiasm to carve a great future for themselves out of the wilderness. Together, the Strongs and the Stantons themselves would work to clear the land; there was no one else around them for miles and miles. One day, while exploring the woods to the south, Jacob Stanton noted many sap-bearing maple trees growing. Excitedly he rushed back and informed everyone of his find. The Strongs clearly indicated they were not interested, so Jacob took his young wife aside, and instructed her in the fine art of syrup harvesting.

Eight years passed. More and more land was put to the plow, and life was pleasant; both families lived as one. Then, on a stifling hot day in late July of 1778, almost a month after the massacre at Forty Fort, Jacob Stanton proposed a picnic in the woods, among his cool, tall maple trees. He didn't really expect the Strongs to join him; in fact, he would have been surprised if they had. His wife packed a picnic basket, and, with their children, they set out. The deeper they went into the woods, the cooler it felt. Laughing and running, they at last found a spot to their liking. Lunch was consumed, and then all was silence as the family dozed contentedly in the filtered sunlight.

A small party of marauding Indians, fresh from their success at Forty Fort, never knew of the Stantons' existence when they attacked the Strong family at Little Meadows. Those frightened, bewildered settlers put up a brave resistance, and managed to kill several of their attackers, before they, too, were massacred.

The Stantons, returning from their pleasant interlude in the woods, took one look at the carnage before them—the twisted bodies, both red-skinned and white—and started to run. They ran and ran, and never stopped running until they reached the Hudson River.

Like the Blackmans, Jacob Stanton could not put his beautiful maple trees, nor the graciously flowing Wallenpaupack River, out of his mind. He also felt a great responsibility to his dear friends, the Strongs, whose bodies were lying back there on the ground. He knew where his duty lay, but dreaded returning.

The Dutch settlement, in which the Stantons had finally stopped, welcomed them with understanding. The Stanton children were maturing, and it wasn't long before their oldest daughter, almost seventeen, attracted the eye of one of their Dutch neighbors, the restless Moses Dolph. So by early 1781, when Jacob Stanton and his family set out on the return trip back to Little Meadows, he had, marching proudly beside him, a brand new son-in-law.

Everything was just as it had been on the day the Stantons had left three years earlier. Jacob, his sons, and his son-in-law cooperated in burying the skeletons of those killed; then they set about rebuilding. More and more land was cleared and farmed. The trees were tapped again, and syrup sold to passing travelers; they were still the only ones in the area. Jacob thought of Moses Dolph as the most industrious of his sons; Moses admired and respected his father-in-law. Fifteen years elapsed, and in that time, Jacob Stanton became a grandfather several times over. He watched his daughter bloom into a lovely, elegant matron. At times, he couldn't believe her to be a child of farm and forest. Perhaps, he reflected, that was because his son-in-law was cleverer than he in getting the best prices for their products. Moses, he observed, also seemed to have a knack for appraising fox pelts and deerskins more accurately than anyone else in the family.

By the year 1795, there had been several changes. Jacob Stanton had passed on, while still in his fifties. He had left the charge of his family to his eldest son, William. But it was a charge that William didn't particularly want. However, Moses Dolph was on hand with an offer, and William sold out to Moses. Worth more than twice as much as anyone else for miles around, Moses concentrated all his energies on building up around the trail junction three miles to the north rather than in developing Little Meadows itself. The trails were in constant use as the nineteenth century approached. There were more people to be seen, and

Moses, who had opened a general store there, preferred the busy crossroads. The intersection was known as Salem Corners.

In 1797, Moses sold a four-hundred-acre tract located near Little Meadows to a Major Theodore Woodbridge and his son-in-law, Charles Goodrich, Jr. These two families were the first of about twenty to arrive in Salem Corners from Wethersfield (now Glastonbury), Connecticut. The Major subsequently purchased another four-hundred-acre parcel.

The years passed into the new century. Moses was busier than ever, selling land all around the outskirts of the Salem Corners intersection. In 1800, Francis Nicholson arrived with his wife and children; they were a part of the group from Wethersfield (Glastonbury). He had been a member of the Continental Army, and had fought in Pennsylvania. He had been looking forward to the time when he would have the opportunity to settle in the new territory. One of the first things that Nicholson did on arriving was seek out Moses Dolph. Moses readily obliged, and sold him a choice tract about a mile west of Salem Corners on the east-west trail. Later, others arrived, and soon the respected Dolph had disposed of a thousand acres in bits and pieces.

In all, Francis Nicholson had ten children; this was not quite up to the twelve at the Dolph residence, but still a goodly number. Of his ten children, the one of which he was most proud (he dared show no favoritism however) was Fandani or Fanny, born in 1791.

The year 1801 was the one in which suit was brought by the Republic, that is the government of the United States, against Francis Nicholson. Nicholson was not the first; Major Woodbridge had had that honor, and for that he never forgave Moses Dolph—after all, he was a member of The Cincinnati!

The controversy revolved around the old question of the Pennsylvanian versus the Connecticut rights to the land. Loud noises had come from Philadelphia, referring back to the Charter of 1681. Philadelphia families busily waved land-grant deeds from William Penn. But the New Englanders' right to settlement, stemming from the reconfirmed 1662 Charter, had also been proven valid. One by one, starting with Major Woodbridge, Francis Nicholson and others were brought before a grand jury, accused of "intrusion on the land." The justice of the peace who officiated, Justice Gibbon, solved the issues speedily, levying fines whenever he could. He had found, early in his political career, that cash in hand was more likely to satisfy a complainant than anything else. And to those defendants who complained about paying out money, he quickly retorted that perhaps they would prefer to lose all they had worked for if an appeal were to go against them.

And Moses Dolph—well, he was another matter. His neighbors, of English ancestry from Connecticut, took a decided dislike to the Dutchman. Dolph, relying on the inheritance from Jacob Stanton, believed that he had a just claim to all the land; but when his neighbors were accused of "intrusion on the land," they relegated Moses to the lowly position of "real-estate trickster."

More settlers seemed to appear, apparently out of nowhere; Salem Corners was growing fast. However, down the north-south road, Major Woodbridge had not forgotten what had happened. Imagine, he had been accused of "intrusion on the land" when he was a member of The Cincinnati! He rented one of the rooms in his house to George Harberger and encouraged and counseled him on the operation of a first-class store. This was in direct competition to Moses Dolph's store at the corners where the two trails intersected.

Thus time passed. What happened at Salem Corners was soon matched at "Little Meadows," and whatever activity took place around Major Woodbridge and his son-in-law, Charles Goodrich, soon appeared in duplicate at Salem Corners.

Into this, Henry Heermans walked in 1808. Henry was a cousin of Moses Dolph. Like him, Henry had been born along the Hudson River—Dutchess County, New York. Also like Moses Dolph, Henry's family had caught the feeling of excitement and love for the Wyoming Valley from the settlers as they had fled eastward from the massacre in 1778. Later, when Moses Dolph had written back to his family, describing his enormous land holdings acquired from his Stanton brother-in-law, as well as smaller parcels from a William Stark and an Isaac Tripp, the Heermans reacted as could be expected. Almost without delay, John Heermans, Henry's father, moved his family into the Wyoming Valley. Within a year after hearing of Moses' successes, in 1796, the Heermans were settled at Pittston, a community about seven miles up the Susquehanna River from Wilkes-Barre, at the point where the river bends sharply north in its preparation for leaving the valley.

It was shortly after 1800 that Henry's oldest brother, Philip Heermans, had married Mary Fellows. In a few years the frugal couple had saved enough so that Philip was able to go over to Salem Corners to acquire some land from Moses Dolph for his new family. The ground Moses sold to Philip was not too far from Pittston, about seven miles further up the valley at a place called "The Corners," later Providence. Providence was the sixth town on the original map drawn by The Susquehanna Company of Connecticut.

Henry Heermans had learned the trade of carpenter. Accompanying his brother Philip, and Mary, to Providence, he helped him to build a house large enough to serve as tavern and general store at the intersection of two roads, similar to what Moses Dolph had at Salem Corners. In return for his labors, Henry acquired half-interest in the property. But once his work was done, Henry grew restless and cast about for something else.

The year is now 1808. It is late March. In Salem Corners there is a knock at the Dolph door, and Moses rises from his seat to answer.

"Cousin Moses!"

In his surprise, Moses almost shuts the door in his cousin's face, for a strapping, good-natured seventeen-year-old man is grinning at him. Henry Heermans has arrived in Salem Corners!

The Dolphs made him welcome, and offered him lodgings with them. Henry lost no time in traveling around the area, introducing himself as a carpenter, and soliciting business from his new neighbors, starting with his second day in Salem Corners. Henry was affable and progressive. The neighbors responded, and gave him work. His pleasing personality was reflected in the frame houses he built. Prior to his arrival, the architecture had been mainly original log. These buildings, the residents of Salem Corners commissioned the young Heermans to replace. Building quickly, he did well, giving the houses an air of substantial respect. Even today there still stands in and around Salem Corners, now Hamlin, a frame house or two built by H. Heermans. All of his customers were well pleased, most calling him Henry, a few Harry, none of them the Dutch Heinrick; and they all paid.

He quickly acquired the reputation of a practical business man, especially after he took the early fruits of his labor and purchased ground at the crossroads. Within a few years, Henry had become a landlord as well as a carpenter, renting to Dr. Asa Hamlin, Salem Corners' first permanent physician.

Fandani Nicholson was the same age as Henry Heermans, precisely two months, to the very day, younger than he. Slender, with light brown hair, she fastened her eyes on Henry Heermans almost as soon as he arrived in Salem Corners. Henry was also working in Moses Dolph's store; in fact, he was in the process of buying Moses out. Fanny kept her eye on the construction work around Salem Corners and knew when Henry would be in the store and when he would be out building. Every day when there was no outside work, she would walk the road east to Henry's store, supposedly to inquire or purchase an item, to give him a long, long look, and then would return the same mile west, back to her home.

At first, Henry was amused. He always had a smile for her; after all, she was good for business. And business was very good; he didn't count his money every night, but he did keep a running total in his head.

All the Dolphs were soon aware of Fanny's many trips to the store. The younger Dolphs took to standing just inside the doorway and giggling whenever she arrived. Knowing Henry could well support a wife, Moses Dolph prodded him, on more than one occasion, to marry. But Henry always veered away from the subject; there was something he wanted to do first. He wanted to return to "The Corners," where he had left his brother and where he had a half-interest in the tavern and store. He had hurried so when he had left Philip and Mary for Salem Corners and Moses Dolph that the area and the land were only a blurred impression in his mind.

Since coming to Salem Corners, Henry had been so busy working that he had never traveled away from the immediate neighborhood, even though the distance between Salem Corners and "The Corners" was about twenty-five miles. So, on the day Henry realized he was looking forward to Fanny's daily visit, in fact even looking up every time someone crossed the store's threshold, hoping it would be she, he decided he had better take his long postponed journey.

It was a warm sunny day, near the end of the second week of October, when Henry started out. He packed his saddlebags with three day's supply of food and said good-bye to the Dolphs. When he cantered past the Nicholson farm house, Fanny was in the front yard playing with her younger brothers and sisters. Henry appeared to be concerned about something on the road ahead, and so missed the wave of her arm.

The grandest, most beautiful colors of nature were on display for Henry as he followed the road west. Even today, there is nothing as beautiful in nature as the Pocono mountains at the height of their autumn coloring. Henry was alert to every change in scenery: this was the first time he was following the west road and old enough to appreciate and understand what he was seeing. (He had been only five when he had come through originally with his family.) Ascending a ridge, Henry gasped at the display immediately before him and extending to the next ridge. And then at the next ridge he gasped again, and so it went until he had his first sight of the great Wyoming Valley as he broke through the mountain wall at Cobb's Gap. He was so moved by its beauty, the strength and the majesty, that his artist-craftsman's soul sobbed silently, sending a tear down his cheek.

Henry followed the road down the valley for a while and then turned right to leisurely cross the gentle Lackawanna River towards the great tree. It was here, he had heard, that Capouse had held his pow-wows. Henry dismounted and sat on the ground, his back resting against the tree's trunk. He sat there for a long while, and thought and thought. He thought of the past, and all that he had done. Then he thought of the future. Finally, he made camp for the night.

Henry was well aware of where he was, that he was only twelve miles from Wilkes-Barre and about seven from his parents' home at Pittston; that Salem Corners was twenty-five miles eastward. But the quiet and serenity at Capouse Flats fascinated him. He had the feeling he was in totally virgin wilderness stretching for miles and miles. The topography of the Wyoming Valley was responsible for the apparent isolation of Capouse Flats. Several small hills rose from the valley floor, and transversed the valley at its midsection. One of these hills was so broad and flat at its top that the present day international airport for the Wilkes-Barre/Scranton area is located there.

Because of the natural bisection created by the hills, people would, from time to time, attempt to divide the valley into two valleys taxonomically as well. Thus Capouse Flats (Scranton) was said to be in the Lackawanna Valley, from the Lackawanna River which flows through Scranton and empties into the Susquehanna approximately a mile north of Pittston, leaving only Wilkes-Barre to be in the Wyoming Valley. However, the true natural rock formation of the mountains encloses only a single valley, the Wyoming. This valley extends from Carbondale in the northeast to Nanticoke in the southwest, including both Scranton and Wilkes-Barre.

The entire valley was also treated as one unit politically; the boundaries of Luzerne County, erected in 1786, encompassed all of the valley. For many years, Luzerne was to be the largest county in the Commonwealth of Pennsylvania, as other counties of approximately the same area or a trifle more, split into two or more smaller counties. When Luzerne County was formed in 1786, Wilkes-Barre became its county seat, thereby giving greater power and prestige to the town.

The next morning, Henry Heermans rose early, and using the great tree as a base, started to explore the area. He talked to a couple of the residents nearby and learned Capouse Flats was across the Lackawanna from Slocum Flats. For a while he rode along the flat land on the southern side of the river. Occasionally he would turn and look across the Lackawanna and in a northerly direction, to the other side and the high ground where he knew his brother Philip had settled. Retracing his steps, Henry crossed back over the river by Capouse's tree and climbed the mile or two to his brother's house.

Henry was given a warm welcome at the White Tavern, and the first meal together, at noon, was passed in catching up with each other's activities. In the afternoon, Henry walked around, checked on his carpentry job, was satisfied, and then continued walking, in ever-increasing circles, exploring the area at "The Corners" or Razorville as it was sometimes called. Providence, as the official name of the community, was not to come for several years. Henry found there were no more than seven families who had settled in the area. He talked with many of them on his walk and found them all to be friendly and kindly people. Satisfied, he returned to Philip and Mary, and after a quiet evening, rose early the next morning and departed for his return trip to Salem Corners.

Of all the sights he had seen, those at "The Corners" impressed him the most. He loved looking down across the Lackawanna to Slocum Flats. He also had a panoramic view of the valley's width. As the valley spread out before him, he experienced almost the same excitement and wonder as when he had broken through into the valley at Cobb's Gap. But Henry carried a sad heart away with him. He was astute enough to realize that, for the time being, "The Corners" could not support a young man with a new wife in the business Henry loved most, managing a general store. For the moment, at least, he knew where his future lay.

Henry didn't comment much about his trip, when he returned. He told everyone that he was happy he had gone, but was happy to get back, too. Only Fanny detected a slight change in him; he didn't seem to tease her quite as much as before. She wasn't sure, but she even thought that there was a tone of respect in Henry's voice when he asked, "And what would Mistress Fanny like today?"

Henry laid his plans carefully; time passed. When Henry first asked her to go riding with him, Fanny was so excited that she ran the whole mile back home to tell her mother. The news was well received in the Nicholson household; Henry was held in esteem among all the settlers of Salem Corners. When he asked for Fanny's hand in marriage, it was a foregone conclusion that the answer would be yes.

Life at Salem Corners was a busy and happy one for Henry and Fanny, to which a good deal of the credit belonged to Fanny. From the first, when she had learned that she and Henry had been born the same year, 1791, and on the same day, the twenty-seventh, although two months apart, she had been convinced there was a special purpose to their lives. Not long after their wedding, the children started to arrive, the first two being boys.

While Fanny busied herself with the family cares, Henry devoted more and more time to his store and building up his savings. Henry and Moses Dolph were very compatible. Being the only two residents of Dutch descent in the community, they gravitated naturally towards each other and spent most of their time in each other's company. Moses had been noting, with growing pride, the steady advancement of his relative and compatriot, appreciating Henry's business astuteness. When Henry inquired about the reason for the two general stores and the two schoolhouses, Moses broke down and took him into his confidence. They were never officially partners, but from then on, they worked together as one.

"They are English and we are Dutch," explained Moses. "Major Woodbridge feels that I have insulted him. So, when we have a school here, he has a school there. Can you imagine, forty-seven families and two schools—East School, West School? We have a store here, he has a store at his place. We charge so much, he charges less. So we lower our price and then we charge less. I don't know where it all will end."

Henry appreciated his Cousin Moses' predicament, understanding it completely. Henry came from a long line of Heermans, recognized for their independence of spirit and thought, and their ability to resist the pressure of a domineering personality in the New World. Ever since August of 1666, when on sighting an English frigate in the Bay of North River (The Narrows at New York City), Henry's great-great-great grandfather had told his neighbor Petrus Stuyvesant (former Director-General of New Netherland) to harvest his own grain and carry it into the fort himself because he, Jansz Focke (Heermans), was too busy tending his own crops, the Heermans had pursued that course best suited to their own interests, undeterred.

The two men, Henry and his Cousin Moses, were puffing contentedly on their pipes, watching a lone rider approach from the east as they talked. Moses continued to explain the situation at Salem Corners to Henry while their eyes followed the man on horseback. The rider came abreast of them, and inquired as to where he could find Postmaster Woodbridge.

Postmaster Woodbridge! Moses Dolph turned a stricken face towards his cousin. The Major had done it again!

All through the early part of 1812, the United States and England were fighting. Some of the great naval battles in American history were occurring. The country's beautiful new executive mansion, the White House, was burned to the ground. Dolly Madison had become a living legend. The new nation was getting its national anthem. The War of 1812 was making heroes, but bringing sorrow to many. But in northeastern Pennsylvania, there was, and still is, a curious apartness from the rest of the world; possibly it stemmed from the lateness of the period in which the area was settled. Ohio had been opened up, Harrisburg and Pittsburgh were thriving cities, and parts of southern New York and the Delaware River Valley had become advanced industrial areas, when the first settlers arrived to open up the one strip of northern Pennsylvania, still using pioneer techniques and living the primitive lives of pioneer families.

So in 1812, while the war between England and the United States raged all around, down the north-south road Major Woodbridge had an extraordinary piece of good luck; he was able to get himself appointed as postmaster of Salem Corners. And Moses Dolph and Henry Heermans spent their time watching the mail rider arrive at Salem Corners and turn left towards the post office. Moses Dolph observed the new activity with growing displeasure. It got so bad, finally, that Henry arranged to spend the day somewhere else than with his cousin, whenever the biweekly delivery of mail was expected. His cousin's dour face was enough to blacken the brightest of sunshine days.

At last, he could stand it no longer. Henry went to his cousin with a suggestion, and it was agreed to put the plan into action immediately. On the mail carrier's next delivery Moses and Henry were waiting. They hailed the rider to a stop: "We'll save you the trouble of the extra run down to the Major's."

The first couple of times Henry showed up, instead of the carrier, with the mail pouch, Major Woodbridge remained deep in thought after Henry's departure. He couldn't quite put his finger on it, but he knew he should be alert; something was afoot. He finally understood what the two Dutchmen were up to when a neighbor child came in one day with a message: the mail had arrived, but Henry wasn't free to bring it down, would the Major mind coming up to the crossroads? Shortly afterwards, the post office moved to Salem Corners proper, and Henry Heermans was officially installed as postmaster. And Moses Dolph had a smile back on his face again.

In 1818 Henry Heermans was elected Constable at Salem Corners, was licensed to keep a public tavern, and his daughter Catherine was born. From then on, life was a steady uphill success for the Heermans. Life had prospered for his brother at Razorville, too ("The Corners"), and Henry spent some time each year traveling back and forth through Cobb's Gap looking after his interests at both places. Then strange new sights were to be seen in the area. Men from outside the territory came in to begin surveying for a water canal transport system, similar to the Erie Canal in New York State; Henry, with his brother-in-law Zenas Nicholson, built a sawmill on the Pike County side of the Wallenpaupack (Paupack) River at Sliding Falls and shipped lumber out in every direction. Now making more money than ever before, Heermans and Nicholson realized even greater profits when a year later they sold out to Fuller and Company. The time had at last come. Henry went to Fanny, and for the first time, revealed his love of the Wyoming Valley to her.

"Come with me now, Fanny, and I will build you the grandest house you could ever live in."

Fanny was aghast. She had had no idea her husband had treasured such thoughts from the time of his first trip, shortly before they had married. At first, she did not know what to think or say. However, when she did speak, it was as if they were bride and groom again, nineteen years earlier. "I have lived almost all of my life here at Salem Corners. I've never been anywhere. And, Henry, I adore you. I'll go wherever you want to go."

The matter was settled. Henry made arrangements with the Hamlins to buy his store, and for Oliver Hamlin to take over as postmaster. With his carpenter tools neatly packed, all of his money carefully hidden, Henry, with Fanny and the children, said farewell to the Dolphs and the Nicholsons and to all of Salem Corners that turned out to see them off. As they drove away, Mrs. Heermans snuggled trustingly against her husband as if the world was theirs, as if they were young again and love would conquer all.

Fanny was like Henry. When she had her first view of the Wyoming Valley, she said, "Oh, how beautiful!" and gave vent to her emotion by implanting a loving kiss on Henry's lips, to the interest and delight of their children. They, in turn, found their parents' actions more interesting than the sweeping, exciting vastness of the panoramic display before them.

3

"In the service of their country" best describes the Beaumont family. They produced statesmen, soldiers, and sailors; they fought in wars around the globe; and they paraded the new Republic's might before all the world. The Beaumonts were the one window in the valley that looked outward, the ones who tied the valley to the rest of the world, the ones who kept the valley's settlers from being too insular. Yet they were not among the first arrivals in the valley.

Andrew Beaumont had the largest head in the entire valley. He came to the Wyoming Valley in 1808 at the age of seventeen, his parents enrolling him as a student in the newly opened Wilkes-Barre Academy (later known as Wyoming Seminary). The Beamonts themselves were not valley people; they lived some fifty miles to the north of Wilkes-Barre, along the Wyalusing Creek. But they had pretensions, and a certain standard. The creation of a private school, in their area, would appeal to them; it would be something that they would want to relate to. Besides, Fear Beaumont, Andrew's mother, saw a spark glowing deeply whenever she looked into her oldest son's eyes. She wanted him to have the best she could provide; she wanted to equip him as well as she could in their limited circumstances, for whatever moment of history was to be his. She felt certain that he had a special destiny.

Almost from the beginning, Andrew's father, Isaiah Beaumont, opposed the special schooling. He could see no reason for his son to leave home. But his wife stood firm, and, as usual, had her way. The outcome had been predictable from the beginning; even Andrew knew that.

Andrew very rarely paid much attention to his father's grumblings, for he knew what really bothered his father: it was his mother's family. The father stood just a trifle in awe of them. Actually, he had no reason to; but he did. Fear's great-grandparents were Priscilla Mullins and John Alden. They were a legend, woven into the very earliest history of the new country. How could one do any better than, "Speak for yourself, John"? All America knew the story. How could one achieve, with his own life, something that would not only equal, but surpass and mean even more to Americans, than the story of John and Priscilla Alden? In unconscious defense, Isaiah had developed the outward characteristics of the typical drifter: life was against him. This unwillingness to persevere, in turn, created situations that then reinforced his outlook. He was a preconditioned failure.

In truth, Isaiah Beaumont was really a soldier of fortune, always looking for new lands to conquer, always restless, constantly on the move. He had enlisted in December of 1775 in a Connecticut Regiment that was leaving for Boston under the command of Colonel John Durkee. He had fought all the way from Boston, through New York, and down into New Jersey. There, when his enlistment period ended, he toyed with the idea of returning home to Fear and his daughters in Connecticut, but at the last minute changed his mind. He marched into Trenton, fought at Princeton, where he was wounded, and rejoined the army in the spring. But in spite of all his fighting, Isaiah kept complaining how fate was dealing him a short deck of cards. Someone else, he knew, would always have better luck than he.

Always on the alert for another opportunity, Isaiah joined Major General John Sullivan's 1779 march, through northeastern Pennsylvania and lower New York, to clean out the Iroquois. Sullivan and his men ranged all over the area, fighting until there wasn't "a single town left in the country of the Five Nations." The miles and miles of virgin timberland, and mountain ridge after mountain ridge, fascinated Isaiah as he marched. It was all so different from the seacoast town of Saybrook in Connecticut, where he had been born, had grown up, and had married and started a family.

In spite of his grumblings, Isaiah stayed with the Continental Army until the end of the war, when he was honorably discharged. He returned home to Saybrook, and told his wife about his travels. He described the places he had been, and the sights he had seen, instead of describing the battles he had fought. He talked mostly of the rolling mountains of northern Pennsylvania, and of the picturesque, fast-flowing Susquehanna River.

By 1791, just after the birth of their first son Andrew, Isaiah finally convinced Fear to leave Connecticut. He claimed his reward, virgin western land, for his years of service in the Continental Army, in the form of a tract on the Wyalusing Creek in northeastern Pennsylvania, some fifty miles due north of Wilkes-Barre and the Wyoming Valley. As soon as the baby Andrew was born, the family trekked westward. There was a purposefulness, now, to Isaiah's step.

The activity and excitement of moving to a new land, of clearing the ground and of building, satisfied the restless, wandering soldier. Better yet, Isaiah received a nice pension from all his years of service in the army. If the family was careful in spending the money, he could provide his wife and children with an air of gentility and respectability. He could be very much the gentleman; for with his pension, in this unsophisticated milieu, he wouldn't have to work as long as their wants were modest. Isaiah sighed contentedly, and settled down for pleasant living on the banks of the Wyalusing. He could never have achieved this, had he stayed in Saybrook.

At first, Fear was satisfied just to have her husband happy, and not restless or complaining. Then, gradually, as harmony continued to dominate the family interactions, Fear slowly returned to her own girlhood personality. Instinctively, she began reflecting her husband's mannerisms and airs of gentility. The Beaumonts lived a quiet, refined type of existence. Since they brought no harm to anyone with their genteel manners, their pioneering neighbors were willing to leave them alone. Everyone else in the area was actively homesteading, and had little time for tea with the Beaumonts. In turn, the Beaumonts didn't seem to mind; they were content as they were.

Each year passed into the next, until one day Fear Beaumont suddenly realized her oldest son Andrew had become a man. She stared reality in the face, and was upset beyond words. Her son was fifteen; what did he know of the world? He knew only the wilderness around them, the untrampled beauty of the stoic mountains. Was that what he was to be the rest of his life, a woodsman? She thought back to her girlhood days of society in Saybrook; they were a part of her, she had grown up with them. Therefore, she could choose, with her husband, to go elsewhere and put them behind her. But Andrew...what choice did he have?

Fear mentioned her thoughts to her husband, but Isaiah stared stonily at her for a moment, before walking into the "library." It was about this time that Fear began noticing the brief articles which appeared occasionally in the weekly paper from Wilkes-Barre. According to the news items, a group of men were interested in starting a private school in the Wilkes-Barre area. She followed the progress of the new school intently, but kept her thoughts to herself. She wasn't quite ready to let her husband know what she had in mind.

By the year 1807, there were approximately four hundred families in the Wilkes-Barre area. Wilkes-Barre itself was a well established, thriving community, a county seat, and had an active local government. The education conscious New Englanders had seen that there was an ample number of one-room schoolhouses scattered throughout the valley. There was seemingly no need for a tuition-funded educational institution. To understand the calm acceptance of a private school in the limited environment of Wilkes-Barre in 1807, it is necessary to review the founding philosophy of The Susquehanna Company of Connecticut, the original developers of the "Western Lands" (northeastern Pennsylvania).

Whenever The Susquehanna Company sold shares in its land ventures, it routinely set aside a certain percentage of the land for educational institutions, similarly allotting another percentage for religious usage. One of its most successful attempts in this respect, reserving a portion for community service, had been in the development of its Northern Tract, now part of New Hampshire.

At the same time as the original shares in its Western Tract (Pennsylvania) were being sold, those enterprising Connecticut settlers who had bought shares in the Northern Tract and had traveled north had organized Dartmouth College in 1769. That no such educational institution existed in the Pennsylvania area, was ascribed to the effectiveness of the Wyoming Massacre, and to the legal battle with Pennsylvania over the ownership of the land. The interest in education was nevertheless present, and the settlers recognized that it was only a matter of time before something constructive was done—if not another Dartmouth, then something of equal caliber. The climate was then right for the establishment of specialized schooling. Looking only to the future, the inappropriateness of a private school, in 1807, among only four hundred families in almost isolated wilderness, never occurred to the citizens of Wilkes-Barre.

Fear Beaumont followed closely each new development of the burgeoning school, as it was announced. Every scrap of gossip that reached her concerning Wilkes-Barre Academy was stored in her active mind. A look of purpose entered her face, to remain there for days, when she read that the Academy's trustees had written to Yale University, requesting the college to send them a teacher-headmaster. Shortly after the new school opened in September of 1807, rage and sadness replaced the purposefulness that her eyes had shown. A visitor had been idly gossiping with her over tea one day, and had passed on the information that the new teacher at the Wilkes-Barre Academy had not yet arrived but had forwarded a curriculum, for his students to follow until he did come, that was the equal of any school patronized by the cosmopolitan inhabitants of Boston, New York, Philadelphia or Baltimore. Fear almost wept openly that her Andrew was not among the first students.

By the time the Academy was ready to open its doors for its second session, Fear Beaumont had achieved her goal. With a hug and a kiss, admonishing Andrew to do his very best, the Beaumonts drove to the town square in the center of Wilkes-Barre, and there entrusted their son to Mr. Garrick Mallery, Wilkes-Barre Academy's headmaster. Mallery took an instant liking to Andrew. His training as a teacher enabled him to appraise Andrew quickly. Like Fear Beaumont, he perceived a glimmer of something greater hovering under the surface of the boy's character. For Andrew, the school year got off to a good start, an omen of a whole year of happiness for the seventeen year old boy. He was bright, and pleased Mr. Mallery in many ways. In turn, his instructor allowed him to pick up a little extra money, carrying out assorted tasks around the school. He knew that Andrew was on a tight budget from home.

For the Beaumonts at home, however, the year went anyhing but well. True, Fear had had her way, and Andrew was off to school, as befitted an Alden and a Beaumont. But it had awakened the old restlessness and resentment in Isaiah. An undercurrent swirled faster every day; the feeling of quiet harmony had disappeared entirely.

In early summer when Andrew returned to his family at the close of school, he found a white-faced mother and a silently stalking father. The tension burst forth in a series of fast-paced events on Andrew's third evening at home. The family had just sat down to their last meal for the day. For the first time since he had been home, Andrew's father spoke to him about school; it was more of a statement than a question: "I hope you enjoyed your year at school."

Andrew's reply in the affirmative was ignored by Isaiah. His father spoke again, "Son, I'm glad you've had the experience. It will be something to carry with you when we go."

Before answering, Andrew looked questioningly at his mother. She lowered her eyelids briefly, and, ever so slightly, moved her head from side to side. Andrew said nothing.

"All right, Beaumonts," Isaiah said to his assembled family around the dining-room table, "it's time we moved on! Get packing! We want to be settled in our new place in Ohio before the first snow."

Ohio!

Two days later, Andrew saddled up one of the family's horses, and, with provisions packed by his mother, rode down to see Mr. Mallery at Wilkes-Barre. He explained the situation to him, and asked Mr. Mallery to advise him.

"You've enjoyed it here at the Academy, haven't you, Andrew?"

"Yes, Mr. Mallery. It's a real pleasure to be with the others, and when I'm studying, the time passes so quickly that I never wait around for the dinner bell."

"I know, I know," Mr. Mallery nodded his head, thoughtfully.

He was attracted to Andrew, as any true teacher is attracted to any bright but modest student. He felt the loss would be as great to the Academy as it would be to Andrew.

"Andrew, busy yourself for a while. I have a letter I want to write."

Almost too docilely, Andrew did as he had been instructed. He selected a book at random from the five spread out on the round reading table at the far end of Mallery's study, and settled himself in a chair near the window. Mr. Mallery's eyes narrowed, briefly. If Andrew Beaumont had a weakness, this was it: he would never be a troublemaker. It wasn't that he wouldn't accomplish great things; but never would he flash the fire of resentment at setbacks or open opposition.

Andrew read silently; the only sounds in the room were the continuous scratching of Mallery's pen and the occasional turning of a page of Andrew's book. Andrew wondered what had caused his mentor to seemingly take leave of his senses. They had been discussing a problem of great concern, to Andrew at least, when suddenly, in the midst of the conversation, Mallery must immediately sit down and apparently resume some long-overdue social correspondence. Andrew was indeed confused.

At last the letter was finished and sanded. Mallery rang for his housekeeper, and instructed her to see that the letter was delivered immediately. Only then, after the housekeeper had left the room, did Mallery call Andrew back to a chair beside the desk.

"Now, Andrew, I'll tell you what I did. I have just written to the trustees of the Academy. You may or may not have been aware of it this year, but the workload here at Wilkes-Barre Academy has become too much for one teacher alone to handle, especially if the iob is to be done properly. I mentioned something along this line at the last trustees' meeting. But nothing much came of it, for no one had a constructive suggestion.

"In the letter I wrote just now, I have made a formal request to the trustees of The Wilkes-Barre Academy, to appoint you as my assistant, to help with the teaching, especially in the lower grades."

Andrew's mouth broke open involuntarily. His eyes moistened, just to the point of forming a tear: "Thank you, Mr. Mallery. It will be an honor to assist you."

The Beaumonts were packed, and within a day of leaving Wyalusing when Mr. Mallery's letter, confirming Andrew's appointment, reached them. The family scene was violent and ugly; but Andrew stood firm, making it clear he wanted to accept the appointment. In the few remaining hours that followed, Andrew met his father's eyes with a hostility that told Isaiah that his son was lost to him forever. To his mother, Andrew was silent. He loved her, and when he thought of how she had encouraged him, of how she had always stood behind him, he visibly faltered. When he helped her with the packing, he could barely speak to her.

Andrew was so tied in his own knot, so choked with emotion at the thought that they would be soon parting, that some time passed before he realized that his mother had not once pressured him to go with the family. Once he had come that far out of his self-imposed emotional shell, enlightened awareness of his family's life passed before his eyes; he saw how his mother was ever obedient to his father's wishes. His mother's life was tied to her husband's; she wanted what he wanted. That was one of the intents of the marriage vows.

But, Andrew thought, I'm not married to my father. I'm not a wife; my life is not a shadow of his life. I have my own life, and my own shadow to find.

Without question, then, he was not going to go with his parents. He would return to the Academy. In his short, one year stay at the Academy, Andrew had loved what he had seen of the Wyoming Valley. He could not leave it—not ever.

When the final day came, and his parents and his sisters and brothers left for Ohio, Andrew headed south to Wilkes-Barre, to become, for the valley, the window that faced onto the rest of the world.

In 1813, Andrew Beaumont married Julia Colt, the daughter of Arnold Colt and Lucinda Yarrington Colt, both Wilkes-Barre settlers from the 1780s. In the intervening years, from 1786 to 1812, Colt had served successively as Wilkes-Barre's town clerk, sheriff, and finally as president of the town council. Arnold Colt was very much pleased with his daughter's choice. He had been impressed with Andrew from their first meeting in his position as a trustee of the Wilkes-Barre Academy, and reinforced later when they had shared many hours of work during the building of the *Luzerne*.

The great ocean-going ship *Luzerne* was built on the banks of the Susquehanna River in 1812. It was to be Wilkes-Barre's major contribution to the war effort; unfortunately, it never reached the sea. After the christening, with all of Wilkes-Barre attending in a wild and jubilant mood, the *Luzerne* floated down the Susquehanna; the patriotic citizens of Wilkes-Barre had instructed the captain to join the American fleet on the Potomac River. But the falls at Connewingo (Conawego) proved too much for the ship, and the *Luzerne* came to a premature end on the rocks there.

Julia and her older sister Temperance often visited the shipyard to watch the *Luzerne* as it was built. At first, both Temperance and Julia vied for Andrew's attention. It soon became obvious, however, which sister he preferred. (Five years after Julia's marriage, Temperance married a grandson of Colonel Zebulon Butler, the leader of the American defense during the Wyoming Massacre.)

After his marriage to Julia, Andrew left his post at the Wilkes-Barre Academy; he was then twenty-three. On the advice and encouragement of his father-in-law, he successfully petitioned to President James Madison, who appointed him collector of revenue for the twentieth (Wilkes-Barre area) Collection District. Two years later, Andrew moved into the county prothonotary office; this was also the year that he joined the Ancient Order of Freemasonry. In the same year, 1816, Elizabeth Colt Beaumont was born. The following year, Andrew formed the nucleus committee which founded St. Stephen's Episcopal Church in Wilkes-Barre. A year later, he took time to serve on the committee which built the Wilkes-Barre firehouse.

In another two years, Andrew Beaumont rode the stagecoach to Harrisburg as the newly elected representative from the Wilkes-Barre area to the State Legislature. Before leaving for Harrisburg, Julia presented her husband with a boy, their first—John Colt Beaumont. He was an able public official, and was conscientious; and his constituents appreciated all he was doing in their behalf. He managed to survive one reelection. But there were other things in store for Andrew.

After his two terms at the state capital in Harrisburg, he was named postmaster for Wilkes-Barre. In the early days of the U.S. Government, the position of postmaster was one of the most coveted. Obtaining government jobs by civil service examinations was not to go into effect until the 1870s, so one of the first patronage opportunities, at a federal level, was with the local postmaster. Many active men, with an eye to their own future, desired the postmaster's job because it placed them in the position of being able to hand out federal government employment where they pleased. Andrew enjoyed his power as Wilkes-Barre's postmaster but political campaigning for state representative had whetted his appetite for more. He used his years as postmaster for some subtle politicking, and, in 1832, entered the congressional race, seeking election to the U.S. House of Representatives from the Luzerne and Columbia Counties District.

He had just opened his formal campaign, when the news that some Masons had forcibly abducted a William Morgan from Batavia, New York, because he was writing a book revealing the order's secrets, swept the nation. By the middle of August, the Wilkes-Barre Masonic lodge had had its last meeting. Andrew and his election bid were caught up in the public's backlash. He had run as a "Jacksonian Democrat," but he was also known as a very active Mason. Aside from the Masonic issue, the popularity of Jackson's government should have easily swept Andrew into office. Instead, there was a long, long wait for the vote count to be tallied. When, at last, the judge of election announced the results, Andrew Beaumont had won by only eighty-eight votes.

Andrew Jackson was in his second term when the Honorable Andrew Beaumont and his family arrived in Washington. The new country's capital was a very exciting place to be. These were boom times (the first of two successive, devastating depressions was not to come for five years, in 1837). The chamber of the House of Representatives, with its rich red coloring and impressive columns, was alone worth a trip to Washington. There were rarely absentees when the House was in session; on any given day, besides Andrew Beaumont, a visitor could listen to Henry Clay, Davey Crockett, or ex-President John Quincy Adams. Across the hall in the Senate, Daniel Webster, John Calhoun, and Thomas Hart Benton held forth.

Even the inauguration of the newly elected legislators, in January of 1833, was a suspense-filled and dramatic event. What would John Calhoun do? Vice-president during Jackson's first term, he had fought bitterly with Jackson, over states' rights versus a strong central government. So strongly had Calhoun felt, that he had resigned the vice-presidency and had returned home to South Carolina to campaign for a senate seat. An audible sigh rippled over Washington at the swearing-in, when, as the others had done, Calhoun raised his right hand and swore to uphold the Union before taking his seat. Andrew Beaumont could not have arrived in Congress, nor participated in the Congressional sessions, at a more momentous, more exhilarating time than he did, with regard to having a part in the first steps along the road of this country's political philosophy, a road that has continued all the way to the present.

In his political philosophy, Andrew Beaumont supported President Jackson; he had more than just a first name in common with the President. Jackson, as George Washington had been, was a Mason, and throughout the furor of the Morgan abduction, had held steadfastly to his membership in the organization. Impressed, Andrew Beaumont showed his own support by fitting out a room in his Wilkes-Barre house in proper Masonic style. It was to be used by the chapter members as their meeting place, for the entire duration of their "underground period."

President Jackson had been an orphan from the age of fourteen, and Andrew Beaumont considered himself more or less an orphan, too, on the basis of his complete separation from his parents since their departure for Ohio; in effect, he had been on his own since his seventeenth year. Much of Jackson's political strength derived from his image as a frontiersman. The frontier was also where Andrew Beaumont had grown up; they both thought of themselves as self-made men.

There were three big issues that dominated Congress while Andrew Beaumont was a member. Besides the furor over the supremacy of states' rights over federal law, as asserted by the "nullification" vote of South Carolina (the state voted to ignore, within its own boundaries, any federal law it did not agree with), there was also the passage of the "gag rule," forced through the House by a pro-slavery faction (debate was barred on any slavery petition).

John Quincy Adams rose in righteous protest over the newly passed rule, and suddenly found himself in the role of champion of the people, a characterization that had never been attributed to him during his years as president. Overnight, as a by-product of his fight for justice, Adams was miraculously transformed into a popular hero, full of charm, sought after by all, and the object of much adulation.

But the greatest furor, and the one that involved Andrew Beaumont the most, was the challenge thrown out by Nicholas Biddle, head of the Bank of the Unitcd States. When Biddle boasted of being "daily in the exercise of more personal authority than the president habitually enjoys," the die was cast. Andrew Beaumont was more than happy to support and work closely with President Jackson as Jackson built his campaign against the bank and Biddle. Beaumont's enthusiasm for Jackson's crusade can probably be traced to some of the old antagonism felt in the Wyoming Valley from the years of dispute between the Connecticut and Pennsylvania settlers. That Nicholas Biddle descended from early Philadelphia settlers, the very group that had laid absentee claim to northeastern Pennsylvania, ensured Andrew Beaumont's opposition.

At night, the social activities in Washington echoed the excitement of the day. Washington society had suffered a temporary disorganization, at the hands of President Jackson, over the Secretary of War's wife, Peggy Eaton. In the throes of indecision, no clear feminine leader had yet emerged. Andrew was not the only Beaumont who was busy; daughter Elizabeth, now seventeen, had immediately stepped into the social activities. She had a naturally friendly personality, and her speaking mannerisms created much the same effect on her listeners as bubbling champagne. For the new waltz and polka dances, she was in great demand. Elizabeth had a fair amount of freedom, too, for her mother's main interest seemed to be increasing the Beaumont brood.

While her mother stayed at home, Elizabeth soon became "a reigning belle of Washington society." It wasn't long before she had a lengthy line of suitors trailing behind her. Just about the most dashing was Captain John Charles Frémont (The Pathfinder). This attraction was to have serious consequences for the Beaumont family in later years.

As Andrew supported Jackson, and Elizabeth graced the social gatherings of Washington, his constituents back in the Wyoming Valley smiled in the reflected glory that the Beaumonts had achieved for them. Andrew was easily returned to Congress by the election of 1834. However, the 1836 vote was a different matter.

In 1836, the boom times were beginning to give way to a feeling of despondency. The Specie Circular (only coinage or hard cash would be accepted as payment in the sale of public lands) was starting to make the East poor. Public figures associated with good times were unpleasant reminders to those who were straining to make ends meet with what they did not have; the Beaumonts were not to return to Washington.

In bidding them good-bye, their friends wrote in Elizabeth's memory book, revealing themselves much as they were known to be in those challenging days of the mid-1830s:

> The best wishes of the undersigned is presented to Miss Elizabeth Beaumont that she may have a long, useful life and a happy immortality.
>
> 1836 Andrew Jackson

With the tender of my best wishes for the future happiness and prosperity of Miss Beaumont, I shall be happy to be esteemed as one of her sincere friends.

Washington, Jan. 28, 1837 James K. Polk

But John Quincy Adams reserved, for himself, the show of affection and warmth that caused Elizabeth to be counted among the young ladies who were depositing kisses on his face:

To Miss Elizabeth Beaumont

Fair maiden, whom the sacred page
The words of kindness would impart,
The Friend, the Lover, Father, Sage
Speaks, says the Volume, to the Heart.

But how shall one in Life's decline,
Laden with threescore years and ten
Speak to that tender Heart of thine?
Or greet thee with an iron pen?

Let thy own Heart fair Maiden frame
The words thyself would most desire,
Fraught with a Lovers fervid flame,
Chaste with a fathers holiest fire

Then to thyself the words apply
Believe them from my Heart to flow.
Yet shall they not one half supply
The bliss my wishes would bestow.

John Quincy Adams
Washington 25 January 1837

The poem reads:

To Miss Elizabeth Beaumont:

Fair maiden, when the sacred page
The words of kindness would impart,
The friend, the Lover, Father, Sage
Speaks joys in volumes to the heart;

But how shall one in life's decline,
Laden with three score years and ten,
Speak to the tender heart of thine
Or greet thee with an iron pen?

Let thine own heart, fair maiden, frame
The words thyself would most desire,
Fraught with a lover's fervent flame,
Chaste with a father's holiest fire.

Then to thyself the words apply,
Believe them from my heart to flow,
Yet shall they not one-half supply
The bliss my wishes would bestow.

Washington, Jan. 25, 1837 John Quincy Adams

The farewell that was the most difficult, however, was Elizabeth's parting from Captain Frémont. He pressed her to stay, to remain with him. Elizabeth hesitated; she couldn't bring herself to say yes. Perhaps it was the long shadow of Jessie Benton falling over them. Both Elizabeth's father and hers were ardent, active workers for President Jackson, Thomas Hart Benton in the Senate and Andrew Beaumont in the House; consequently, they were very friendly. But, many times, Elizabeth's quick eyes had caught Jessie's face watching hungrily, as Elizabeth and Frémont had danced, flirted, or shared a refreshment together.

Or, Elizabeth's hesitation may have been simply a repetition of the previous generation's cry—when asked to leave the Wyoming Valley for Ohio, father Andrew Beaumont could not; when asked to leave the Wyoming Valley for Washington, daughter Elizabeth Beaumont could not.

The Beaumonts returned home to Wilkes-Barre. Just in time, too, for Elizabeth acquired another brother; Eugene Beauharnais Beaumont was born the Second of August, 1837.

The following year, Elizabeth wrote to Frémont to tell him that she had married Samuel Phinney Collings of Wilkes-Barre.

4

Who was Samuel Phinney Collings?

The question was never "Who was he?" To ask that brought forth no satisfactory answer. But, if one inquired along the path of "What did he do?", the results were much more rewarding.

What Samuel Phinney Collings did was to bridge a gap, to bring together two powerful, active, valley forces, the Blackmans and the Beaumonts. Yet, incongruously, his joining force was not of equal intensity.

The Blackmans and the Beaumonts were the true pioneers. They had come to the valley area when there had been absolutely nothing. There was no gamble in their decision to carve a home, a place in society for themselves out of the virgin forest, provided they had the stamina. And this they proved that they had. If they were not gamblers then, what were they? They were givers.

They gave their strength, sometimes their lives, always their time, and all of their energies to build and make a habitable community. If they could endure the physical hardships, the rewards were automatically waiting: wealth, in the form of large areas of land; prestige, in being recognized and accorded all the privileges due a founding first settler; honors, from executing and administering public offices; and an enormous amount of self-satisfaction, from being responsible for something that grew successfully.

The Collings were not among the first settlers, at least not in the Wyoming Valley. Daniel Collings was in the second wave of wanderers to the valley. He had come specifically because the settlement was already well established; a pioneering community could never have supported him. His way of "making his fortune" was by taking from others—not by building, not by creating something that had never existed before, not by "adding to"; instead, his way was to "take from." Oh, he was willing to work for it. The fact that he was a taker in no way affected his honesty. In truth, Daniel Collings was a very honest and sincere person, as was his son. But Daniel was a taker; and to some extent, he instilled the same characteristics in his son Samuel.

When Daniel's parents migrated from England to the New World, they came to Easton, Pennsylvania and began their homemaking there. Shortly afterwards, when the fighting began (Revolutionary War), Thomas Collings, Daniel's father, enlisted almost immediately. Thomas fought from the beginning of the hostilities almost to the end. (This Thomas Collings is not to be confused with Thomas

Collins (*sic*—without a "g") who arrived in the Wyoming Valley from Ireland in 1845. The confusion was later compounded when Collins had a son, Francis D. Collins, who became a Congressman in 1877, and who was a very close friend of A.H. Winton.) In 1787, his son Daniel was born in Easton.

Easton was a well-established community by 1787; settlers had been living in the area since 1740. There was security, and little trouble from the Indians, because no matter what direction the 1737 Walking Purchase's disputed line took to reach the Delaware River, Easton had always been south of the boundary. The glowering Blue Ridge, set just north of the town, forced the inhabitants to link with Philadelphia. Easton was not an isolated, single community of frontiersmen, a last outpost of civilization, but was instead a part of the highly sophisticated Princeton, Trenton, and Philadelphia milieu. Easton marked the upper end of civilization along the Delaware River; it had even sent a delegate to the Continental Congress.

In such an environment of well-established homes and businesses, there was definitely a need for a clockmaker. The residents had long ago solved the problems connected with procuring the necessities of life; by 1800, the eastern seaboard cities concerned themselves with the niceties of comfortable living. Clocks and watches were certainly in that category; a graceful long-case for a hall, or a tinkling pocket watch was very much in demand.

Daniel Collings learned the clockmaking trade in Easton and would probably have stayed there all his life, gracefully decorating, with his clocks, the homes of the well-to-do, and the dress of affluent business men, as well as their office walls, if it had not been for the stagecoach.

The early 1800's were full of bustling activity. Travelers were everywhere. Stagecoach lines sprang up daily to carry the overabundance of passengers. Enterprising men banded together to build and operate turnpikes. Improved roads, replacing Indian paths, and improved coaches were two lures travelers could not resist. At the close of the Revolutionary War, the new republic found itself to be a country that needed everything. It needed a government, and speedily took care of that with four months of hard work in Philadelphia, producing the Constitution.

It also needed communications. The new Republic was a union—not a confederation, but a union. Fearful that a state might pull out of the newly created union too easily, links were forged at every level, as quickly as possible, to bond the union together in a physical way. This need, to link all the towns of all the states together, was the force inspiring road improvements. Any good idea, to be really worthwhile and to succeed, has to involve some personal gain. The concept of the turnpike—fast, well maintained stretches of road, with "turns" for the collection of tolls at stated intervals, satisfied all these requirements. Easton to Reading (Pennsylvania), Easton on to Stroudsburg (Pennsylvania), and Stroudsburg to New York City were all instant successes as fast travel routes. Lighter and faster, the new stagecoaches, with glass windows and an air of officiality about them because they carried the mail, were a temptation few citizens could resist. Thus, the new union's bonds were forged by bands of roadway, and these were more effective in welding the states together than any bands of spring steel could have been.

One person who could not resist the temptation to try the new coaches on the new roads was Eleazer Blackman. All he needed was an excuse; this, his wife supplied him in a most unexpected manner.

In the intervening years, since that awful July 4th of 1778 when Eleazer Blackman had fled from the Wyoming Valley with his family, the Blackmans had returned and spread powerful roots for the growth of Wilkes-Barre. Like all the Blackman men, Eleazer farmed a large tract of land (later called Blackman Mines). He and Corinda were very happy. Their first child was a girl; they christened her Melinda. Because he had missed out in the actual fighting of 1778-82, Eleazer devoted most of his spare time to Wilkes-Barre's defenses. He was commissioned Captain of First Troop of Horse. Later, in the War of 1812, he served as a major in the militia.

Eleazer Blackman had just finished seven years of public service, five as a county commissioner and two as the county treasurer, when his wife commented on the number of leisure hours he was spending at home. Corinda's aristocratic air had never ceased to fascinate Eleazer, and he had almost no resistance to her suggestions.

"This clock of Mamma's," she said one day to her husband, "it's been so long since it worked. Now that you have a spare hour, do you think you could do something about it?"

Eleazer looked at his wife a moment before speaking, weighing the matter. He knew that she knew that he didn't have the faintest idea about what made a clock tick.

"I'll look into the matter," he said. That reply had always worked at county commission meetings in the past; he thought he would try it at home. It did, for Corinda gave him a fleeting smile and departed for another room.

Actually, Eleazer did exactly that, looked into the matter. When he saw an ad by a Daniel Collings, clockmaker, in an Easton paper left behind by a visitor to Wilkes-Barre, he decided to act.

The stage came into Wilkes-Barre weekly. Eleazer mentioned to his wife that he thought it would be best to take the clock to Easton. Corinda was surprised, but said nothing; she recalled that she had asked him to get it going again.

The clock in question was an ornate tortoise-shell and ormolu mantel clock (with an accompanying shelf), in the "Grand Style." Corinda's mother had brought it with her when she had left France. Ornate and heavy, and terribly out of place in their primitive frontier dwellings, she had cherished the clock as a symbol of her France, the world of refinement she had left behind. Because her mother had cherished it, Corinda cherished it, too. Several times she had been on the verge of discarding it, for she couldn't ever remember hearing it tick. But each time, a vision of her mother's face looking at the clock would appear to her and stop her.

Eleazer helped Corinda take the clock down from its shelf, wrap it in a piece of cloth, and place it in a box that Eleazer had made. The next day, he boarded the mail coach for Easton.

Daniel Collings was intrigued, the moment Eleazer unwrapped the clock in his shop. He wanted to start work on it immediately.

"I don't expect any difficulty with it, Mr. Blackman. It's a handsome piece if ever I saw one. Been in your wife's family, you say?"

Eleazer had Mr. Collings write a receipt for the clock, and instructed him to return-ship the clock by stage as soon as it was ready. Instead of spending three days in Easton waiting for a return coach, he hired a horse and rode west to Bethlehem; there he picked up another mail coach going into Wilkes-Barre. The trip had been brief, but satisfactory.

A little over six months passed, and Eleazer forgot about the clock. A passing whim of his wife, which, with little effort and certainly enjoyable traveling on his part, had been taken care of. Thus Eleazer dismissed the matter of the clock.

Daniel Collings worked almost every day, if only for fifteen or twenty minutes, on the clock, for it fascinated him. It seemed to attract him, if it can be said that an inanimate object has such power. About six months after Mr. Blackman had brought the clock into his shop, Daniel finished working on it. After he had satisfied himself that it was in running order, he hesitated. He wasn't too certain that it was wise to ship it. The longer he hesitated and thought, the stronger grew the impulse to deliver the clock in person. Daniel's impression of Eleazer, from his brief visit, left him with strong doubts as to Mr. Blackman's ability to unpack the clock properly. But the main reason for the personal delivery of the clock was that, as with Eleazer, it would satisfy an urge to travel. It would give him a chance to see Wilkes-Barre; he had never been there.

It took Daniel almost a whole day to properly prepare the clock for traveling. He removed the pendulum, and wrapped it separately. Next, with soft twine, he tied the various gears in place. He also secured the small hammer, and packed cotton around the vibrating chime. Then, he was ready to go.

Once in Wilkes-Barre, Daniel found that he would have a three-hour wait before someone with a wagon would be going past the Eleazer Blackman farm; he spent the time looking about. He was quick to note that Wilkes-Barre had no clockmaker.

His reception at the farm was cordial. He arrived just as the family was preparing to sit down to supper; a place was made for him immediately, and he joined them gratefully.

After supper, he unpacked the clock, and placed it on its shelf. Corinda was thrilled to have the clock functioning after so many years of silence.

While Daniel untied the twine from the various gears, Melinda Blackman stared at his hands in fascination. They were so white and gentle looking; no one had hands like that at the farm. They weren't effeminate hands; she was quick to notice that. They were strong, as strong, she suspected, as her father's, in spite of their soft skin.

The Blackmans put Daniel up for the next two nights, until he could take a coach back to Easton. During this wait, of this two and a half days, he spent most of his time with Melinda.

On his ride back to Easton, Daniel decided that he wanted two things very badly: he wanted Melinda Blackman, and he wanted a clockmaker's shop in Wilkes-Barre. Confidence in himself convinced him that both were attainable.

Twelve times, at once a month intervals, Daniel Collings rode the stagecoach between Easton and Wilkes-Barre. At the year's end, he was married to Melinda, and had opened his own shop. In the course of their married life, his wife presented Daniel with eleven children; a son, born in 1816, was named Samuel Phinney Collings.

Samuel was an alert child; he was always planning and dreaming. Sometimes, his dreams resembled schemes more than anything else. He was quick to see an opportunity, and was never hesitant to cry "foul play" if he thought someone was taking advantage of him. He was also very mature for his age. Consequently, Samuel never exerted himself too much. He adored his maternal grandfather, and was always willing to listen whenever Eleazer told a tale about his years as county commissioner.

Public life fascinated Samuel; at sixteen, he worked on Andrew Beaumont's election campaign committee. The Beaumonts were like a shining star to Samuel, and he tried never to let the star out of his sight. No sooner had Andrew Beaumont arrived in Washington than Samuel began writing him, asking for his help in obtaining an appointment in the War Department. He felt he was as well qualified as others who were being appointed, because, like the others, his grandfather Thomas Collings had fought in 1776. Andrew Beaumont liked the boy, but felt he was too young for Washington political life, and to be of much service there; instead, he encouraged Samuel to pursue his studies.

Samuel's letters, importuning the Hon. Mr. Beaumont to find a position for him in bureaucratic Washington, were apparently never intended to be taken seriously; maybe the schoolteacher in Andrew recognized that. The copious correspondence was really Samuel's undirected first steps in pursuing his vocation. The letter-writing soon gave way to story-writing, and two years later in 1835, Samuel brought out the first issue of the *Republican Farmer*. A fine newspaper, for seventeen years performing a service to farmers and others in the valley, it brought to its publisher and editor everything he desired.

Whenever the Beaumonts returned to Wilkes-Barre from a session of Congress, Samuel Collings was on hand to interview them and report on their doings in the nation's capital. He could never keep his eyes off Elizabeth Beaumont; had he printed his interviews with her in their entirety, there would have been no space left in the *Republican Farmer* for any other story.

Elizabeth was amused by Samuel's open adulation. She tossed her curls whenever her father teased her about her home town beau. When she had all of Washington at her feet, one more swain made little difference.

The key ingredient responsible for bringing this couple to the marriage altar was that Samuel was always there. Not in a hang-dog, hanger-on fashion—he could never adopt that pose! It was just that he was always around. Just as today's billboards are always around, waiting to stare us in the face whenever we look up, Samuel was always at hand. Whenever Elizabeth Beaumont looked around, Samuel Collings was in the landscape. But that is only one of the many, many ingredients needed to transform a couple into a Mr. and Mrs. Elizabeth could have any man she wanted; why did she pick Samuel Collings? The answer was quite simple.

Like beautiful wild flowers that grow only at high altitudes, Elizabeth came from a mountain family. When her father went to Washington as Congressman, it was not to become rich and famous. He was already that, within the confines of the valley. His purpose in the nation's capital was to protect the interests of those in the Wyoming Valley area.

Mountain people, particularly those in northeastern Pennsylvania, are a little softer, a little kinder, a little less hard in their relationships with others, than people in cities such as Philadelphia. If Elizabeth were to marry someone her equal, living outside the mountains would put her into an environment that would be stifling to her. To marry someone not her equal would not be fair to her. In order for her to retain that one quality of human warmth and softness, in order not to stunt her personality, she had to find someone from her own area.

When the Beaumonts returned home to Wilkes-Barre in the spring of 1837, Samuel Collings pursued Elizabeth shamelessly and relentlessly. He called at the Beaumont home daily, each time with a new suggestion for a series of articles about what the Beaumonts had done, and whom they had seen while in Washington. That all the minutia of their lives were of the utmost importance to him and to the readers of the *Republican Farmer*, he was quick to assure any member of the family who hesitated.

It was his aggressiveness that Elizabeth responded to. She had become accustomed to men on the move, men on the way up, in Washington. But on the whole, they had frightened her a little. Too much ruthlessness lay submerged just under the surface of their polite manners. She found in Samuel the push, the drive, but not the hard core. Just as advertising on billboards is effective, so Samuel succeeded. When his senses told him that this was the moment, when his newspaper nose told him that the timing was right, that Elizabeth was vulnerable, he proposed. She replied in the affirmative.

The year they were married, 1838, Elizabeth's oldest brother John Colt Beaumont received his appointment as midshipman in the U.S. Navy. John corresponded regularly with his sister, and Samuel always found newsworthy items in his brother-in-law's letters for publication in the *Republican Farmer*. Two years later, almost every letter John wrote to his sister found its way into print; he was then aboard the *Constitution* as she sailed on her round-the-world cruise. Samuel featured the letters on the front page of his paper. There was great interest in these articles; the *Constitution* had become a national legend ever since Oliver Wendell Holmes had written (in 1830) his poem "*Old Ironsides*" describing the ship.

The newly married Collings were very busy; it was an exciting time for Samuel. His father-in-law was still involved with politics. In the same year that John kept them informed of the *Constitution*'s progress (1840), President Martin Van Buren wrote to Andrew Beaumont, to ask him to assume the post of Treasurer of the U.S. Mint at Philadelphia. Samuel became very excited at his father-in-law's prospects, and gave full coverage to the appointment in his paper. Not until Andrew had formally declined did things calm down.

The Samuel Collings were to have a total of five children, four girls and one boy. In 1845 Alice Muhlenberg Collings was born.

Throughout most of her married life, Elizabeth continued to live very much as Elizabeth Beaumont. Even with the birth of her five children, she still lived her life as Andrew Beaumont's daughter. She was never the mother of children; she was always the daughter of parents. The excitements and accomplishments of her father's life were her triumphs, too. Unknowingly, her husband encouraged this attitude. All the Beaumonts, beginning with Andrew, were still Samuel's star to keep in sight. It was a very subtle thing, this immature attitude of Elizabeth's; even she wasn't aware of what she was doing. Elizabeth thought of herself as a loyal and devoted wife. She was proud to be known as Mrs. Samuel Collings. What's more, she had confidence in her husband and his ability. But in her heart, she was still Elizabeth Beaumont, daughter of the Honorable Andrew Beaumont.

When, in 1847, President James Polk, the third to follow Martin Van Buren in office, appointed Andrew commissioner of buildings and grounds for the District of Columbia, Elizabeth was thrilled. She told Samuel that she wanted to take the children and accompany her parents when her father assumed his new post, for Andrew had accepted this one. The Collings' latest child, John Beaumont Collings, was a year old, and she thought that the children would enjoy their sojourn in Washington. Samuel agreed wholeheartedly with her plan; he arranged to join the family later. He was as excited as Elizabeth at the thought of living in Washington.

But the long shadow of Jessie Benton came slithering out of the forgotten past and slowly fell across the Beaumonts as they entered Washington. It crept so slowly that they were never aware of losing the light until it was too late.

Andrew arrived in Washington in late March, just in time to take up his new duties. Those of his family that were ready had come with him. Samuel planned to join them in early September. The spring and summer months passed quickly. The women and children were busy settling in. Andrew traveled over most of the city every day to familiarize himself with the area under his control. Whenever he saw the need for an immediate improvement, he authorized the work begun at once. The first of September brought Samuel; there was excited rejoicing all around when he arrived. Simultaneous with his coming was a letter from John Beaumont. He had safely survived the battle at Veracruz, Mexico, and expected to put into Washington in time for Christmas, as the Mexicans had accepted an armistice. He wrote to say that the brief Mexican War was over.

But the happy time of Christmas in Washington, 1847, never materialized. When Congress reconvened in the middle of September, only weeks after Samuel's arrival, Andrew's old ally and friend from the Jackson days, Senator Thomas Hart Benton, stood up in the Senate and launched a violent attack against Andrew's appointment!

The cast of characters was the same as a decade earlier but oh, what a difference! Elizabeth Beaumont was now the wife of Samuel Collings. John Charles Frémont was married to Jessie Benton. Andrew Beaumont was still a political figure, but no longer subject to voters' whims. Once his appointment was confirmed, he would become a permanent resident in Washington. Only Thomas Hart Benton had remained the same; he was still a senator. However, there were changes in some of their positions. This was the time (late September) when Frémont was on trial for his seizure of power in California. Jessie was no longer following Frémont hungrily around a ballroom floor. Instead, all eyes were turned towards her as she sat in the courtroom each day trying to shield her husband.

With all of her emotions tied up in her husband's trial, Jessie could not stand the threat of having Elizabeth near Frémont again. Her emotions were already stretched too taut from the weeks of arrest and uncertainty her husband had endured. Jessie lashed out, in violent anger, to her father concerning the Beaumonts. It fell on fertile soil. Benton's reputation was at stake over his alliance with his son-in-law, for he had sponsored Frémont on his trips. Senator Benton allowed his daughter to goad him on. He, in turn, unleashed his own version of Jessie's anger at having Elizabeth around again. Before the Senate he turned on Andrew Beaumont and demanded that Andrew's appointment not be confirmed. Aghast, the Beaumonts and Samuel Collings stood in the wings, unable to fathom Benton's attack on Andrew.

Jessie had her way. Andrew's appointment was not approved, and the Beaumonts left Washington, returning to Wilkes-Barre. But it was an empty victory for her. The court-martial found Frémont guilty of inciting Americans to revolt in California, and of undertaking an unauthorized campaign of conquest, among other charges. Enraged over the interpretation of his actions, Frémont left for the West immediately. Senator Benton, having so successfully hounded Andrew Beaumont out of office, and continuing to reflect Jessie's frustrations, next turned on his son-in-law's rival. For thirteen successive days, he filibustered in the Senate against a Stephen Kearny and his promotion to the rank of major general, in this instance without success.

The final discordant sound of the melee came via John Beaumont's letter, this time from the ship *Columbia*. After two weeks of peace negotiations, the Mexicans had disavowed the truce and resumed fighting. He concluded his letter by writing that he had no idea when he would be able to get to Washington.

The journey back to Wilkes-Barre was made in silence, with each traveler reviewing the events, trying to fathom what had gone wrong. No one suspected

Jessie Benton Frémont of being the cause. Once home, the family gathered strength and held a council of war. Andrew spoke quite bluntly. He was sensitive to political environments, and he knew that he personally was finished in Washington. He proposed sending Samuel, to take over where he had been forced to leave off. "First, Samuel, we'll enter you in the House race," Andrew told his son-in-law.

The two men called on a neighbor, Colonel Hendrick Wright. Wright was in a strong position in the political life of Wilkes-Barre in 1847. He had been chairman of the national Democratic Party convention when it had met in Baltimore three years earlier. This was the same convention that had nominated James Polk; and Polk had gone on to win the presidency. Chairman of a successful convention, Wright carried a lot of weight in the twentieth election district.

The three men discussed the wisdom of running Samuel Collings for Congress. "I think we stand a good chance with Samuel," the colonel agreed with Andrew, "from what I hear, the Whigs are planning to put up Chester Butler."

So it was agreed. Samuel ran for Congress on the Democratic ticket. Most people in the Wyoming Valley were acquainted with him through his newspaper, and liked him. *The Republican Farmer* was generally recognized as one of the best Democratic papers in the area. As the campaign approached the final weeks, Samuel's election committee reported to Andrew Beaumont that it looked as though Samuel would win a large majority of the vote.

But in early October, Colonel Wright was openly referred to as the "Great Bobtail Leader" by Andrew, Samuel, and their campaign staff. This was not the first time that Andrew Beaumont and Hendrick Wright had clashed, but it was Wright's first public act of treachery to his friends and the Democratic Party.

What Wright did was to proclaim himself an independent or "stump" candidate. The outcome was predictable. Many of the staunch Democratic voters in the valley became confused. They had clearly identified Wright in their minds with the Democratic Party, since the national convention in 1844. But, at the same time, handbills all over the district, even more clearly, proclaimed Samuel Collings to be the Democratic nominee. The vote split, and the Whig Butler was elected; Samuel had lost.

Hendrick Wright's behavior to Samuel Collings and Andrew Beaumont, in the 1848 campaign, was certainly not unusual. Politics and political campaigns have always involved deals, counterdeals, and vote-stealing, both legal and illegal. And by Wright's subsequent history in area politics, such would certainly seem the case: namely, a typically crude politician's display of his *modus operandi.* However, disposing of the cavalier Mr. Wright so casually should be questioned. And it was unfortunate that the Hon. Mr. Beaumont, widely recognized for a superior intellect, also had not thought to delve more deeply into Wright's actions than the surface interpretation.

Until 1787, ownership of the northern quarter of Pennsylvania had been hotly contested between the settlers from Connecticut and those from Pennsylvania.

Until the decree issued by the Continental Congress in that year was implemented, the claim to ownership had been backed by physical force. There were times when it seemed more preferable to fight Indians, as being the easier course to follow. But Congress had settled the question once and for all. Neither faction was entitled to exclusive possession. The fighting ceased, and those with a Connecticut heritage opened up the wilderness side by side with those who were native Pennsylvanians.

Yes, they did live in harmony, side by side; that is, they lived in physical harmony. But did the contest of claim authenticity manifest itself in other ways? When Andrew Beaumont and Samuel Collings first approached Hendrick Wright, it was with the odor of Connecticut and the *Mayflower* clinging to them. And the one on whom they called, their neighbor in Wilkes-Barre, the one who so courteously welcomed them into his home, was the child of those who had sailed on the *Welcome* with William Penn. He was the one who shared a law office with Wilkes-Barre's Judge Conyngham, a grandson in a family that had aided in the building of Christ Church in Philadelphia. So, the question arises, was the old battle still showing itself—this time, not in terms of square feet and grains of dirt, but in a contest of wills, of minds, for control of the valley?

The newspaper that Samuel Collings edited and owned, the *Republican Farmer*, was highly respected and revered in the valley. The valley's best writers contributed to it, and were proud to do so. But another newspaper made its appearance in the valley—the *Luzerne Democrat.* The owner and editor was Hendrick Wright. He was not as fortunate as Samuel Collings in his editorial staff. He had men writing for him like former Sheriff Steele of Luzerne County, who described such things as a package of processes as "leven rits."

Was this rivalry, with Andrew Beaumont and Samuel Collings on one side, and Hendrick Wright and his law mentor, Judge John Conyngham, on the other, simply a clash of personalities? Or was it the old struggle: Connecticut against Pennsylvania? It is hard to say. One of a suspicious nature would say the first. A kinder person would believe that the men were merely challenging each other. However, as time would show, whenever there was a divergence of opinion, two sides to an issue, it would always be thus: Wright and his Pennsylvanians challenging those who could trace back to Connecticut. Had it been mainly a matter of men pitting their strength against each other, it would certainly seem more logical that they make their differences more marked. Had one group been leaders of the Whig party, and the other adherents to the Democratic party, the question of motivating factors could be more easily answered. But they all espoused whatever philosophy was for the ultimate good of the valley; thereafter, they competed with each other as to who was to lead the way.

For the remaining years of his life, Andrew Beaumont returned to the Pennsylvania State Legislature. He formed a committee to strengthen the ties between federal and state governments: he was still espousing the old Jackson philosophy of a strong central government.

The end for Andrew Beaumont came very quickly, in 1853; Julia Colt Beaumont was then a widow. At the time of Andrew's death, her oldest son

John was stationed at the U.S. Naval Observatory in Washington and her youngest son, Eugene Beauharnais Beaumont, had entered West Point. Julia turned to her daughter, Elizabeth Collings, for support. Elizabeth stepped in immediately, and managed the funeral arrangements on her mother's behalf.

Elizabeth notified many of her father's old friends of his passing. Franklin Pierce had just become President of the United States. When he learned of Andrew Beaumont's death, his thoughts turned back to the days when he himself had first been elected to the House of Representatives. He and Andrew had both been elected the same year (1832), and had begun their Washington careers in the same crimson chamber simultaneously. He remembered how he had moved on to the Senate, just in time to witness Benton's violent outburst against Andrew's appointment. Now he, Pierce, was president, and Andrew was gone. He remembered Elizabeth's fresh beauty, her charm and warmth at Washington social functions.

Pierce was just beginning his term; he had great plans for his country. At this moment of reflection on things past, he had a great urge to do something for his old friend of Congressional days. It would also fit in with some ideas he had for his country's foreign policy, he noted. He appointed Samuel Collings, because he was Elizabeth's husband and Andrew Beaumont's son-in-law, to be the U.S. consul in Tangiers, Morocco. The year was 1854.

It is interesting to note that, when the appointment was announced locally in Wilkes-Barre, Hendrick Wright lost no time in telling anyone who would listen that he, Wright, had at last silenced Samuel Collings with a foreign appointment. The expression of Hendrick Wright's hostility to Samuel Collings, in this instance, gives greater insight than any other incident as to the underlying cause of the factiousness. Had it been personal animosity, Wright would most certainly have decried Collings as unfit for the office. But this he did not do. Instead, in a backhanded fashion, he was really expressing pride in a Wyoming Valley resident receiving the diplomatic appointment. What he tried to show was that he, Wright, of Pennsylvania heritage, was making the decisions for the valley.

Tangiers was an important post, about to become even more important. The city was directly across from Gibraltar. Tangiers and Gibraltar were the two gates that controlled access to and from the Mediterranean. Known only to a few, word had been brought to President Pierce that the Vice-Roy (Viceroy) of Egypt had just given a French engineer, Ferdinand deLesseps, the charter to open a passage through the Egyptian Isthmus of Suez, at the other end of the Mediterranean.

Pierce realized the portent immediately. The canal passage would restructure world commerce the moment ships could pass through it and thus avoid completely the treacherous Cape of Good Hope passage. England was already in possession of Gibraltar. If he could establish supremacy for the United States, on the opposite shore of the Straits of Gibraltar, his country would have powerful leverage on world shipping. Pierce did not know Samuel Collings, but he did know his wife. He had great confidence, and instilled high hopes in Elizabeth.

Once again, Elizabeth was on the road to Washington.

There, Samuel received his credentials and instructions for Morocco, and the couple, with their children, prepared for the ocean crossing to Tangiers. They were put aboard the *San Jacinto* as it was leaving for duty along the coast of Europe. To everyone's delight, John Colt Beaumont welcomed them aboard, for he had just been assigned to the *San Jacinto.* After two years on land, at the Observatory, John was thrilled to be back at sea again. Adding to his pleasure was the realization that his first task was to escort his sister and her family. It was the promise of wonderful things to come.

President Pierce waited patiently for news about Morocco. When early reports confirmed that his appraisals and estimates, of both the Mediterranean situation and Elizabeth and Samuel Collings, were correct, he couldn't have been more pleased. He, too, like John Beaumont, felt the promise of wonderful things to come.

The Collings were immediately successful with the Moroccans. Though they were from the Western culture, they did not rub these Arabs the wrong way. In a vague sense, there was a general similarity of temperament. Arabs are friendly, not naturally aggressive or hostile, although they are instinctively suspicious. They appreciate independence of character, and can be simple and direct in their dealings with others if they so decide. All of these qualities, to some degree, are present in mountain people, especially those from the Wyoming Valley area. Samuel achieved amazing results in his first year as U.S. Consul. Then suddenly, in June of 1855, he became ill with a fever. In less than two weeks he was dead.

The *San Jacinto* sailed into Tangiers harbor to take Elizabeth and the children home. John and his sister were very silent. What could be said to ease the pain? Before boarding the ship, John escorted Elizabeth to the emperor's palace, where she paid her respects in a formal farewell to the ruler. The emperor handed John a packet, to be delivered to President Pierce.

The *San Jacinto* sailed gently back across the Atlantic; it seemed to match the mood of the grieving sister and her brother. The crew remembered the Collings children. They made much of them, and allowed them to wander over the ship.

When they reached Washington, Elizabeth remained with the children, while John was instructed to turn her husband's papers over to the Secretary of State; included was the packet from the Emperor of Morocco. In the packet was a eulogy to Samuel Phinney Collings. The emperor praised Samuel, in elegant, formal language. That he had high regard for Samuel was obvious. With a flourish, the emperor had emblazoned his signature across the bottom of the paper. It was there for all the world to see: what a whole country thought of Samuel Collings, and how much it admired and respected him.

John was given an extended leave; he escorted Elizabeth and the children back to Wilkes-Barre. There, she and her mother, Julia Colt Beaumont, embraced each other. They had both been widowed within the space of two years. Alice Collings, now ten, watched silently at the reunion of her mother and grandmother.

5

W.W.W.

William Wilander Winton.

Like a two-headed penny, no matter how he was tossed about, W.W.W. always landed face up.

This description of W.W.W's character fits in quite nicely with the description of his arrival in the Wyoming Valley; W.W.W. was more or less tossed into the Valley and came up smiling.

During the years the Blackmans, Beaumonts, Colts, Yarringtons, and others were planning and building in the Wyoming Valley, a substratum of society was developing, too. This latter group was based on coal. The inherent beauty of the Wyoming Valley, its expansiveness, meant nothing to those interested in coal; they came to plunder. Daniel Collings, on the other hand, may have been a "taker," but he expected to give a full day's labor for what he took. And he did, too. He served as postmaster of Wilkes-Barre for a six year period, from 1835-1841. He worked for the Democratic Party. He felt responsible for the condition of his community. Just as you and I keep our front lawn neat and trimmed, the grass cut and free of littered papers, on a larger scale he did his part to keep his local government functioning smoothly and for the best interests of all. Daniel Collings may have taken a Blackman for a wife, and he may have taken the hard earned profits of the pioneer settlers, gained by having survived Indian attacks and converting virgin forest soil into farm land, in order to provide himself with an income, but in return he gave back service and responsibility to the Wyoming Valley inhabitants. The difference between the two is that the settlers gave first and received in return; as for Daniel, he took first before giving.

The coal people, though, came only to take. They also served the community in government posts, but only to improve and protect their own profit and comfort. If a law, passed to enrich their own pocketbook, also improved the community, fine. But the unwritten code was never to approve a law for the general good, unless it was certain to put a few extra dollars their way. There was never any thought other than "what would it gain them personally?" Eventually, two separate societies came to exist side by side in the Wyoming Valley area. To the outside world, outside of the valley that is, only the "coal robbers" were recognized; they were called the "coal kings." And the only significance the Wyoming Valley had to them was as a spot on the face of the earth which provided them with their wealth.

Coal was not a miraculous, overnight discovery in the Wyoming Valley. The first abortive attempt at settlement, in 1762, had gained the knowledge of the black stones; a few of the friendly Indians had shown the settlers, even then, that the black stones would burn. The larger settlement that followed, the one that was destroyed by the Indians in the Massacre of 1778, had also known about the black stones. Darius Spofford, Lovinia Blackman's husband, who had worked as a blacksmith before losing his life in the massacre, had often used the black stones to help build his fire for his work. The Blackmans had first-hand knowledge of the black stones, from having watched Darius at his forge. It was commonly known among the Wyoming Valley settlers, regardless of their Connecticut or Pennsylvania origin, that the black stones would burn. There wasn't a blacksmith in the area that didn't add a few to his fire. This was particularly true in the 1787 to 1800 resettlement period. Then why the silence? Why were the black stones ignored? Why weren't they mined immediately and sent to the industrialized coal market, where big profits were to be had? Why did the main activity in the valley remain farming?

Simply, because nobody recognized the black stones for what they were—the finest grade of coal to be found anywhere in the world.

At that time, England had a monopoly on the coal trade. By the year 1800, she was taking eleven million tons of coal out of the ground annually. Most of the coal was shipped by wagon to English cities. The rest of it was shipped to the United States, because the new country didn't have any coal. The coal mined was in great demand. It was valuable for two purposes: to produce steam to power the machines in factories, and, on a lesser scale, to heat houses. James Watt's steam engine, patented in 1769, was such a great improvement over earlier attempts, that the manufacturing methods for consumer goods changed almost immediately. Factories, with steam-powered machines, their assembly lines, and seemingly limitless mass production ability for producing goods cheaply, created cities all over England. The steam engine was necessary to drive every power tool and every complicated machine used; English coal was necessary to power every steam engine. So, coal was as synonymous with the industrial revolution as Watt's steam engine and all the other patented machinery that had sprung from the newly acquired ability to mechanize. Coal was king!

Northeastern Pennsylvania's "black stones that burn" were never considered to be coal, positively. Sometimes they were called coal, but more often they were referred to as the "black stones that burn." The first attempts, made by a few Pennsylvanians, to put the product across to the public, had ended disastrously; a Colonel George Shoemaker had been denounced as an impostor by his Philadelphia customers (one went so far as to swear out a warrant for his arrest), and Colonel Shoemaker was reduced to giving away the remainder of his nine wagon loads of "stones that burn." The trouble was that the customers were used to building fires with English coal, and could not get the Pennsylvania "coal" to keep burning after it was ignited.

Another earlier attempt, in 1803 by the City of Philadelphia, to substitute Pennsylvania "coal" for English coal had also resulted in disaster. When the black stones were thrown on the fire under the boilers at the city waterworks, they succeeded only in extinguishing the fire, instead of burning quickly and easily as the highly desired British coal did. Disgusted with the results of the experiment, the city had the black stones broken up and thrown on the sidewalks nearby in place of gravel.

However, there was always some interest in the black stones; note that the blacksmiths of northeastern Pennsylvania were nevertheless using them in their fires. On the strength of this, towards the end of the Revolutionary War, Pennsylvania "coal" had been shipped to Carlisle, Pennsylvania, where it had been used to build the fires at a forge making arms for the 1776 hostilities. While most Philadelphia customers were distrustful of the black stones from "upstate," there was a very small group who felt otherwise. Eventually, their interest was to be rewarded because of Jesse Fell, a blacksmith.

Jesse Fell had come to Wilkes-Barre with the first wave of settlers returning after the Wyoming Massacre. In 1788, he had a small forge in operation and was busy making nails for the new housebuilders in the area. Jesse, like the other blacksmiths, knew enough to scratch the surface of the ground around him, and throw a few of the hard black stones he found onto the fire; that was the extent of his knowledge.

The idea that the black stones could be used as coal stayed with Jesse for twenty years. Whenever there was a recurrent surge of interest in finding a profitable way to use the "stones that burn," Jesse would be like the other blacksmiths and their friends. He too would try, only to be laughed at, the same as his co-workers. In one such surge in 1808, Jesse again threw some of the stones onto the fire, but this time he utilized an iron grate. He also experimented at night, for he was getting tired of being laughed at. He piled on enough of the stones so that he was able to ignite them. The stones were burning when Jesse fell asleep. They were still burning when he awoke, several hours later! The thrill of discovery was much greater when he became conscious of the large amount of heat still coming from the stones after having burned unattended for so many hours.

Jesse demonstrated the firing and heating capacities of the black stones to his friends and neighbors, On the strength of Jesse's success, John and Abijah Smith of Plymouth (across the Susquehanna and five miles down towards the end of the valley) formed the Abijah Smith and Company coal supply firm, and by 1812 were making shipments down the Susquehanna to Havre de Grace, Maryland. Once the coal arrived, it was distributed elsewhere by a quickly formed New York City coal firm, Price and Waterbury. But these few people were the only ones able to sell the "black stones that burn" and consequently to derive a monetary profit. There was no other coal activity in the valley at that time.

The reason for the long delay in getting Pennsylvania's black stones to burn was due entirely to man's own mental state. His frame of reference had blocked his creative vision, to the point where he accomplished nothing. As long as the black stones were treated and handled in the same way as English coal, there could be nothing but failure. English coal was bituminous, whereas Pennsylvania's coal was anthracite. Man had retarded himself because, for no other reason than his frame of reference, he insisted on using English coal standards in evaluating the new Pennsylvania coal. He knew the new coal would burn, because both the Indians and local blacksmiths had demonstrated it. If he had taken the black stones and approached the task of getting them to burn in any way be could, instead of trying to get a satisfactory reaction by following existing standards, then success would have come much earlier.

In today's modern world, with years of scientific research behind us, the structure of coal and its characteristics are quite well established. Coal is organic, plant in origin. It consists of varying proportions of carbon, plus mineral matter and moisture. The higher the percentage of carbon, the greater its fuel value is to man. English coal is bituminous. The lowest form of coal is peat; peat has a high degree of moisture and crumbles easily. Next in ascending order is lignite, followed by subbituminous or black lignite. Above the lignites in desirability, because of their relatively high carbon to moisture ratio, are the bituminous and semibituminous (a high-grade bituminous) coals. Little effort is needed to start a fire of bituminous coal; it burns easily and quickly, sending out a fair amount of heat. This was the coal used to power the English factories, and it was also shipped to the United States.

The finest coals, almost pure carbon, are semigrade anthracite (a low grade of anthracite) and anthracite. When the settlers coming in to northeastern Pennsylvania from Connecticut followed the valley-created paths, the terrain swept upwards from the valley floors into mountains of pure anthracite. It was there waiting for man, provided he came with no inhibiting prejudices nor restricting frames of reference, ready to power the country and part of the world into comfort, warmth, and industrialization.

The northeastern Pennsylvania coal beds formed the upper end of a vast coal region, stretching through the Appalachian mountains from Pennsylvania to Alabama. In later years, as this country spread westward, many other coal deposits were found, but their discovery had first to wait for the westward expansion of the people. However, of all the places where coal was found, only northeastern Pennsylvania had the highly prized coal, anthracite coal.

Once it was learned that an anthracite coal fire had to be built differently from one composed of bituminous coal, it was almost impossible to keep up with the demand, for anthracite coal is far superior to bituminous. Anthracite gives off more heat and is longer burning. Thus, much less coal has to be consumed to produce a greater amount of heat; it is ideal for heating houses. Another feature, unknown then but important today, is its relative purity. When anthracite coal burns, it causes very little pollution because of its low sulphur content. Pollution from bituminous coal, with its high sulphur content, can be controlled but at great expense. And as Jesse Fell, who eventually became Judge Fell of Wilkes-Barre, wrote, "I find we have various qualities of coal, but our best specimens are said to be superior to any yet known, and we have it in sufficient quantity to supply the world." And a good thing it was, too, for the world's need for coal compounded daily.

One coal transporter alone, the Delaware and Hudson Canal Company, increased their shipping from 7,000 tons in 1830, their first year of operation, to 122,000 tons, nine years later in 1839. And in 1843, it seemed as if the millennium had been reached: a ship on her maiden voyage, the *Prince Albert*, took on as freight anthracite coal to be delivered to England!

The demand for coal produced another great problem, one the world had never faced before: cartage! Before utilizing coal, man had always been able to live on what his immediate environment could supply him with. Whatever type of stone and wood he found in an area he used. Only rarely would heavy, bulky materials be transported from one place to another. But with the use of coal, all that was changed; what had been true for hundreds of years no longer held. Not since the days of the temple and pyramid builders, when they were bringing the giant cedar trees down from the mountains of Lebanon, did only one place in the world have something that people everywhere else had to have.

Universally, coal was first transported by wagon. Next, from the Wyoming Valley area, a canal was constructed to carry the coal, from a point on the outside wall of the mountains enclosing the valley, over to the Hudson River. However, the coal was still brought by wagon from the mines to the canal's terminus at Honesdale, Pennsylvania. Farther south, in areas through which the Lehigh or Schuylkill Rivers flow, the locally mined coal was floated down these tributaries to the Delaware River (these two areas were the first to get their anthracite to market). The wagon, previously the sole method of conveyance, gave way to the barge. But the raft idea was unsatisfactory, for canals and natural waterways were limited. A lot of places, at both ends of the coal's journey, still had to be reached by wagon.

It was about this time (1804) that Richard Trevithick, an Englishman, ran a small steam locomotive on a circular track. He enclosed the area, and admission was paid by the curious to see the engine run. His idea was taken and developed, but another twenty years passed before George Stephenson, another Englishman, built a locomotive that was commercially practicable. From that point on, the growth of the railroad and the demand for coal developed simultaneously; the history of one was the history of the other.

The railroad was the first method of transportation that brought coal from the miner to the consumer with ease, quickly, and with a profit for all along the way. Not only did the railroad carry coal to the customers, but it was also a customer itself, for it was coal that fueled the locomotive engines.

There was no question that the railroad was superior to the canal. Tracks could be laid in any direction. The locomotive was strong; ascending or descending grades were traversed with equal ease. In the U.S., railroad lines sprung up everywhere between 1825 and 1830, but none of them was longer than ten miles. That railroads existed at all, however, did worry the Wintons. The Wintons, in this particular instance, were Andrew Winton, his brother, and his son.

A family characteristic of the Wintons was that they appeared to be opportunists, "fast-buck artists." To some extent this was justified; they sensed where the action was. They were always *au courant* with the times. There was one big difference, however; the Wintons were givers, never takers. And in no way could they ever be classed as plunderers and robbers.

When the War of 1812 had come to an end, Andrew Winton sensed that money and action were to be found in travel. The Wintons were originally from the part of Connecticut along the Naugatuck River near Waterbury. Andrew moved into New York State at Butternuts, now Gilbertsville, in Otsego County, and established a stagecoach line running from Albany to New York City, sweeping west to link Coopertown and Oneonta with the two Hudson River cities. It was a profitable business, and soon he married Fannie Glover. In 1815, he became the father of a boy, William Wilander Winton. William was the delight of his father; Andrew took the boy with him wherever he went. William was as much a part of the stagecoach business as his father and his uncle.

Andrew watched his boy grow with pride. At the same time, he was also watching the growth of traffic on the Hudson River. Both William Wilander and the descendants of Robert Fulton's steamship *Clermont* seemed to be progressing at the same rapid, healthy pace. The Erie Canal, which wasn't finished until 1822, had never bothered Andrew Winton. In fact, the canal had been one of the reasons for setting up the stage line. He had rightly deduced that people would want a reliable means of connecting with the waterway (it was that Winton ability for going where the action was).

But there was something about steamboats that disturbed Andrew; he even went as far as to confide his thoughts to his son. William was interested, and his father went into a detailed discussion of steam engines, steam boats, and how they worked, and how it was all so different from the sailing vessel Andrew had always known.

William was nine, and on the precocious side. His years of sharing interests with his father had sharpened him into an alert as well as gregarious lad. Enlightened by their conversation, William called his father's attention to an advertisement in a New York City newspaper, the *Commercial Advertiser*; the year was 1824. The ad was from the Wurts brothers, inviting interested New York City businessmen to examine and test "Lackawaxen" coal, which would soon be brought into New York by a canal they were building.

The Wurts brothers, William and Maurice, could be described as the first of many who came into the Wyoming Valley to plunder and rob and give the valley nothing in return. In 1814, they came from Philadelphia looking for coal. For two years, they had searched the wilderness at the upper end of the Wyoming Valley. The Wurts were different from Jesse Fell and John and Abijah Smith; the latter had lived all their lives in the Wyoming Valley; theirs was a case of finally finding a use for something they had always had. On the other hand, the Wurts were looking for only one thing—money. It made no difference to them where they went or what the locale looked like; it mattered only that it would provide them with large sums of money.

The two-year search for coal, up and down the southeastern mountain wall of the valley, led them to David Nobles. He was willing to sell them a large tract of land, with "curious black stones" on it, for payment of a $15 debt. This debt, incidentally, was to a son-in-law of Major Woodbridge, Moses Dolph's and Henry Heermans' old competitor. The Wurts brothers knew this tract, some 70,000 acres, by its popular name, the Holland Tract. In all probability, this area was part of the original holdings of Moses Dolph, hence the local reference to the Holland Tract.

Those of English origin, whether from Pennsylvania or Connecticut, were antagonistic to those of Dutch descent if both moved into an area at approximately the same time. The internecine squabbling, between Moses Dolph and Henry Heermans on one hand, and Major Woodbridge and his relatives at Salem Corners on the other, was typical. Equally typical was the lack of respect accorded the early settlers of Dutch descent. For example, when the first ministers came into Salem Corners (Hamlin) to establish churches, the records describing the meetings in full detail refer to Major Woodbridge and his family by name. But as for Moses Dolph and his family, they speak only of "the Dutchman" assisting at the meeting, implying an inferior position.

The Wurts took possession of the land from David Nobles, and opened the first coal mine in the Wyoming Valley. They called their firm the Grassy Island Coal Company. Once they started to mine the coal, they were faced with the problem of finding a market and getting the coal to it. South of the Wyoming Valley, in the Lehigh and Schuylkill River areas, barges were carrying coal from just north of the Blue Ridge to Philadelphia. The Wurts then thought of New York. They conceived the idea of building a canal from just outside the valley's mountain wall, at Honesdale, and extending it to the Hudson River. They planned to connect with the Hudson at Rondout, approximately Kingston, New York. The Wurts were very successful in both Pennsylvania and New York state legislatures; the two states gave the brothers the authority to make use of local area rivers wherever necessary in the routing of their canal. Soon a mayor of New York City, Philip Hone (after whom Honesdale is named), and Benjamine Wright, who was also an engineer in the building of the Erie Canal, joined the Wurts, and the Delaware and Hudson Canal was begun.

The Wurts Brothers' original intention was to extend the canal from the Hudson River all the way to the mines in the valley, but Benjamine Wright, after surveying the route, recommended going no farther than Honesdale with the waterway. He saw no way of passing through Moosic Mountain. There were only a few possible gaps in the mountain, none of which were practical to use. One of these gaps was quite far south of Honesdale; this was Cobb's Gap, which had been part of Henry Heermans' path to "The Corners" (Razorville).

The idea was then put by Benjamine Wright to the other principals, namely, William and Maurice Wurts and Philip Hone, that the remaining miles from Honesdale to Carbondale, and eventually to Archbald and Olyphant in the valley, be covered by railroad. By 1828, Wright was no longer with the canal company, but following his suggestion, another engineer, Horatio Allen, was sent at company expense to England. Once in England, Allen contacted George Stephenson (who had made the first successful commercial railroad run) and after much study, Allen arranged for the purchase and shipment of three engines to the Delaware and Hudson Company. On their arrival in New York city, they were exhibited, and one of them, the *Stourbridge Lion*, was then shipped to Honesdale, where plans for a test run were made.

This trial took place on August 8, 1829. Just before the Lion was to start on the run, grave doubts arose as to the success of the trial. Track timbers (ties) had cracked from the hot August sun, and one curve, less than four hundred feet, was too short. At the last minute, no one would operate the engine except Horatio Allen, who stepped forward and calmly climbed into the cab. He safely passed over the curve, and then continued on for another two to three miles, where he reversed the valve and returned to the starting point. It was "the first railroad trip by locomotive in the western hemisphere," a great moment in American history!

At this point in the latter part of 1829, the men involved in creating the Delaware and Hudson Canal Company, including a new president by the name of John Bolton as well as the Wurts brothers (who also owned The Grassy Island Coal Company), had in their hands the opportunity to become the most powerful economic force in the United States. They were the first to bring the railroad to this country, and to unite Queen Railroad with King Coal!

They were truly far-sighted financial genuises who thought on the grand scale. They were in a position to become supreme giants of industry. For they, and they alone, had had the vision to spend approximately $10,000 on commercial research in the year 1829. And of the $10,000, the sum of $3,837 had been spent just for traveling expenses. Horatio Allen had been allotted $4.50 per day, in addition to his ship passage. Truly, they were admirable men.

Or were they?

As soon as the *Stourbridge Lion* made its successful and thrilling run, the canal, any canal, was obsolete. Intuitively, the men at the head of the D&H Canal realized it. They had already spent a million and a half dollars building their canal. It had been carrying coal less than a year, only since December of 1828. Unfortunately, the men of the canal company were not really big men after all; they only appeared that way. Instead of going forward, they tried to turn back the hands of time. They declared the run of the *Stourbridge Lion* to be disappointing, and stored the locomotive in a shed in Honesdale. It remained there until 1849, when they removed its boiler, using it in their shop at Carbondale.

They were so fearful of losing the dollars already spent, that they would not put out a few more, even after they had had proof of limitless profits for the future. If only they had been big enough, they would have written off the cost of the canal and forgotten it, and laid railroad track everywhere in the United States. If only they had been like Andrew Carnegie and willing to stake all their money on the new railroad, as he had been willing to do with the Bessemer process for steel!

Andrew Winton was interested in the advertisement that his son showed him for "Lackawaxen" coal. He felt certain that something was going on that he should watch. He followed the building of the canal. For some time, he even toyed with the idea of extending their own stagecoach line down to connect with the Delaware and Hudson Canal. But he dismissed the idea when he learned of a triweekly run from the Wyoming Valley to New York, via Stroudsburg, Pennsylvania; this was in addition to another stage that made daily runs along the valley, from Wilkes-Barre to Carbondale and Honesdale. Too much competition, he decided.

Andrew Winton's interest in what was going on in the Wyoming Valley intensified when he read the June 12, 1829 story in the *Morning Courier and New York Enquirer*, which described an exhibition of the *Stourbridge Lion*, in New York City before it was shipped to Honesdale. Andrew showed the article to the other members of his family. All the Wintons were very thoughtful. As owners of a stage line, they were wondering just what was in the future. The Wintons became confused, however, when they heard in August that the locomotive had performed successfully at Honesdale, but the canal company was going to transport its coal over the mountain by means of an "up and down hill railroad," or gravity railroad, instead. Andrew Winton had no answer for William when his son asked, "What kind of a railroad is an 'up and down hill' one?"

The Delaware and Hudson Canal people had had their chance, and had thrown it away. In the next few years, railroads sprung up everywhere. The Baltimore and Ohio put its *Tom Thumb* engine into service in 1830; others soon covered over the void left by the canal people. Almost a thousand miles of track were laid, although usually not more than ten miles at a stretch.

By the time the year 1833 came up on the calendar, Andrew Winton felt that it would be foolhardy to delay any longer. He wanted to get a look at the coal that was powering all the steam vessels on the Hudson, and all the locomotives along the railroad tracks that could be laid anywhere, independent of land formations, as was not the case with water transportation. The railroads, he felt, were the biggest threat to his stagecoach business. He wanted to be where that action was, and he didn't believe that there was any more action left in stagecoaching.

The same year (1833) when Andrew Beaumont was taking his seat in the House of Representatives, Andrew Winton and his son William, now eighteen, set out for the Wyoming Valley. It was just a short trip to look the situation over; they traveled by stage. When the coach pulled to a halt at its midvalley stop, Andrew Winton looked around. They were in front of a large white tavern, at a crossroads called Razorville, in the middle of the Wyoming Valley. He decided to get out. "Let's stay here for a few days. This looks like a good place to stop. It will give us an opportunity to look the area over," he suggested to his son.

The two men got out, and climbed the steps of the inn. They crossed the porch, and entered into warmth and spaciousness. The proprietor came forward to greet them. "Good afternoon, Gentlemen. Welcome! Welcome! I'm Henry Heermans. Can I be of service?"

Four years had passed since Henry and his much loved Fanny had departed Salem Corners (Hamlin), with their children, for Razorville. When they had arrived, they had gone straight to The White Tavern to stay until the mansion Henry had promised Fanny was ready. Knowing they were coming, their new neighbors, including Philip's family, had turned out to give them a warm welcome. A party atmosphere prevailed throughout The White Tavern; the Henry Heermans were acknowledged as the wealthy family of the area.

In the midst of all the gaiety, Henry had drawn off to a quiet retreat. He thought back to when he had first come with his brother Philip and Philip's wife, Mary, and to the sadness he had carried with him when, after his exploratory trip before marrying Fanny, he had realized Razorville could not support him and a wife. Razorville, then, could hardly have been designated a village. At an intersection of two cart roads, including a blacksmith shop and a wagon shop, it had seven buildings in all; these were occupied by the Washburns, Knapps, Merrifields, Taylors, Tripps, and Squire Fellows and his sons, the latter being Mary Fellows Heermans' family. Two miles to the south, down on the flats (Slocum Flats) were the Slocums and the Vaughns. North of the intersection, the Watres family had a carding and fulling mill.

Now, a little over a decade later, the change was remarkable. Razorville was a thriving intersection with almost two of everything. The White Tavern, as Philip Heermans's place was known, was busy night and day, largely because of the stagecoach. A few years earlier, when a stagecoach run had been established between Wilkes-Barre and Carbondale, from one end of the valley to the other, Heermans House or The White Tavern (it was known by both names) became the changing place for the horses, and a dinner station for the travelers, for Razorville was approximately fifteen miles from Wilkes-Barre.

The area around The White Tavern had developed nicely, too. In 1826, a Harvey Chase came from Hyde Park, New York and settled just west of "The Corners" (Razorville), naming his area Hyde Park. So there were now two fast-growing communities side by side.

Someone brought Henry back to the present, for he heard his name being called. It was his first born, Alva. He was coming towards Henry, escorting an attractive-looking girl. "Pops, do you know Sarah Slocum?"

The signs were unmistakable. Henry decided he had better get to work on the mansion house he had promised Fanny immediately, if he didn't want to do the work himself. It was a good thing the large "Homestead" was built quickly, for Fanny lived to enjoy only two years in it. In 1831 she passed away; Henry was disconsolate. The mansion, as he privately thought of the house, was unbearable without her. He moved into The White Tavern, and for the first time, began to exercise his rights to the tavern and store he had helped to build so long ago. Managing them took his mind off his sorrows.

The White Tavern became a meeting place for everyone in the area; elections were held there as well. Andrew Beaumont and his future son-in-law Samuel

Collings could often be found there, passing pleasant hours campaigning. Henry Heermans also supplied the community well, with items from the store. He had a genuine understanding of farming and was able to provide farmers with practical advice as well as seed and fertilizer. In fact, Henry specialized in fertilizer, contending it could make or break a farm's income.

Thus it was that, when the door opened that afternoon in 1833 and the two Wintons, just off the stage, entered The White Tavern, it was Henry Heermans who was there to come forward, greeting them automatically. When Henry was quite close to them, he peered curiously. He thought it strange that he was aware of a complete absence of tension among the three of them as they stood in the entrance. Henry could not sense any desire, or intent on the part of the two facing him, to establish or impose their personalities over his, of bearing down on him as if to impress him into submission—a feeling that he had often experienced with other prosperous looking travelers. Instead, he felt a special rapport with these two particular travelers.

Andrew Winton expressed the desire to lodge several nights. Their affable host showed the two Wintons to a clean, attractive room on the second floor. Supper, they were told, would be around five. Andrew and William remained in their room until a few minutes after five before returning down the stairs. They descended to the dining room; Catherine Heermans, Henry's oldest daughter, was setting the places at the table for the guests when Andrew and William entered.

William Wilander Winton took one look at Catherine Heermans, and that was that! For the rest of his life, he never wanted to look at another woman. From that first glimpse on, until the day he died, he had the greatest love and respect for her. His world would always revolve around her.

Andrew Winton left a week later, alone. William stayed behind to teach in the schoolhouse. On the last day of the year 1835, he and Catherine Heermans were married. In March of 1837 their first child, a girl, Elnorah, arrived. On November 17th, 1838, their second child, son Aretus Heermans Winton, was born.

William had taken the teaching position because it had been the only means open to him of remaining in Razorville and near Catherine. He taught for a short while; when he married Catherine, he joined his father-in-law in Henry's store. For now Henry had remarried, returned to his mansion house, and was proprietor of his own store adjoining the house. Henry Heermans, for his part, liked Catherine's husband very much. In fact, for all the children he fathered, he looked on William as his only son, and often acted that way. William genuinely liked Henry, too. They were very compatible in the store. William was quite an entrepreneur, and he gave early evidence that merchandising was his "cup of tea."

When Henry Heermans had remarried and moved back to his mansion house, he lived a life of ease, doing very little physical work. Many of his responsibilities he turned over to Catherine's husband, William. Henry and his first son Alva had parted in bitterness, and his second son was to die in 1842, leaving a wife Mahala Jane Tripp Heermans and two children. On her husband's death she returned to her family, leaving Catherine to all intents and purposes Henry's oldest child. It was not only by choice but also out of necessity that Henry relied more and more on William.

When the two Wintons, father and son, had separated in 1833, they had already concluded that whatever future there was in coal and railroading, it was then too ill-defined for them to consider. True, they saw that coal was being mined, and that a canal was transporting it. Everybody in the valley knew that; it was no secret. But the attitude expressed by the residents was of the "So what?" variety. It was just a few men's method for putting bread on their families' tables.

Andrew and William Winton had also taken a close look at the "up and down hill" railroad. It struck them as a rather primitive method of transporting the coal. Their own thoughts were confirmed whenever they spoke to a valley native. A slight grin of amusement would curve the lips of whichever speaker the Wintons were questioning. The coal and canal men were not natives of the area, and, in the opinion of the speaker, if they wanted to come in with a hare-brained scheme and a lot of money, and were willing to pay hard cash for digging a trench or hauling logs, the people in the valley were more than willing to help out. Satisfied with the information he had obtained, Andrew Winton had been ready to return to the stagecoach line and New York when William told his father that he was in love with Catherine Heermans, and would not leave until he married her.

Until his decision to remain at Razorville, William's only experience at making money had come from the family's stagecoach line. He had taken the teaching post because it was the only job available at the moment he wanted to stay. He taught no more than a couple of years, for he found he enjoyed helping Mr. Heermans in the store much more. William showed he had a real flair when it came to selling, and when he married Catherine, he became Henry's sole assistant.

These years were a busy period; Razorville was growing daily. At about the time of William and Catherine's marriage, a young lawyer, Charles Silkman, came into the area and married a daughter of Holden Tripp, one of the Heermans' earliest neighbors. Soon afterwards, Catherine's sisters began marrying. Isaac Dean, the son of James and Catherine Tripp Dean, married her sister, Polly; her first cousin, Philip's son Edmund, married Sarah Slocum. At this point the Wintons decided to strike out on their own; they moved a few miles to the west, and William opened his own general store.

William's first year in business was profitable—so profitable, in fact, that when Henry Heermans came for a visit, the conversation took an odd turn. Shortly after arriving, Henry had centered most of his remarks on how much he missed William in the store. Feeling powerful with his first year's profits in his pocket, William quickly asked Henry whether he missed him enough to sell out to him? Catherine was busy playing with little Elnorah and Aretus, and her attention was distracted; thus she missed that part of the conversation when her father replied yes, he would sell to William, as well as the look on William's face as he found himself agreeing. (Henry had acquired sole ownership from his brother in much the same fashion, buying Philip out.) William sold his own burgeoning business for a profit, and the Wintons returned to Razorville.

Henry Heermans had gone to William because his second son had just passed away. When William gave him the opportunity to sell out to him, he was delighted. It was what he had been hoping to accomplish by his visit to them. When he offered to sell out to William, it was because he knew of no other way to lure the enterprising merchant he sensed in his son-in-law to return to Razorville ("The Corners"). And he wanted them back in Razorville very much.

He was thankful his scheme worked. In the past months before going to see William and Catherine, he had been compiling a reference book for farmers. He had entitled it *The Farmer's Mine, or Source of Wealth.* In it, he shared his vast knowledge on the importance of fertilizer to a profitable farm. Henry felt strongly about the farmer, especially the farmer in the Wyoming Valley. As coal was bringing more and greater wealth to valley coal land owners than to the original settlers who had come for farming, Henry wanted to give the farmers an encouraging message; that if they understood, and used, proper farming techniques, they could reap material benefits from the valley comparable to what the coal land owners were getting.

It was while working on his book that Henry saw himself begin to slip. Sometimes he would sit blankly for up to five minutes before completing a sentence he was working on. At first, he attributed it to the effect of his son's death. But later he had a premonition. It was then he had decided to go and see William and Catherine and ask them to return. Henry's fears, it turned out, were well founded. No sooner had *The Farmer's Mine* been published in New York City than he passed away. In November of 1843, William W. Winton assumed the duties of administering his father-in-law's estate.

When he had returned as the store's proprietor, William became W.W. Winton. He soon hired C.T. Atwater to clerk for him; later they were partners. When Atwater left, A.B. Dunning became W.W.'s partner, and the firm became Winton & Dunning.

Abram B. Dunning was also an enterprising merchant. He was originally from northern New Jersey, across the Delaware River in Sussex County, about eighty miles due east of the Wyoming Valley. Abram Dunning's first contact with the Wyoming Valley was as a student at the Wilkes-Barre Academy. After graduating, he went to work in a store in New York City. But his few years at school in the valley had left their mark, and, with a little capital saved, he returned to the valley and opened a general store in Razorville, giving W.W. competition.

The situation changed quickly, however, when W.W. met the competition head on and one of his sisters-in-law, Mahala Heermans, caught the eye of Abram Dunning. A double merger entwined Abram securely into the history of Razorville. And if one ever wanted an illustration for "mighty oaks from little acorns grow," there could probably be none better than the Wintons' innocent relationship with Abram Dunning. It took many years to grow, but the seed of an idea, begun by Abram, was to take root and grow in the hands of the Wintons beyond anyone's imagining.

With Abram Dunning as both business partner and brother-in-law, W.W. concentrated on his store. As with his first store, it wasn't long before the profits began to mount up. This was the first time W.W. felt secure; he was sure of his income and, even more important, he was sure Razorville was where he wanted to settle permanently. He started to look around for places to invest his money. In a relatively short time, he was able to purchase several adjoining pieces of land, and by 1848 had built his holdings up to a large tract.

The most interesting thing to note about this tract, W.W.'s first as a large landholder in his own right, was that each component part, as it was acquired, was deeded to W.W. Winton and wife, Catherine being specified by name. It was not a common practice at that time to record deeds jointly; thus, it is an interesting question why W.W. so specified. If this story were fiction, a fabrication of the author, an explanation would be readily at hand to justify some future event as the author unfolds his tale. But since this is the story of real people, and their lives just as they lived them, from day to day and without advance knowledge of what the future had in store for them, one can only interpret W.W.'s actions as a revelation of the kind of a man he was, how fine and honorable a person. Catherine had contributed to the purchase prices from her father's inheritance; W.W.'s love for his wife was deep and genuine; and he respected her as a person—this was not a common philosophy in 1840. He was all the more remarkable, when one remembers that there were no such things as joint tax returns and deductions in the 1840's. Divorces, too, were a rarity then. With husbands and wives remaining together until parted only by death, the need to list a wife's name on a deed was superfluous.

About this time, towards the end of the 1840s, the inhabitants of "The Corners" stopped referring to their area as Razorville; it became known as Providence. Some of the other communities' names changed, too. One, Slocum Flats (or Slocum Hollow) gave way to Harrison.

The year was now 1850; two more sons had joined the Winton household: Walter Winthrop Winton in 1845, and Byron M. Winton in 1847, bringing the total of children to four. At this point, W.W., who always seemed to know where the action was, proposed to Catherine that they move to New York City; he wanted to try his luck with a store there. In this move, W.W. reflected the temper of the nation. Affluence was everywhere; men were more concerned with the prices of perishable goods, the dividends on stocks, and the expansion of factories, than with politics or the strength of the union. Reflecting the new philosophy, W.W. sensed that the action had shifted to the large mercantile cities in the country, especially New York, and there he proposed to go, even though he had just invested in Providence real estate.

Hastily, before anyone could dissuade them, the Wintons packed and departed from the valley, after W.W. had sold his store again, this time to his latest partner, Abram B. Dunning. His land purchases, though, he held on to.

Once they had reached New York, W.W. decided the locale would not support a general merchandise store; instead, he opened a shop on Cortlandt Street that dealt exclusively in hats, caps, and furs.

Soon after they had settled in their New York home, and the household was once again running smoothly, Catherine Heermans Winton, as another mother (Fear Beaumont) had done many years earlier, realized with a start that her eldest son was now fifteen. She turned to W.W. and asked him what he thought should be done about Aretus's education? The New York store was nearing the end of its second year of operation; because of the store's success, the Wintons had attained that economic level best described as affluent middle class. W.W. therefore proposed sending Aretus off to a private school.

When the suggestion was put to Aretus, he refused to go anywhere—unless it was back to the Wyoming Valley. He had very much missed Providence, his aunts and uncles, and his many cousins. Any parent who has ever had to contend with a determined child knows what an exhausting experience it can be. W.W., who saw in his oldest son an extension of himself, acquiesced first; Catherine was able to hold out a little longer. When she too conceded defeat, it was with one condition: Aretus's sister Elnorah was to go to school with him. The two Wintons were enrolled in the fall term of 1853 at the Wyoming Seminary, the old Wilkes-Barre Academy, renamed in 1838 and relocated at Kingston, some four miles to the northwest, and directly across the river from Wilkes-Barre proper. Shortly after his arrival at the seminary in Kingston, Aretus wrote this to Isaac Heermans:

> Dear Cousin,
>
> Perhaps you will be surprised at seeing a letter mailed from me at Kingston. Elnorah and I came here a week ago last Monday. Olive Leach, Helen White, the two Miller girls and Harriet Heermans are here; but not any boys from Providence. Henry Heermans (Aretus' uncle, a son of the original) says he is coming in 4 or 5 weeks. I wish you were here to room with me. I room in the boarding house now, as the Seminary rooms are not all fitted up. When I first came here I was very lonesome, but last Saturday I went up to Holden's, on my way to Camp Meeting, and there I found H. Atwater, H. Heermans, I. Tripp and several other boys and girls from Providence. H. Atwater and I came down here and saw the girls and got back to Holden's about six o'clock, Isaac Henry Tripp and I went up to William Shoemaker's and staid all night. Here we saw your Mother who that day had baked sixty-three loaves of bread. Next day, we all went up to Camp Meeting and before noon your Mother had to come down and bake forty-two loaves more, besides a great many cakes. I staid until Monday morning and came back, feeling very well, and since then I have not been very lonesome. I want you to answer this letter as soon as you can. I have not time to write anymore tonight. It is now study hour and most 8 o'clock. Write soon and give my love to Uncles, Daniel and Andrew.
>
> Yours in Haste,
> A.H. Winton

Thus did Aretus announce his return to the valley that was home. He was very happy to be back, within easy reach of his heterogeneous Heermans relatives. He also announced his new freedom, for he had signed his letter with his initials: A.H. He wanted everyone to know who had returned; it was A.H. Winton.

A.H. was a very simple, sincere, and direct personality, even at the age of fifteen. He was also a very normal boy, even by today's standards. The only news he thought worth relaying to his cousin Isaac was about the girls at school and the rather staggering number of loaves and cakes baked and consumed!

Wyoming Seminary was only the beginning of A.H.'s education. From Kingston, he moved on to the Phillips Academy at Andover, Massachusetts. He then spent some time at the Williston Seminary, still in Massachusetts, before transferring to Mount Washington College at Number 40, Washington Square, New York City. This last move brought A.H. back to his parents. The Winton family was together again, and would remain so, although somewhat larger, for William Henry Winton had been born in 1855.

The world and its affairs had progressed while A.H. had been away at school. National events of the highest significance had taken place while W.W. had been selling his hats, caps, and furs on Cortlandt Street. Although, in all fairness to W.W., these events had not gone unnoticed by him. With the same, almost gifted, business intuition that had endeared W.W. to Henry Heermans so many years earlier, W.W. guessed correctly the portent of each passing year's activities.

The various incidents proceeded in a logical order, starting with the publication of Harriet Beecher Stowe's "Uncle Tom" stories and the popularity of their anti-slavery message. Next was the emergence of the newly formed Republican Party. The new party carried eleven of the northern states in the 1856 election, a strong show of force. Then there was the excitement in Kansas over John Brown's raid. Finally, and when he considered this W.W. frowned intently, there was the incident in the Senate chambers when Congressman Preston Brooks thrashed Senator Charles Sumner with a cane! W.W. wondered what a country's future could be, if a Congressman would beat, almost to the point of death, a Senator as he sat at his appointed seat. No, W.W. decided, that was not good. He had also heard that, since that beating, there had been many other occasions when various members of Congress had fought each other.

But what was nagging W.W. the most was the old thought that had been cradled in the back of his mind since its premature birth so many years ago, the reasoning that had taken him and his father into the Wyoming Valley originally; this was their concern over coal and railroads. They had concluded, after that initial visit to the valley, that there was nothing to be concerned about; but that was almost twenty-five years ago! Now, W.W. knew for a fact that there were about twenty-five thousand miles of track in the United States. One of the strong points of the new Republican Party was that it had promised to authorize the building of a transcontinental railroad, provided it was given the presidential nod in '56. W.W. knew something else for a fact, because he observed it every day in

New York: immigrants were arriving daily by the hundreds, and although most of them stayed in New York as factory workers, a great many were shipped to the coal mines in Pennsylvania.

Finally, desire tugged at his heart, too. He and Catherine had been away from home for a long while. All things considered, W.W. knew that it was time to go—time to return to the Wyoming Valley.

W.W. did not expect any difficulty in selling his business; this was a period of boom times. With one more year for A.H. at Mt. Washington, W.W. estimated that, if he delayed the final transfer of the business until graduation time, the entire family could return to Providence (Razorville) together. But a buyer appeared sooner than W.W. expected, almost as soon as he announced his intention to sell out. W.W. settled at once, only because it had always been his practice to do so. He had always followed the rule never to delay when offered money. How fortunate that turned out to be for W.W. and the Winton family, although at first they chafed at the ill-timing!

For no sooner had W.W. signed the agreement of sale, than the boom evaporated, like Cinderella's coach, into one enormous burst bubble. The depression of 1857 was far worse than any that had occurred in 1837. The 1837 effects of Jackson's specie circular had been nothing compared to the disaster which resulted when banks halted specie (hard currency) payments in 1857. While waiting for A.H., W.W. had fortunately gathered his assets about him, in readiness for the move back to Providence. After the bubble burst, W.W. stood at the window of their temporary quarters in New York and watched the unemployed wander threateningly about the city. He thanked God that he did not have to be out on the street, protecting his shop.

Patiently, the Wintons waited for A.H.'s Commencement Day.

Graduation finally took place in the last week of June, 1858; all the family attended. They were very proud; A.H. was the class valedictorian. His father embraced him after the exercises. W.W. had been much impressed by A.H.'s speech; "What now?" he asked.

"The law, father."

6

The return to Providence was jubilant and noisy. Heermans relatives by blood and by marriage welcomed the Wintons back. With everyone assembled, almost the entire Providence-Hyde Park population was there. What a joyous homecoming it was, too. Everyone clustered around the Wintons, interested in hearing about New York. The Wintons, on their part, were just as interested to hear about home. They had noticed many, many changes on their arrival. They couldn't believe that it was the same place they had left almost nine years earlier. Everything was so different! This was true not only for Providence but for Harrison (Slocum Flats) and the entire valley as well.

Railroad tracks crisscrossed the valley. Black grime gave a slight tint to the clear valley light. W.W. and Catherine looked for the open fields where a dear and valued neighbor had farmed. Two-story, front-porched pretensions to the better life in the New World clustered like haystacks up and down the former fields. "What is this?" they asked each other.

Momentarily, W.W.'s heart was arrested. Had the vision, that he and his father had had, been lost forever? Had he been careless with his ambition and drive, a squanderer? Was he to have been there first, only to walk away when he should have stayed? W.W. shuddered slightly, and shifted his position. He lightly touched the back of his wife's hand; he gathered strength from this act. The moment of self-doubt and questioning passed.

The big, sprawling, active family gathered gladly to welcome the Wintons back. W.W. had a long conversation with his brother-in-law Isaac Dean (married to Catherine's sister, Polly Heermans Dean) and his first cousin by marriage, Edmund Heermans, Sarah Slocum Heermans's husband. One of the first things that W.W. inquired about was what had happened with the Post Office. He remembered that just before leaving for New York, the Providence postmaster had been asked by the residents of Harrison (Slocum Flats) to verify the fact that almost all of the mail that came into Providence was addressed to Harrison residents.

Isaac Dean did not reply directly to W.W.'s question. Instead he asked, "Had Merrifield sold before you left?"

W.W. thought he remembered hearing something about it but couldn't recall exactly, "A George and Joseph Scranton offercd to buy Merrifield's property down at the far end of Slocum Flats. Seemed they liked the place for some iron and coal work they had in mind."

Edmund Heermans interrupted, "Wasn't long after, that Dr. Throop came around asking the Providence postmaster for a survey on how much mail stayed here and how much went down to Harrison."

W.W. wanted to know how they had handled it.

"Oh, he got his survey, all right. In fact, the survey showed that seven-tenths of the Providence mail actually did go to Harrison people. But you know how sharp we Razorville boys are," replied Edmund Heermans.

This time Isaac Dean interrupted, "I think someone had a talk with Andrew Beaumont when the Honorable Mr. Beaumont stopped in at the tavern. I remember hearing Throop coming around a year or so later muttering something about how President Polk's postmaster general didn't pay attention to people."

W.W. next commented on the physical change of the area, "I think when we left, there was just about two thousand in population around here,"

"They come in every day by the trainload," answered Isaac Dean.

"By 1860, there'll be ten thousand at least," added Edmund Heermans.

"Who are they?" W.W. wanted to know.

"Mostly Irish, about one German for every two Irish, and then maybe half again as many Welsh."

"They work in the mines?"

"Can't get them up here fast enough."

"I'm not surprised," said W.W., "I used to see them get off the boats in New York and hop right on to the railroad."

"Oh, the big news, W.W. I remember now," again interrupted Edmund Heermans, "Right after you left, the two Scranton brothers legislated Harrison (Slocum Flats) into Scranton borough."

"How did that go here?" W.W. wanted to know.

"Well, some fancy footwork turned Providence into a township, and then Hyde Park became a township, too."

W.W. chuckled; he nodded his head approvingly, then added, "That new bunch down at Slocum Flats seems to be giving us a lot of competition."

A slight vertical nod of the other two heads showed complete agreement.

"How's that boy of yours, W.W.?"

"You mean Aretus? Fine—he's thinking of taking a turn at the law. Always been a great talker. This time, he'll get paid for it. Who do you think will be good for him to study under?"

Edmund Heermans suggested David Randall. "He's a good man and he read law with Charlie Silkman here in Providence."

"How about Eugene, Edmund?" W.W. always remembered Eugene Heermans. He had been born the same year as his own son, Walter Winthrop Winton.

"Coming along, coming along."

W.W. then turned to Isaac Dean and asked the same question of him. Only for Isaac, it was about little Arthur Dean. Arthur was a Heermans grandchild

W.W. remembered well, because the boy had been born just before the Wintons had departed for New York. Isaac Dean gave the same reply as Edmund Heermans had.

The three men mused lightly on the possibility of southern rebellion.

Edmund Heermans said, "I can't see any fighting up here in the valley. Everybody's much to busy with the coal and the railroad to go to war."

Again W.W. experienced that spaceless moment. "Why didn't you get into it, the coal and the railroad, Edmund? You were right here all the time. You weren't restless and didn't have to go and spread your wings outside the valley like I did." W.W. turned to Isaac Dean to show that he was including him in the question.

Edmund Heermans was the first to reply, however, "I don't know, W.W. You were here at the beginning, same as we were. I guess we were always too busy farming and selling to see what the other fellow was doing. No one ever said anything or showed any interest. All of us have always made more than enough from our land. The rail and coal men just sneaked up on us, I guess. We were rich, but they wanted to get richer.

"You know, one minute we'd be standing on a rise to get a better look at all the newfangled activity going on, and then, all of a sudden, we'd be scrambling off the rise before it caved in under us from the tunneling that was going underneath, or else we were jumping off right before a rail spike was driven through our boot."

"We missed it, W.W.," and Isaac Dean did nothing to resolve the self-doubt under W.W.'s shirt front.

W.W. looked at his two relatives. He had always liked them. And to Isaac Dean he had always felt especially close. He gave them a warm, friendly smile.

Isaac Dean said, "What are your plans, W.W.? Going to open another store?"

"I thought I wouldn't rush into anything."

"We could use another general store around here, what with all the immigrants coming in. Remember Pop's first store, animal skins hanging from all the rafters, and sacks of seed? Now it's shovels and picks."

"I had been thinking along other lines," W.W. offered in lieu of any other comment.

Isaac Dean and Edmund Heermans looked at him sharply. Isaac said, "What do you have in mind?"

"Well, I've been thinking. We've been here a long time, in the valley. Yet all the really big money, everything, is going to outsiders. Of course, they come to us for their living supplies, but that's small change compared to what they get.

"Normally, we'd be getting a comparable return from the land, but everyone here sold property rights without knowing enough to ask a high price."

His audience nodded agreement.

W.W. continued, "I've been toying with the idea of still providing services to the newcomers; that's the role we've always played. But give them service on a level they understand."

"How do you mean?" Isaac Dean wanted to know. "I follow you, but I can't see where you are leading."

"Back in the days when our parents were selling supplies to the settlers, it went over big, because they were offered something that they really wanted. Now there's no more opening up of the wilderness. The needs of the settlers have changed. They aren't settlers any more; they've become residents. In the beginning when they were settlers, they needed the tools necessary to create something out of nothing. They have that something now. So their needs have changed. What they need now is money. Now they need money so they can expand and refine and improve on their original creation. To put this into practical terms, I was thinking of a bank."

"A bank!" both men stared incredulously at W.W.

"Yes, a bank. You see, I've come back in a superior position, especially now with the panic and hard times. And what is so special about my position, is that I have money in the form of specie currency. And what is so extra special about my particular specie currency, is that it isn't valley money. I'll give you an illustration of what I mean by valley money. Valley money is money earned—let's say by you, Isaac—by working for Pop, assuming he is still living. The money you get from Pop, you turn around and give to Edmund here, in exchange for a shot of whiskey over the tavern bar that Edmund operates. Again in turn, Edmund comes to me and gives the same money to me, when he picks up his sack of seed from my store, that enables him to grow the rye that he makes into liquor, which you, Isaac, drink. I, in turn, take the same money, and pay it over to Pop, for rent due on my store. Then Pop takes the money, and hands it to Isaac as wages for working for him, and so on it goes, around again and again.

"The only way one of us gets richer is if Isaac can be persuaded to drink more liquor, so that I sell more seeds. In that case, Isaac becomes poorer because all of his money is going out to buy drink. All the extra money you take in from Isaac, Edmund, you put right out again for supplies, seeds, etc. But if I sell more in the way of seed, it doesn't affect the amount I have to put out for rent. So I become richer, while Edmund and Pop stay approximately the same, and Isaac becomes the poorest. But the important thing is that it's all done with the same money; just the distribution changes. It's a circular chain that goes around and around.

"I have now, however, extra capital to throw into that closed circle. And by breaking into that chain, at any point I choose, I can upset that particular chain, and then reorganize it into a new circle that's even more in my favor than before.

"This time, though, instead of liquor and sacks of seed, we'll be dealing in terms of specie currency against stock certificates and credit loans used for expansion."

Isaac Dean and Edmund Heermans had followed W.W. with rapt attention.

Edmund said, "Wouldn't it be better, with a large amount of cash, to take the same cash and buy as many shares as you can of, let's say, the Delaware and Hudson Canal Company? You know, through all this depression, their stock has held around $200. It's never dropped more than a few cents on the dollar." He turned to Isaac Dean at this point, "Almost all the other stocks are now paying a few cents on the dollar, that is, if you're lucky enough to find a buyer." And he concluded with a small chuckle.

"No, no," said W.W., "The bank is better. For one thing, I don't think the D & H Canal will ever amount to much more than what it is right now. That darn fool gravity railroad of theirs is a waste. Canals are on the way out, too. It's railroads; they're the only thing that's going to count from now on."

Once again, W.W. had displayed his business acumen. The year 1872 was to be the best the D & H Canal Company would ever have, and from then on it would be a steady downhill drift until the canal shut down completely in 1898. (Today, the old canal bed is a constant attraction to numerous antique buffs, and the old gravity railroad bed is especially attractive to railroad collectors, who enjoy attempting to trace out its exact location.)

W.W. continued, "Railroads need coal. If they're going to grow bigger, expand, they're going to need more money. If I break into the railroad-coal chain at this point, here in the valley where the coal is, I'll be getting returns on my money investment from every link in the circle. The coal miner will want to improve his house, and will come to the bank for a loan. The coal-carrying railroad will want to lay down more track to reach more customers, and will come to the bank for a loan. In case a loan is not repaid, the land posted for collateral will come under the jurisdiction of the bank. Interest on the loans will be bringing in more money. All the time, the bank will be performing a service, helping these people to improve their situation.

"If I put my money into one company, I'd have to put in enough to gain control. Once I've gained control, the company is my responsibility. And if nobody wants what my company makes, I'm out of everything. Money, on the other hand, is one thing that never goes out of fashion."

"No," concluded W.W., "I've given this a lot of thought, especially while we were waiting for A.H. to finish school. Something tells me handling merchandise over a counter is not what it was. I'm going to leave that for somebody else."

Isaac Dean and Edmund Heermans were visibly impressed by W.W.'s reasoning, Isaac in particular. He had always been aware of the high regard Henry Heermans had for W.W.; now he understood why.

Edmund Heermans, on the other hand, was of a much more cautious nature. He had always dealt in the tangible—things he could touch, always from the practical side. He expressed his personality by asking W.W., "How are you going to go about this?"

"Edmund, I am going to start simply by spreading my money around."

"That could be the same as throwing it away."

"No, I'm going to spread it around where it will be the most effective. You wait and see; I'll have my bank."

That evening, when they were alone, W.W. related some of his conversation with his brother-in-law and cousin to Catherine. He was more direct with her, and gave expression to more of his thoughts than he had with Isaac Dean and Edmund Heermans. With them, he had dealt in terms of statements of facts, rather than feelings and intimations. "Catherine, I feel the time is ripe for something big to happen. There are thousands of miles of railroad all around, but none of them lead anywhere, really. They're just little snatches of track here and there. There is no cohesiveness, no unity; that has to change. People are going to grow up and see what the railroad can really be made to do."

"Coal can be used everywhere for everything. Yet how much is being mined?" W.W. concluded, "I keep getting the feeling of a swirling storm, whose vortex is right here in this valley."

The first thing W.W. did was to deliver A.H. to Mr. Randall, to clerk in Randall's law office. Next, he traveled around the valley renewing old associations. He let it be known that he had some capital and was interested in spreading it around. He also drew up subdivision lots on the tract of land he had bought in 1848. Part of it, he conveyed to the New York and Pennsylvania Coal Company. The lots he held for sale to individual home buyers. From then on, W.W.'s grand plan gathered momentum at a pace almost faster than he could control.

Word reached the valley of John Brown's raid, this time (1859) at Harper's Ferry, West Virginia. The drama and significance of Colonel (later General) Robert E. Lee's rush, by train over the Baltimore and Ohio's track from Washington, to contain and capture the raiders, was not lost on the residents of the Wyoming Valley. It was the first time that a railroad had been used to affect the outcome of a battle. Soon, some of W.W.'s money found its way into Durque Locomotive Works at Pittston, a small town seven miles upriver from Wilkes-Barre toward Scranton.

Shortly thereafter, A.H. went before the Luzerne County bar in Wilkes-Barre. In August of 1860, he passed his bar examination with ease. Judge Garrick M. Harding asked A.H. to join him in his law office. A.H. accepted immediately.

The Wintons were now on their way. The foundation built by the father's fair dealings as a mercantile tradesman, his true and genuinely gregarious personality, and his obvious respect and devotion for his wife, now surfaced as a single picture: a portrait of one of the area's leading citizens. W.W. was honestly liked by everyone. Adding to this was the interest and stir created by A.H.'s arrival on the scene. A.H. was now twenty-two—full of vigor, bursting with energy—a lawyer.

The two men, father and son, blended together, each an extension of the other. When one fell short in ability or knowledge, the other filled in. For A.H., the competitive pace was far more arduous than it had ever been for his father or grandfather, Henry Heermans. The increase in valley population alone put a greater demand on the individual. A.H. reached forward to accept the gauntlet, with his father running right behind. The atmosphere of the times, with the war just beginning, permeated the valley. A.H. and W.W. vibrated in noisy exultation over the quickening attention focused on their home.

A.H. was completely unlike his two other brothers, Walter W. and Byron M. When the three of them posed for a photograph in 1863 at Mr. Simpson's studio, the dissimilarities were amazing. A.H. didn't look at all as if he belonged to his brothers. He was taller, broader, and more healthy looking than they. A.H. was truly an extension of his father, in physical appearance as well as in temperament and interest as to how the community grew. He was a portrait, slightly larger than life, of flamboyant conservatism; so was his father. Byron and Walter, the two oldest of his three younger brothers, on the other hand, seemed thin, delicate, and introverted by comparison; always they walked in their brother's and father's shadow—a fact that apparently never bothered Byron. But Walter Winthrop did have his moments of rebellion, and eventually his vengeance.

As 1860 faded into 1861, and the nation was scrambling to establish as much railroad power under military control as possible, W.W. was building his own power base from which to operate. Astute land purchases quickly turned into Winton's addition to Hyde Park and Winton's addition to Scranton. W.W. was very busy in the land development business for a while. He sold lots as quickly as buyers knocked at his door; but whatever was unsold remained that way. He was just as happy to hold onto the land. In hindsight, one mistake that he made at this time, was that when he sold a lot, he sold it in toto. Later, through his son's legal astuteness, he learned to reserve the mineral rights below the surface of the land. But W.W. was satisfied; it was a beginning.

An unexpected dividend, due to one of his free-wheeling and far flung enterprises, came from the Durque Locomotive Works. They informed him that they were naming one of their locomotives the *W.W. Winton*. It was a 4-4-0 American Standard, with a bulbous, onion-shaped exhaust stack, and similar in design both to the famous *General* of the Civil War and the *Jupiter*, Central Pacific's locomotive at the golden-spike ceremony in Utah when the transcontinental railroad was completed. The Winton family was interested in their father's locomotive, as it was referred to, and all turned out to view it before it departed for future war service.

W.W. himself was quite modest and said very little. But as noted earlier, W.W. and A.H. were extensions of each other; where one fell short, the other took over. The *W.W. Winton* locomotive was probably the last thing W.W. was ever able to be quiet about. A.H., with his lawyer's courtroom sense of the dramatic, forced his father into being an extrovert; that is, if W.W. wanted to keep up with his son. And he did. They might best be described in the following terms: what one did not think of, the other did.

Fort Sumter had just been fired on by the new Confederate government when A.H. tried his first case in court, a murder. William Corwin was accused of killing his wife. Little attention was paid to the young, neophyte defense lawyer as the trial began. However, as the sessions continued from day to day, more and more spectators arrived. Word of A.H.'s golden-tone oratorical powers had spread, and the visitors were anticipating a "show." Local newspaper reporters were ordered to cover the trial. They did so, and gave a glowing description of A.H.'s maiden speech, giving him the reputation of a "talented, gifted, powerful debater and orator." This reputation was to stay with A.H. forever, and over and over again he proved it a true and just accolade.

A.H. succeeded in getting Mr. Corwin acquitted, and then, flushed with his success, contracted with a printer to produce 1500 copies of his description of the trial, a pamphlet entitled "The Trial of Wm. J. Corwin for the Murder of His Wife." The cost of the printing was sixty dollars, which A.H. himself paid to the Wilkes-Barre printer. A.H. next contacted several of his acquaintances in Scranton, and had them sell copies of his pamphlet, paying him fifteen cents for each copy they sold and promising to return all unsold copies to him.

Now all this activity may make A.H. seem like a very, very brash young man, almost too smart to be tolerated. But this is an excellent example of that Winton characteristic of always bouncing back, almost serendipitously, with a golden aura around them. Spawned by the enthusiasm over his first case, A.H.'s pamphlet gave rise to the *Luzerne Legal Journal*. This magazine satisfied a need of the county's lawyers and judges. It continued to be published long after A.H. stepped down as editor. Eventually, the journal was renamed the *Luzerne Legal Register*.

W.W. was able to pace his son pretty well. He began to reap from some of his prudent sowing. During the Civil War, the Confederate States were not the only ones with paper money. War scrip was issued everywhere. One Scranton borough bank, George Sanderson and Co., floated an issue backed by some of W.W.'s money. They thought they were flattering W.W. when they included a picture of the *W.W. Winton* locomotive in the design of the paper money. W.W. was delighted, but not for that reason—he now had a toehold towards his bank.

The Civil War was now raging throughout the Southlands. It was in its second year, 1862. Trains and railroads were playing an integral part in the fighting. Never before in man's history had a war been fought with the movability that was now available. Troops were moved by train. Supplies were sent to the front by train. In turn, battles were fought over the railroads themselves. Possession of a railway junction meant control of the flow of men and supplies, and consequently control of the direction of a battle.

The war itself, that is the actual fighting, never touched the Wyoming Valley directly, but it was a key area. The North's strength to do battle was gathered from the Wyoming Valley. Coal poured down from the mountains of northeastern Pennsylvania like a volcano erupting. Like black lava flow, it spread along the curves, crevices, and ravines that were the railroad tracks, throughout the Confederate States. W.W. kept in rhythm with this flow of coal. He was not a war profiteer, for a profiteer holds back vital goods for the highest bidder; he was a war opportunist. If some people were going to make money supplying the military, he wanted to be among them. Soon, he would have enough to start his own bank.

For A.H., however, the war was a problem. Just how he would have decided to handle it, will never be known. He himself probably never knew what he would have done, because the decision was taken out of his hands. Suddenly, all lawyers were required to be licensed if they wanted to be recognized as accredited, bona fide lawyers. Once licensed, these men were called to handle situations requiring their specialized legal knowledge. They were expected to meet demands other than physical combat. A.H. certainly had to have himself licensed. If he didn't, it was the same as saying that he was not a real, genuine lawyer. But once licensed, he would not be expected to enlist as a foot soldier in the infantry.

On the bleak and cold, although snowless, day that was the tenth of January, 1863, A.H. rode from Providence down to the County Court House at Wilkes-Barre, and there paid his ten dollars to be licensed as a fully accredited lawyer. Actually, he was four months late in doing this; all the lawyers were supposed to have registered by September of the preceding year. But Joseph Hand Scranton, the county clerk, was glad to see him anyway. While filling out the license, they had quite a discussion. Scranton wanted to put in A.H.'s full baptismal name. "No, no," insisted A.H., "A.H. will do. It's perfectly legal. Take my word for it." Never again would "Aretus Heermans Winton" haunt A.H.

It was afterwards, as he was coming out of the Court House, that he ran into a young law clerk and acquaintance of his. John B. Collings wanted to know what he was doing.

"I've decided to be licensed as a lawyer."

Everyone knew that this meant the licensee would probably not fight in the war.

"Well, good for you!" declared John Collings, seeing the mournful face before him. "It's a big decision, I know. But when you are a practicing lawyer, how can you come to any other decision, or pursue any other course of action, than to register?"

"I know, that was how I reasoned it, but still—" and A.H. let his voice trail off into silence.

"I'll tell you what, come home with me and have a bun or two. It's too cold to stand here, and once you're warm with some food inside you, you'll feel happier about your decision. Come along. Now that I think about it, this really calls for a celebration."

A.H. walked with John Collings back to the Collings home at 124 Union Street. Once inside, John led him into the parlor, and introduced him to his older sister, Alice. Just like his father, A.H. fell in love with her right there on the very spot.

To complete the introductions, Alice, in turn, took A.H. over to a corner of the room near a window. He was aware of a shadowy figure seated on a sofa. Long fern and green plants, draped behind the chaise, created a bower of mystery and seclusion.

"Mama, I'd like you to meet a young lawyer friend of John's. This is Mr. A.H. Winton, from Providence."

A.H. tried not to peer too curiously at Mrs. Collings as he bowed slightly and said he was very pleased to meet her. Mrs. Collings, Elizabeth Beaumont Collings, the daughter of the Hon. Andrew Beaumont, the wife of Samuel Collings, was legendary; and A.H. had heard much gossip about her, and her exciting days in the nation's capital and, later, in Morocco. He would have loved to have been able to talk to her alone.

Cocoa and buns were soon brought in, and the three younger people sat near the fire and chatted agreeably, inquiring into each other's interests. John Collings noticed how much perkier A.H. was looking than when he had first seen him an hour earlier. What he didn't realize was that A.H. had always enjoyed feminine companionship, and with the exciting Mrs. Elizabeth Beaumont Collings in a nearby corner, and the newly found love of his life seated opposite him, A.H. was at his excited best.

Almost another hour had passed before A.H. took note of the darkening sky outside. He begged leave to depart, alluding to the long return ride to Providence, which he was not looking forward to with enthusiasm. Before leaving, he asked whether he could call again.

"Please do, Mr. Winton. We would be most happy to have you. You have so lightened a most dreadful and dreary day for us," responded Mrs. Collings.

A.H. floated up the valley to Providence, not quite unconscious but nearly so. 1863 was going to be a big year.

1863 was a big year; W.W. Winton & Co. opened its banking office in Scranton borough. It was only a small bank, but W.W. had made a start at last. He called on Isaac Dean and Edmund Heermans as soon as he was open for business. He invited them to visit him at his banking office.

"You see," he told them, "I have the bank."

Isaac Dean was much impressed and very interested. "I most certainly will be in, W.W."

Edmund Heermans was just as enthusiastic, but the bank had less personal meaning to him. He wished his cousin-by-marriage good luck.

The spring and early summer days were spent by A.H. in riding back and forth between Providence and Wilkes-Barre. When court was in session, he went to Wilkes-Barre daily. On every trip, even if there were only five minutes of unaccounted time, he would pop in at the Collings house to see how the ladies were doing. Sometimes, he would entertain them with stories of court activities. Sometimes he would have the mother and all four of her daughters as an audience. Sometimes he would just posture elegantly before the two who interested him most while they were busy preparing the tea. Alice was aware that he was courting her, but hadn't decided how far she wanted to encourage his advances.

Early in June, after an exceptionally pleasant visit with Alice and her mother, A.H. returned to Providence and found the place in an uproar. All the great Heermans clan were gathered at the White Tavern, in the public room. W.W. had been watching for his son's return, and saw him as he opened the door. He moved over to him immediately.

"A.H., thank God you're back. What are we going to do?"

"What is it, Father? What's happened?"

"We're bankrupt!"

"Bankrupt! How can that be? What do you mean, 'We're bankrupt!'?"

"We are! I'm telling you, we are! The books have been balanced, but there is nothing to balance them with. Oh! What are we to do?"

How typical this was of mountain people. The whole country was at war. The history of a nation was hanging in the balance, yet, at the very source of the war supplies, the concern was over a bookkeeper's ledger. A.H. was struck by the insular outlook of the valley. An entirely different world existed outside the mountains. And the two worlds did not appear to relate to each other at all. What was important in one place had no meaning whatsoever in the other. For a moment, A.H. was truly speechless, his orderly mind in total confusion. Where did he belong? Which was the real world? He was conscious of his father's voice again.

"I'm telling you, we're bankrupt."

A.H. replied flatly, "I don't believe it. You've been too careful."

"Oh no, no, not me, not us, not your mother and I. Providence! I mean Providence!"

"Providence?"

"Yes, the township of Providence is bankrupt! What will we ever do? How can we pay our bonds? Oh, this is horrible!"

A.H. agreed with him on that. It was horrible, especially with Scranton Borough breathing down their necks, ready to pounce. The war was forgotten. The immediate needs of the problem at hand, like the mountains surrounding, closed in on A.H., and cut off any attempt to relate with what was going on elsewhere.

The meeting was called to order. One by one, those involved stepped forward and presented their facts. Providence Township was indeed insolvent.

At the conclusion, A.H. stood up and remarked, "I see, Gentlemen, we suffer only from being too kind. We have been too considerate of the poor, the needy, the unfortunate. Is there a greater crime to be accused of? I think not!"

Whistles and cheers greeted his comments.

When the applause had subsided, someone asked him what he thought should be done.

"We are a responsible body. We most certainly shall not run and hide. Therefore, my considered opinion is that the township itself should file for bankruptcy."

"Hear, hear!" approved A.H.'s audience.

The unofficial meeting was adjourned. Later, when the official Providence township meeting was convened, A.H.'s suggestion was adopted. The township filed for bankruptcy, and the court appointed three commissioners to ascertain the indebtedness of Providence township. A.H. was one of the commissioners named. The three commissioners decided to hold their court of investigation at the banking office of W.W. Winton & Co., in Scranton.

The commission opened its hearing at ten in the morning on the eighteenth of June, 1863. They met daily, listening to all creditors who presented themselves. They were beginning to gather an approximate idea of the total of accounts owed when, on July 1, 1863, Pennsylvania's Provost Marshal, Capt. S.N. Bradford, dispatched a wire to Scranton. The Battle of Gettysburg had just begun, and every available man was needed. Reinforcements were needed desperately to stop the Confederate invasion into the North. Bradford had remembered that a squad of deserters was being held in Scranton; he wanted them brought down to Gettysburg as soon as possible. Bradford's deputy in Scranton called on A.H. and appointed him special provost marshal on the spot. A.H. departed immediately for Harrisburg, where Bradford would be waiting.

A.H., with his squad of deserters, reached Harrisburg on the following day. There, on the second of July, he handed them over to Capt. Bradford. Every one of the men in the squad had been on the army's muster roll for the month of July. Bradford then gave A.H. a written order, instructing him to return immediately to Scranton via the Northern Central Railroad. It took A.H. a few hours longer to make the return trip. Once back in the valley, A.H. again experienced, but this time more strongly, the feeling of existence in two separate worlds: the valley world, and the real world outside the valley walls.

NOTICE!

The undersigned Commissioners appointed by the Court for the purpose of ascertaining the indebtedness of PROVIDENCE TOWNSHIP, will meet at the

BANKING OFFICE of W. W. WINTON & Co.

IN SCRANTON, PA., ON

THURSDAY, the 18th June, 1863, at 10 o'clock A. M.

for the purpose of organizing their Court of investigation, at which time and place all parties having claims against the said Providence township are notified to present them for adjudication.

Andrew Bedford,
David L. Patrick,
A. H. Winton,

Scranton, June 15, 1863. ***Commissioners.***

Other than the short interruption for his trip to Harrisburg, A.H. and his two fellow commissioners, Andrew Bedford and David Patrick, passed the whole of the summer of 1863 working on Providence's insolvency. It was as A.H. had summarized at the informal meeting in The White Tavern: the township was bankrupt because of too generous support to the destitute. Instead of providing a minimal "widow's mite," the township fathers had in fact been providing a widow's fortune. The three men were also aware of an added pressure as they worked. The rapid growth of Scranton Borough had been placing Providence and Hyde Park in a precarious position. The men at the helm in Scranton were newer arrivals to the valley, and were both competent and aggressive men. The three Providence commissioners knew all about the rumor that was circulating: Scranton intended to incorporate itself, plus Hyde Park and Providence, into a city. A weak, impoverished Providence would almost automatically bring about its own dissolution. Should Providence come under the domination of Scranton, the city charter for Scranton was as good as in effect. Providence would be swallowed up, losing its identity forever.

The three commissioners were also aware of the significance of Scranton as a city. Wilkes-Barre, fifteen miles down the valley, was the county seat; it was also the oldest community in the area. But it was not yet a city. If Scranton could achieve city status, with the accompanying tax privileges, before Wilkes-Barre, the power center in the valley could be shifted from its lower end to its geographical middle. Increased powers and added taxation revenues would be available to the railroad and coal barons operating out of Scranton. In time, they would probably be able to transfer the county seat to Scranton.

A.H. was cognizant, as was his father W.W., of the issues involved. Neither the Wintons nor all the Heermans clan were adverse to bringing about a shift in power from Wilkes-Barre to their own area, but not at the cost of losing Providence's and Hyde Park's identities. The sentiments of all concerned in the township teeter-tottered from predestined gloom to pugnacious gloom.

As the commission's investigation progressed, A.H. began to notice a pattern emerging. It was only a suspicion, but he was intrigued enough at the possibilities it presented to mention it to his father.

"Father, I am detecting a relation between excessive disbursements on the part of a couple of board members and Scranton borough's increasing demands for city status."

W.W. stared at his son thoughtfully. "There's no question, it's inevitable; Providence is doomed. Who would ever have confidence in our bond issues again? But this may give us an ace to play against complete dissolution. Give me some time; let me look into it. In the meanwhile, say nothing more about it."

Green leaves had given away to reds and light yellow greens of autumn before A.H. was able to get down to Wilkes-Barre to see Alice Collings. The work on the bankruptcy had become so involved and demanding that he had opened a small office next to his father's bank in Scranton. He notified Judge Harding of the move, and added that he would probably remain in Scranton until the work was completed, unless the judge needed him. At the same time, A.H. also wrote a brief note to Alice, telling her of his change of plans.

When at last he did arrive at the Collings' on one warm afternoon in early October, he was greeted with pleasant politeness. A.H. sighed a sob of sadness to himself; he had hoped that Alice would have reacted otherwise. He thought, also to himself, that perhaps Miss Alice Collings had better remain in Wilkes-Barre after all, and that he should confine his feminine activities strictly to local Providence residents.

He looked at Alice longingly. She was on the tall side, near his own height, slender; she had a rather large-boned frame, but was agreeably distributed in the most eye-appealing places. She had a level-headed directness that set his legal mind at ease. A.H. never felt that he had to lose time in conversation with Alice, pondering her every statement. Did she mean what she said, or had she really meant the opposite?—this was a game A.H. had frequently found himself playing when in conversation with members of the opposite sex. Alice also had a sophisticated, mature manner, the combined result of her voyage to Morocco and of her part in supporting her widowed mother and grandmother. This appealed to A.H., too. Looking at Alice, he wanted very much to put his arms around her and crush her to his chest, but he was not going to be toyed with.

The visit was an exercise in balancing a cup of tea with one hand while eating cake with the other. As much as Alice meant to him, and as much as he was fascinated with Mrs. Elizabeth Beaumont Collings as a possible mother-in-law, when he walked down the front steps of the house on Union Street afterwards on that particular afternoon in October, he felt that he would not be at all surprised if it were the last time for him to do so.

After that particular visit, A.H. very rarely left Providence or Scranton. The commission was in its final days, preparing its list of recommendations. It was a lengthy list, too. Some of the debts that they decided to recommend for payment extended back to 1840, a span of almost twenty-five years. This would be a decision typical of mountain people—this display of a lack of a hard core. The softness at the center of their personalities, either individual or collective, would make such a decision inevitable and, for them, correct. A similar decision would never be considered, much less tolerated, in a long-established community elsewhere. But locked up behind a mountain wall, out of sight, the people were free to adjudicate as they felt they should.

Just as the pressure from the bankruptcy proceedings lightened, A.H.'s father, W.W., came to him and requested his services in reorganizing W.W. Winton & Co., Bankers, into Winton, Clark & Co., Bankers. W.W.'s first tentative step into the world of finance and banking had become more surefooted. Myron Clark, a friend of W.W.'s, was bringing added capital. The extra money was put to use immediately. The war was now going into its fourth year; railroads, and the energy generated by King Coal, were coming into their own at last. W.W. handed out money to everyone everywhere, or so it seemed. People flocked to do business with him. W.W. had such an air about him that, after a session arranging amounts, interests, and collateral, the borrower left the bank feeling like the guest of honor at a banquet. W.W. also remembered old friends and old times. One such friend who came to him was Lewis S. Watres. W.W. was disturbed at Lewis Watres's appearance; he had not seen Watres for several years.

"No, I'm not well," Lewis Watres replied to W.W.'s inquiry, "But don't take my word for it; I think I'm fine. It's the army. I raised two volunteer companies, the Fifty-second and Fifty-sixth, and took them to Harrisburg, and both times they sent me back. Said I wouldn't be able to stand up in the field. Took everybody I sent down but me. Me, they sent back. Anyway, W.W., it's not my way to complain; you know that."

W.W. answered, "It would be out of character for you to complain—you, who have heard at least one complaint from everybody living between here and the Delaware River.

"I can remember back to when Charlie Silkman married Holden Tripp's daughter, and he kept leaving her to go see you. He was the only lawyer between Razorville and Carbondale, and you were the only justice of the peace. Charlie's wife used to keep Catherine in laughter all the days you'd be holding court. She was so mad at you."

Lewis S. Watres held up a silencing hand. "Please, W.W., don't remind me; the pain is too great."

"What's the matter?" said W.W., alarmed.

"To remember back to all the good, when I have fallen on such evil times."

"I don't understand. What's happened?"

"To be struck such a low blow—and none of it my own doing."

By now, W.W. was quite alarmed. "Please, my dear friend, calm yourself."

"I'm all right, W.W. Don't worry. You have brought to mind again too clearly, what I have deliberately forced myself to forget."

W.W. remained silent, wishing in no way to further upset Lewis Watres. Lewis Watres, too, was silent. He stared intently at W.W., preparing himself for a role unfamiliar to him. At last, he began to talk.

"About the same time that we were speaking of, I purchased the coal and timber lands at Mt. Vernon with some money I had gathered together." (Mt. Vernon was a dreamy, tiny hamlet approximately twelve miles north of Scranton, nestled at the base of the southeast, Moosic Mountain, wall of the valley.)

"By every indication, there was supposed to be an excellent vein of coal on the property. Well, you know, W.W., the estimates were correct, and from the very beginning I've been getting excellent coal; it's just about the finest in the valley. After the mine was producing, I handled most of the arrangements for The Pennsylvania Coal Company to construct their own gravity railroad from Pittston through Cobb's Gap over to Hawley, where it joined up with the D & H Canal. Everything I mined was shipped out on the gravity to Hawley, and then onto the canal.

"And you know how the D & H stock held up during the '57 panic. That gives you a fair idea of the amount of income I was getting out of the mine at Mt. Vernon."

"What's the problem, Lewis? I don't seem to understand. Everything you've told me so far, anyone would envy."

"I didn't understand at first, either, W.W."

Again, W.W. waited quietly for his visitor to continue. When he did, a supercilious smile twisted his ordinary elegant features. "My uncle—my Uncle Charles in Philadelphia."

"Your uncle?"

"Yes, I had endorsed him. And apparently he was caught terribly in the panic. Before I knew it, every cent of cash I had was gone—to cover him."

"But Lewis, that was almost seven years ago."

"I know, but at first I just delayed my own payments, hoping to balance cash receivable against what I owed—payrolls and the like. With the way the coal was coming out of the mine, I was confident that I would be caught up in a few months. But I never caught up. First, it would be a new piece of equipment that was needed. Then there would be an explosion, and extra expense to open the tunnel up again."

"What do you want me to do, Lewis?" —a most pertinent question to come at this point in the story. It was pertinent questions, such as this, that had endeared W.W. to every borrower who had ever passed through his bank doors.

Lewis Watres produced several sheets of figures, and the two men passed more than an hour studying them. In the end, W.W. agreed to underwrite whatever was needed.

W.W. was still sitting at his desk, mulling over Lewis Watres's visit, when A.H. stopped in.

"Father, tell mother not to expect me for supper this evening. I'm on my way to take the train for Wilkes-Barre, and I'm not sure when I'll get back."

A.H. appeared to be in a somewhat agitated state. W.W. said as much, and wondered, "Why the haste?"

"I've had a note from Alice Collings. She's in distress, and apparently believes I can be of some assistance."

Before W.W. could reply or ask further questions, A.H. had gone. When W.W. got home later, he relayed the message to Catherine. "I think we are about to have a wedding."

"It's about time," replied Catherine. "I was beginning to think they were all hopeless. A.H. is twenty-six, Walter is nineteen. We should have had a grandchild by now."

"Now don't be in a hurry. As soon as one goes, they will all go."

"And I will have you all to myself," Catherine answered, leering at her husband.

"Ah, my dear Catherine," W.W. said, and kissed her lightly on the forehead.

After A.H. left W.W., he went directly to the station. He was fortunate; he waited no more than five minutes for a train. The ride was a relatively short one, but it gave him time to compose himself. He chuckled slightly at the impression which he was sure he had left with his father. To say that Alice was in distress had been a little strong. No, he reflected, that was not quite right either. The intent had been one of distress; the excuse that she had employed perhaps had not. For he had read the unwritten message between the lines of her note. She had come to a decision; that was why he felt it imperative to see her at once.

The train reached Wilkes-Barre a little after three o'clock. A.H. went directly to the Collings. He mounted the steps leading to the front door, and had just pulled the door pull, when he heard a voice call from behind.

"Mr. Winton!"

He looked around, and saw Alice turning in from the pavement. He walked back down the walk towards her.

"Alice—it was so kind of you to think of me."

The last moments of a bright January sun enveloped the two in a microcosm of their own as they stood on the walk facing each other. The emotion that A.H. felt as he looked at Alice so near caused him to sway slightly towards her. Alice, too, had eyes only for the strong, powerful, energetic man before her. It had been such a long time since she had seen him. She had missed his visits very much. Now to have him before her again, made her oblivious to her surroundings.

At last, she spoke, "It was so good of you to come." And then she faltered slightly, "I did not know if you would."

"I think of you often."

Alice brightened slightly, "You do? I think of you, too."

This time, they both swayed towards each other, as if to kiss. The yearning and the longing was that much greater, because the two dominating personalities had at last admitted openly their need for each other.

"You did not think my request too forward? At first, I was almost too ashamed to write. I did not know what you would think."

"Oh, Alice, all that I have been waiting for is something from you to show how you feel about me. I thank God that you did."

He slipped his hand through the crook of her arm, turned and escorted her back up the walk to the door. Alice opened the door, and the two of them went in.

"Mama," Alice called into the parlor. "Look who's with me! Dear Mr. Winton!"

Mrs. Collings was in her usual place—her bower of repose by a south window.

"I'm so glad to see you again, Mr. Winton. We do need your help."

"How do you do, Mrs. Collings. It's a pleasure to be of service to so charming a family. Now tell me, please, what do you want me to do?"

"As Alice has already written you, my daughter Mary will marry this spring, and we do need a gentleman, dear Mr. Winton, to help guide this bevy of females through all the arrangements and ceremonies. One whom we can depend on. If you would be so kind?"

"I would be delighted, Mrs. Collings. And I'm honored that you have such trust in me, as to consider me a part of your family."

"Thank you. It is such a relief to know that we will have you to depend on. Mary is to marry Jacob Dillinger from Allentown [Pennsylvania]. There will be so many out-of-town gentlemen; I would never know what to do with them. My son John will of course stand in the place of his father and give Mary away, but we do need one with a wiser head to direct us all.

"Ordinarily, my brother, Commander Beaumont, would be the one, but he cannot be here, because he is in charge of the *Mackinaw*. And my other brother, Eugene Beauharnais Beaumont, cannot be here, also due to the war. He is with General Grant, and will not be given any kind of leave at the present. I remember that after the fighting at Gettysburg, he was able to get away for a few days and visit with us. But we have heard from him, and he says that it is impossible now; all leaves are being cancelled."

One by one, the other members of the family came in and greeted A.H. warmly. John Collings was quite open in showing his pleasure at seeing A.H. again.

"It's been damned lonely around here without you," he whispered.

When A.H. had first read Alice's note, he had thought the pretext used to summon him a very flimsy one. With Blackman and Beaumont relatives nearby, he felt sure that the family could have turned to someone more appropriate than him. He was not angry, however; he was really thankful for any excuse. He had wanted Alice from their first meeting a year ago. Only Alice's failure to express herself to him had kept him away. It wasn't until Mary had joined the family group that A.H. dropped the mental reservation that he had had about the validity of the Collings' appeal. Mary's fiance was the prothonotary, that is chief court clerk, for Lehigh County. He was very well liked in Allentown, and the Collings knew that many of the legal minds from Lehigh County would be invited to the wedding. With John Collings in charge of his sister and the wedding party, the family had turned, in real need, to A.H. for the entertainment of the out-of-town guests.

For the first time since October of the previous year, A.H. relaxed. He allowed himself to be caught up in the excitement over the wedding plans; and soon everyone was spending more time laughing at him than coming up with constructive suggestions for the wedding. Mary wanted to be married at home, but some of A.H.'s suggestions as to what to do with the various guests had reduced the serious planning session to one wild, improbable fantasy of ideas. When dinner was announced, no one would allow A.H. to do other than stay.

Afterwards, Alice walked A.H. to the darkening recess that was the vestibule, just to the inside of the entrance door. They bid each other a polite "Good-bye." But by now the intensity of their restrained emotions was a deafening roar in their ears. A.H. leaned toward Alice, and lightly brushed his lips across hers. The sensuousness of her rather full-bodied lips anguished him; he erupted from the house as if in pain. He almost ran down the walk to the street, and then hastened along the paving.

A.H. had quite a wait at the station for a train. The first one to come along was carrying coal. He climbed in with the engineer, who knew him by name, and rode back to Scranton.

In Scranton, the night was still and silent after the train had puffed off. A.H. had a fairly long walk ahead of him, a little over two miles, to get back to his home. He had forgotten about the distance in the coziness of the engineer's cab. But after a few minutes he recognized that there would be a value to the walk in spite of the cold; it would give him time for reflection.

He had been right. He had interpreted Alice's note correctly; the unwritten message between the lines had been the important one. The plea for help with the wedding had been only a pretext to see him again. He was very glad he had gone to see her immediately. But there had been another side to the evening that required additional thought; this had to do with a part of the conversation at the dinner table, which had not gone unnoticed by him. He knew what daughter and mother had had in mind, although he had feigned ignorance at the time. Unconsciously A.H. slowed his walking pace while considering this, despite the near-freezing temperature.

He did not like being manipulated. And he knew that mother and daughter had been attempting to manipulate him. He had seen his own mother do it too often with his brothers Walter and Byron, especially Byron who was still young, not to recognize the signs. "Damn it," he was not going to have it happen to him. "Oh, Alice, why is there always a problem?" "No," and he corrected himself, "I am wrong to call it a problem. Problems are solvable. It's Alice; she and her mother have been alone for so long, have had their own way for so many years, that they expect to direct everything." A.H. was so deep in his soliloquy, now, that he was mumbling aloud as he walked.

Other girls that he had known paraded, one by one, before his mind's eye. "No, no, no," he said, as each one passed from his vision. A.H. had always thought on the grand scale. He had a big, expansive personality, and he needed someone to match him, with enough of a challenge to hold him.

"Oh, Alice, what attracts me is the very thing I deplore. Very well, I'll give your way a chance. I'll try it once. And after that, on my terms."

In truth, even to himself, A.H. had resorted to the lawyer's bluff. He had agreed, at least mentally, to let Alice manipulate him once, but only once. But he would be bluffing her. He had come to the decision to try things her way, for another reason. This reason derived from his own desires as much as hers, although he was going to lay his actions at her feet as if they were solely of her direction and responsibility, regardless of the outcome.

He had been well aware what daughter and mother had been suggesting at the dinner table. Actually, they had been rather obvious. He knew that their talk of their days in Washington, and their description of political figures, had all been for his benefit, had been meant for him. To make sure that there could be no doubt, Alice had even said to him, "Have you ever thought of serving in Washington?" He had let it go by, but he knew that it would have to be answered. It would definitely have to be answered, and if they were to marry, it would have to be answered before they married.

A.H. had turned a corner, and could see his parents' home. A light was lit downstairs, and, like a beacon, it guided him in the dark. He continued with his thoughts. What was Alice asking of him? What was she really asking? Was it something that he had never considered on his own? He knew that she wasn't demanding something completely foreign to himself. That feeling, he had had from time to time—that feeling of two worlds: one in the valley and one beyond. All Alice was really asking him to do was to join the world beyond the valley. He knew that she would marry him tomorrow without question, if he said he were going to Washington. But he wasn't going into a marriage, that way. Yet, what was wrong with leaving home?

He himself had been aware of the provinciality of living strictly in the valley and for the valley. A.H. remembered how happy he and his family had been to leave New York and return home. But then he remembered the suffocation he had experienced at The White Tavern, when they had been discussing Providence's debts as if that were the only thing that mattered, even with the war only two hundred miles away. Of course, out of that meeting had come his appointment as commissioner; he certainly was enjoying that work. But, perhaps, it was only the beginning. Perhaps he was destined for greater things, beyond the valley, and Alice was the catalyst to get him out and going? "All right, Miss Alice Collings, we'll try it your way once; but after that, what I say."

A.H. stepped into the warmth of his home. The light that he had seen from the road had been coming from the parlor room windows. He looked in before going up to his room. His mother and father were sitting at the center table, each reading a book.

"You're still up?" he greeted his parents.

His father was the first to put his book aside. "Come in, A.H. Let me get a look at you. You have something to tell us?"

"No, Father, not yet."

"Not yet? An errand of mercy to help a fair maiden in distress! And there is nothing to tell? Mother, what do you think of that?"

For the first time, Catherine raised her eyes from her book. "Now. now, W.W., leave him alone. I'm sure he will tell me in time to have a new dress, if I am to go to a wedding."

A.H. came in and went over to his mother and kissed her on the top of her head. "She's right, Father. Alice and I will marry, but we haven't set any time yet. We have to get her sister Mary married first."

The following week, the last in January, A.H. returned to Wilkes-Barre and called at the Collings.

Providently, no one was about when he arrived, except Alice. "Alice, I would like to talk to you."

"Let me get some tea first," and she ran off toward the back of the house.

A.H. followed her, and caught up with her in the pantry. He gently, but with a sure grip, grabbed hold of her hand, and led her back through the hall into the parlor.

"No, sit here with me first. We can have tea afterwards."

Obediently she sat on the settee beside him. A.H. turned to her, and put his other hand over the hand he was already holding. With his two hands, he gently turned her palm up and raised it to his lips. There was not a sound as he kissed the softness of her palm—first once—then a second time.

"Alice, my dear, I love you very much. I have ever since I first saw you that afternoon John brought me here. I am not interested in having any other woman but you for my wife. Do you understand what I am saying?"

All the while he was speaking, Alice had been looking intently at his face. Her eyes were dark and luminous; excitement gave them fire and sparkle. She nodded her head yes.

"But Alice, my whole life is Scranton and Providence and Hyde Park. If you marry me, you may return to Wilkes-Barre only for a rare visit. Do you understand this?"

A slight frown crossed her face, but still she did not speak.

"I mean, my dear, that your allegiance, once you are my wife, will be to me, to my interests and to where I am. I have always lived in Providence, I will always do what I think is best for it, not for another place—not for Wilkes-Barre. You would have to feel the same way."

"I...," Alice faltered.

But A.H. interrupted, fearful that she would say something he did not want to hear, "Wait; let me finish." He was so anxious to have Alice come with him, that he was resolved to keep talking until she answered his way. He did not want to hear her commit herself with an answer that could not be changed.

"Both you and I, Alice, have been away from here for a period of time. We've both come back. I'm going to decide it one way or the other. If there is an opportunity for me in Washington, I will take it. But if there is no opening, then the issue is closed. All of my energies will be concentrated in Scranton.

"I am asking you to be my wife, Alice. I want you to be my wife very much. But I want you to come as my helpmate. You inspire me—you give me confidence, but if you are not proud of who I am and what I do, it will be the destruction of us both."

It was probably the worst possible way for a man to declare his love and ask a woman to marry him, if judged by the effect A.H.'s speech had on his listener. A silent flow of tears was running down Alice's cheeks. A.H. put his arms around her, and pressed her close to him. At length, he drew away enough to raise her head and kiss her.

"Will you be mine?" he asked.

"Yes."

The following day at his desk in his office in Scranton, A.H. composed a letter addressed to The Honorable George W. Smith.

A reply came almost by return mail. A.H. took the unopened letter with him when he went down to Wilkes-Barre to call on Alice.

He showed her the envelope and remarked, "I've waited to read this until I was with you. This will be our future together, and I thought we should find out together."

A.H. opened the envelope and read the enclosed letter aloud to Alice, "'Washington, February 4th, 1864, A.H. Winton, esquire. Dear Sir,'

"Before I go on, Alice, do you want to change your mind? Should we talk again? Do you have any reservations?"

"No, my love. Our future is together, whatever it may be. My love for you is my promise. Let us hear what The Honorable Mr. Smith has to say."

A.H. resumed reading:

> In reply to your note of February 2, I would say that you might succeed in getting employment here that would suit your taste, and you might not. There is a constant rush of both worthy and worthless persons here who are importuning for employment in all the well paying positions, and the worthy ones are not always the successful ones.
>
> If you were to come here and get a place at $1200 or $1400 per annum, it would not be as well for you as to stay in Luzerne County. Cause why. You are well fitted for a successful lawyer. As you say in your note you are

apt at both hand and head work. And you are sufficiently eloquent and now is the time for you to study hard in your profession and lay by those stores of learning which you would not have time to acquire if you were full of business. You have only to *fit yourself* for a lucrative and honorable practice and in Luzerne County it will surely come. You stand a better chance to secure wealth and position by pursuing your profession, than in any other way, and you can do it sooner that way than by shifting from one thing to another. Come to Washington, if you choose but do not come here to stay, so as to lose one client at home. My fortune was spoiled by not sticking to some one business and mastering it when I was young. Do not spoil yours in that way. Almost every man of any note connected with the government has been a successful lawyer first and a politician or office holder afterward.

Yours truly, George W. Smith

P.S. I will give you a job now. Find me a customer to purchase the whole or part of my farm in Scott [nearby community in the Wyoming Valley]. It contains 160 acres and is worth $5000. About one half is improved. It is good land and is conveniently watered. I will sell the whole or a part to suit the purchaser.

Almost before A.H. had finished reading the postscript, Alice had placed her hand on his forearm. The moment he stopped, she spoke, "I love you, my darling. It will take me a while to prepare—dresses, linens to embroider, initials—would next spring be all right?"

"In May?"

"May."

(Note: In July of 1858, A. H. Winton married Mary Abbie Sawyer, a daughter of another early family in the Wyoming Valley. She died in December of 1860. They had no children. A. H. was twenty at the time he married, and whether because of his age or because of their brief time together, his papers indicated she was a very dim memory compared to his "beloved wife, Alice.")

7

Isaac Dean passed across the front of Winton, Clark & Co., Bankers, every day. Not a day went by, when they were open for business, that he didn't attempt to estimate the number of customers going in and out. In a way, Isaac thought of it as his bank; he had been a part of the conversation during which W.W. had first announced his plans. Isaac Dean was also proud of what W.W. had accomplished. W.W. was the first of the Heermans clan to actively compete with the valley's aggressive immigrants on their own terms. The settler was gone; a new look predominated, but W.W. had been able to carry the taint of the settler with him as he mingled with the money men.

Occasionally, Isaac would actually enter the bank and visit with W.W. briefly. Whenever Isaac did come in, W.W. would greet him warmly. He had always liked him as a brother-in-law. W.W. would show Isaac around the bank, and introduce him to whichever cashier was on duty at the time. W.W. was proud of his bank, and enjoyed showing it off to Isaac. Isaac was always amenable to the idea.

One particular day when Isaac Dean came in for a visit, he found A.H. in deep conversation with his father.

"Come in, Isaac. Sit down and join us. A.H. and I were just going over some financial ideas."

"Don't let me hold you up, W.W.; A.H., nice to see you again. How's that law business of yours?" Isaac clapped his nephew soundly on the back.

"Fine, Uncle Isaac. Will you give Arthur a message for me, please? He was talking to me the other day about the future. Tell him that if he would like to spend a day going around with me, it should give him an idea about the law."

"Good boy, A.H., good boy. Thank you. Now, don't let me interrupt. I'll just sit here and puff away on my stogie, while you two talk."

A.H. looked at W.W. "What do you think, Father? Shall we?"

"Why not? I think it would be good."

Isaac Dean had just lit his cigar and looked up, conscious that the two men were regarding him with interest. He stood up quickly, "Wait a minute; wait a minute. You two are concocting something. On second thought, W.W., I think I'll just step outside. You and A.H. are busy. I'll stop in tomorrow."

W.W. and A.H. laughed conspiratorially, having been discovered.

W.W. said, "No, stay, Isaac. You might enjoy this. And don't pretend no. You come by every day. You're as interested in this bank as I am. Now come back and sit down. Hell, you may actually enjoy it."

To show their good faith, A.H. and W.W. both sat down and waited expectantly for Isaac Dean to do the same.

"Isaac," and W.W. directed his conversation to Isaac Dean exclusively, "I asked A.H. to stop in today because I want him to help me with the bank. I'm telling you this in confidence. The money is pouring in. The loans I grant for purchasing war materials are paid off in months, and then they're right back asking for even larger amounts. I've decided to go for something big. That's why I brought A.H. in. I was just asking him to begin the arrangements, and to help me to follow the proper procedure."

"What?" was Isaac Dean's only comment. This was something he had been secretly and wishfully hoping for, from the day W.W. Winton & Co., Bankers, had first opened for business—to be a part of the banking and financial world.

"A national bank," was the terse reply by W.W.

Astute lawyer that he was, A.H. removed himself from the conversation.

"A what?"

"A national bank."

"But what about this place here, Winton, Clark & Co.?"

W.W. turned to his son, "A.H., you explain to your Uncle Isaac."

A.H. took over from his father, "Uncle Isaac, it's this way. When Father opened W.W. Winton & Co. in '63, all he had to do was agree to abide by a few rules. They were referred to as 'charter conditions.' Once he promised, the state, whichever state he was going to operate in, gave him a charter to operate his bank.

"With his charter and his bank, Father was then in the position to issue 'Bank Notes'—you know, our paper money. Now technically, every bank note printed was supposed to be balanced by specie; this means that the exact same amount printed on the note was also sitting physically in the bank's safe, in the form of specie currency.

"But who was around to see if that was really so?

"What the chartered banks started doing was printing a bank note, putting ONE DOLLAR amount on the paper, when in truth there was only a fifty cent piece of specie currency sitting in the safe."

All the while A.H. talked, Isaac Dean was nodding his head in understanding.

"Then last year, in '63, the National Bank Act was passed. That's what Father and I were discussing when you walked in."

"And you think, A.H.?"

"Father thinks, and I concur—to follow along and hop on the bandwagon."

"Which means?"

W.W. took over, "We're not sure, Isaac. That's what A.H. and I were discussing. Which way should we go?"

"Where does the national bank come in?"

"Oh, I see. All right, A.H.; go ahead."

"Uncle Isaac, the National Bank Act means that the federal government is also going to charter banks, and what's more, we've just learned that the federal government is going to give the banks they charter the authority to issue bank notes, too."

Isaac Dean interrupted, "What's the difference, then?"

"Up to this point, essentially no difference. But we hear that, at the same time they give their own banks the authority to go ahead and issue money, they are also going to levy a very large tax on the bank notes issued by the state-chartered banks. This, in effect, will make the state's notes more expensive to issue, and following logically from there, put them out of business."

"Ohhhhhh, I see," said Isaac.

W.W. smiled at Isaac Dean, "You get the picture now, don't you, Isaac?"

"Wait, wait, Uncle Isaac. There's a little more to this than what I've told you. It goes a little deeper. There are some banks, the savings banks or 'banks of deposit,' which have never been able to issue bank notes. So, in daily practice they will be unaffected by the new ruling."

"Oh, I see," said Isaac Dean, again.

"Well, there you have it, Isaac. I had just asked A.H. to get me a copy of the rules and regulations I'll have to meet if I do decide to go under federal supervision."

"Count me in."

"What?" The two Wintons both looked at Isaac Dean.

"I said, count me in. I'm no fool, W.W. The requirements are going to be stiff. So, as I said, count me in."

There was silence in the office as W.W. digested his brother-in-law's offer.

"Wait, Father; this presents another very interesting possibility."

Now it was A.H.'s turn to be stared at.

"Why not have it both ways? If Uncle Isaac brings in extra capital, why not run both kinds of banks simultaneously?"

"How about it, Isaac?" asked W.W. of his brother-in-law.

"Fine with me."

"A.H., get all the information ready. Then we'll have another go at it with your Uncle Isaac."

After A.H. left the bank, he stopped in at the telegraph office and sent a wire to Alice, telling her that he would not be able to get to Wilkes-Barre for a while. As he wrote the message, he chewed his lower lip nervously. This was the first test. If Alice did not know how to handle it, it would be the end.

When the wire reached Alice, she read it in consternation. It had been only two days since A.H. had been with her and they had read George Smith's letter. Alice Collings was also a Beaumont and a Blackman, and she was nineteen years old—the prime marrying age. She was popular in Wilkes-Barre, and had her choice of friends and dances. She did not need A.H. to make her a complete person. She wanted him, she loved him, but she didn't need him. Unfortunately, she realized that the same was true for A.H. That he didn't really need her, she was aware. He would go on doing whatever it was he was doing, whether she were there or not. "But he loves me, I know," she whispered to herself. The emotion that had passed from him to her, as she had sat beside him on the sofa two days earlier, had been stronger than anything she had ever experienced from any of the many friends she had known. He was a man stronger than any she knew—stronger than her own dominant personality.

"Oh, my darling," she sobbed, barely audibly, "I love you." And she admitted defeat.

It took A.H. almost a week to gather the information needed. When he had finished, he stopped in at his uncle's home and told him that he and his father would wait for his arrival at the bank. Shortly after noon, Isaac Dean appeared.

A.H. addressed the two men, "Uncle Isaac, Father, basically the more money you have to put in, the stronger your position, and the greater the amount of credit you can float.

"The most practical way would be to organize on a stock basis. I'll draw up your application, stating the total number of shares, how they are allotted, the amount of capital represented by each share, etc., and file it immediately. I suggest haste, because we stand a good chance of getting the city's first charter."

As soon as he had finished speaking, W.W. and Isaac Dean went to work. Without question, W.W. advocated going for the federal charter.

Isaac agreed, "But what about the bank of deposit?"

"We'll go into that afterwards," replied W.W.

A.H. let the two brothers-in-law wheel and deal. As counsel for the bank, he intended to abstain from any actual financial involvement, anyway.

"Just don't forget to include my legal fees in your proposed expenses," he said as he moved over to a chair at the far side of the office; there he sat relaxed for most of the afternoon. Occasionally, he allowed his mind to wander to Alice. In the back of his mind, there was a constant worry about what her reaction would be when he finally returned to Wilkes-Barre. In spite of their new understanding, the cool reception to his October visit, after a similar absence, was still too vivid in his memory to be ignored.

"A.H., listen to this," his father's voice broke into his reverie, "We're thinking in terms of $300,000 capital. We'll divide the shares of stock equally between us."

"How many shares?"

"A thousand?" W.W.'s voice expressed uncertainty.

"Five hundred for you and five hundred for Uncle Isaac?"

"What do you think?"

"I think each share costs $300."

W.W. regarded his son thoughtfully. The old business magic, which had always intrigued Henry Heermans, came to the foreground. "That's too unwieldy."

Isaac suggested cutting it in half.

"All right then," A.H. summed up, "I'll try for a charter as the first national bank in the city, $300,000 in capital and 2,000 shares of stock. The list of stockholders, for the present, will be Isaac Dean, 1,000 shares, and W.W. Winton, 1,000 shares.

"I think you're definitely better off, doing it this way. It gives you more latitude. Both of you can still raise another $150,000, by selling off half your holdings. That should give you tremendous credit leverage, bringing the capital up to almost half a million.

"Well, I'm off to do my part now. Wish me luck."

A.H. got to work immediately. But as fast as he was, he wasn't quick enough. The charter they were given was for the second national bank in Scranton.

When the actual charter arrived, W.W. called Isaac Dean and A.H. to a meeting in his office, without telling them why. When they were all assembled, he brought out a bottle of fine whiskey.

"To the Second National Bank of Scranton! May she be second to none!"

The three of them savored the mellow liquid.

Isaac Dean proposed the next toast, "To Winton, Clark & Co.!"

"Hear, hear," echoed the Wintons, father and son.

Again there was silence in the office, as the three savored the mellow liquid for a second time.

W.W. refilled the glasses. It was heady stuff, building a banking empire. "To the next," he said.

"To our savings bank," responded Isaac Dean. "How soon, W.W.?"

"As soon as we can raise the capital. Isn't that correct, A.H.?"

A.H. nodded his head affirmatively.

"While we're waiting, A.H.," instructed his father, "make all the necessary preparations. Then we won't be delayed when we're finally ready."

"I will, Father."

It took almost two hours to consume the bottle's contents. But W.W., Isaac, and A.H. felt that they were deserving of a little celebration. Then too, they were celebrating more than just the opening of a new bank. They were allowing themselves the extra few minutes of luxury in which to enjoy their success in moving from a first settler, who knew only the farm he had cleared with his bare, rough hands, to the role of elegant gentlemen of finance.

A.H. was the first to leave the little meeting. Now there was nothing to delay him; he was free at last. He could ride the train to Wilkes-Barre.

In his absence, Alice had admitted her defeat. After that, she had waited quietly for A.H. to return to her. The last time she had seen him, when he had brought the letter, the understanding was that he would return in two days. With his return visit so near, Alice had decided to wait until he came back before speaking to her mother about their plans. She had wanted A.H. with her, and had also thought that her brother John should join them, because more was involved than a mere ritualistic request for a maiden's hand in marriage.

Alice had been the one to manage the household almost as much as her mother, since the death of her father, Samuel Collings, in Morocco. The shift in responsibility had been a natural one, too. Earlier, Elizabeth Beaumont Collings had temporarily turned everything over to Alice when she had gone to the support of her mother at Andrew Beaumont's death. Then, within a year, she had joined her mother as a widow. Alice had only to extend her responsibilities to handle the everyday minutiae for both widows. More than just remembering to set one less place at the dinner table would be involved, when her time came to depart for Scranton with A.H.

When at the end of the two days the telegram had come instead of A.H. himself, Alice continued to remain silent and said nothing of their plans to marry. Consequently, the family had no idea of the seriousness of the relationship. This presented Alice with further complications. She was expected to participate actively in all the festivities preceding Mary's wedding. In fact, weddings were regarded as the ideal environment for young people to meet each other, and, in turn, prepare for still more weddings.

Alice had admitted her submission to A.H. privately, but she still had enough strength of character left to hide it from outsiders. She had not dismissed as unthinkable the possibility of standing in her wedding gown on her wedding day, receiving a telegram saying that the groom was still in Scranton and could not get down to Wilkes-Barre for a week or two. At all costs, Alice wanted to protect herself from ridicule such as that. But at the same time, she knew that A.H. was the only man who could control her and love her in a way such that she would always have respect for him.

Consequently, Alice did nothing or very little. The bride-to-be, Mary, accused her of putting a damper on her prenuptial parties, and John never knew whether to coax his sister to go on an outing with other young friends or not. Alice turned into a silent shadow, moving unobtrusively from one room to another about the house. It was the only defensive mechanism to protect her pride that she could think of. Should A.H. fail to return, no one would ever know, for there would be no radical change in the outward expression of the way she lived her life. But of course A.H. would return. Alice's subdued demeanor was only the expression of her own frustration in not being able to control him.

The day when A.H. finally caught the train for Wilkes-Barre, Alice was in the parlor embroidering on some linens for Mary, who had gone out to luncheon with two of her friends. Her mother was also out. At the sound of the doorbell, Alice pricked up her ears; she wondered who could be calling at so unusual an hour. Soon, she thought she heard the beautiful musical quality that described A.H.'s voice. Alice tiptoed to the parlor doorway and watched as A.H. stood at the far end of the hall asking whether Miss Alice was at home. Now that he was here, now that he had returned to claim her, Alice collapsed into a frenzy of nervousness and self-consciousness. In great haste, she scrambled back to the settee and hurriedly picked up the embroidery hoop. She seated herself on the formal furniture at an angle, presenting her back to the doorway—an erect, somewhat forbidding figure—with a light motion to her arm as the threaded needle was drawn through the linen. This was the picture confronting A.H., as he prepared to enter the room.

He paused at the doorway. Not a sound came from within the room. The only movement was the slight motion of Alice's arm. From where he stood, he could not even see what she was doing. A.H. experienced complete dismay. Alice had deliberately chosen not to be understanding of his message. At a loss, he hesitated, wondering what he should do. But "he who hesitates is lost" is a really sound and worthwhile piece of advice. Gathering strength from every part of himself, A.H. strode over in three enormous, quietly powerful steps to stand before Alice—still, she failed to acknowledge his presence. He leaned over her, placed his hands on both sides of her face, raised her face towards him, and kissed her hard and long. Alice wriggled back on the settee and out of his grasp. A.H. dropped to his knees immediately before her and circled her waist with his arms. He nuzzled his face at the base of her throat.

"Oh, no you don't, my lovely Alice. Give me a kiss, or I'll make love to you right here and now."

He raised himself back up to a standing position and pulled her with him. Still holding her, he waltzed briefly around the room.

"When you haven't seen me for a while, I want to be greeted by a kiss." And he kissed her. She responded, equalling him.

Alice never apologized for her rudeness or lack of greeting. A.H. never expected her to. But their relationship had now become stronger than ever.

"Sit down beside me, my long absent Mr. Winton, and I will tell you all that you have missed. You know, you did promise to help with Mary's wedding."

The battle had been fought. The battle had been won. The month of tension had been swept away. A.H. almost collapsed on the settee, as hard as it was. He sat beside Alice, and held her hand. He stretched his feet out before him, and, as she talked, he closed his eyes. Who was to know, assuming Alice's recital was long and involved, that he lightly slumbered.

The Collings had everything quite well planned. A.H.'s chief function was to take care of the legally minded guests and to make them feel welcome. He felt a slight pressure on the hand holding Alice's.

". . . to since I last saw you?"

A.H. dared not ask her to repeat the whole of her sentence. He kissed her where a wave of her hair followed the curve of the ear nearer him; it gave him time to gather his wits.

"Oh, let me see. Yes, I know. Elnorah has been astounding us all again."

"Elnorah? She's your sister?"

"Yes."

"What did she do?"

"She came home one evening about a week ago with a young man, and told everyone they were engaged to be married."

"Uhhhh! Good heavens, what did your mother say?"

"I don't know. Father and I were working at the bank, and Elnorah had already departed for a visit somewhere by the time we had gotten back."

"Who is he? After all, we will be brothers and sisters. I should know his name and something about him."

"Thomas Livey. Elnorah met him when we were living in New York. Apparently they have been corresponding all this time. That's all I can tell you."

A.H., having supplied Alice with a fresh subject to muse about, went back to relaxing. He had almost forgotten about Elnorah; he had been so busy with the banks and with his own worries concerning Alice. As they sat there, the warmth and nearness of the woman he had asked to be his wife reached him, and began to stir a desire within him for their life together.

He interrupted her, "We must set a day, Alice. There are too many days in May just to say 'May.' Tell me one. And then I want to talk with your mother and brother."

Suddenly, Alice was frightened. The future that was waiting for her became too unknown, too strange. Faced with it, she felt inadequate to explain to her mother that she would be going to Scranton, and that Wilkes-Barre was to be a part of her past only.

"Oh, A.H., just tell mama that you have asked me to be your wife. I will be with you when you do, and I will tell her that I do love you. Then I will ask her whether it's all right. John already guesses. He will agree, I know."

"But Alice, you are so close to your mother. I think we should talk with her a little more than that. After all, you'll be coming to Scranton."

"No, no, my love. It is better this way. Really, that is all that will be necessary."

"What day?"

Alice reached out hurriedly, to lead A.H.'s thoughts where she felt safest. "The ninth. The ninth of May."

And so it was arranged. Elizabeth Beaumont Collings gave her blessing to the union. John welcomed A.H. as an older brother. "Soon there will be two lawyers in the family." A.H. thanked him, but wondered if he was referring to joining the family or to the near future, when John expected to pass his bar exam.

Alice's final suggestion to them all was that, in view of the nearness of Mary's wedding, very little ought to be said about her own, so as not to compete with Mary.

A.H. said that he was willing, but regarded Alice with curiosity. He was certain that she was up to something. He was right; but it was Alice's own insecurity and nothing more. Because she did not dominate A.H., she was not certain of him. It must never be said that a Beaumont-Blackman-Collings was left waiting at the altar, even if it was only until the next train arrived from Scranton.

And so, very few were aware that, in the near future, Alice Collings would be the bride of A.H. Winton.

Of course, the Wintons were included in Mary's wedding guest list; when they arrived for the ceremony, their presence caused no great stir. Like the Collings, they were long time valley residents, and their attendance seemed natural to the Wilkes-Barre guests. A.H.'s presence, as a rising young lawyer among other members of the bar, also created no stir.

A.H. talked with Mary's new husband at the reception. He found Jacob Dillinger to be a court clerk with admirable qualities, and said as much to John Collings, shortly afterwards when the two met at the punchbowl.

"There is someone here who admires you too, A.H.; I've heard him say so on several occasions."

"Who is he?"

"Come; I'll introduce you," and John Collings guided A.H. to a well dressed young man, who had just left a group talking at the other side of the table. John called out, "Frank! I'd like you to meet A.H. Winton of Providence."

The two men shook hands.

The newcomer said, "Winton, how do you do? I'm Frank Collins."

A.H. acknowledged the handshake cordially, "Collings? A relative?"

"No," Frank flashed an engaging smile, "I'm the 'Collings' from the other side of the alphabet, I guess. I'm the Collings without the 'g'".

"Aw gee, that's too bad," bantered A.H. "Tell me, Collins, what do you do? You look familiar. Have I seen you around?"

"If you spent more time in the court house, I'd look even more familiar to you. I passed my bar exam recently."

"Good to hear. You're in Wilkes-Barre then?"

"I'm looking around. My father has his place in Dunmore [a small community about four miles up the valley from Scranton], and I haven't decided where to settle yet."

"The next time you're in Scranton, stop in. I'll be glad to show you around."

"Thank you, Winton. I'll take you up on that."

Shortly after his conversation with the Collins without the "g," A.H. told Alice his parents wanted to leave.

"I'll take them home, Alice. When I come again, we will talk about ourselves. Mary's wedding is over now."

A.H. did come again—and several times again after that. In the summer months following the wedding, Alice would usually pack a simple picnic basket and the two of them would spend a lazy afternoon on an outing. Alice loved to tease A.H., because he would lie quietly for up to an hour if she would read to him from a book of poems.

"What kind of a lawyer can you be if you are a poetry lawyer?" she would mock. "What would Judge Harding say if you presented your case in rhyme? I can see it now; he would say, 'Who is this Wintin who is a speakin?'"

As an answer, A.H. would roll over and pull Alice down beside him. Sometimes, he would kiss her loudly; other times, he would smack her smartly on the rear. "No, he wouldn't. He would say, 'Who is this man who speaks in rhyme? Let the court convene on time.'"

When the days started to get a little chilly, A.H. did not come as frequently. But this time it was more of Alice's doing than any absorption in work on his part. Alice still did not have complete confidence in A.H. In fact, every time he did arrive, Alice looked on it more as a chance occurrence than as a deliberate plan on his part. She was completely happy when she was with him, but because he was not hers to command as she pleased, she imagined that she could not depend on him. This was foolish reasoning; just because he would not let her lead him around as a pet on a leash, it did not mean that he was not hers to command. But, anyway, this was how Alice felt. And she felt that she must keep their love a secret. To publicly participate in any activity that indicated she was expecting to be Mrs. A.H. Winton, was something she wanted to avoid at all costs, for the present.

A.H. already owned a small property in Scranton. Alice suggested that they make their first home there, at least temporarily, until she was more familiar with Providence and Scranton.

As far as furniture was concerned, she really thought that only a few pieces were necessary. "I'm sure we have a chair or two too many here. Perhaps your mother has something she is not using right now, that we could borrow temporarily?"

Having noted the comfort in which the Collings lived, A.H. was a little surprised that Alice could be content with such simple furnishings. But the thought of the resulting savings to his pocketbook caused him to remain silent. So in the cold winter months at the end of '64 and the beginning of '65, A.H. went less often to Wilkes-Barre and did as Alice suggested, from a distance.

He engaged the services of his brothers, who helped him move a few pieces of furniture into the modest, although two-story, single dwelling, located a block from his office and the new bank. His mother sent over a pleasant serving-girl by the name of Bridget Malia, who cleaned and scrubbed. A.H. found her so agreeable that he asked her to stay on and help the new Mrs. Winton.

Alice, meanwhile, was doing her part. For the most, this involved assembling a trousseau of clothes and linens. To be proper and correct, the table linens, the bed linens, and those used in the bath all had to be initialed. Alice's mother shared a few large silver serving pieces with her daughter and, from her own account, Alice purchased the rest. While Alice did not participate in the usual round of festivities that winter, she did on occasion go to a hop or dance with her brother. Thus, it never crossed anyone's mind that Miss Alice Collings might soon be disappearing from the Wilkes-Barre scene, only to emerge as Mrs. A.H. Winton of Scranton.

The atmosphere of the times aided and allowed Alice and A.H. to plan as they did. The tragedy of the bitter deaths of the twelve thousand men at the Andersonville Prison in Georgia was not unknown. The war wounded who had been discharged and returned to the valley had described the burning and spoilage of the South in ugly terms. The general mood was as grim and hard as the "black diamonds" rushing down from the mountains. The war was uppermost in everyone's mind. Then, suddenly, miraculously, the news came—General Lee had yielded. Lee had decided that there was no sense in continuing to fight against a limitless supply of men and equipment. The date, April 9, was one month before the wedding.

8

Alice Muhlenberg Collings was married to Aretus Heermans Winton at eleven in the morning in the chapel at St. Stephen's Episcopal Church, Wilkes-Barre, on the Ninth of May, 1865. Captain John Colt Beaumont, USN, between commands, had arrived suddenly to give his niece away. The assembled well-wishers were few in number: the bride's family and the groom's family. Grandfather Henry Heermans' second wife, Sarah Ann, was there, as were Isaac Dean and a few other Heermans relations, including Abram Dunning and Mahala. Missing was Colonel Eugene Beauharnais Beaumont, another uncle of the bride. He had been fighting in the battle at Selma, Georgia, on the second of April, and had gone from there to Macon, as soon as word had been received of Jefferson Davis's capture. Col. Beaumont was required to wait there until Jefferson Davis arrived and was turned over to him. Again, he would miss a niece's wedding.

Alice changed her mind. At the last minute, she sent everyone scurrying in every direction, because she suddenly decided that she wanted to be married at St. Stephen's instead of at home. A.H. was perhaps the person most tolerant of her apparent whim. But he probably recognized it for what it was: her last, farewell gesture to her family, her town, and the part of her life already lived.

"It will bring me closer to Grandpapa," she had told everyone simply, referring to Andrew Beaumont.

As for A.H., he remained calm even to the moment when he stood beside the rector, waiting for his bride. When at last she entered, on the arm of her much beribboned uncle in his navy dress uniform, he was amazed that his desires had been so content during the past months. He thrilled when he saw her; Alice was as beautiful a woman as any he had ever seen. Even her dignified modesty, which she expressed as she walked towards him, was a challenge to him. Unconsciously, he straightened himself; his male ego strove to dominate her. To the family gathered before them, all that was apparent was how A.H. flowed with strength and grew in demeanor, just at the sight of his bride, the lovely Alice.

After the ceremony, the family reassembled back at the Collings' home. The gathering glittered and sparkled like brilliant diamonds—not because they were self-conscious of their surroundings, for after all they treaded on "black diamonds" every day—but because of who they were, in the sense of what they were: a gracious mother-of-the-bride, yet one who had held all of Washington society at her feet; a friendly father-in-law, yet one who had wrested a banking empire from those who considered themselves far more cosmopolitan than he; the daughter of a man who had grown from a wilderness settler with a few carpenter's tools, to a wealthy patriarch who had known the importance of a post office and was the connecting link of a clan that covered half the valley; and lastly, a doting uncle, yet one who had commanded ships and men around the world, who had been a part of the sea blockade that had controlled the Confederate States—in fact he had just come from capturing Fort Fisher. And what made this gathering even more remarkable was that all these people were no more than one generation removed from those who had fled in terror to hide in river banks from massacring Indians.

The guests, once at the reception, moved about talking to one another. Captain Beaumont sought out A.H.; something about him appealed to the captain. He had been commanding men for several years, and he had guided ships across oceans; he knew a responsible junior officer when he saw one. "I've been looking forward to meeting you, A.H. My sister has written to me on several occasions about you. I want to welcome you to the family. Alice is my favorite niece; always has been. I've often wondered who would capture her heart."

A.H. responded quickly to his newly acquired uncle. Capt. Beaumont was a change from his many Heermans relatives. Astutely, the two men, one a seasoned career naval officer, the other a young, brilliant lawyer, sized each other up simultaneously. They both saw an honesty and a directness of mind in the other. Neither one flinched at the other's gaze.

Before moving on to speak to someone else, the Captain shook A.H.'s hand again, "Yes, sir, welcome aboard, A.H. Take good care of Alice. But then, I know you'll do that." And he gave A.H. a wink of friendship before departing.

John Collings acted the seasoned veteran, having already ushered the family through one wedding. He spoke to the bride, "If you need me, Alice, just send a wire. I'll come immediately. You may be the man's wife, but remember you're still my sister."

"Oh, John, you're so silly. Thank you. Of course I would, if I did. But I don't think I will. Just come and see me lots of times. I don't think Mama ever will. It's going to be terribly lonesome for a while, you know, not to see your dear face."

All of the Heermans, for their part, were on their best behavior. They politely refrained from inquiring into Alice's cooking ability, or asking if she had thrifty habits. They even refrained from expressing too loudly the hope that the children would wait a while before starting a family.

At one point, Elizabeth Beaumont Collings gave A.H. a moist kiss on the cheek, and whispered, "Take care of my little girl."

So really, for all their glitter and hardness and sparkle, their conversation was quite ordinary; basically they were simple folk concerned about the happiness and welfare of two of their children.

But to an outsider passing by, it was the grandest of all grand affairs. Gathered together as relatives, were Wyoming Valley people in whose veins flowed the blood of half the valley's original settlers—the blood of the people who had first seen the valley, and had loved it enough to endure everything, whatever hardship was meted out to them: Blackmans, Yarringtons, Colts, Beaumonts, Collings, Heermans, Wintons, Tripps, and Slocums.

If that intangible thing called the history of an area could have been embodied or captured and put into a human form, then one could say that the marriage of Alice and A.H. was far more then just two people uniting. In allegory, Wilkes-Barre and Scranton had plighted their troth, to live together in love and harmony forever. Both Alice and A.H. carried to their wedding bed not only their love for each other, but also the story of the two great cities of the Wyoming Valley. In many ways, Wilkes-Barre, like Alice, was the more cultured, sensitive, elegant, striving to dominate; Scranton, like the male, was bolder, brasher, coarser than the woman, but powerful enough and virile enough to resent domination, strong enough to break free of her wiles and to demand cohabitation on his own terms.

There was still an hour before sunset when A.H. and Alice stole away. They had planned to begin their married life in the little house that A.H. had prepared. The sun was a golden glow behind them, as the train made Alice a stranger to Wilkes-Barre. The northeast view, that was their path ahead, embraced them with the beauty that comes when a landscape is caught in the sun's soft rays at the end of a day.

"I've made arrangements for a light supper at the Wyoming House; it's on Lackawanna Avenue. We'll go there first."

"Whatever you say. You are my guide, now." Alice smiled at A.H.

The train lurched, and A.H. went to wipe a cinder from his eye. He reached into his pocket for his handkerchief. As he did, he felt the letter that had been thrust into his hand just before he and his father, as best man, had gone to stand by the rector in St. Stephen's.

"Alice, what is this? Not until after I had opened it and begun to read, did I realize it was not meant for me."

"I'm sure I don't know. What does it say?"

"It's addressed to you. I think perhaps you had better read it." A.H. was so insistent because he already knew the contents.

"No, no, the train moves too much. Please; you do it." Alice was equally as insistent—perhaps because she could guess at the contents.

Only a few hours as husband, and A.H. was already slightly annoyed with his wife. Her calm indifference to the letter that had been hurriedly and mistakenly placed in his hands, because the messenger boy had only been told to deliver it to the one who was getting married, agitated his legal mind into suspicion.

Turning large, luminous eyes to him, Alice said, "If you do not care to read the letter, then tell me about the Wyoming Hotel."

A.H. unfolded the note and read the following:

Monday, P.M.
Miss Alice,

I think I may say that I entertain for you no other feelings than those of friendship. I do not feel at liberty to accept your invitation. Sad news has just reached me from home.

Hoping that your path in life may be strewn with heaven's sweetest flowers—allow me to subscribe myself, most I am yours.

E.L. Merriman

A.H. refolded the letter and handed it to Alice, who accepted it wordlessly. A.H. waited, hoping she would speak. But a good witness knows when to remain silent before the opposition's lawyer.

At length, A.H. inquired, "You invited him to our wedding?"

Alice replied, "Please, Mr. Winton, do not be concerned. Mr. Merriman has been a friend for a long while. He often pressed me for feelings that I could not honestly say were mine.

"I will admit, there were several occasions, when you were not in Wilkes-Barre, that he called, but it was always as a friend. I never thought of it otherwise. Although, I believe, he may have.

"That was why I sent him the note, inviting him to our wedding. It seemed more kind that way. If I showed that I had always thought of him as a friend, he could pretend the same and not be embarrassed."

The chord of compassion that Alice struck in him moved A.H. deeply. He leaned back in his seat and squeezed her hand. "You know," he said, "I am very lucky—very lucky indeed—to have such a beautiful wife, with such an understanding soul, and to be so intelligent. Yes, I am very lucky indeed. Perhaps we could skip supper and go straight home. I do feel rather tired."

Alice's look pulverized A.H.; it was the kind of look a school teacher uses to handle an erring boy.

A.H. had arranged to have a cab waiting for them at the train stop. They climbed in and it clopped quietly down the road the short distance to the Wyoming Hotel. A.H. dismissed the cab at the entrance. The spring evening was fragrant and pulsing with the new life of the delicate and tender green buds bursting from the bare branches.

"Our home is only a short distance from here," he said, "I thought we could walk afterwards. It is a beautiful night."

The entire staff of the Wyoming Hotel assembled in the dining room to welcome the new Mrs. Winton. It seemed to Alice that everyone knew A.H. The other guests in the dining room were quickly caught up in the spirit of the welcome, and came forward to congratulate A.H., too. He received each one, known or strange, in a courteous fashion, and in turn introduced his wife. At last, they were allowed to sit down. With great flourish, one dish after another was placed before them. Alice had always been accustomed to attention, but this ostentatious show of affection embarrassed her; she really wasn't sure whether it was seemly or not.

A.H. must have read her thoughts, because he leaned over and whispered, "You're in Scranton now, my dear."

Afterwards, they walked through the darkened streets to their home. It was a very short distance, but A.H. moved so leisurely that Alice could not judge the length by the passage of time. The warm spring evening was fraught with promises of love and excitement—it matched the mood of the strollers. When they came to the modest two-story frame building, A.H. fitted the key into the lock. Wordlessly, he picked up his bride in his arms and carried her across the threshold—and on up the stairs to the bedroom.

They passed the whole of the night loving each other, with fits of light sleep in between, until, in the first gleams of the new morning, they fell at last into a sleep as if drugged.

A.H. was the first to awaken; it was almost noon. He regarded his beautiful sleeping wife for a while, and when she did not stir he lay back beside her. He moaned, just audibly enough to be heard, until Alice awakened.

"What is it?" she asked, sitting up in alarm.

A.H. feigned sleepiness. "Nothing. I was wondering; perhaps we should get up. I'm certain the time is very late. Would you like a little something to eat, Alice?"

Alice darted a penetrating look at him, but said nothing. She leaned over, pinning him to the bed, "If I get up, you will have to, too." And then she was gone before he could grab her.

They chased each other, laughing and screaming, through the house until they were exhausted; they found each other in the kitchen. Their first meal together was a joint effort.

And so, one day passed into the next.

In the afternoon of the third day, Bridget came to prepare the dinner. With her arrival, the magic vanished. Now they became the very proper Mr. and Mrs. Winton and had only the bedroom for their moments of passion.

Bridget was only the beginning of the pressure to return them to their surroundings. Late in the morning of the fourth day, John Collings arrived. Alice and A.H. were preparing to sit down to a noonday meal when they heard his knock at the door. They welcomed John gladly and encouraged him to stay. Alice introduced Bridget to her brother and had her set another place at the table for him. It was a happy, light-hearted meal. All three of them refused to be serious. Afterward, John announced his intentions to depart. He noted to himself how he was not pressed to stay. But Alice and A.H. were aware of the reason behind his apparently nonchalant call. So as John got up to leave, A.H. suddenly remembered something that he had forgotten and excused himself momentarily, leaving brother and sister alone.

Alice took the opportunity, and said to her brother, "Tell Mother that I am very, very happy. He is a wonderful man."

John left, satisfied.

Before their wedding, when they had been making plans, Alice had not been able to draw out of A.H. exactly how long their honeymoon would last.

"Couldn't you possibly give me an idea?" she had pleaded about three weeks before the wedding day, "If we are to send out 'At Home' cards, I will have to have a date to put on them."

But A.H. had always managed to sidestep the issue. His platitudes had silenced her, but they had not satisfied her, "Pick any date to tell our friends when we will be glad to receive them. If you want to wait until September, I will not mind." He had added, after a pause, "Do you realize that when I come to call on you on the ninth of May, it will be a call that will never come to an end? I am sure that in all our hours together, we can always find time to greet a friend. But if you must have a date, then you decide when to tell the world that our 'honeymoon' is over."

Alice had pursed her lips and frowned at that. A.H. had retreated into silence, delighted with the neat way in which he had side-stepped the issue.

There was a real reason behind A.H.'s reticence about setting a date. The Providence Bankruptcy Commission had decided to announce their final decision on the twenty-sixth of June. This open meeting was scheduled to be held in his law office. A.H. did have enough sensibility about him to question the wisdom of implying to Alice that her wedding had been scheduled before a business appointment. As for himself, A.H. saw nothing wrong; an interval of a full six weeks separated the two, his wedding and the meeting. The fires of bridegroom and love should have been sufficiently quenched by then to allow him to conclude the commission's work, he reasoned.

After almost two weeks of living exclusively for each other, A.H. grew restive. He was anxious to return to his work and to the forthcoming bankruptcy commission session. He left Alice for a few hours each day, to rummage around in his office. Alice did not mind; in fact, if questioned, she would have admitted that she welcomed the brief time alone, for it gave her a chance to attend to the little things that she had pushed aside in the last minute rush before the wedding. A good portion of her free time was spent in catching up with her correspondence. There were many who still did not know that she was Mrs. Winton. One such note, to her friend May Wright in Allentown, who had introduced her sister Mary to Jacob Dillinger, brought a quick reply.

After going through the mail, the day in early June when May's letter arrived, Alice went to the kitchen to discuss the evening meal with Bridget. Bridget had just come in from shopping, and had a bag of fresh groceries and a newspaper with her.

Seeing the paper, Alice reached for it and said, "Do you mind, Bridget? I'll return it to you as soon as I check through the advertisements. It's my way of learning which store sells what in Scranton."

While Bridget unpacked the food, Alice stood by the kitchen table and hastily glanced through the paper. Among the ads, her eye picked out the notice for the commissioners' meeting on the twenty-sixth of June.

"Ohhh!"

"Did you say something, Miss Alice?"

"No, no, Bridget. You must be mistaken. Here, take your paper. Thank you for letting me see it," and Alice started to leave the room.

"Wait, Miss Alice. What about dinner?"

Alice hesitated. For a moment, she was ready to tell Bridget to throw the pans at her husband if he wanted to eat, but collected herself in time—a little more dignity was probably in order. She retraced her steps back into the kitchen, and, with Bridget, inventoried the contents of the icebox and the just-purchased items spread before her on the table. Between the two of them, they arrived at a satisfactory menu of chilled soup, a meat and a pudding for desert. Alice then left for the front of the house, to await her husband's return.

When A.H. arrived, her greeting was cordial but not as warm as it should have been. She observed that the subtle difference was lost on him. Not until they were at the dinner table and consuming their dessert of pudding, did Alice begin to advance on the subject of greatest interest to herself at the moment.

"I received several fine letters today, my dear. One friend in particular was most eloquent on our marriage. Oh, Bridget—" Alice interrupted herself to address Bridget, who had come in to remove the plates, "Do you have the paper for Mr. Winton? Please get the paper for him. He would like to read it, now that he can sit here and relax." Finished with Bridget, Alice returned to A.H., "And while she is getting the paper, I will go and get my dear friend May's letter. You will enjoy hearing it."

Alice hastened from the room to get the letter, and hurried back in time to intercept Bridget, who was returning with the newspaper.

"I'll give it to him. Thank you, Bridget."

Alice folded and placed the paper before her husband, the small commission notice in the portion facing up. After a glance, A.H. ignored the paper and, instead of picking it up, followed his wife's progress with his eyes as she returned to her seat. He waited for whatever was to come next.

Alice took the letter from the envelope and read aloud:

Allentown, May 28th.
My Dear Alice,

Accept our sincerest congratulations. We received your cards telling us you were no more Alice Collings. I need not tell you I was very much surprised. I had a little hint about it sometime ago but had no idea it was to be so soon. It is not necessary to wish you happiness. I know it will be yours. You would never have married him, I am sure, did you not know him to be worthy your love and confidence. I was disappointed you did not come to Allentown. I sent word with Mr. Lenard that I would be happy to see you. I watched every train after we received your cards. Shall you go directly to housekeeping? Will it be in Wilkes-Barre or Scranton? Write to me, dear Alice, and tell me all about it. You know I am interested in all that concerns you. Did you have any wedding? Who were your bridesmaids and groomsmen? I have a very slight impression that you once promised that honor to Mr. Sturdevant and me. I expect you forgot it, just as all my Wilkes-Barre friends are forgetting me, Mr. Sturdevant with the rest. All the family send much love to you, Father included, provided Mr. Winton does not object. My sincere regards to your husband. Tell him I hope someday to make his acquaintance. With much love for yourself,

Affectionately,
May

After Alice finished, the silence hung in the room like a blanket, smothering any attempt at sound.

At last Alice spoke, "Wasn't that a lovely letter from May? You will have to meet her." There was a pregnant pause, "May is so sweet. Did you note that part where I read, 'You would never have married him, I am sure, did you not know him to be worthy your love and *confidence*'?" Alice emphasized "confidence" when she reread.

A.H. knew what was in the newspaper. He didn't have to read it. As for the letter, Alice's first reading was sufficient. She didn't have to verbally underline her drift of thought.

At length, he spoke, "That was a lovely letter, Alice. Perhaps you would like to ask her to visit us soon?" Then he picked up the paper and refolded it to another section.

"You might, at least, have told me."

Again the silence, before an answer was given.

"Yes, I suppose I could have."

The two combatants glared at each other. Nothing more was said; nothing was resolved.

Inwardly, A.H. was in agony. Now that it had come out this way, he was sorry that he had not braved the risk and told her about the bankruptcy meeting before. He had learned his lesson, however. He would never underestimate Alice. He would never ignore Alice. Then, he took pride in her, in her behavior at something that must have been very upsetting to her. But his pride in her made his shame of himself all the more acute.

"Here is a truly beautiful woman," he thought to himself.

She had expressed no censure of her husband's act, nor any criticism of what he planned to do—only a reminder that he had excluded her, had demonstrated that he did not have trust in her, only a reminder that he had not shared a confidence with his mate. Had Alice stopped at this point, all would have been well. In his estimation, she would have been almost untouchable, so fine a woman did he consider her, who had become his wife.

Unfortunately, after a brief respite, Alice continued to belabor the point. All evening, or what remained of the evening, A.H. felt her pressure, her accusing look placing him in the wrong—a feeling he did not share. He knew that he should have told her, but the decision to actually hold the meeting carried no wrong.

It was a battle of the sexes and by the time they were ready to retire, the battle between the sexes had not lessened.

Later, in the dark when he turned to her, he loved her and used her as if he had bought it. Alice was passive, and perhaps a little frightened, before the onslaught. But before long she was returning his own primitive passion with a fire that matched his. Afterwards, A.H. fell back exhausted and slept deeply. Alice lay there, awake, restless. Finally she crept from the room, like a silent white shadow, and wandered about the house, at last coming to rest on the sofa in the parlor downstairs.

She had not been gone too long when A.H. awakened. It was a minute or two before he realized that she was not there beside him. He called her name softly, "Alice?" and listened for a reply. Gravely disturbed when he heard none, he rose, put on his robe, and went in search of his wife. He found her on the sofa, a graceful, limp figure. He knelt beside her and gathered her two hands in his. They were alone in the house, but still he whispered.

"Alice, my darling, what is it?"

She did not answer.

To himself, A.H. cursed his passion. He truly loved her too much to make her unhappy.

"Alice, please dear, what is the matter?"

"I'm so ashamed," she whispered back, fresh tears running down her already stained face.

He showered her with tender, light kisses, and murmured, "Ashamed? Ashamed of what?"

"What you must think of me. I was so gross. I was like a savage."

The legal mind reeled in amazement. In his pursuit of woman, A.H. was glad that he had never tried to understand her as well.

"No, no, darling. There is nothing to be ashamed of. You only showed you love me."

Tenderly, he gathered her up in his arms. Tenderly, he carried her back upstairs. Tenderly, he lay beside her. And tenderly, he showed her how tender their love could be.

Afterward, she clung tightly to him, in trust. He would not disturb her for any reason, and so lay there the rest of the night without moving.

This was the turning point in their relationship together. They had bared every emotion, and each had found the other understanding and loving in return. Very rare, and very beautiful indeed, are these marriages.

Thus did Alice's and A.H.'s honeymoon end. It was a time in which they laid a foundation of rock as hard as the "black diamonds" they lived on, and so strong that their trust and love would be able to carry them forward through whatever obstacles were to fall across their way.

9

W.W. had listened well when A.H. had spoken of his suspicions concerning Providence's bankrupt status. Almost a year and a half had passed since that conversation; during that time W.W. had been very alert. He had doubted that anyone involved would be careless enough to openly admit any wrong-doing. All he was hoping for was enough information to make his own references accurate when it was his turn to talk.

On the day before June 26, the day of the commissioners' open meeting, W.W. visited A.H. in his law office. It was the first time that he was to mention any of his findings to his son.

When W.W. came in, he made no reference to the change in A.H.'s mode of living other than giving his son a good hearty clap on the back. His fatherly eye had discerned a deeply satisfied contentment in A.H.'s eyes. W.W. didn't have to ask how married life was with Alice. Instead, he went directly to the purpose of his call.

"Well, A.H.," he said, "you were right. It was a concentrated effort to force a city merger."

"Do you have anything specific we can go on? I could bring it to trial. Once out in the open, we could hope for a public outcry, and perhaps get some money back into the treasury."

"I don't think we'll ever be able to pin it down that closely. No, I'm afraid Providence is licked. All I can see is that we may not have to go down ignominiously."

A.H. snorted in disgust.

"No, now be patient. The important thing is to handle it right. I have confidence in you. I'm sure you'll think of something. This bunch in Scranton is sharp. Their idea is sound. It's just that we old time Razorville boys used to consider ourselves the sharp ones, and we sort of resent having to move over and play second fiddle."

A.H. changed the subject briefly, "We [referring to his fellow commissioners and himself] decided to pay interest on the debts up to the first of this coming August, then freeze the amount from that date on."

"Very good. That's more than fair," but W.W. was more interested in the broad scheme of things, "A.H., Seldon Scranton and Dr. Throop want a city classification badly. What's the size of Providence now?"

"Five thousand."

"Our five thousand can give it to them. Wilkes-Barre isn't anywhere near that population. The war is over, but one thing it has done: it's made the railroad and the coal all-important. And we have both here. The iron works are turning out track, and the mines are fueling the whole country, almost. If ever there were a moment to shift around, I would say that this is it. I'm going to talk to everybody, and see what we can arrange. While I'm doing that, see what you can work up in terms of an actual agreement." W.W. started to leave, but then came back in. "On second thought, I think I'll ride out and have a talk with your Uncle Abram first."

"A.B. Dunning?"

"Yes."

"Why Uncle Abram?"

"Because, while we were in New York in the 1850s, he was fighting for a new county status in Harrisburg."

"A new county? Uncle Abram?"

"He was a state representative then, and he tried to divide Luzerne County and bring us out as another county. He was able to pass it through the House, but Buckalew was in the Senate and squelched it irrevocably. Yes, now that I think about it, I'm sure I want to talk to Abram before I do anything else."

The tiny little acorn that was to turn into the mighty oak had started to grow.

W.W. departed to visit his brother-in-law, who was now living about eight miles south of Scranton in a community bearing his name: Dunning (now Elmhurst).

Shortly after his father departed, A.H. returned home. He related most of his conversation with his father to Alice. She listened attentively; she was interested in his affairs, but mostly she appreciated being taken into his confidence. When he arose early on the twenty-sixth, she got up with him to see him off. A.H. departed for his office and the commission meeting a very happy man. At last, Alice was working with him; the only battles and problems he had to face were outside the home.

The list of creditors and amounts due were on view. Everyone was satisfied, and Providence's bankruptcy came to a satisfactory conclusion. The commission was dissolved. However for many years thereafter, A.H. continued to keep a controlling or supervisory hand in its Poor Board, the source of the bankruptcy trouble. For a while, he was one of the directors of the Poor Board, but mostly his activity was as a very interested observer. He had learned the power of a deficit welfare agency and its far-reaching effects. If it was ever going to happen again, he wanted to know ahead of time.

As a young lawyer fighting his way for a place in the legal arena, A.H. had two major credits to his name. But handling Providence's indebtedness and setting up the Second National Bank for his father were not even enough to keep a man in pocket money.

Frank Collins, whom A.H. had not seen since the time of Mary's wedding, stopped in to see him.

"You see, Winton. I told you I would look you up."

"I'm glad you did."

The two men shook hands cordially. A.H. liked "the Collins without the 'g.'"

"Now that you're here, tell me what you've been doing."

"I've been busy; in fact, our whole family has been busy."

A.H. elevated his eyebrows in mock surprise.

"First off, I'll give you the big news. I've taken an office at 306 Lackawanna Avenue. So you'll have to watch it now, Winton; you're going to have some real competition."

"That's good news, Collins. If my space were larger, I'd have asked you to come in with me."

Frank Collins was deeply touched by A.H.'s remark. "Well, maybe we will some day. The other news, and this is for your ears alone at the present time, is this: my father is going to run for associate judge in next year's election."

"Now that is really good news. We need every man on the bench from this end of the valley that we can get."

"Agreed. Don't forget, Winton, Collins is in town."

The two laughed.

After Frank Collins had left, A.H. gave the matter of earning an income some thought. He reached into his desk drawer and brought out his box of business cards:

Aretus H. Winton
Attorney at Law
and
Shorthand reporter
office with Garrick M. Harding, Esq.
Wilkes-Barre

No emotion showed as he consigned the box to the wastebasket beside his desk.

"I'm on my own, trying to maintain my own affairs," he thought, "I'd better see what I can do about earning some money." After more reflecting, he decided that no fee would be too small.

It was shortly thereafter that he ran into S.N. Bradford, the provost marshal to whom he had delivered the squad of deserters at the time of the fighting at Gettysburg. A.H. wanted to know what had brought him back to Scranton.

"Winding up the aftermath of the war," was the reply.

A.H. looked surprised.

It was then Bradford's turn to be surprised at A.H.'s surprise, for he hadn't been aware of the peculiar insular outlook of the valley. The great era of Reconstruction that was sweeping the south was unfelt by those living in the Wyoming Valley. It is difficult to imagine it thus, but that was exactly what happened: carpetbaggers and scalawags were unknown to the residents of Wyoming Valley. Perhaps earlier, before A.H. and Alice had come to terms,

A.H. would have blushed at his display of ignorance of what was going on in the world. But now he was committed to the valley; so instead he smiled tolerantly at Bradford. Let Bradford adjust his perspective, decided A.H.

Bradford assessed A.H.'s calm assurance and was impressed. He proceeded to explain the legal maneuvering over the fate of the South.

"There's money in it, even for people like you and me up here in the North," he concluded.

A.H. was immediately interested and asked for more detail. Bradford explained that he himself was no longer with the military, and consequently no longer provost marshal for Pennsylvania. He detailed the advantages derived from being a claims agent for the federal government. The work appealed to A.H., and he and Bradford formed a partnership on the spot. They announced their joint venture with a placard:

Claim Agents
all claims for exemption
or claims against the government for
Back Pay and Bounty
will be promptly attended to by

A.H. Winton and
S.N. Bradford,
Late Provost Marshal

All those wishing to Enlist or Volunteer or Substitute
or
Those who are Drafted or expect to be, will receive any
information at our office free of charge.
Office opposite Provost Marshal's Office

They also had business cards printed to read the same. A.H. closed out his temporary office, which he had set up to handle the bankruptcy, and moved in with Bradford, across from the provost marshal's office, also in Scranton.

A.H. was attracted to this line of work because he regarded it in the same light as he had his work for the Providence debt. It was an expression of service to the community. When he handed out his new business cards, he was advertising that he would assist his fellow valley residents and would play the role of intermediary, as he had on the commission, between his government and his neighbor. Only in this instance the work would be far more lucrative.

The months following the commission's last meeting were a period of consolidation for A.H. and Alice. A.H. worked hard to establish his law practice. Besides handling military claims, he acted as a collector of unpaid debts for various local merchants. In these cases his fees ranged from $40.00 to about $150.00. It was also a period of consolidation in his home life. He and Alice used the time to settle themselves into a well-organized household. However, when he arrived home one evening to find his brother Walter parading a young lady, albeit an attractive one, past his home as one would show off a P.T. Barnum curiosity, he almost lost his matrimonial maturity.

On this particular occasion, Alice, hearing the commotion, came out, and seeing Walter and the girl, invited them both in for a visit. Walter introduced Alice and A.H. to his current friend, Ella Tunstall, and said that she was a new arrival from Peekskill, New York, that her father had come to Scranton lured by the opportunities of a coal region, and that the father, Stephen Tunstall, had opened a small foundry across from Dr. Hollister's establishment. Afterwards, when the couple had left, Alice chided her husband for his surly behavior. To this, A.H. politely reminded her that, as his brother was twenty years of age, this was exactly how he would behave towards him until Walter decided to put his shoulder to the grist mill of life and engage in some worthy pursuit.

As the cold winter months turned into the soft breezes of spring, a look of expectancy lighted the faces of the A.H. Wintons. There had been no fruit from their initial union, but by the time they were ready to celebrate their first wedding anniversary, parenthood was only a month or so away. Alice expressed a desire to return to Wilkes-Barre at that time.

"I would feel more comfortable if mama were with me. I love your mother, A.H., but she must take care of your father and the boys. At home, mama can be with me all the time."

A.H. saw her logic, and reluctantly agreed to let her go. Only once did he give an indication as to how he was thinking; this was when he asked Alice, "I wonder if our first child should be born on Scranton soil instead of Wilkes-Barre?"

Alice squeezed his arm and said, "Please, this time?"

They decided that it would be best if Alice moved to Wilkes-Barre at the end of May.

"You can have the whole house to yourself, and you can work as hard and as late as you like," she told him. "Besides, no one wants to see me in the hot summer months, especially you. I might lose all my fascination for you."

A.H. vowed, however, that he was going to join her in Wilkes-Barre when her time was imminent.

When Alice had first learned of the forthcoming new arrival, and its expected date, she had blushed in hot embarrassment. For she remembered back to the night when they had been together. They had come from a celebration with A.H.'s family and some of the Heermans clan. Alice had been feeling particularly lonely that night, in spite of the laughing relatives around her, for it was her first big party away from her own family. When they had returned to their own little house, A.H. had wasted no time preparing for bed. Full of food, he dropped off to sleep almost immediately, snoring slightly, while Alice, still feeling sorry for herself, had sat up in bed and regarded her sleeping husband.

Looking back on it, she wondered whatever had possessed her. Maybe it was because A.H. had looked so healthy and happy as he lay there perfectly relaxed while she felt so miserable. Alice remembered how she had leaned over and kissed him, gently at first, and then with an increasing intensity. It had been with no little effort and many caresses on her part that she was finally able to arouse him. Remembering, her blood throbbed vibrantly through her whole body as she thought of the part she had played in creating the new life.

At the end of May, Alice and A.H. decided that it was time to travel to Wilkes-Barre. It was quite a homecoming. Coinciding with their arrival was that of her uncle, the seagoing Captain John Beaumont.

"I've come for my namesake!" the captain called out.

A chorus of, "Why?," "What's the matter?," answered his demand.

"Because I'm leaving for Russia immediately, and I'm going to take John with me!"

Captain John Colt Beaumont hugged his sister Elizabeth Collings exuberantly, and before the eyes of the rest of the family the years seemed to vanish, and it was as if it were 1832 again and they were preparing to leave for Washington with their father.

Elizabeth pushed her brother away, "John, be serious. Please tell us what this is all about. What are you doing here in Wilkes-Barre? Why didn't you tell me you were coming?"

"I told you, Elizabeth, I'm leaving for Russia immediately, and I'm going to take my namesake with me."

John Beaumont Collings, Elizabeth's son, stepped forward, "Uncle John, what do you mean? Why am I to go to Russia with you?"

"Because it will be a wonderful experience for you. Because I can take you. Now pack your gear. I can't delay a moment."

In spite of the commanding ring to his order, no one moved. A.H. had been as excited as everyone else, but even he did not move.

Elizabeth put a restraining hand on her brother's arm, "John, I really do think we had all better sit down, and you can explain more calmly. John can't go running off to Russia just like that. He has his law career to think of. He has even been talking about taking his bar exam soon."

Everyone recognized the wisdom of her suggestion, and found seats about the room. Only Captain Beaumont remained standing.

"Word has just come from Imperial Russia to Washington, via the transatlantic cable," he began in a formal tone.

"The transatlantic cable?" A chorus of voices interrupted him.

"Yes, Cyrus Field did at last accomplish the impossible. A permanent cable has been laid and is in perfect working order this time. The news came over the cable that an attempt had been made on Tsar Alexander II's life, and that he had managed to escape unharmed. Congress is dispatching me and Assistant Secretary of the Navy Fox to present our government's congratulations to the tsar on his escape from the assassins. And I am to be in command of the *Miantonomah*! It's a double-turreted monitor. My orders also include instructions to the effect that I am to proceed leisurely on the return trip and display the monitor to all the European countries, as they have never seen a monitor before!"

A ripple of "Ohhhhhhs" responded to Captain Beaumont's announcement.

Alice was the first to turn to her brother, "Oh, John, how fortunate you are that uncle has thought of you and wants to take you with him."

John Collings's eyes were shining lights. "I'm going, Mother. Do you mind?"

Elizabeth Beaumont Collings yielded gracefully, "You must write to us regularly, John."

"I will," he promised.

The two seafarers packed, and were off the following day. A.H. departed shortly afterwards. Once the men had gone, the Collings household settled down to quiet waiting. The arrivals of John's letters were the only breaks in the monotony. He was as good as his promise and kept them informed of the *Miantonomah*'s progress. In his first letter, a brief note just as they were preparing to depart, he made reference to the importance of the voyage. He was quite excited, for he had learned that naval men all over the world would be following the progress of the ship; a monitor had never before undertaken an ocean voyage of any length. How the *Miantonomah* would behave, and whether she could cross the Atlantic at all, were of great interest. His official position, he wrote, was private secretary to the ship's commander, Captain John Colt Beaumont.

When A.H. got back to Scranton, he stopped in at his father's banking office. W.W. had a message for him from his mother: they would expect him for dinner, and he was welcome to move back into his old room for the "duration." But A.H. declined. The role of waiting husband was a new one to him, and he wanted to enjoy it to the utmost. Free to roam as he pleased, he spent most of his time with his fellow lawyers, visited Frank Collins a great deal, and made quite a show of eating a solitary meal at the Wyoming Valley Hotel. Probably, if the truth were known, half of Scranton was following him about and waiting along with him.

All A.H.'s attention was turned towards Alice. Her time was drawing near; the first week of June was already past. He took to spending half the week in Wilkes-Barre with her and the remaining three days at his office in Scranton. By good fortune, he was in the Wilkes-Barre part of the week when Alice felt her first pain. The following afternoon a beautiful baby boy was born.

The new father came over to kneel beside the bed. He looked into the wondrous face of his wife, "I love you," he told her, filled with emotion.

Alice felt the outpouring of his emotion surround and engulf her and the baby as they lay there. She gave A.H. the most beautiful smile he had ever seen. "Aren't you proud of me?" she asked, "See what a beautiful son I have given you!" This first moment of their parenthood was the most tender time of all their married life.

Later, A.H. left for Scranton, to bring the good news to his family. Congratulations and toasts were definitely the order of the evening.

W.W. was the most proud. He kept repeating, over and over again, "My little grandson, my little grandson."

A.H. remained in a daze of pride and happiness. He returned to Wilkes-Barre a day later for his second look at his son. Cautiously, Alice allowed him to hold the baby.

"What is his name?" she asked her husband.

"What would you like to call him?"

"After you."

"No, I don't want to wish that on him."

This upset Alice, for she had been planning to make him a Junior.

"Well, we'll have to think about it for a while," she replied, hoping that in time A.H. would change his mind.

They discussed their return to Scranton and decided to wait until the end of the summer.

As for naming the baby, Alice found her husband obstinate and stubborn, to say the least. The new parents finally reached a compromise: James Collings Winton.

On one of A.H.'s many visits with Frank Collins while Alice was in Wilkes-Barre, the two concocted the idea of feting the judges in the county. A.H. and Frank sounded it out on the other county lawyers, and everywhere they mentioned it, the idea was received with enthusiasm. Invitations were sent out to the judges of Luzerne County for a complimentary dinner in their honor, at the Wyoming Valley Hotel in Scranton on Tuesday evening, the twenty-sixth of June. A.H. liked the neatness of the date; it was exactly a year from the day on which he had concluded the Providence Bankruptcy case.

It was a very gala affair, with a hundred in attendance. Two long tables extended the length of the dining hall. Colonel Hendrick Wright presided; Judge Woodward sat on his right and Judge Thompson at his left. At the far end of the table was Judge John Conyngham, with Justice Read beside him. Justices String and Agnew were at the other table. A.H. and Frank Collins were also at the second table, sitting near the exit. They had placed themselves there in order to be free to attend to any last minute arrangements. The Scranton barristers had given a great deal of thought to the dinner, and had tried to make it as nice an affair as they possibly could. A congratulatory letter from Governor Curtin was on hand, to be read to the judicial guests of honor. Hendrick Wright, as master of ceremonies, was full of charm and wit; and as the supreme compliment to the Luzerne County judges, he quoted a letter from Eli K. Price of Philadelphia, in which Attorney Price referred to the Luzerne judges in the most complimentary terms.

Wright concluded his opening remarks with the toast: "The Supreme Court of Pennsylvania—alike distinguished for its ability and integrity."

Chief Justice Woodward was the first to respond. "For the first time in my life, I find myself in an equivocal position here tonight. I scarcely know whether to look upon myself as one of the entertainers or as one of the entertained—as host or guest. This is a dinner given by the Bar of Luzerne County to the Judges of the Supreme Court of the State, and I have the great honor of being a member of both bodies."

The judge continued to talk at great length, extolling the virtues and responsibilities of a lawyer. A.H. sat relaxed, and let his eyes wander over the room. He was proud to be a member of such a distinguished looking group. One speaker followed after another until almost midnight. But before long, A.H. grew rather tired of the praising and self-congratulations, for interspersed with compliments to the judges were praises of Wilkes-Barre.

Even Common Pleas Judge Agnew had had to include in his remarks, "Wilkes-Barre—underlaid with hospitality, cultivation and beauty."

A.H. frowned at that. They were assembled to honor the judges; what did Wilkes-Barre have to do with it? If they were going to pay tribute, why not to Scranton, where they were sitting at the moment? Then he remembered Hendrick Wright's implication in his opening remarks, that only a Philadelphian carried the proper authority to bestow a compliment.

When a student of history researches his subject, and precisely lists the causes and effects through centuries of living, no matter how many factors or forces he may list, he will always find that one specific, usually infinitesimal action is the trigger that sets all of history off in another direction. Such was the role of the complimentary dinner, that Tuesday evening in June of 1866.

Until that evening, A.H. had been opposed to making Scranton a city because he didn't want to see Providence and Hyde Park lose their identities. He had felt that the two communities should be preserved at all costs; he had never been in favor of the merger with the Borough of Scranton. But that evening, after hearing everyone talk, he changed completely. Scranton and Providence and Hyde Park—each was as fine a place as any on the face of the earth. Then and there he committed himself totally to the fight for city status.

The following day, he told his father W.W. about the change in his thinking. He also had a few suggestions to throw out to W.W., "They can't make Scranton a city without Hyde Park's and our help. We could also stir up a storm over the way the Poor Board was administered.

"I would bargain with the Scrantons and Throop and Sanderson; in exchange for city classification, I would demand that Providence and Hyde Park be allowed to keep their own post office designations, and that we have first opportunity at managing the Poor Board. Also, when we come in, we are to comprise the first and second wards of the city.

"And I think it would be best to include a statement to the effect that we came to the unification voluntarily, and that we have the right to withdraw if the union proves unsatisfactory or detrimental to either Hyde Park or Providence."

"Good for you, A.H.!" W.W. exclaimed, and beamed with unadulterated pleasure at his son's perceptiveness. He also smiled at A.H.'s reference to the post office. Everyone knew that a post office was looked on as a political prize, but in this instance he felt that it was in memory of A.H.'s grandfather, Henry Heermans.

Only fifteen men knew of the plan afoot to unite the three communities into a third-class city. Another consideration was included as the men planned the advancement into city status for Scranton—The Mayor's Court. The Mayor's Court was a special and unique judicial entity; it was to be a Scranton-based court of record. Ordinarily all state courts of record are county-based, and are held at county seats. But in the city status petition submitted to the State

Legislature, there was the request for this special court, to meet at Scranton, and to be presided over by the mayor of the city.

This unique court was to have jurisdiction over criminal cases, such as forgeries, perjuries, and various types of assaults, as well as over actions which would ordinarily be tried in a common pleas or orphans court. Even appeals in certain civil cases could be heard. To make the court official, one of record, the president judge of the particular judicial district Scranton fell under, the eleventh, was to be the court recorder. To Judge John Conyngham fell the first honor.

A.H. considered the establishment of the Mayor's Court the one biggest gain resulting from the merger of the three communities into a city. Not to have to take the nine o'clock or court train to Wilkes-Barre was almost worth the bankruptcy of Providence.

The petition for city status for Scranton passed the Harrisburg legislature. All that was needed to complete the deed was the governor's approval. The fifteen men sponsoring the bill were going to take their chances that there would be no wholesale objection on the part of the voters living within the area. They got the governor of Pennsylvania's approval in August, when Governor Curtin signed the proclamation designating the boroughs and townships of Hyde Park, Providence, and Scranton united, thereby creating a third-class city.

The news trickled down to Wilkes-Barre, in time for the October 9 balloting lists. The town reeled in shocked amazement, but said nothing. They closed ranks at the court house and ignored the matter. Dutifully, however, the change was noted in the ballot lists sent out to the printer.

In the merger, Providence and Hyde Park did become Scranton's first and second wards. In all, there were a total of twelve wards, some divided into districts. The transition was effected quietly; there was no opposition. Providence and Hyde Park were allowed to keep their post offices. The Mayor's Court was approved. Having just begun its new life, the city barely flexed its muscles. The move had been made, however, to shift the balance of power in the valley. Edmund Heermans was named to the Select Council of twelve, the smaller of the new city's governing bodies. Equally as important, various tax revenues were no longer forwarded to Wilkes-Barre, as the county seat. With Scranton as a city, more money could now remain in Scranton for use there.

Throughout the summer days of July and August, when A.H. was free of work, he looked forward to his trips to Wilkes-Barre to see Alice and to enjoy his son. On his trip on the last week in August, it was agreed that Alice and the baby would return to Scranton when he came again. But instead, on A.H.'s next return trip to Wilkes-Barre, Alice called his attention to a faint rattle in the baby's breathing. But Elizabeth Beaumont Collings, the baby's maternal grandmother, silenced her daughter.

"When you have had your fifth, Alice, you will know when to be alarmed and when not to be," she said.

The visit was brief, and again A.H. rode the train back to Scranton. Between his clients and his son, he wondered whether he shouldn't rent lodgings on a train car and just shuttle back and forth. On the twenty-fifth of September he was preparing to ride again the now familiar route, when a letter arrived from another client. It was a simple collection action, involving a watch and a chain and $25, that the client was requesting of A.H. But the man was a friend, so A.H. wired Alice that he would stay in Scranton another two or three days to clear up the case. Her reply telegram reached him on the twenty-eighth at his parents' home in Providence:

"Baby very much worse. Come. A. Winton"

A.H. dropped everything and hurried back to Wilkes-Barre, but the worry and the waiting that he and Alice went through the next two days were futile; on the day of their intended homecoming, A.H. solemnly handed the gravedigger $2.00. Then two very lonely and forlorn figures returned to Union Street and the Collings home. Back inside the house, Alice gave way to her emotions. For quite some time, A.H. held her while she sobbed tears for both of them.

Finally, A.H. said, "We had better think about getting packed and going home. Your mother has been very hospitable, but I think it's time we leave."

"I'm not going back," Alice said quietly.

"Alice?" A.H. wasn't sure what he had heard.

"I can't. I'm sorry, but I can't. I can't bear going back, empty."

"What are you going to do?"

"I don't know. I just can't think of going back now."

A.H. tried reasoning, and then pleading, but neither accomplished the desired result. In desperation, he sought out his mother-in-law. Elizabeth Collings wasn't able to get anywhere with Alice, either.

"Let her stay a little while longer," she finally advised A.H. "She loved the baby very much and was so proud of him. Give her a little more time."

Completely at a loss, A.H. returned to Scranton and went to his parents' home, hoping that his mother could advise him. When he reached the house in Providence, the place was a beehive of excitement and activity. His glum countenance was diametrically opposed to everyone else's mood. A.H. went into a rage at the lack of sympathy extended him.

"How can you all be so callous?" he stormed at his mother.

Catherine turned from examining several of her husband's jackets in the window light, and bade A.H. sit down beside her.

"My son, my dear little boy," she crooned, almost as if A.H. were five years old again, "I know you're upset. It's natural to feel that way. But your grandfather and your grandmother and I, and yes, even your father, learned a long time ago that when you are out in the wilderness, when you are all alone, you observe, you see life come and go, you find that sometimes you have to destroy life yourself in order to survive. Dying comes to have no more meaning than living. Do we ever question our living? We look forward to new life. In the wilderness, dying comes into the same focus. After a while, you grow accustomed to the fact that what is here today may not be here tomorrow. That is one of the experiences of living, too. It is then that you learn to live for just the time you are here. You stop storing up days as credit to be used ten years later, when you think you will be richer or happier or feel better.

"For the short time you exist, you learn to live as fully and as well as you can.

"Now, come and help me get your father's things ready. He must look extra nice tomorrow night."

A.H. had been listening attentively while his mother was speaking. He tabled judgment on it, however, as his curiosity got the better of him, "Why tomorrow night? What's going on then?"

"Oh, your father was so pleased. Mr. Hitchcock asked him to be on the reception committee to receive General Geary when he arrives tomorrow evening."

Just then, W.W. came in. Outside of a perfunctory "That was bad luck, A.H., sorry to hear about the baby," he concentrated his attention on the following evening's event.

Thus are parents ever leading and instructing their children, even long past the time when their children have felt themselves far above any such need. In their casual and calm acceptance of life's events, they were showing and training A.H. just as surely as when they gave him a fork at the age of two.

W.W. spoke again, "Do you realize what this means, A.H.? One week before the elections, and Geary thinks Scranton's vote is so important to him if he wants to win the governor's race that he's coming here. Oh, it was a great day when we decided to become a city. Byron is bringing Mother, but, now that you're here, go with them. I'll have to leave early. The reception doesn't begin until nine, but everyone on the reception committee has to be at the Wyoming House [Wyoming Valley Hotel] an hour earlier."

A.H.'s father bustled off to check on his shirt studs; A.H.'s mother had already disappeared. A.H. was left in the parlor alone. He sat there for quite a while, sorting out his thoughts. For months, all his thinking, all his activities had been centered around the baby's arrival. Now the emptiness was enormous. But, he finally decided, his mother was right. This would not be their only child. Life did indeed come and go. And one should be thankful for whatever time they did have on earth, whether it be long or short.

"I would rather it be said of me that I lived to the utmost of my capacity for a year, than that I sat waiting in a chair by the window of my parlor for my eightieth birthday," concluded A.H.

The reception for the gubernatorial candidate was glittering and exciting. Scranton was thrilled at her new importance to the political king-makers, and her residents reflected their acknowledgement of the honor. W.W. introduced Frank Collins's father, Thomas Collins, to General Geary. Both were running for office—Collins for associate judge of Luzerne County—but on opposite tickets.

At the actual balloting, seven days later on the ninth of October, Scranton's first and second wards, the Providence and Hyde Park areas, supported Geary wholeheartedly, but the city as a whole did not. It was a Democratic city, and with little or no ticket-splitting, the Republicans fell behind by almost a third when the vote was counted. On the whole, A.H. was very pleased with the election. His friend's father, Thomas Collins, gained the associate judge post, and, with all of Pennsylvania polling a majority for the Republicans, Geary went in as governor. A.H. was so pleased over the election, Scranton's first as a city, that he almost didn't bother to study the returns. However, he did take the time to clip the published results from the newspaper, and prepared to file them in a desk drawer. Before putting the list away, he read it over quickly. Scranton's first and second wards, Providence and Hyde Park, had gone Republican and voted for Geary. But the city as a whole had recorded a Democratic majority, as had Wilkes-Barre. For a minute A.H. frowned. "Was it a coincidence?" he wondered. Scranton hadn't been a city for a year yet. Was it too early to tell, or was this an indication of how things were meant to be? He had no answer.

"Time will give me one, however," he said to himself.

Again, A.H. was back in Wilkes-Barre. He was as bright and as cheery as he could be, but it fell on deaf ears. Alice was as depressed as before. He tried some of his mother's logic on her. This was met with large dark eyes filling with tears, but not a word in response.

At last, Alice spoke, "It's not that. It's that my love seems to destroy. Every man I've ever loved has been taken from me. I thought my grandfather [Andrew Beaumont] was the most wonderful man in the world. There was nobody like him. I loved Papa [Samuel Collings] the most of all his children; I felt the closest to him. Our little baby son, I loved him, maybe even more than you. They're all gone."

"But I'm here, Alice..."

"Ohhhhh," she sobbed at him, "that's just it. That's just what I was saying."

A.H. felt utterly miserable and confused, and looked it.

Alice blurted out, "Maybe you'll be taken from me, too. Everyone I've ever loved has!"

He folded his arms around her and drew her close to him. "If that's all that's bothering you, then it's nothing. No, I'm here to stay. I can assure you of that. I have to be here to take care of you and all the other children that we will be having."

It was a touching scene, an emotional scene, but in the end, A.H. decided that very little had been achieved. Alice still would not come back to Scranton, and their empty home, with him.

The next one to call on Alice was her mother-in-law. Up to this point, Catherine Heermans Winton had refrained from injecting herself into her married son's life. But A.H.'s miserable expression, which he had worn daily on his face throughout all of October, was more than she could stand.

"A mother's love is amazing," she told Alice. "I worried about A.H. every day of his life, right up to the day of his wedding. But after that day, all responsibility fell from me as if it had never existed. When he married you, Alice, I was in essence turning him over to you. I speak to you now, because I see him and he looks so miserable, so unhappy. What are you doing to him?"

"I'm sorry, but the baby...," and Alice's voice trailed off as if that explained everything.

"But Alice, the baby is gone. 'For the children shall inherit the kingdom of God.' It is A.H. that you must think of now. He is here. You have so much to be happy about. Many couples never have a child. Be glad that you don't have that problem. No one would blame a husband, if he put his wife aside because she did not bear him the children he wanted.

"Don't forget that I, myself, am one of ten children. Our mothers had as much responsibility in settling the wilderness as did our fathers who cleared the land and fought the Indians. We are not so far removed from those days that we can ignore them.

"Please, do not destroy your husband for something that is already lost."

In the end, Catherine Winton came to the conclusion that she had met with about as much success as A.H.

When reasoning and talking produced no results, A.H. tried coaxing Alice back to Scranton.

"Look," he said on one of his visits, "see what came in the mail today? Cards from cousin Eugene Heermans and Miss Sarah Finch."

Alice showed a little interest.

Encouraged, A.H. plunged on. "The wedding will be after Christmas, and I'm sure that it will be a very fashionable affair, Alice. Eugene's mother was Sarah Slocum, a grandfather was Benjamine Slocum and a grandmother was Mary Fellows. The Finches are relatively new to this area, but I hear that they do very well in their mercantile businesses. Just think of all the new gowns that the ladies will be wearing. Eugene said something about there being a band for dancing at the reception." A.H. darted a quick look at Alice, and thought that he had at last gotten through to her.

But when he had finished talking, Alice merely said, "We'll see."

Alice's mother joined them at this point, waving a letter. "We have news from John. Stay a minute, A.H., and hear how our sailors are doing." Then she read:

Dearest Mama,

Nothing could exceed the cordiality of the reception extended to us in Russia. The Emperor was deeply affected by the action of the United States, and took occasion to show his gratitude by personal attentions of the kindest character toward Capt. Beaumont and his officers. The monitor lay at Cronstadt [Kronstadt], where the people crowded on board and examined every detail of the iron-clad with great interest. After lying a week at Cronstadt [Kronstadt], notice was received that the Emperor Alexander was coming on board. The imperial yacht steamed down the Neva, and there was a great stir when the Czar of all the Russias made his appearance attended by forty officers in blazing uniforms. At the Emperor's request Capt. Beaumont introduced him to all the American officers, and he was a splendid host. He had a magnificent presence, was over six feet high, and his eye was like the eye of an eagle. I watched him closely, and watched also his officers, and I noticed at the time that every man of them evaded his glance as if they feared to look him in the face. The adage "the cat may look at the King" did not seem to apply to those Russian nobles. Upon the departure of the Czar the *Miantonomah* fired a salute and there was an interchange of the most effusive and demonstrative friendship all around.

The Emperor then sent his staff and took us in yachts up the Neva to St. Petersburg. Every American officer was attended by a distinguished Russian and our lightest wants were anticipated. We were housed in imperial style at the "Cross of Gold," an elegant hotel to which we were conducted in carriages along the Nevskoi Prospekt. I rode with an Admiral who wore a cocked hat, and who really acted as my servant for the time being and it occurred to me as we drove along, that if some of the Wilkes-Barre and Scranton boys should see me then they would think I was putting on a heap of style.

The banquet with the nobility was a brilliant affair and in all respects our visit to Russia fairly overwhelmed us. The generosity was universal and unbounded. I could not go out to buy a pair of gloves that a Russian officer was not at my side to pay for them. We were not allowed to pay for anything during our stay, and before leaving we each received a massive medal from the hands of the Czar. I have mine and consider it one of the choicest treasures in my possession. Were I to tell you of half the attentions that were showered upon us it would weary you. Our reception was royal beyond description. My love to you, dear Mama. The Captain sends his also.

John

A.H. had been watching Alice as her mother read. It was an exciting and interesting letter, but other than an occasional flicker of the eyelids, Alice acted as if she had not heard a word.

It was Walter Winton, A.H.'s brother, who achieved what none of the others had been able to accomplish. He showed up in Wilkes-Barre, carrying a small suitcase, with Ella Tunstall, the girl who had been with him before. He was looking for Alice. It was December 1 when the couple rang the bell at the Collings house.

"Hello, Alice," Walter kissed his sister-in-law on her cheek. "You remember Ella, don't you? Well, I've come to ask a favor of vou. We were married last week, and I have to go away for a few days, so I told Ella she could stay with you. I thought you were in your house at Scranton, but I know you have room here. It won't matter to Ella where she is." Walter turned to his bride, "I'll be off, my love. Don't you worry about a thing. Alice is very good at managing. Just do whatever she says, and I'll be back as soon as I get the money from your father." Walter gave Ella a quick kiss and was gone, out of the house, leaving behind his bride and a speechless Alice.

As soon as she could, Alice excused herself, and, leaving Ella alone, went in search of her mother.

"Mama, what are we to do?"

Elizabeth Beaumont Collings restrained herself remarkably well considering the situation. "This is a little too much, Alice," she said as calmly as she could, "Just get her out of here."

By five o'clock, Alice was back in Scranton with Ella.

A.H. had just closed up his office, and was on his way to the Wyoming House for a solitary dinner, when he decided to stop off at the house and leave some papers he had brought from the office. A light coming from the upstairs startled him, and he picked up a stout branch from the wood pile before going in. The door was unlocked, and he entered cautiously and quietly. The sound of feminine voices drifted down to him from above.

"Who's there?" he called.

Alice and Ella appeared at the top of the stairs, "A.H., what are you doing home so early?"

A.H. didn't answer immediately. For one thing, he looked as if he had seen a ghost. Secondly, he felt rather foolish, standing there clutching the branch and looking up at his wife.

Alice came halfway down the stairs. "Are you all right? You don't look very well. Oh, my dear, sit down quickly! I'm worried about you. Ella! Please go and fetch a glass of water."

As simply as that, Mr. and Mrs. A.H. Winton were at home again.

"What's going on?" A.H. whispered, as soon as Ella had disappeared from view.

"Oh, A.H., let me introduce you," Alice giggled.

"I know who she is. She's that friend of Walter's," he whispered back.

Alice shook her head, "No—she's your sister-in-law!" she replied, in a similar whisper, enjoying the consternation and disbelief on her husband's face. "Be careful, she'll hear you," Alice admonished sharply, as A.H. started sputtering and fuming.

"What's Walter been up to now?"

"She really is a very nice girl. She'll be staying with us for a few days, until Walter gets back."

A further explosion from A.H. was prevented by Ella's reappearance. To gain time, for something to do, A.H. slowly sipped the water she brought. Composed, he turned to Ella.

"Ella, Mrs. Winton tells me congratulations are in order. I understand that my brother has had the good fortune to marry you. I extend a welcome to you, on behalf of the whole family. Now sit here beside me, and tell me all about it." A.H. patted the cushion beside him invitingly.

Alice gave Ella a little push. "Go ahead, Ella, sit down and tell him everything you have told me." Alice knew how A.H. regarded Walter; this was a perfect opportunity to get Walter Winton back into his brother's good graces.

"Where would you like me to start?" asked Ella.

A.H. tried not to assume the guise of counsel examining a witness, although he certainly felt like one, "Why not with your wedding?"

"We were married last week, on the twenty-second of November. Father had never been able to make a go of the foundry here in Scranton, and when we returned to Peekskill, New York, this fall, Walter followed us. He is so marvelous. I adore him more than anything else in the whole world."

A.H. chose to ignore the latter, "You were married in Peekskill?"

"Oh, yes. It was a beautiful ceremony; we had it at home. Afterwards, when we were ready to leave, my father said that he would advance Walter money to open a store in Scranton. Wasn't that wonderful of him? That's where he is now; Walter, I mean. He went back to Peekskill to make the arrangements with my father."

A.H. raised his eyes to look at Alice, to see what she was thinking of the whole matter. He detected a glimmer of laughter in her eyes. Suddenly A.H. realized that he had his wife home again; the problems connected with Walter receded into the background. If Ella hadn't been present, he would have grabbed Alice and smothered her with kisses. He restrained himself, and instead proposed that he and Alice take the new Mrs. Winton to dinner at the Wyoming Valley House, in celebration.

10

It was after 1866 that the most extraordinary fortune followed all the Wintons; it seemed everything they touched turned to money. This was true not only for W.W. but also for A.H. and Walter Winton as well. Stephen Tunstall, Walter's father-in-law, advanced Walter a large enough sum so that he was able to open a very fine dry-goods store, Winton & Tunstall, at the corner of Lackawanna and Wyoming Avenues. It was Walter's first effort in business, and, from the beginning, he showed every indication that he had inherited his father's, W.W.'s, merchandising acumen. The dry-goods business brought in a sizable income, and Walter and Ella were very happy, especially after their children started to arrive.

A.H. was also prospering. He and Bradford parted, each going their separate ways. A.H. moved his office to Washington Hall, at the corner of Penn and Lackawanna Avenue. He remained a claims agent, but enlarged his practice to such an extent that the war claims business was but a small percentage of it.

The Second National Bank was also prospering at 318 Lackawanna Avenue. Isaac Dean remained very much in the background; he preferred to play the role of gentleman farmer, and turned the actual administration of the bank over to W.W. As his family enlarged, W.W. sold a few shares from his portion of the bank stock to Walter's wife, Ella, and to her father, Stephen Tunstall. Byron, W.W.'s third son, got married, and a few more of the bank's shares went to the new couple. Elnorah and her husband, Thomas Livey, were also brought into the family bank by their purchase of almost fifty shares of the Second National from W.W. The only ones who were members of the Winton family but not included in the family bank as share owners were A.H. and Alice, because of A.H.'s position as bank's counsel.

Byron was the next of W.W. and Catherine's children to marry. Through him, more intricate threads were woven into other valley families. Byron Winton married Frances Silkman, a daughter of Daniel Silkman. Her sister Helen married Edmund Fuller, the son of Alderman Fred Fuller. Frances and Helen were also the nieces of Charles Silkman, the area's first lawyer, who had arrived in Razorville in 1835 and married into the Tripp family. To complete the circle of marriages, Charles Silkman's son Francis, who had become a lawyer following his father, had married Jane Fuller.

Byron also went into partnership with his father-in-law, just as had his brother Walter with Stephen Tunstall. The new firm was Silkman & Winton Wholesale Grocers, at 107 Franklin Street. It, too, prospered like all the other Winton enterprises, although not without some help from W.W. and A.H. in the beginning—they switched the purchasing of provisions for the Poor Board over to Silkman & Winton.

A.H. did not think of this action as charity toward his brother; instead, he regarded it as a precautionary move. The arrangement was highly satisfactory to A.H., because he felt that he could exercise control over the quality of the food delivered to the indigent, and also could easily gain access to the records of the supplier, thereby negating any easy attempt at overbilling.

To those more experienced in the ways of the world, especially the world of politics at the city level, this last analysis of A.H.'s activities (awarding his brother a city contract) may seem as the most absurd of all naivetes. But please do not scoff, nor loudly proclaim "humbug!" Keep in mind the Winton background. By thought, marriage and blood, they were tied to the first settlers of the area. While these early arrivals had come because the land was cheap, it gave them an opportunity to build a community and to create the environment they wanted and that was desirable to them; and because they were the first settlers, they were on their honor to establish and administer a government and schools that were for the good of all. They were the only people there, they were the only ones responsible for what happened, and if they did not deal in terms of personal integrity, they were cheating no one but themselves. In order for the first settlers and their children to continue to live in the valley they had chosen, they had to preserve what they had; they could not afford to destroy or plunder.

To those who came in afterwards, after the discovery of the coal and its worth to the rest of the world, this philosophy actually became a hindrance. For these later arrivals came into the area only because there was something there for them to take away: the coal. Their primary interest was definitely not to create a self-perpetuating community. They viewed everything in the frame of reference of "how will I benefit?" either in the immediate future, preferably, or in long-term gains. To them, awarding the contract for supplying the poor with their food would most certainly be interpreted as graft. But to the men who had started a community, and then had seen it lost, swallowed up by another because of excessive handouts to the poor, it was nothing more than a protective measure. The strength of the system lay in the caliber of the men still in control, and the "black diamonds" they dealt in represented their word of honor.

The philosophy of the settler, that ability to draw from nothing a working, cohesive assemblage of people into a town or city that would endure, was the factor that prevented these same people from stepping into the high-paced world known later as the "industrial giants and robber barons." These kings of industry used their creativity only to take profits for themselves, with neither concern for the future nor for what effect their actions would have on the future.

Every act of the pioneer settler, on the other hand, was tempered by its enduring qualities. If those who had come first to settle had also had a little of the "taking" about them, the valley would most likely have become like a fortified castle impervious to any attack, the greatest wealth in the United States being concentrated there among those first families from Connecticut and Pennsylvania. Instead, the pioneers had divorced themselves from those who had come to "take," and had watched, almost with derision, the newcomers scrambling about digging holes. Because the newcomers were giving nothing in return to the valley, the pioneer settlers could not see them as a threat to their way of life and to their community. Then, suddenly, it was too late; the gap had widened, and the very, very rich were not the pioneers who had staked their very existence for material comforts and freedom.

In Scranton, W.W. was one of the very few to bridge the gap between the old and the new. Henry Heermans had been right when he had appraised his son-in-law as the most valuable of his children's generation. Now, as the Wyoming Valley was marching at the forefront of the rush into the age of steam and steel, Henry's confidence in W.W. was showing itself to have been well placed. Of all of Henry Heermans's children, Catherine and W.W. were the only ones to move with equal ease among both the farming settlers and the railroad and coal overlords. The wealth generated from the coal-iron-railroad revenues was on a far grander scale than the most prosperous farmer or merchant could ever hope to achieve. The early settlers knew that they were losing out to the coal entrepreneurs, and held on to as much as they could. But W.W. rose on beyond, joining the new breed wherever possible. His years as a merchant in New York City had probably prepared him for this better than anything else could have. But it was his understanding of human nature that helped him the most. Whether it was from Henry Heermans's early guidance, or whether he had instinctively known, W.W.'s practical application was resoundingly successful. He knew that to keep control, one had to join with those encroaching, but at the same time play at the game better than they. "If you can't lick 'em, join 'em"—and join them W.W. did.

For instance, W.W. was aware that Dr. Benjamine Throop had returned to the general area in the 1840s, to Scranton from Honesdale via New York City, for the purpose of assisting the Scranton brothers in their purchase of land and in dealing with the natives such as the Merrifields, Slocums, Tripps, Heermans and others; and he was also aware that Dr. Throop always seemed to be found where the opportunity for making money was the greatest. Many years earlier, Throop had matched the opening of his medical practice at Honesdale with the early days of the Delaware & Hudson Canal at its terminus, also in Honesdale. But in spite of all this, W.W. was the best of friends with Dr. Throop. They worked together on many projects, and valued each other's opinions. In a similar fashion, W.W. related to almost everyone who was active in Scranton. Generally, he was very well liked.

W.W.'s fancy was tickled one day, so much so that he delayed his reply a day in order to share his private amusement with Catherine. At the close of business of a hot day in the beginning of August, he hurried home to his wife.

"Catherine," he called as soon as he entered the house.

She came running, alarmed, "What is it?"

"I thought you might enjoy seeing something," and W.W. handed her a piece of paper.

Catherine automatically accepted the paper, but still asked, "What is it?"

"One of the doctors in town wanted a recommendation—Dr. Masser. He's a good chap; I've known him for several years. Very friendly, very likeable. Very responsible, too. He wants an insurance agency, and needed some people to vouch for him. Here, look, see whom he went to. I thought you might enjoy seeing whom he asked to recommend him."

Catherine turned the paper to better see it, and W.W. bent over her, pointing to the signatures at the bottom.

"See, here's Brisbine's signature, as president of the Delaware, Lackawanna & Western Railroad. And here's Mrs. Dickson's as president of the Delaware & Hudson Company. And the other two Dicksons for the Dickson Manufacturing Company. Archbald's as president of the Lackawanna & Bloomsburg Railroad."

W.W.'s finger moved quickly from name to name. There were only nine on the recommendation, but he was enjoying calling them out to his wife, and Catherine understood the message W.W. was conveying.

"This one is Galusha Grow's—he was the speaker of the House of Representatives—and these two, Albright as general agent for the Union Coal Company, and Storrs, the general coal agent for the Delaware, Lackawanna & Western.

"And do you see this last one here? See whom else Dr. Masser thought was necessary to have, along with Brisbine, Dickson and the others? W.W. Winton!"

Catherine didn't say anything, but W.W. detected a gleam of approval in her eyes, as she handed the paper back to him. They understood each other remarkably well. The pleasure that these two were taking in the roll call of names was not in personal satisfaction over W.W.'s reaching a circle composed of presidents of railroads and coal companies, but that of all the names on the paper, who all controlled natural resources leaving the valley in one form or another, except for W.W., not one of the people named had come to the valley because of his love for it. That Dr. Masser considered W.W.'s recommendation desirable was further proof of the inroads the Winton family was making in bridging the gap between the land-rich, locally-educated settlers and the sophisticated, city-traveling, coal and railroad barons.

"I told Masser to stop by tomorrow for the paper. I thought you might enjoy seeing this," W.W. added.

Other than for the little light touches, such as was provided by Dr. Masser's request, the post-Civil War years leading up to 1870 were comparatively dull and uninspiring for the Wintons. About the only sound heard from them was the hum of profitable commerce. Almost in amazement, the Wintons watched their money mount higher and higher. During this period, Silkman & Winton, Byron's enterprise, was working its way up to an annual gross of over $50,000. Walter and Ella were doing just as well with their dry-goods store. And it was not unusual for A.H. to total $3,000 annually from his $40.00 fees: a sum more than double the amount of a government salary, had he gone to Washington. The name of Winton seemed to be everywhere. In less than ten years (nine to be exact), dating from their return to Providence after their sojourn in New York City, W.W. and his family had built a financial empire, and, through his sons, W.W. had formed a powerful conglomerate yielding enormous returns.

The easy flow of money into their pockets was in keeping with the boom times following the war. While the South was struggling under its imposed reconstruction, the North abounded with industrial expansion. The Wyoming Valley lived the exhilarating life of boom times. Enormous sums of money poured into the valley daily, and, with his Second National Bank to lend money for further expansion, and his sons, Walter and Byron, to provide basic supplies (after all, everyone had to eat and everyone had to wear clothes), the Wintons reaped a harvest that catapulted them to the top of a great mountain of wealth. Watching over all their activities was A.H. He made sure that accounts due were collected, a chore commonly overlooked when more money is coming in than going out. He kept them free of all legal entanglements, no simple task with their mushrooming businesses; and, if a charlatan or parasite showed intentions of preying on them, he mounted an impregnable defense. Profit was everywhere.

Into all this new affluence, John Collings's letters to his sister Alice were a welcome addition, fitting their new life style. His description of the *Miantonomah*'s progress along the coast of Europe echoed the new standing of the Wintons; every letter spoke of royalty and royal receptions as common, everyday occurrences for Captain Beaumont and his nephew, now on the return leg of their fourteen-month voyage:

> I must not forget to tell you of a thrilling incident on our return trip. At Stockholm, on our way back, the King and Queen of Sweden came on board, and were very hospitable and gracious.

A.H. was perhaps the most calm of all, amidst the newly acquired, enormous purchasing power of his family. And whenever Alice or his mother would make mention of John's latest letter, he would always call in a loud voice for the portion that followed, the one he enjoyed the most:

> We touched at a number of ports, and although something of interest occurred at each, I must let them pass to tell you of a peculiar adventure at Toulon [France].
>
> We staid there three days. One day while on deck talking with the Doctor, First Lieut. John J. Cornwall complained of feeling very sick and turned in to take a nap. Four or five of the party went where they could take a smoke, and were chatting there pleasantly a few minutes when the Doctor came up with a frightened face and explained that Cornwall was dead. Of course we were horrified. He was such a brave and splendid officer. The seamen all were more or less superstitious and thought something terrible would happen. Capt. Beaumont sent Ensign Alcorn on shore to purchase a

metallic coffin. The sea was rough at the time and there was great difficulty in getting it on board. All declared it the heaviest coffin they had ever seen or handled. Once the boat gave a lurch and the coffin had a narrow escape from being thrown into the sea. It was a lucky thing for us it wasn't. The men wondered why it was so heavy, but they realized the reason as soon as they took off the lid. There was the body of a beautiful French girl dressed in white and covered with exquisite flowers. You can imagine what a sensation this caused among us. We had not as yet recovered from the shock occasioned by Cornwall's sudden death, and now here was another corpse on board. The men asked each other in frightened whispers what could it all mean, but the matter was soon explained. In a few minutes we saw rowing in the direction of our ship a boatload of Frenchmen. As soon as they came within earshot, we could hear them swearing savagely and vowing vengeance. They could scarcely control themselves long enough to get on deck, and when they did, they pointed to the open coffin and demanded in angry tones why this outrage had been perpetrated—why the crew of the American monitor had stolen the body of this beautiful French woman for some base scientific purpose. Capt. Beaumont was calm and said he thought the matter could be satisfactorily explained. He then pointed to the body of Cornwall, told of his sudden death, and of having dispatched a party on shore for a metallic coffin. The stupid fellow in charge of the boat saw a metallic coffin at the depot, and thinking that it had been sent on from Marseilles by Ensign Alcorn took it along without asking any questions. This in some measure calmed down the mercurial Frenchmen, and so, after screwing up the coffin, they took it and went away growling, and looking very much as if they would like to declare war against the *Miantonomah*. I can assure you that the grim mistake of the thick-headed marine made us all feel nervous enough, and we did not get over it for some time. Capt. Beaumont was naturally very indignant over the mistake. I believe a sensational paper in Marseilles did actually accuse us of trying to steal the body of the young lady, whose name I heard but have forgotten. After all the royal ovation we had received this incident was a damper, and we did not feel entirely comfortable until we got away from the shores of France.

Afterwards, the listeners usually agreed with A.H. that this story was more in keeping with boys from Wilkes-Barre and Providence than the accounts of being received by Kings and Queens in pomp and glory.

When the money first began to accumulate, W.W. was content to just let it lie in the Second National; he had a couple of bad debts that he was anxious to cover. One of these was from his old friend, Lewis Watres. The coal vein at Mt. Vernon had run out, and the former justice of the peace had moved into Scranton. With the change to city status, Watres had fitted naturally into the post of an alderman; but there was little that could be done about the tiny coal mining community of Mt. Vernon, some twelve miles northeast of Scranton. The Second

National, fortunately, was in such a profitable position that the loss had no effect. It did annoy A.H., however, who liked to keep all accounts in a credit-worthy status. He remarked as much to his father on repeated occasions, but W.W. would never give him a satisfactory answer.

It took W.W. some time to become accustomed to the fact that the pile of money before him was not only permanent but was actually growing larger. Once he perceived this, he took off on a spending spree of unbelievable magnitude. He had A.H. accompany him, and every purchase was thoroughly researched by A.H. before any money was handed over. Father and son traveled everywhere together; name it as you like, a partnership, a team, they were good for each other and worked well together. As W.W. would point out to A.H., "I'm not really spending money, I'm simply converting from one form of wealth to another." For W.W. seemed to have turned into a sponge that was soaking up bankrupt and estate-settled real estate at an unbelievable rate.

"We're going to get ourselves a coal mine yet, A.H.," W.W. boasted exuberantly, "That's where the real fountain of money is."

A.H. might have been as optimistic as his father, if he had been privy to all of W.W.'s acquaintances and the customers of the Second National. But most of the people who dealt with the Second National Bank were only account names to him. And probably, if he had known what W.W.'s ears had been filled with, he would have been more upset than optimistic. In the almost 40,000 population of Scranton, George Filer and W.W. Winton had managed to find each other. That they did was only right. W.W. was the standard-bearer of the early settlers' traditions into the era of exploitation, and George Filer was without question the best mine engineer in all the Wyoming Valley. If the area could be mined for coal with as little damage as possible to its ecological environment, these two men were the ones to do it.

In 1846 George Filer had come to the United States from England at the age of twenty-five. He had worked the coal mines in England, and found employment as soon as he arrived in America, in the coal mines in Schuylkill County, Pennsylvania, an area outside and south of the Wyoming Valley near the coal town of Mauch Chunk (now called Jim Thorpe). From there, George Filer eventually migrated to Scranton, arriving just about the time that W.W. and his family moved to New York City. He was an intelligent and shrewd workman, and in short order became exceedingly knowledgeable about mines and mining operations. Shortly before the Wintons returned to Providence from New York City, George Filer was sufficiently confident of his ability in sinking shafts and driving, or opening up, tunnels, to strike out on his own, leasing land from its owner for the right to mine coal.

To do this, George Filer needed capital, and was fortunate to find a partner, Spencer, and later Hunt and Davis. But by 1867, he had established his reputation as the best mine engineer in the valley. and was determined to go it alone. Filer met W.W. through the Second National Bank. Independent, competent, and confident, all because of his ability, Filer accepted W.W.'s financing gladly, for W.W. had offered it on the best of all terms—a loose alliance. It was a tenuous friendship at first; Filer was only six years younger than W.W., and did not need a fatherly, guiding hand. Their common ground, the interest that brought them together, was a sound one—mutual respect. Filer appreciated W.W.'s easy approach in money matters, and W.W. recognized him for the master workman he was. In describing the first days of their business relations, even the term "loose alliance" was almost an overstatement. For it had been left up to Filer himself to determine the amount of profits, and who should receive how much. However, these two men were the very best the valley had, and they knew how to act accordingly. Periodically, Filer, of his own accord, specified at deposit time certain amounts to go to W.W. Perhaps W.W. would not have been so casual if it had been "hard times" or if he had been short of cash, but whatever the reason, it was certainly the right way to handle George Filer. Acclaimed everywhere as the best mine engineer living, he was continuously flattered, bribed, and begged to join a coal company, and work for its owners. To all of this he turned a deaf ear. The possibilities of an association with W.W., however, were as pleasing to him as they were to W.W. For several years, the two men were careful not to publicize their friendship. No one, not even A.H., was aware of just how closely these two men were involved with each other. It was, to say the least, a loose alliance.

A.H. should have been aware that there was more to George Filer than just an account at the bank. For all the apparent indiscriminate purchase of lands that he supervised for his father from the legal point of view, the pattern of many parcels having once been worked for coal should have told him that his father was getting guidance from someone in selecting his purchases. As anxious as the Wintons were to break into the coal owners' club, A.H. knew perfectly well that W.W.'s knowledge was nowhere near detailed enough to enable him to be an accurate judge of what was or was not a profitable vein of coal, particularly when, repeatedly, W.W. cheerfully laid out cash for land in which, it was commonly conceded, the coal vein had run out. There was another clue to W.W.'s and Filer's association, which A.H. also failed to pick up; for from time to time, he was called upon to handle a legal problem for George Filer.

The two men succeeded in guarding their secret—a wise move considering the vicious scramble there would have been for high quality coal mines, had their association been a matter of public record. Every time that W.W. would have so much as taken a second look at a foot of land, its sale price would have skyrocketed, or else the owner would suddenly develop second thoughts about selling. Any time that George Filer and W.W. Winton would be seen talking and W.W. would afterwards evidence an interest in some particular parcel of land, definitely the logical conclusion of the busybodies would have been that the land was coal rich.

In the meantime, 1866 became 1867 and 1867 became 1868. And after 1868 came 1869. In that period, John Collings returned home from his successful voyage aboard the *Miantonomah* to his mother in Wilkes-Barre, and resumed his law studies. His uncle, Capt. John Beaumont, made his official report to the U.S. Congress on the mission to Russia, and then retired from the Navy. He had served his country for thirty years, of which almost twenty-five had been spent at sea.

This was also the time when cousin Eugene Heermans, Edmund Heermans's son, announced that he was taking his bride Sarah and himself to New York City, because he wanted to study medicine at Bellevue Hospital Medical College. In this period too, Arthur Dean, Isaac Dean's son, came to the decision that he wanted to pursue a legal career. Should he persist and pass his bar exam, there would be three lawyers in the family: he, A.H. and John Collings. And also during this period, as each October circled around again on the calendar, A.H. carefully clipped Luzerne County's voting results from the newspaper. At each successive October, he spent less time in concentration over the figures, but more effort in pursing his lips firmly together and in forming successively deeper furrows to his frown. What he was observing from year to year, however, did not bother him enough to make him speak out. Nor did he speak out or evidence unhappiness on another matter: the fact that he and Alice were still childless.

For this was the time when nothing really bothered any of the Wintons. They were all so rich, and getting richer every day. Nothing really mattered; to have so much money made them all very, very content. They were so well fed and so comfortable mentally that they could feel no pain. Even the few empty spots, whenever they occurred, caused no discomfort. On the whole, life's events and life's problems just did not seem to touch these descendants of the early settlers.

It was as if they had been placed on one side of a sheer veiled curtain, where they could observe all that was happening without really getting involved. It was as if nothing could reach out through an opening in the veil and affect them, touch them so as to leave an indentation on their skin. Oh, they laughed, or cried, or said, "How lovely!" Or, as A.H. and Alice did, they listened rapturously on one particular Tuesday evening in February of '68 to Charles Dickens as he stood before them and read his poems and his stories. But it was all done in a mechanical way, as if they were automatons. For they had not yet learned to live or act as one does when one is very, very rich.

Even as late as June 1869, A.H. was poring meticulously over the account sheet for his Masonic Knights Templar's excursion to Philadelphia. Eighteen knights from the Coeur de Lion Commandry, Scranton, were going to take part in their semicentennial celebration on the fifteenth of June. As treasurer for the trip, A.H. soon discovered what a difficult task it was to collect the $318.23 he had laid out in advance. That half of them still owed him various amounts, ranging from $8.81 down to 23 cents, at departure time, almost spoiled the trip for him. And when he gave his accounting at the next monthly meeting, he concluded with the comment, "I have mailed notices to the above Sir Knights." Fortunately, William Monies, who was to be elected mayor of Scranton in October, escaped A.H.'s censure, as did W. Connell, J. Gillespie, Fred Mason, G. Winans, F. Amsden, M. Orr, W. Carling and E. Hill; but from one poor, unfortunate, delinquent knight, A.H. finally collected his $8.71 debt while standing at the bar in the Wyoming House (Wyoming Valley House), on the thirteenth of January the following year. No, definitely not—for all their purchasing power, the Wintons had not yet learned to live as one does when very, very rich.

A.H. was apparently the only one in the family who did not seem to be sure or confident of their wealth, or the firmness of their money's base as was the rest of the family. The few delinquent accounts at his father's bank bothered him. He had asked his father more than once about the solvency of Lewis Watres, but his father had always silenced him with a "don't worry, A.H." And so, A.H. put aside his worry, not because his father told him not to worry, but rather because his father gave him no free time in which to worry. On September 24, 1869, W.W. consummated his most spectacular real estate purchase to date. He acquired the coal rights to the Allen Ande property at Dickson City, about one mile up the valley from the Scranton city limits. There was much jubilation and celebration among the Wintons; they had a coal mine, at last!

That was on the twenty-fourth of September, but by the fifteenth of October, A.H. was ranting and screaming at his father. The elder Winton was not to be outdone. No longer father and son, they locked horns as if they were two enraged bulls fighting over a female, their male vanity at stake.

The cause of the tiff was in the newspaper A.H. had been brandishing when he arrived at his parents home after dinner on the fifteenth of October. The fact that he had had to bottle his rage all day, until after banking hours when he could speak to his father in private, had made him all the more angry.

The basic cause of the tiff, however, was the fundamental difference in their personalities over handling financial matters—W.W. always optimistic and A.H. ever cautious. The fight was so intense because they were really attacking each other's vanities.

When A.H. came into the room, he was, on the surface, calm, The house was quiet; his parents were in their usual places around the elegant, bulbous kerosene lamp on the table in the center of the parlor. He kissed his mother briefly on the cheek, and said, "Good evening, mother."

After waiting almost the whole of the day, at last able to confront his father, A.H. stripped himself of feelings he did not feel; his mask of calm composure fell away. The newspaper, that he had held behind his back while greeting his mother, he now brandished in the air, violently.

"Did you see this, Father? Did you see this?" He was almost screaming.

Taken aback by the explosion, W.W. stared up at his son and his odd behavior.

"Here! Read it! See for yourself!" and A.H. projected the paper forward into W.W.'s line of vision.

Still, W.W. said nothing. He had no idea what was going on, or what was exciting A.H. so much.

"Here! Here!" A.H. excitedly jabbed his forefinger at an advertisement in the paper.

Watching the events, Catherine rushed in, hoping to calm her son, "What, is the matter with you, A.H.? What's in the paper? Read it to me, please;"

Catherine's request was in the firm voice of mother to child, that brooks no disobedience regardless of age. A.H. complied:

Peremptory Sale
To close a concern
James A. Freeman, auctioneer
Valuable coal lands
Luzerne County
Penn.
on Wednesday, Oct. 20, 1869 at 12 o'clock noon
at the
Merchant's Exchange
In the city of Philadelphia
The following described real estate, viz:

A valuable tract of land containing four hundred (400) acres, and allowances, in Blakely township, Luzerne Co., adjoining and bounded by lands of the Delaware and Hudson Canal Co., George Hollenback and others.

It is very advantageously situated being on both sides of the Lackawanna, about one mile from the town of Archbald and about 12 miles from Scranton, and it is believed to be entirely underlaid by all the veins of coal known in that region.

It is easily accessible by railways and canals both from New York and Philadelphia. The Lackawanna is a reliable water power and there is on the land, pine, oak, and hemlock timber; also a number of dwelling houses. The town of Archbald is extending toward the tract. The title is perfect. Parties desiring to examine the premises are invited to call upon Mr. John Gardner at Archbald. Plans and surveys can be examined at the Auction Store. Sale absolute to close a concern. Terms liberal.

$500 to be paid when the same is struck off.

James A. Freeman, auctioneer
store 422 Walnut Street

In the silence after A.H. finished reading, Catherine started to speak, "What—?"

But W.W. interrupted her with two words spoken quietly, "Lewis Watres."

A.H. finished the thought; just as quietly, and with finality, he added, "Mt. Vernon."

As long as no one moved, no one spoke, but when W.W. shifted slightly in his chair, A.H. turned and glared at him. W.W. glared back defiantly. Wisely, Catherine made no effort at conciliation or peace.

"What's going on, Father? It says here the title is perfect. What kind of an agreement do you have with Lewis Watres?"

From then on, neither one would give an inch. Each defended loudly his right to criticize the other, and each, just as loudly, expressed his resentment at the other for criticizing his judgment and behavior. The strange part was that, while it was a "fight to the death," at the end, when neither man had any more passion left, the two, in spirit, drew close together. They would brave the common danger together.

Through it all, Catherine remained silent, never interrupting, her eyes traveling from face to face following the speaker. As he was preparing to leave, A.H. came over and kissed her on the cheek again.

"I'm sorry, Mother," he said, "but we will have to find out what is going on. Father is going to speak to Lewis tomorrow."

"Don't say anything about this to anyone," cautioned W.W., "Come back here tomorrow evening, A.H.; I'll tell you what I find out, then."

It was lunchtime the following day before W.W. located Lewis Watres. Together they went into the Wyoming House to eat. The two men chatted amiably; it was a typical business men's luncheon. When W.W. got around to the subject of Mt. Vernon, Lewis Watres was open and frank.

"I saw an ad in the paper yesterday, for four hundred acres going up at auction in Philadelphia. Is it yours?" politely inquired W.W. of his friend.

Sadness settled across Watres's features. "All my life, W.W., has been centered around Mt. Vernon. But there isn't a thing I can do about it. Believe me, I am very happy to be here in Scranton and doing something worthwhile."

"I'm still a little confused. Exactly how did all this happen?"

"Well, frankly, I was a little surprised, too. The bank just sent me a notice that they were going to put the property up at auction. I had always been hoping that someday, well, you know, someday, somehow, something could be done. But after the vein petered out completely, I just didn't bother to say anything more or to renew the lease."

A sinking feeling within him, brought on by the sudden clarity of thought that accompanies insight when solving a difficult problem, caused W.W.'s lunch to sit like a lead balloon in his stomach. He didn't need to hear Lewis Watres's voice, to tell him what he, W.W., had done; he knew. He had lent Watres money on Lewis's coal lease, and not on Lewis's ownership of the land. Hadn't he just done a similar thing a month earlier, purchased the coal under the ground at Dickson City and not the property itself?

The old Winton ability to come up smiling came to the fore. W.W. was quick to recognize a loss, write it off, and move on. He had always philosophized that, while he was taking the time to dwell on a piece of bad luck, the other fellow was going to be in there, picking up the next buyer's dollar. W.W. returned his attention to Lewis Watres.

"I loved Mt. Vernon, W.W. That little town was everything to me. It almost broke my heart when I realized the bind I was in—and through no fault of my own! Uncle Charles..." The finest actor could not have read the last two words with more emotion, more scorn, more futility than Lewis Watres expressed.

W.W. let his friend talk on. In the years since he had first opened his bank and had offered to help Lewis Watres, W.W. figured that he had come a long way. Now, looking back at his almost adolescent enthusiasm when he had decided to go into the banking field, it was a wonder that he hadn't been tripped up on more mistakes than this one.

"When my uncle said he needed cash in a hurry, I didn't have a thing on hand. I remember, I can still see myself—I went over to the safe in the mine office while I was talking to him; I was going to look through it, and then my hands touched the deed and pulled it out of the safe before I was even aware of what I was doing."

W.W.'s ever active mind began to cast around for some way out of the mess he was in. His first thought was to see whether something could be worked out with the creditor.

"Where did your uncle raise the money?" he inquired.

"I had promised to stand as guarantee for him. When he started to go under, the best course seemed, at the time, to let the Farmers' and Mechanics' National in Philadelphia hold the deed. We would have made it, too, if the coal hadn't run out at Mt. Vernon."

W.W.'s stomach was a lead mass again. "Are you sure the vein is exhausted?" he asked.

"Oh, no question about it. We haven't been able to get anything out of there for three years. And before that, I guess for about the past ten, we were mining less every year. It was still plenty, but nevertheless the tonnage was progressively smaller. I used to think those lazy fellows weren't working as hard as they could, but I guess I was only fooling myself," Lewis Watres heaved a heavy sigh.

W.W. echoed him and heaved a heavy sigh, too; the picture was getting darker and darker, "Are you sure the vein has run out?"

"Oh, yes—positively. Everybody knows there is no more coal at Mt. Vernon."

After lunch, W.W. parted sorrowfully from Lewis Watres. His friend's sad plight, and his forthcoming session with A.H., made him feel as if he did indeed carry the burdens of the world on his shoulders. He had already dismissed the idea of talking to the creditors. If there was no more coal, they would be interested only in selling for cash. The unfortunate part of the sad plight of W.W.'s friend was that his loss of Mt. Vernon was only a coincidence. Mt. Vernon happened to be caught, by chance, in a bigger game that had just been played.

Jay Gould, New York financier and owner of the Erie Railroad, had used the suspension of gold sales by the federal government to push up the price of gold; by this, he intended to make a lot of money. To get the government to stop selling gold, he first had had to convince President Ulysses Grant that the suspension of gold sales would force the business world to deal in grain, by selling wheat abroad. Gold would then come into the U.S. as payment by the foreign buyers. Gould made use of this scheme because it would, on the surface, benefit the American farmers, people for whom Grant felt empathy, as he himself came from a farm state.

When gold had risen to a certain high price, Gould intended to sell all that he could lay his hands on, even selling short. Gould's price was reached in the early part of September. On September 24, "Black Friday Panic," the government resumed selling gold and the price fell. Gould came out of his maneuver with more money than ever before, but financial houses all over the country had to scurry to put themselves in a sound position; they raised cash where they could. The four-hundred-acre tract was expendable, and Mt. Vernon was one of the first to go on the auction block. But in terms of reality and the Wyoming Valley, it was a sad day for Lewis Watres and W.W.—especially W.W., as he thought of his forthcoming session with A.H.

At home, A.H. was waiting for his father when he came in. Catherine had had the good sense to see that supper was ready. She had reasoned that a repeat of the previous night's emotional outburst would be difficult if the two combatants were well fed. A.H. waited until the three of them were seated at the table.

"Were you able to see Louis Watres today?"

"Yes; we had lunch at the Wyoming House."

"What did he have to say?"

"I had lent to him as coal lessee."

For some time the three Wintons devoted their attention to the food before them. Finally, A.H. broke the silence.

"What do you want to do about it?"

"I'm not sure."

"We could try filing a claim against him, *in personam*."

"I told you, A.H. I'm not sure yet what I want to do. Let me think about it for a while."

The three returned to eating again. After dinner, Catherine excused herself and left the room, leaving her husband and her son sitting in silence. At length, W.W. spoke.

"I think I know what we should do, A.H. First, I'm going to speak to George Filer."

"The mining engineer?"

"I'll speak to him tomorrow, and then, depending on what he says, I'll know whether to forget the whole thing or to start some action."

Fortunately for W.W., and probably for A.H.'s blood pressure as well, George Filer came into the Second National just before closing time the next day, the seventeenth. W.W. had been looking for him since early morning, and had almost despaired of finding him. He asked George about the mine at Mt. Vernon.

George Filer replied, "I don't know much about it. I've never had a look at it. I've heard it's completely dry—has been for three years."

"What do you think?"

"Can't say until I get a look at it."

"How soon can you do that?"

"What's involved? I can ride out tomorrow morning and ask for a tour of the place."

W.W. shifted about uneasily, "No, no, I wouldn't recommend that."

"It will take some time then."

"How much?"

"Two or three weeks."

Again W.W. displayed discomfort, "No, no, I wouldn't do that either."

"We could take a look at it tomorrow night. I can't get ready in time tonight."

W.W. relaxed, "There's a little bridge there over the Lackawanna. I could meet you there."

"Fine. Better make it two hours after dark."

"How about nine o'clock?"

"All right with me."

"I'll probably have my son along."

The two men parted, W.W. this time in search of A.H.

But he searched in vain, because A.H. was again waiting for him at home. When W.W. got in and saw A.H. waiting for him, he brightened. This was the first break he had had in the sticky mess of the past two days.

"I saw George Filer and he's agreed to take a look at the mine at Mt. Vernon," W.W. told A.H.

"That's fine. When?"

"Tomorrow. We're to meet him there at nine."

"Tomorrow morning?" queried A.H. somewhat querulously.

"No, tomorrow night."

It took A.H. a while to digest the implication, "You don't want anyone to know?"

"No, I don't. The quieter we keep this, the better it will be. I told George I would probably be bringing you."

"How do you plan to accomplish all this?"

"Well, I don't know about George, but I thought you and I could take the afternoon off tomorrow and do a little hunting."

Shortly after two o'clock on the eighteenth, the third day after he had seen the newspaper notice, A.H. rode with his father, both carrying their shotguns, out of Scranton towards Cobb's Gap. Their departure went unnoticed. The rest of the time until nightfall, they spent in working their way back through the woods, down Moosic Mountain towards Archbald and Mt. Vernon. At the last half mile before reaching the little bridge that crossed over the Lackawanna, they tied their horses to a tree and waited until eight-thirty, when they started out on foot. George Filer was waiting for them at the bridge. Silently, he handed a lantern to A.H. to carry, and divided a small pick, like a geologist's, and a shovel between himself and W.W.

Wraithlike, the three forms flowed along in the dark towards the mine entrance. Once inside, George Filer led the way, feeling and groping until they were more than fifty feet into the tunnel. Only then did he stop and strike a match, lighting his miner's lamp and the lantern A.H. was carrying. Eerie, distorted shadows danced on the tunnel walls with each movement of the lamp A.H. held.

For more than an hour, W.W. and A.H. followed George Filer as he moved methodically from tunnel to tunnel. Periodically, he paused to chip at a spot on the wall, sometimes up near the ceiling or more often down near the floor of the tunnel. They were deep into the mine when he finally spoke.

"I've never seen anything like it, W.W. This is the richest vein of coal I've ever come across."

"But everybody says the vein ran out."

"No, not by any means. They've missed it completely. The initial shaft they sunk went down neatly between two branches. From then on, it was the same story everywhere they cut. They kept opening in between, just nipping at the fringe so to speak, without ever finding where the lode was spread out all open and waiting."

The men spoke in whispers. As conspirators, even the echoes of their own voices unnerved them.

"How do you feel about it, George?" asked W.W.

"I'd like a chance to open it up. That's how I feel about it."

"It's coming up at auction in two days in Philadelphia. You think it's worth getting?"

"Definitely."

W.W. turned to whisper to A.H, "A.H., I think you had better ride the train to Philadelphia tomorrow. You don't want to be late when they start the bidding." He faced George Filer again, "What kind of a limit would you put on the price?"

"None."

For the first time, A.H. spoke, "None?"

"I told you, this is the finest vein of coal I've ever come across. And by that I mean for both quality and quantity."

"How far do you think it runs?"

"Probably all the way through the mountain to the other side of Moosic."

Again A.H. spoke, "But this is only four hundred acres and that includes part of the village. Some of the miners' houses we passed on the way to the entrance are a part of the tract."

W.W. spoke, "George, can you be patient? Given a little time, I think we can put the whole thing together."

Excitement made A.H.'s lantern jump shadows all over the tunnel, the walls, the ceiling, and the floor. It was as if a crowd of a thousand people were pressing in on them, listening, and watching everything they did and said. The three men swore each other to secrecy.

The way back to the mine entrance was a quick, silent progression. All three had their heads full of the part that each was going to have to play in the future, if what they had just seen was to bear fruit. Again, as before, about fifty feet in from the entrance they extinguished their lights, and George Filer led the way as they groped out into the chill October, starlit, but not moonlit, night. At the bridge, the three parted company, W.W. and A.H. going back to camp beside their horses, and George Filer drifting off into the darkness up towards Archbald.

The Wintons made haste the next morning to get back to Scranton before sunrise; A.H. had a train to catch. In Philadelphia on Wednesday, the twentieth of October, at fifteen minutes after noon, four hundred acres in Blakely township, Luzerne County, were knocked down to the high bidder, whose name was W.W. Winton.

11

The purchase of the ground at Mt. Vernon passed essentially unnoticed. The three men, A.H., W.W., and George Filer, were understandably nervous about W.W.'s newest land acquisition. To succeed in what they had in mind, it was necessary to quadruple the four hundred acres, at least. If anyone was to "get wind of it," or suspect what they were up to, they might as well cancel the project.

W.W. had fairly well decorated the area around Scranton with his real estate developments. Starting with the tract of land held from when he had purchased it in 1848, he was more or less famous for his "additions": the first had been Winton's addition to Providence, then there had been Winton's addition to Hyde Park, Winton's addition to Scranton, and with his son-in-law, Elnorah's husband Thomas Livey, Winton & Livey's addition to Scranton. One more large piece of land in W.W.'s hands could only mean one more "addition," as far as the public were concerned.

The acquisition of the property at Mt. Vernon had a moral and ethical aspect to it that pleased W.W. and convinced him that he was pursuing the right course. When Moses Dolph had come to Salem Corners (Hamlin) with his father-in-law Jacob Stanton, after the Strongs had been massacred in 1778, he had laid claim to many acres of land, covering many square miles. Honestly believing the ground to be his, he had sold off four hundred acre lots to various settlers as they had come into the area, Major Woodbridge being his most famous purchaser.

Salem Corners (Hamlin) was not too far distant from the southeastern, outside face of Moosic Mountain, part of the wall of the Wyoming Valley. Moses Dolph considered the area that later became Mt. Vernon to be within his domain. When William and Maurice Wurts had been looking for coal land to buy, they had done so from David Nobles, for payment of his fifteen dollar debt to Thomas Goodrich, Major Woodbridge's son-in-law. At the time, the Wurts brothers were aware that they were acquiring the Holland Tract, Moses Dolph and his cousin Henry Heermans originally coming from Holland. Through his wife Catherine, W.W. was directly related to Henry Heermans. So, in a sense, what W.W. acquired in Mt. Vernon was something that had originally been in the family.

W.W. next cast around as to how to acquire all the ground the three men wanted. Here a stroke of good fortune awaited him, further proof that what he was doing was right. The adjoining property on the valley side of his four hundred acres was owned by Edward Dolph, Moses Dolph's grandson, and his wife. With A.H. supervising, Edward Dolph sold his tract of 464 acres to W.W. at a reduced price. In return, W.W. and Edward Dolph set up Winton & Dolph's addition to Peckville, Peckville being the community at the far edge of Dolph's land. The building lots close to Peckville sold quickly. Edward Dolph soon had more money than he knew what to do with, what with the money from selling to W.W. as well as his percentage from the individual building lots; and W.W. had his first addition to Mt. Vernon without it costing him a thing. The Peckville lots that were sold reimbursed him for the money he paid to Edward Dolph. In the development of Winton & Dolph's addition to Peckville, A.H. and W.W. showed that they had profited from their past experiences. Even though the lots down near Peckville were far from the coal mine at Mt. Vernon, they nevertheless retained the mineral or coal rights to every lot sold.

Other things then crowded on W.W.'s horizon, and his activities at Mt. Vernon temporarily receded. He joined with Joseph Scranton, Thomas Dickson, Moses Taylor, John B. Smith, H.S. Pierce, John Brisbin, Ira Tripp, and H.B. Phelps to put together a half million dollars for capital in order to open the Scranton Trust Company and Savings Bank on Wyoming Avenue. Full of enthusiasm, W.W. offered twenty-four shares of his own Second National to Ira Tripp, thus bringing Ira into his banking family.

It was the second of March, 1870; the valley was still bare from the cold winter months. The days were getting longer and spring was coming soon, but it was only in the air that blew. All the Wintons journeyed to Wilkes-Barre, for a family celebration with Mrs. Collings. John Collings had at last finished his apprenticeship, and on that day was admitted to the Bar of Luzerne County.

A.H. wanted his brother-in-law to join him in Scranton, "There's plenty of room in Washington Hall," he told John, "We could join into a partnership, or, if you prefer, just have your office there."

But John declined. He had lived all his life in Wilkes-Barre and was committed there. It was also the county seat, so most of his law work would be centered there also, "Thank you, A.H., but not now. Maybe some day, if you don't change your mind about your offer."

"Change my mind! How could I change my mind about my own brother-in-law? That's as if I were to change my mind about Alice," A.H. began to scoff incredulously at the idea just presented, but ended suddenly on a feeble tone.

He was beginning to have second thoughts about himself and Alice. He knew something was terribly wrong somewhere. In a couple of months, they would be celebrating their fifth wedding anniversary, and they were still childless. It wasn't that he loved Alice any less; she was still as desirable to him as on the day he had first seen her. And in spite of the five years he had been playing the husband, there were still times when he looked into his lovely wife's eyes and could think only of their bedroom waiting for them. But something was wrong. He thanked God it was not physical; the baby that had been born discounted that as a cause.

As John Collings turned away to receive the congratulations of Byron Winton and his wife, A.H. nervously fingered the card in his pocket. He realized how desperate he must be, to have even read the advertisement, much less be planning to do something about it. At first, he had tried to fool himself, rationalizing that the notation at the end of the ad, inviting inquiries from prospective selling agents, had been the cause of his interest. But now, after having carried the advertisement around with him for six months, he admitted to himself that he was desperate enough to seek help anywhere. Dr. E.C. Abbey, of Buffalo, New York, in addition to inviting agents, was selling his book, *The Sexual System and Its Derangements*, directly to the public. For ten cents, total insight and remedies regarding any matter from sex education to impotency because of nail-biting, were promised.

In the midst of the party gaiety, so busy was A.H. with his private thoughts that he was not aware that Alice had joined him. She surprised a look on his face that confused her. For the first time in their married life, she had the feeling that A.H. was deliberately hiding something from her. This was not like the affair of the Providence Bankruptcy Commission; then he had been silent, only waiting for the appropriate moment to tell her that their honeymoon would be interrupted. Now, however, he could not let her guess how unhappy he was that they did not have a child.

Alice drew back within herself at the unknown look on her husband's face. Unsure of herself, she turned away without speaking. These abortive meetings were happening more and more frequently between them. The difference this time was that A.H. reached out and touched her on the arm as she started to move away.

Almost involuntarily, he spoke out; "Alice, I've been looking for you," he said.

She turned to him, everything a man could desire. Suddenly she seemed very vulnerable to him. He wanted to protect her.

"I was looking for you, too. Your mother said to tell you she and your father were leaving. I told them we would take a later train. Is that all right with you?"

"Remind me to tell you about the lot," he called over his shoulder as he went in search of his parents to bid them good-bye.

When A.H. returned, Alice was in approximately the same spot she had been standing when he had left her. His promise to tell her about "the lot" took precedence over everything else.

"I didn't have a chance to tell you on the way down, but I think we can have our choice of several lots."

Alice and A.H. had talked tentatively from time to time of building a house of their own. But they had never gone any further than talking because, without children, the need had never been there to move to larger quarters.

"I'm so excited," said Alice. "I didn't realize that you were going to do something about it now."

"The opportunity has presented itself, and I don't think we should risk letting it go by. The two most promising locations are on 7th Street, towards Hyde Park, and at Wyoming and Mulberry."

"Can we look at them when we get back?" Alice was quite excited.

She smiled and purred at her husband. The prospect of building their own house brought unexpected, but genuine, pleasure to her countenance. She gave voice to her feelings.

"You've made me so happy, Mr. Winton."

Again A.H. experienced the new, and consequently strange, feeling of wanting to protect Alice.

"If we are going to have a lovely new house," she continued, "we must do something about having children to put in it."

Alice's eyes mocked her husband, challenging his male ego. Momentarily, A.H. was too shocked at his wife's very private suggestion, while standing in the middle of a room full of people, to do anything, much less reply. Had Alice been aware of the advertising card burning a hole in A.H.'s pocket, she might not have been so playful. His nascent emotion, of wanting to protect Alice, vanished. In its stead he almost reached out to turn her over his knee and spank her, but remembered where he was in time.

Suddenly contrite at her outlandish remark, Alice drew back within herself, "Oh, A.H., forgive me," she said.

But remember, these were two people who loved each other so deeply as to have almost total understanding.

"No, Alice," answered A.H., "forgive me."

At last, he was aware how badly she wanted a child, so badly that she would speak out as she had just done. Unconsciously, he put his hand into his pocket and fingered the advertisement again. Perhaps he would not reply to it quite yet.

The next morning, A.H. took Alice to see the various lots. When she had so much difficulty in deciding, A.H. resolved the matter in the only proper and correct way possible when one is part of a very, very rich and enthusiastic family: he bought both lots, the 7th Street and the Wyoming Avenue. Shortly after, A.H. invited Messers Gardner and Forepaugh to set up their two tents on Friday, the seventeenth of June, at his 7th Street lot, as their circus traveled through Scranton from Carbondale on its way to Pittston. It was a first-class circus, including a menagerie housed in twenty-two dens, and with a magnificent wardrobe made by the first class Clothing House of J. Wanamaker at Nos. 918 and 920 Chestnut Street in Philadelphia.

After the arrival and departure of the circus, A.H. calmed down. He remained calm for the remainder of the summer months, until September, when Alice told him a baby was on its way. On hearing the news, A.H. knew the proper and correct thing to do. As soon as he was alone, he tore Dr. Abbey's advertisement neatly in half and then half again. In other instances, he also knew what to do. Without regrets he declined his cousin L.W. Heerman's invitation to Heermans Dancing Academy, a series of hops to be held during the coming season. The first hop was scheduled for October 25 at the Wyoming House. When he showed the invitation to Alice, she suggested that he attend the first ones without her. A.H. pointed to the "Gentlemen are expected to bring Ladies."

"I have nobody to take," he said, "Besides, I would much rather spend the twenty-fifth with you."

He and Alice talked at great length. Under no condition was he going to allow her to go to Wilkes-Barre. This time, Alice agreed with him wholeheartedly. They also discussed their new house, which now had a real meaning. It was also September before Alice decided on the Wyoming and Mulberry lot. A.H. was more than satisfied with her choice. He passed along the information to his parents: the fact that they were anticipating an addition to their family, and their intention to build a house at 436 Wyoming Avenue, almost at the corner of Mulberry. The idea appealed to W.W., and he gave some serious thought to doing some building of his own. But before he could get a design down on paper, he had another stroke of good luck: he was offered a parcel of 403 acres at Mt. Vernon. This new tract did not adjoin either of his two previous acquisitions, but for his joint plan with A.H. and George Filer, it couldn't have been better. The four-hundred-odd acres were in the shape of a long narrow strip up and over Moosic Mountain.

"Don't quibble at settlement time," he instructed A.H.

For a business man, surprisingly W.W. was showing signs of tension. Too much was involved, too much was at stake, and the pieces were coming together so nicely that he was almost fanatical in his worry that something would interfere or go wrong. A.H. supported his father beautifully. They clung to each other all through the fall and up to Christmas, when the holidays diverted them. On later analysis, though, it was questionable as to who was supporting whom. In his own way, A.H. was just as nervous as his father in the intervening months before the baby was expected to arrive; A.H. became almost as fanatical as his father in his worry that something would go wrong. But somehow or other A.H. and W.W. managed to survive the winter.

Then suddenly, miraculously, on the eighteenth of May in 1871, tiny, elegant Catherine May Winton made her appearance.

A.H. passed the remainder of the eighteenth, and almost all of the nineteenth of May at the bar of the Wyoming House, celebrating.

The sun was just starting to set, although the hour was past eight. The lamps had already been lit against the dark that would come. Frank Collins (the Collings without the 'g') joined A.H., and offered him his congratulations. There wasn't a person in Scranton who didn't know what had happened in the A.H. Winton household.

"I'm going to be looking for a new office," Frank threw out to A.H., hoping the latter would be interested.

"The offer is still open," A.H. replied expansively, viewing everything in the light of new fatherhood.

Frank Collins was embarrassed at the ready generosity of his friend; "I might as well confess," he said, "I have an ulterior motive."

"One usually does;" A.H.'s intellectual prowess had not been dulled by his round of celebrating.

"Because I want to ask a favor of you."

A.H. waved his hand grandiosely, "Ask away."

"I'm going to run in the election this coming October, and, truthfully, I want your help."

A.H. straightened himself up from his slouch with one elbow resting on the bar. He picked up Frank's glass and handed it to him; picking up his own, he said, "Come, my friend, let us go into the dining room for a bite to eat."

Weaving ever so slightly, he led the way across the lobby to the main dining room, the same one in which he and Alice had eaten when they had had their first meal together in Scranton.

"Now what's this about you running for office?"

"The Senate seat from Luzerne, Pike and Monroe Counties will be vacant this fall, and I've decided to make a try for it. I need your help."

"On the Democratic ticket?"

"Yes."

They interrupted their conversation while their sandwiches were placed before them.

Frank Collins continued, "A.H., I can make it, I know; but I need your help. The Democrats are in the majority in Luzerne, and if you would swing just a few Republicans my way, to counteract the Democrats that will be voting Republican or Temperance, I'll be in."

Thoughtfully, A.H. munched his food. Frank's proposition had deep implications, but only for A.H. He had never mentioned his thoughts about the pattern of voting in the elections after the Scranton City Charter came into effect. Perhaps Frank's request for aid would be a means of getting answers to the questions that he had been carrying around within himself for the past five elections.

At last, he spoke, "It's not going to be easy. This new Republican party is the popular one, nationally."

Frank Collins was a master politician. Seeing that he had A.H. half sold, he turned to a related matter, "The truth is, the reason why I want to join you is because, if I win, I'll be spending most of my time in Harrisburg. Where I am now, alone, my office would be closed up. I'm not going to move out of 306 Lackawanna, but if I'm also in with you, I'll feel that I have an associate back home, so to speak."

It was Frank's trump card. That he offered it demonstrated how highly he regarded A.H. For what he was giving A.H. was a direct pipeline to the State Legislature at Harrisburg.

Still eating, A.H. remained deep in thought. He was not unaware of what Frank had just offered. But he was more interested in protecting the voters of Hyde Park, Providence, and, to a lesser extent, Scranton. He wanted the answers to the vote pattern after 1866. Perhaps if A.H. had not written to George Smith in Washington so long ago, he would have jumped at the offer and allied himself with Frank Collins on the spot. But very little outside the Wyoming Valley held an interest for him.

At last, he spoke, "I have some ideas of my own, Frank. They don't interfere with what you want. If I go along with you, will you cooperate with me?"

Surprised, Frank hesitated before answering. "Can you let me in on some of your ideas?"

"Yes, but not until the campaign is underway."

Frank still hesitated, weighing the advisability of pushing A.H. for more information. But he was an Irish politician, with all the attributes for being a successful one. Before the pause became too lengthy, he spoke, "Agreed."

A.H. pummelled Frank Collins on the back, "Glad to have you, Frank. Glad to have you.

"Come by tomorrow. There are four corners to the room, take your pick. We'll put a desk and a chair there, and file all messages for you on top of the desk."

Frank came the next day, and quickly settled on a back corner, across from A.H. From then on, he took to dropping in for a few minutes once, and sometimes twice, each day.

At home, A.H. and Alice apprehensively watched the baby. Somehow it was fixed in their minds that if they could get through the first month, all would be well. Kate May did not disappoint them; she grew larger and healthier every day.

With the baby doing well and Frank Collins dropping by every day, life settled momentarily into a routine pattern. A.H. took this time to look for his father. He had not forgotten that he had promised to help Frank with the election; his decision to help Frank had been motivated primarily by his suspicions about Scranton's elections. He was fortunate to find both W.W. and Isaac Dean at the Second National Bank, and asked the two men if they could spare him a few minutes. The three men went into W.W.'s office, and W.W. shut the door.

"Father, Uncle Isaac," began A.H., "I'd like to tell you something that's been on my mind for some time. If you can listen without interrupting, I'll be as brief as possible.

"I don't know how closely you have been following the election returns since we agreed to the Scranton City merger. Before that time, Providence and Hyde Park, as separate boroughs and townships, usually voted opposite to Scranton Borough. We voted Democrat and they went Whig. Then we turned out for the new Republican, or Radical, party, while they were shifting Democratic. Well, that was all right. But before the city merger, our vote, that is Providence's and Hyde Park's, had some power. We were separate entities, and could control our little area, where we lived, the way we wanted.

"Have you realized what's happened ever since we merged with Scranton? Providence and Hyde Park are still voting the way they did before. And Scranton is still voting the way it did when it was a borough. But now our Republican vote has absolutely no weight at all; it's thrown in with the other losing minority votes of Scranton city. We're only a few wards out of twelve. In essence, by merging into a city, we were throwing our votes away. And what's more, we've lost our right to self-government at the level where it concerns us most directly, the local level.

"We might as well be living in Wilkes-Barre. Wilkes-Barre and Scranton always vote the same way. We can't do one thing that Wilkes-Barre hasn't decided or approved first. If they're for it, we get it. If they're against it, we don't. What we want for ourselves, we can no longer have, unless it happens to coincide with what Wilkes-Barre wants, too."

W.W. and Isaac Dean were stunned. They had never perceived this as A.H. had.

"Thank God Pop [Henry Heermans] never lived to see this happen," said Isaac Dean.

W.W. took out his handkerchief and mopped his brow. He had been so busy keeping his eye on the way things were developing at Mt. Vernon that he had completely ignored the political elections. He realized, hearing A.H. speak, that he had been lulled into a false sense of security. From the time of Lincoln's election, the Republican Party, with its stronghold in the North, had been carrying the nation. As Hyde Park and Providence voted, the nation went. Even state gubernatorial candidates backed by the Republicans were voted into office. Something tugged at the back of his mind; he looked at Isaac Dean.

"I think he's got something there, Isaac. I just remembered; when Geary came here for the election in '66, you remember the reception we had for him? You should, you were there!"

Isaac nodded.

"I remember at the time, thinking what a great show of strength we had at the reception, and how our man Geary got the governor's post. But afterwards, I remember thinking that the official vote made us look as if we had not supported him at all, because the city was recorded as turning in a Democratic plurality. It was the vote from all over the state that was as our reception had promised. And, of course, it was the total state vote that put him in office."

"Whenever Scranton votes, it's always three or four wards which come in with a large enough plurality to wipe out the votes from Providence and Hyde Park." Dispassionate, but in despair, A.H.'s voice reached W.W. and Isaac Dean.

The three men stared at each other without speaking. Into the mortar of deeds done, their pestle of analytical mental powers were grinding slowly and thoroughly. Not one of the three, however, had the courage to give expression to their common thought—that Providence and Hyde Park had been done in by the city merger. The biggest question left in their minds was whether or not the Scrantons, Dr. Throop, George Sanderson, and William Merrifield had been innocent dupes as well.

At last, A.H. spoke up, "I think we have a way of finding out whether we're right about this or not.

"Frank Collins tells me that he is going to run for the state senate in October, and he wants me to help him. I told him I would; he's a good man. His father's been on the bench at Wilkes-Barre for some time, and has a reputation for being fair. I don't think we will have to do too much for the election. All that will be necessary will be to spread the word around that he's honest and that we're all for him. Frank's got the makings of a top-notch politician; he'll do the rest himself."

Isaac Dean had a question, "I don't see the connection. How will throwing our influence behind Collins tell us what we want to know?"

"Frank is a Democrat and will be running on the Democratic ticket. If it's widely known that the Republicans at Providence and Hyde Park are solidly behind him as well, he's sure to get plenty of votes. At the same time, if we can keep a watch on the polls for voting irregularities, we'll know the vote count will be an honest one. I know which wards in the city have been coming in strong with the way Wilkes-Barre votes."

"But what will it prove?" queried W.W.

"Father, I don't care whether it proves I'm right or wrong. All I want to do is to find out whether my suspicions are founded on truth or not. I hope I'm proven wrong, if you want my personal opinion.

"You see, with Frank cooperating with us, we can eliminate the one factor that could confuse the picture; Frank himself will not be buying votes or paying men to adjust ballot boxes. Any irregularities that show up we can definitely attribute to the political machine."

W.W. started to pooh-pooh the whole idea; too many things were starting to come at him from too many directions, when all he wanted to do was to complete things at Mt. Vernon. But he held back from saying anything. Experience had taught him that when A.H. started niggling away at something, he was usually right.

He said, "Your idea, then, is to watch the polls; but you aren't expecting any trouble because, the way you reason it, if there are no interested parties, everybody, both Democrats and Hyde Park and Providence Republicans, will be voting for Collins."

"Exactly."

"Then what do you expect to learn?"

"If certain political interests always want something contrary to what Hyde Park and Providence want, they won't be happy when they realize that we are coming out heavily in favor of their candidate. I'm hoping that, at the most, they'll tip their hand. I don't expect any overt activity."

W.W. threw up his hands in a gesture of surrender, "Handle it anyway you like, A.H."

"Uncle Isaac?"

"I was for the city merger, A.H. I honestly thought it would benefit us all here. But the way you've presented things just now has me upset. I'll work with you; just tell me what you want done."

W.W. spoke up before A.H. could leave, "Don't go, A.H. I, too, have something I would like to discuss with the both of you.

"Isaac, A.H. tells me that he and Alice are going to build a house. The thought has occurred to me that we could do with a new bank building—

something a little more elegant; a little more in keeping with the bank's position." The other two just stared at W.W.

He continued, "Anyway, I've been looking into the matter. I think I've found a reliable architect. A.H., I spoke to him about doing a house, and he can do a bank and a house very nicely at the same time. I've also been looking around town, and the lot at 234 Lackawanna Avenue, across from Washington Hall, looks good to me."

A.H. stared at his father in amazement. Then he laughed, "Why not? Come on, Uncle Isaac, let's go take a look at the ground."

He grabbed Isaac Dean's arm, and propelled him towards the office door. Calling back over his shoulder to his father, he said, "Just make sure, Father, he doesn't build Alice and me a bank for our house. I don't want to have to pay that kind of bill."

The next few months were very busy. Isaac Dean was intrigued with the idea of a new home for the Second National. 318 Lackawanna, where the Second National Bank was presently located, no longer looked so desirable to Isaac as his mind's eye envisioned how 234 Lackawanna would look. After that, the new building couldn't go up fast enough to suit him. Alice, who was busy pouring years of mother's love out to the little baby, was just as impatient for the new nursery. Both buildings were designed in the "French taste," with mansard roofs. But the elegant frame structure of the A.H. Winton home was modest, compared to the $115,000 spent on the bank. It was the city's first skyscraper; with five floors and an attic, a combination of stone, marble, and iron, the bank building was as solid as a rock. Each floor, all the way to the attic, was built by pouring mortar, high grade cement, over brick arches. The interior walls, partitioning the space into rooms and offices, were of two inch thick plaster over wooden studding. It was decorated on the inside with fine fresco work, plaster scrolls and embellishments on the ceilings and walls. The main floor was well lighted, both by the two big windows and door which fronted on Lackawanna Avenue, and by the ten large windows running down the side. The plans included a massive burglarproof vault and an intricate fireproofing system.

Shortly after ground had been broken for both the bank and his and Alice's home, A.H. spoke to the Republican County Committee. He did not talk to them in the same way that he had to W.W. and Isaac Dean. To the Republicans, he said that he feared there were some gross irregularities occurring in the Scranton city voting. They were interested, but wanted something a little more specific. A.H. suggested that the Seventh, Tenth, Eleventh, and Twelfth Wards be watched very carefully.

At the Republican meeting in Wilkes-Barre on the nineteenth of August, a Republican Vigilance Committee was formed to cover the whole of Luzerne County. The pollwatchers having been organized, A.H. returned to Scranton, in time to hear from W.W. that another 403-acre tract at Mt. Vernon had been offered to him. This second piece adjoined the last one purchased, and, like it, was long and narrow, also running up and over Moosic Mountain. This last purchase brought the total to 1600 acres at Mt. Vernon.

Then came a lull. Everything was in readiness, waiting for the elections on October 10. Frank Collins was campaigning well, and the word had been passed among the Republicans, in loud stage whispers, that Collins was the man for the state senate seat. A.H. had no doubt that the whisper had been heard wherever it should have been heard.

Finally, election day came—and went. The vote was tallied, and Frank Collins won. All was quiet. A.H. had been wrong; he had cried "wolf" when there had been none. To say that he hung his head and slunk away into oblivion, and that this tale came to an inglorious end, would not be right. A.H. had to keep on living, and living in Scranton, too. He had a wife and child to support, he had a law practice, he was counsel to several firms including the bank, he was surrounded by family, and he was intimately involved with the plans at Mt. Vernon. No, he could not slink off and hide. He had been wrong; he had been proved wrong. So, he shut his mouth and went about the rest of his business—that's all there was going to be to it—until a week later, when the final returns for the whole state of Pennsylvania were published; after Frank Collins' name, as winner, was the notation that he had won by the grossest fraud, and that his election would probably be contested!

A.H. read it and wondered; he had no idea what was going on. At the time of the balloting, none of the Republican Vigilance Committee members had said anything about any questionable behavior at the polls. He inquired around, but got no help; no one knew anything, nor had heard any rumor as to what was happening. It all started to come out in the open when, on the twenty-eighth of October, a complaint on the election was filed with Judge Garrick Harding at Wilkes-Barre. The judge was the same Garrick Harding with whom A.H. had first begun to practice law more than ten years earlier, before he maintained his office exclusively at Scranton.

The complaint was a citizen's complaint, and, in its list, the Fourth, Seventh, Tenth, and Twelfth Wards of Scranton were specifically named as returning illegal totals. A complicated situation had been made even more complicated by this complaint. The complaint actually filed questioned the validity of the election for sheriff of Luzerne County. Frank Collins, in his bid for a state senate seat, had been the choice of his own party. It would not do for his own party to suddenly object to his winning. So, certain members of the Democratic party attacked the situation by questioning the results in a case where their own man had lost. What they hoped to do by contesting the votes for sheriff was to throw doubt on the votes of all the winners, thereby catching the one they were most concerned about in the larger net.

Hastily, A.H. read through the complaint. Of the four Scranton city wards named, he had already predicted three of them. The attached complainants' names were unfamiliar to him; he did not recognize any Republicans among them. As A.H. had not cowered a week earlier when apparently wrong, neither did he gloat when proven right. As he had told his father and uncle, he really hoped that his suspicions would be shown to be unfounded.

The hearing on the complaint was scheduled for November 14 by Judge Harding. Just about every lawyer in Luzerne County crowded into Judge Harding's courtroom that day. They were a gregarious, actually noisy, lot before the judge entered. After court convened and Judge Harding heard the complaint, he appointed Mr. A.H. Winton commissioner to take testimony on the disputed votes and make a report to the court. A large uproar from some of the lawyers greeted A.H.'s appointment. Judge Harding knew that A.H. was an honest man, well-qualified for the task he had just assigned him. He became furious at the objections, "What's the matter?" he roared from the bench.

Several lawyers answered him at once, Col. Hendrick Wright's voice being the loudest in protest.

Judge Harding listened for a minute or two, and then banged his gavel.

"Silence!"

It took a while before everyone quieted down. When there was order, Judge Harding continued.

"I have listened to you just now. I have heard no valid objection on any account applying to Mr. Winton. The Court has appointed him commissioner. Therefore the appointment stands."

Col. Wright opened up a barrage, "No! No! No! He won't do!"

Judge Harding repeatedly called for order but Col. Wright ignored him; he encouraged other lawyers to give voice against Winton's appointment.

Finally, over all the shouting, Harding's voice rose the loudest, "Wright, if you don't shut up, I'm going to give you thirty hours in the county jail!"

That did the trick; silence and order prevailed in the courtroom once again. But by then, Judge Harding was so mad that he called for a recess.

"Court's adjourned until two o'clock," he said.

Hendrick Wright left the courtroom, crying to anyone who would listen, that Garrick Harding had shut him up by offering him thirty hours in the county jail. He was indignant over the affront. He gathered about him those who he knew were with him, and they caucused until almost two o'clock. They were not giving up.

When court reconvened, another lawyer, Mr. Rhoan, stepped forward. There was order now, no noisy outbursts. The opposition had seen that they were not going to unbalance Harding by rushing him. Mr. Rhoan spoke in a dignified manner as he addressed the bench.

"In view of the fact that, on a matter as important as the one that is presently before the court, Judge Harding appointed Mr. Winton without consulting his associates on the bench, we earnestly appeal to the associate judges to revoke Mr. Winton's appointment, and instead appoint Mr. A.A. Chase."

Judge Harding blew a fuse! Right there in front of everyone, he turned red and blue and purple and pink and white and every shade in between. But it was to no avail; the associate judges were called in. Everyone waited while they deliberated. It was Associate Judge Thomas Collins, Frank Collins's father, who announced the decision. Mr. Winton's name was to be withdrawn, and Mr.

Chase, also the publisher of the *Scranton Times* newspaper, was to be appointed the commissioner.

Everything that A.H. had hoped to prove or disprove, when he had agreed to help Frank Collins, had been proven. Politically, the areas formerly known as Hyde Park and Providence had been obliterated. It was another eruption of the old Pennsylvania-Connecticut feud. This time, those with Pennsylvania ties had successfully obtained a stranglehold or the others. The little seed, that was to grow into A.B. Dunning's mighty oak, took another spurt in growth among the Wintons. Hazily, in the far recesses of his mind, A.H. cast around for a way out from under; something would have to be done.

12

Before the Second National Bank could move into its new home, Edward Dolph introduced N. Halstead to W.W.

In the aftermath of the October '71 election, the Democrats involved realized that they had overplayed their hand in Judge Harding's courtroom, and hushed the complaint, the appointment of Chase, and everything connected with the election. This sudden change was mainly because they had gotten something that meant a great deal to them. Wilkes-Barre, actually those politicians interested in Wilkes-Barre's welfare exclusively, were willing to quiet things down, because they had just remedied something that had been a thorn in their side for five years: Wilkes-Barre had finally been elevated to city status. At last, Scranton was not something more than Wilkes-Barre (and, in the eyes of some, would always be a good deal less). If for no other reason than the city designation, it was hoped that all that had transpired at election time would quietly fade from everyone's memory. Which it did—except for A.H.'s. Frank Collins took his seat at Harrisburg, and A.H. returned his thoughts to the Second National Bank and Mt. Vernon.

It was on account of Mt. Vernon that Edward Dolph felt that W.W. should talk with Halstead. Halstead apparently was one of the very, very few men who were watching the activities at Mt. Vernon. By W.W.'s most recent purchase, an enormous and solid block of land had been formed, except for one area like a pocket at the far end of Mt. Vernon village proper. Concerning this missing link, so to speak, Halstead informed Edward Dolph that he thought that he, Halstead, could talk the owner into selling 165 acres. Compared to the other tracts, it was small, being only 165 acres. Dolph, remember, was unaware of the coal mine plans; he was interested only from the standpoint of real-estate development. Halstead, too, had only land development in mind. The mine at Mt. Vernon had been shut down completely for several years; it was generally conceded that whatever coal had been there had been taken out, and that the land was good only for building.

At first, W.W. was inclined to let the 165 acres go by. It was not a vital piece to the Mt. Vernon scheme; it was at the outside edge. But Edward Dolph was enthusiastic, and Halstead declined a commission, insisting that he was not interested in such a small piece of ground. He implied that he was just glad to be of service and pass the contact along to the interested parties. In the late spring of '72, W.W. decided to go ahead and purchase the 165 acres anyway.

The bank building was far enough along towards completion that W.W. started to plan for a gala opening. A.H. suggested certain minor revisions in the administration. After consultation with Isaac Dean, Byron Winton, A.H.'s younger brother, was named Vice-president of the Second National, more or less dividing his time equally between the bank and his wholesale grocery business, Silkman & Winton. When A.H. next considered his other brother, he hesitated; Walter and Ella had not been getting along as well as they should. It was now almost a weekly occurrence that Alice related, at dinnertime, an episode describing some particular unpleasantness by Walter towards his wife. When A.H. spoke to W.W., he found that his father was aware of the situation, too.

W.W. was now fifty-seven years old. If the plan for Mt. Vernon matured, he would have to be in a lot of places, all at the same time. He had rents to collect, a large bank to run, and should George Filer be right, soon a full production coal mine. W.W. was also director of several other companies, including the Scranton Trust Company and Savings Bank and the People's Street Railway of Scranton. Not through nepotism, by installing various family members at the heads of his enterprises to prevent intrusion, but with the philosophy that they were the extension of his own personality, did he plan to direct his conglomerate empire. Whereas previously he and his family had covered a wide area of the commercial market through their own businesses, such as the bank, the real estate, Winton & Tunstall, and Silkman & Winton, the current drive was to shift into one person who controlled and directed from the top. The underlings, in this instance extensions or projections of the director's personality, and not underlings in the strict definition of the word, were to carry out the directives.

Walter Winton could be valuable to his father. But Walter's family knew him too well to be completely sold on him. For the present, W.W. finally decided to put Walter at whatever task needed immediate attention. Elnorah's husband, Thomas Livey, he decided to save for Mt. Vernon, if and when they were to go ahead there. Walter's first assignment was to make the plans for the bank's gala opening. A committee was formed. They named June 17 as the date. In all the flurry and preparation, Alice, A.H., and Kate moved quietly into their new home at Wyoming and Mulberry.

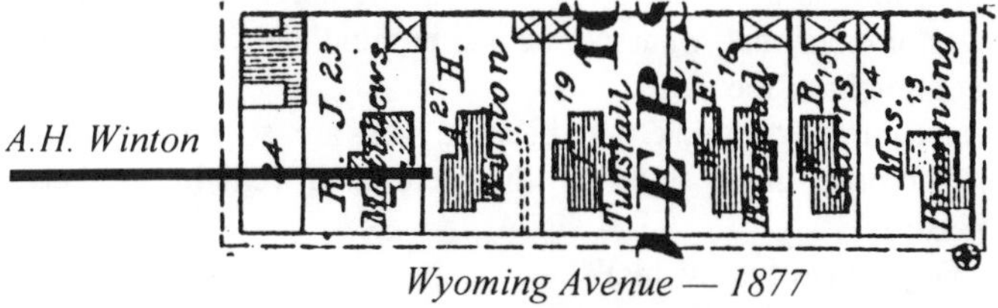

Wyoming Avenue — 1877

They had an open house for family and friends, but it was mild, even dull, by comparison with the anticipated bank opening. In the middle of May, invitations were engraved and mailed:

Compliments
of the
Second National Bank of Scranton, Pa.
requesting the company of yourself and lady at the
opening of their New Building
Monday Evening, June 17th, 1872
(entrance card enclosed)
Ira Tripp
W.P. Carling
Walter W. Winton
E.R. Mills
Committee of Arrangements

At last, the great day came. Both those planning the gala and those invited acted as if they were going to a great ball. All the Winton ladies arrived early, in their most glamorous attire. Gas lamps blazed everywhere. A steady procession of guests toured the vault and marveled at the tumbler lock. W.W. moved everywhere. Isaac Dean, more modest, stood before a cashier's window and bestowed smiles on everyone. Refreshments, a never-emptying punchbowl, and a small band's music buoyed the spirits of every guest. As one travels through life, there are always one or two bright moments that make a whole lifetime seem worthwhile; for W.W., his bank opening was his brightest. A.H. put an added sparkle in Alice's eyes; at one point during the evening, he whispered, "I have a surprise for you," and then vanished before she could question him. It was a beautiful evening, perfectly planned by the arrangement committee.

Quite late, after midnight, when A.H. and Alice returned home, they paused on their veranda.

"Tell me what my surprise is, now. You have had me dying of curiosity, ever since you whispered to me."

"What would you like most to do?"

"Oh, no, Mr. Winton. You're not going to trap me on that. For, whatever I say, you will accuse me of harboring some long-standing disappointment."

In the quiet of the late-hour midsummer evening, A.H. was acting more like a bridegroom than a husband of seven years. His kisses caressed the side of his wife's face towards him as they swayed slightly on the porch swing where they were sitting. It was obvious that, whatever he had in mind, he was delighted with himself at having thought of the treat.

Finally, he murmured, "I think that because you are so intelligent as to discern an ulterior motive in my question, the secret shall remain one between Mr. Doyle and myself."

"Who is Mr. Doyle? Do I know him?"

"No, but I do," whispered A.H. smugly.

Try as she would, Alice could not dislodge any more information from her husband. The success, his excitement of the bank opening, and his delight in his secret plans for Alice and what they held in store for her, made him capricious and teasing.

"I'll tell you what. Let's take it to the judge and let him decide."

"Oh, you're being silly now."

"No, I'm not. It's Judge June Night. Let's hear what he has to say. Mrs. Winton, this is—"

"Stop, please," Alice was laughing.

"Mrs. Winton, if you'll step into my chamber, counsel will give you a clue. It has something to do with Kate."

The next morning, at breakfast, A.H. finally told Alice what he was planning: "We're going to spend the summer by the sea."

"Oh, A.H., how thrilling!"

Alice meant her words. In spite of all her traveling and her ocean crossing, she was basically a Wyoming Valley girl, and, except for her time as a young girl in Morocco and Washington, D.C., she had never frequented any place outside the valley area.

"Alice, you're going to love Nantucket," A.H.'s face was shining as he described the delights of the island community off Cape Cod, "I know you will. It's a beautiful island out in the ocean. I visited the place one time on a school vacation when I was studying in Massachusetts. I told myself I would come back someday. All day, you and I will sit on the beach, relaxing in the sun, watching the waves, and Kate, she will have the time of her one-year-old life."

"Who is this Mr. Doyle, that you said knew your secret?"

"The owner of the Ocean House, where we will be staying."

After the Fourth of July, A.H. packed up his household and departed for Massachusetts. It was almost a three-day trip, first by train to New York, and then by ferry steamer out to Nantucket Island. Once there, it was as he predicted; his family loved the place. On this their first vacation, they acted very much the tourist; they sampled everything, lived lazy days on the beach among the dunes, promenaded on the hotel's piazza, and after dinner explored the community.

Meanwhile, back in Scranton life was going on. Just before the A.H. Wintons were to return home, W.W. heard from Mr. Halstead again. This time, he had a proposition of a slightly different nature. Truthfully, W.W. was not surprised; he had been expecting something since the time he had bought the 165 acres at Mt. Vernon through Halstead's generosity. Again, Halstead was bringing news about land at Mt. Vernon.

"The Hollenback family has contacted me about purchasing their property at Mt. Vernon," he told W.W.

W.W. caught his breath. The Hollenback tract was the last remaining 400 acres there. It included the part of Mt. Vernon that had not been included in the Philadelphia auction purchase. He was going to have to watch his step very carefully, or all would be lost. Possession of this last 400 acres was absolutely necessary before they could go ahead with their plan. W.W. did not doubt Halstead's veracity about the Hollenback heirs wanting to sell to him, but W.W. thought it was more of a feeler thrown out by Halstead than any *fait accompli*. If

Halstead knew how badly he wanted the ground, he would never get it, he knew. W.W. treaded lightly.

"What do you think you will do?"

"Well, I don't know," replied Halstead, "It's a fair size piece there, and the heirs are asking a fair size price to match."

"That last piece of 165 acres that you put me onto was more than I had planned to commit myself to. I don't want to overextend. I don't know, Halstead, this piece you're talking about now is over part of the mine tunnels, isn't it?"

"That don't make a difference—plenty of room to build houses. Wouldn't interfere at all. If you open up a hole while you're excavating, throw in some dirt. You could sell every inch."

W.W. appeared to study the proposition, "I don't know. Have you talked to Dolph yet?"

W.W. wasn't sure, but he thought he detected a flicker of surprise in Halstead's eyes. W.W. felt encouraged. Maybe he could throw Halstead off the scent.

"No, I haven't seen him."

"My suggestion would be to get his opinion. He knows the area as well as you do. I don't. See what he thinks."

The two men shook hands cordially, and Halstead left. Had W.W. been a nail-biter when worried, he would have been fingernail-less over the intervening weeks until he heard from Halstead again, so worried was he that Halstead would try to develop the Hollenback acreage by himself. To keep his sanity, W.W. busied himself with whatever he could put his hands on. He induced the Western Union Telegraph Company and Central Express Company to rent the basement of the new Second National Bank building.

A healthy, sun-tanned, relaxed A.H. caught up with his father at the beginning of September. W.W. described his conversation with Halstead. Now, there were two to worry. Everything else faded into the background, while the two tried to guess Halstead's next move.

Halstead brought Edward Dolph with him the next time he saw W.W. Seeing the two together, W.W. almost cried, he was so relieved. He was pretty sure which way the "wind was going to blow" now. They discussed the probability of selling the Hollenback acreage for development.

W.W. felt so confident of the way things would eventually develop that he played a bold hand, "Halstead, if you're so sold on the place, why not float a loan and do it yourself? The Second National will certainly be glad to finance you. After all, you did me a good turn. I'm more than happy to do one for you."

"Well, that's one way. Of course, I've given it some thought," Halstead acted as if he was thinking it over, "You and Mr. Dolph are already established. You've been in there developing the place for almost three years. People are more familiar with your name." He darted a sly glance at W.W.

W.W. played the game, "Do you have any other suggestions?"

Halstead appeared doubtful. He spoke hesitantly, "Well, I don't know. Maybe we could join forces?"

W.W. almost shook the man's hand, he was so relieved. Now was the time to get down to the real maneuvering. He hadn't invested three years of his life, money, and worry in Mt. Vernon, only to yield to someone else just because that person said he should. W.W. looked at Edward Dolph.

"Think we can work something out?"

Dolph replied, "I told Halstead here, that if the executors of the Hollenback estate were going to sell only to him, I'd be interested in working out a percentage basis with him."

W.W. faced Halstead, "That's how you want to do it?"

"Well, that's one way. Another way, we could go into it equal-like—each one take a third."

Gently, slowly, W.W. followed along the conversational path with Halstead, "Set ourselves up as a company with equal shares of stock? It would be possible to arrange a loan for the full amount, in the name of the company."

"Well, that's good. That's very good," Halstead looked as if he had had a sudden flash of inspiration, "Or maybe we could each put up a third. You know, that way, there wouldn't be any need to float a loan."

Edward Dolph's face expressed dismay, "Count me out if you go that way. I couldn't raise that much cash now without upsetting my other investments."

W.W. watched Halstead closely while Dolph was speaking. He did not expect to see concern or disappointment on Halstead's face, and he didn't. W.W. knew what was expected of him—not by Dolph, but by Halstead.

"I can help you out, Ed—temporarily—until you're more liquid with cash."

Edward Dolph demurred. He was embarrassed at W.W.'s generosity. But W.W. insisted; he would have it no other way.

Halstead seemed relaxed at the outcome, "I'll tell the heirs that we'll meet their price, and let you know when they'll settle."

As before, the three men were extremely cordial when they parted.

Later, W.W. told A.H., "Be patient, be patient. I think everything is going to work out beautifully."

A.H. couldn't see it at first, "How? We don't want Halstead as a partner, do we?"

"Don't worry. We won't have him when it comes time to settle."

"How can you be so sure?"

"Because he wants me to put up his share of the money for him."

A.H. was incredulous; he couldn't believe it.

"Oh yes," W.W. assured him, "He won't float a loan, because then he'd be liable and he'd have to pay interest. But this way, if he gets me to advance him his share out of my own pocket, he'll have no risk—only profit."

October 24, 1872 was finally named as the day for settlement. W.W. notified A.H. of the date, adding that he wanted to have a meeting with A.H. and George Filer on the following day. Everything developed just as W.W. had predicted. The day before settlement, on the twenty-third, Halstead confessed to W.W. that he was having trouble raising the necessary cash for his third. W.W. told him not to worry; he was already covering Dolph, and he could cover him as well. It was either that, or lose the good faith money that had already been put up, which was also W.W.'s. This arrangement now made W.W. the only one to actually hand over cash to the seller at the time of settlement. He insisted that his name be the only one on the receipted bill of sale.

"Just a precautionary measure," explained W.W., beaming at those present, "When we file the deed, we'll list everyone's name who's entitled to a share."

The great day had come at last. For three years, almost to the day, W.W. had courted the muse of good fortune; now, he was rewarded. It had taken three years of his life to do it, but he had accomplished what he had promised George Filer he would do. He had assembled 2,235 acres of first-quality coal land.

When W.W., A.H., and George Filer met the following day, W.W. announced that all was in readiness for reopening the coal mine.

"Start getting your supplies now, George," he instructed, "I'm going to give Halstead a little time to produce his portion of the money, but not too much time. He wanted to use my capital to make himself rich—and not pay a penny of interest in the bargain. But I don't want it to be said that I'm harsh or unjust. If he doesn't pay me back by the end of the year, he won't have a leg to stand on. I told him that the bank would lend him money; but no, he wanted it all for free. Edward Dolph said he couldn't do it, and didn't want the money when I offered. I insisted, because I knew what Halstead was after, and I wanted him to feel secure in his thinking that he would get what he was after."

As soon as he had finished with his speech, W.W. calmed down. The situation with Halstead had been rankling him all during the time the negotiations had been in progress. With his naturally open personality, it had been painfully hard for him to hold back on his thoughts. Finally free of restraints, W.W. unburdened himself. Once spoken out loud, his frustrations left him, and he got to work on the administrative problems connected with developing Mt. Vernon.

There was a lot to do; A.H. worked steadily until the end of the year. When Halstead still had not produced the money by that time, W.W. notified him, at the beginning of 1873, that he was out. To Edward Dolph, W.W. said that he was going to assume full ownership of the 400-acre tract himself, but if Edward ever did repay him, he would adjust profits accordingly.

The future of the little village at Mt. Vernon, and its abandoned coal mine, now lay totally in the hands of W.W. He called on A.H., and together the two of them created a new world for the dreamy, romantic, deserted spot along the Lackawanna River, twelve miles from Scranton.

First of all, Mt. Vernon ceased to exist. They renamed the little community *Winton*.

Second, they decided to separate ownership of the land from the operation of the coal mine. In keeping with his new policy of extending, or projecting himself through members of his family, W.W. brought in Thomas Livey, his daughter Elnorah's husband. A.H. set up the firm of Filer & Livey, coal operators. They were to lease the coal mine from W.W.

Thirdly, as the landowner, W.W. would have the right to lease or sell his land as he chose. This he did; the troublesome 165 acres were leased to the Delaware & Hudson Canal Company, neighbors on the west side. All the rest, he leased to Filer & Livey.

Fourth, they set about constructing fifty miners' houses at Winton for a start, to be leased with an option to buy. Concerning the income from the rents, they decided that the landlords should be everyone concerned: W.W. Winton, A.H. Winton, E. Dolph, George Filer, and Thomas Livey, jointly. Edward Dolph was included as a landlord because he had begun to repay W.W. the money advanced him for the purchase.

Suddenly all eyes, at least those of Scranton, Wilkes-Barre, Luzerne County, northeastern Pennsylvania, and that part of the world peopled by men interested in coal, were focused on the Wintons. Suddenly, everything they did was of importance. Before, they had been very, very rich. Now, suddenly, they were rich people who were very, very important. Wherever George Filer started to dig was news; not only was he digging in a community with a new owner and a new name, but he was also hiring 200 miners.

Suddenly, everyone wanted to meet the new owner of Winton. The Wintons, especially W.W. and A.H., turned their smiling faces to the floodlight that was publicity—and their public adored them. Enough kind words couldn't be said about them. They were courteous, they were of gentlemanly demeanor, they were intelligent, and they had brought prosperity to an impoverished community. In other words, they were universally liked.

As if all the activity and adulation weren't enough, W.W. convinced himself that his image should be that of a kindly, generous benefactor. He had A.H. dig out of his back files the plans they had made, almost seven years earlier, for a savings bank. A charter was quickly obtained from the state, and The Miners' Savings Bank and Trust Company of Providence, in Scranton's First Ward, was opened. W.W. selected one of the buildings that he had owned for some time. It fronted on the town square, dating from the time when Providence had been a township. Workmen were called in, and, while waiting for the charter to come from Harrisburg, the building was quickly remodeled into the savings bank office. The new bank brought to three the number of banks that W.W. controlled: the Second National Bank of Scranton; Winton, Clark & Company; and The Miners' Savings Bank and Trust Company of Providence. This list does not include The Scranton Trust Company and Savings Bank, because W.W., although on the board of directors, did not have control of it.

The miners and the farmers of the northern end of the valley were encouraged to save their money in Mr. Winton's new bank. He promised, and delivered, a generous rate of interest. The depositors responded, and flocked to W.W.'s new bank. They had great faith in W.W.; many knew him personally, others by reputation. It is interesting to see how W.W. was thinking, and what motivated him into opening the savings bank. The old heritage, passed to him from Henry Heermans, and from his association with other early settlers, that personal gain is unacceptable unless accompanied by service to the community, was too strong to be ignored. Finding himself at last in the other stratum of society in the Wyoming Valley, the layer consisting of people whose only interest was coal, and who had come to the valley only to take, W.W. still could not, and would not, adopt their attitude. The community and the people in it would always be his responsibility, just as every pioneer had a responsibility to his neighbors, for together making the place inhabitable. The Miners' Savings Bank was W.W.'s way of showing that he was not exploiting his neighbors who toiled and worked for him underground. It was his way of providing an opportunity to those lower down on the economic scale—a way by which they could move upward.

Suddenly, too, Winton was the most exciting community in the valley. The sleepy little village had become a hum of activity. Rumors were flying as fast as the carpenters' hammers which were creating the fifty new houses. One particular rumor caused some trouble, and things were pretty tense for a while. W.W.'s neighbor, on the southwest side, was the Delaware & Hudson Canal Company; W.W. was even leasing some land to them. They were mining part of the Wurts tract, which had been theirs since the 1820s; they had a proprietary interest in the area. W.W. had always been friendly with the officers of the D & H, and rumor had it that W.W. would be leasing all of his coal rights at Winton to them. The announcement that a new coal company, Filer & Livey, had been formed at Winton came as a shock.

There was another surprise yet in store for the D & H. Rumor again ran wild that Filer & Livey would be shipping their coal to market via the gravity railroad and the D & H Canal. But W.W. and his father Andrew Winton, on their original first visit to the Wyoming Valley many long years ago, had formed their own opinion of such a method of transportation. As George Filer was sending his first crew of miners in to open the mine, W.W., remembering his and his father's early opinion, closeted himself with the officials of the Delaware, Lackawanna & Western Railroad. In return for the right to carry all the coal from Winton, they agreed to build a spur, to be known as the Winton Branch of the Delaware, Lackawanna & Western Railroad. This branch was to run from Winton to Nay Aug on the southern outskirts of Scranton, where it would join the main line of the DL&W from Scranton to Hoboken, New Jersey. This decision was quite a blow to the D & H Canal; they felt that they had been insulted, although much more than that was involved.

The DL&W was only too glad to build the line into Winton. This was the time when railroads were the power ploy of the Wall Street financiers in New York. The financial men of this period dealt primarily in railroad issues. The railroads represented great wealth and power because they carried the coal out of the Wyoming Valley to the rest of the United States, and over to the big eastern seaports for shipment abroad. The DL&W alone had 13,000 coal cars! Some of the railroad's biggest profits came from getting coal from the mines of the Wyoming Valley to the mills and factories, where it was needed to power industrial machinery.

That W.W. and his father were correct in their original appraisal of the D & H Canal and its gravity railroad was obvious. From 1866 on, there were recurring suggestions from the public to drain the canal and install railroad track in its bed. In 1898, the D & H Canal Company closed down completely. However it had built a small length of regular railroad track in the valley, which finally replaced the gravity system in 1885. It is from this small piece of regular track, and from other additions that have survived to the present, that the D & H Company takes great pride today in being the oldest, continuously operating railroad company in the United States, counting from the year the canal was built.

Besides building the miners' houses at Winton, Filer & Livey needed its own buildings from which to conduct their business. The company office was the first to go up. Next came a company store, followed by a blacksmith's shop, quite a few sheds for storage, and other outbuildings. But the most important construction was the breaker; getting it built consumed the attention of everyone concerned.

The most tangible evidence of the existence of a coal mine, other than the large pile of culm (the inferior grade of anthracite, coal dust, slate, and general refuse from the mine), is the breaker. Considerable time and money ($60,000) went into the breaker at Winton.

From the time the miner goes into the tunnel until the coal is thrown on the fire, the coal has passed through quite a process. It is not a simple "one, two" operation. The miner's first task is to cut the coal from its matrix, the stone in which it is imbedded. Once this is done, he throws the large, irregular chunks of coal into an open (gondola) coal car. The filled car is run on track through the tunnel to the opening shaft, and is then hoisted to the surface. At Winton, two engines were installed for the hoisting. These engines are considered to be part of a breaker, although their only function is to lift the coal to the surface, and then hoist it to the top of the breaker proper.

Once it has been brought above ground, the task of preparing the coal for market is begun. The coal has to be broken up into the various sizes that are sold at market. After the coal has been lifted to the top of the breaker, it is dumped into a tip-house, where the lump-size coal is sifted out immediately and sent down a chute to a waiting railway car. This lump-size coal is used to power train engines.

The rest of the coal passes down another chute and into crackers or breakers, which are revolving iron rollers with projecting teeth capable of exerting enormous amounts of pressure. After going through this crushing process, the coal is sifted through screens of successively decreasing mesh size. All pieces of a given size are then conveyed into a trough, known as a telegraph, along which boys stand and pick out the slate and other impurities. From each telegraph, a chute carries the coal off to its proper size storage bin.

W.W., A.H., and George Filer had big ideas; fortunately, they had the money to back their ideas. And even more important, they were willing to actually spend that money to turn their ideas into reality. They ordered R. Godshall from

Scranton to come out to Winton and build them the finest breaker possible. This was no light task; the hardness of the anthracite coal required the use of more than average pressure, and the breaker itself needed correspondingly strong structural supports.

The enthusiasm of everyone at Winton inspired Godshall, and he constructed a model breaker for them. It was considered a model anthracite breaker in every particular; the most economical to operate, the largest in size, with the greatest capacity for passing coal through, and capable of crushing coal in the most rapid manner. To accomplish all this, the two forty-five horsepower hoisting engines were built by Wisner & Strong at Pittston and were designed on the new principle of a frictionless slide valve. The entire length of the breaker was 434 feet. It was 87 feet wide and rose up into the air to a height of just under 100 feet. The structural ironwork was supplied by the Dickson Manufacturing Company in Scranton. Another forty-five horsepower engine was installed to power the revolving iron rollers.

As soon as the breaker was finished and the railroad track laid, at a cost of $30,000 per mile, the coal started to pour out of Winton. W.W. then selected another site about a mile away, up Moosic Mountain and opposite his D & H neighbor. Here he built another, similar breaker, although not quite as large. All told, in the first two years of operation, 250,000 tons of coal were shipped out of Winton, at a price of approximately $2.00 per ton.

Needless to say, in all the excitement and hubbub, with all the trips to Winton, and the trips to Pittston to consult with Wisner & Strong on the engines and to check in at the Dickson Manufactory, Alice saw very little of A.H. On one of the occasional meals they ate together, she mentioned that her Uncle John Beaumont had been asked to return to active service in the Navy. He had been elevated to the rank of Commodore, and assigned to the *Powhatan*. But when she made reference to his command the next day, A.H. looked blankly at her. She decided to give up telling him anything.

As for A.H., other than asking Alice to write to Mr. Doyle at the Ocean House on Nantucket and reserve the same rooms for the same dates as the preceding year, and telling her that his friend Robert McKune had been elected president of the brand new Crystal Hose Fire Company, it must be confessed that he practically forgot that he had a home, wife, and child.

There was one thing, though, that did prove strong enough to draw his mind away from Winton, if only briefly. Wilkes-Barre, having been a city for a little over a year, was finally beginning to flex its muscles, strengthened by a change in the Pennsylvania Constitution. The trouble was that they were very powerful muscles, because Wilkes-Barre had the added authority of the county seat behind her.

Pennsylvania finally finished revising its Constitution in 1873; one of the revisions required that all judicial business be conducted at county seats. This new ruling aided Wilkes-Barre in its uphill progress for supremacy over Scranton, for the former was a county seat. The reason the Constitutional revision had such a devastating effect on Scranton was because it destroyed the

Mayor's Court. The lawyers at Scranton had found a way to handle their most immediate local problems under the aegis of their special Mayor's Court, granted to them in 1866 when Scranton had become a city. Now, the 1873 Constitutional Revision was to deny them this mode of adjudication, although it was not to go into effect for two years, at the end of 1875.

First, Providence and Hyde Park had lost their political identity. A.H. now wondered whether Scranton would somehow be going the same way? His uncle A.B. Dunning's acorn, that had grown into a sapling, made yet another spurt in growth, and was fast becoming a full-fledged oak tree.

Alice M. Collings
(1845 - 1913)

This picture shows Alice at age 18.

A. H. Winton
(1838 - 1896)

A. H. as he appeared ca. 1878.

William Wilander Winton
(1815 - 1894)
W. W. W. ca. 1874.

(opposite page)

Second National Bank of Scranton

Located at 234 Lackawanna Avenue, the building, Scranton's first skyscraper, was razed in 1977. The property later became part of The Mall at Steamtown, opening for business in 1994.

The Women of Andrew Beaumont's Family

Taken sometime after his death in 1853, his widow and daughters strike a formal pose. Julia Ann (Colt) Beaumont, seated center, is in her 60s; back row (from left) are daughters Julia, Hortense, who would die of tuberculosis in 1863, and Eleanor. Elizabeth and Sarah are beside their mother.

Lucinda (Yarrington) Colt
1765 - 1830

Arnold Colt
1760 - 1832

Julia Ann Colt, as a young lady
1794 - 1872

Andrew Beaumont
1791 - 1853

Hairdresser.
hair cutting
Pension

(above) ***Elsbeth Winton****, now a grown woman, had this 1904 formal portrait made in Paris as a Christmas present to send back to her Uncle Walter Winton.*

(left) The same ***Elsbeth*** *in 1881 at age three seated on her father's lap. The once ebullient* ***A. H. Winton*** *now reflects some of the stress of recent events in his face.*

(opposite page) ***Elsbeth****, with a friend, after a session with photographer Reutlinger at 21 Boulevard Montmartre, 2D Arrondisment, Paris, France.*

Louis S. Watres
1808 - 1882

Edward Dolph
1814 - 1890

Isaac Dean
1811 - 1902

Arthur D. Dean
1849 - 1926

Benjamin H. Throop, M.D.
1811 - 1897

George Filer
1821 - 1898

Edward Merrifield
1832 - 1918

Frederick W. Gunster
1845 - 1900

*Widow **Alice Collings Winton**, shortly before her death in 1913, continues alone with the traditions of her youth. Here, she is presiding at a late afternoon tea.*

13

The summer of 1873 at Nantucket was probably the best thing that could have happened to A.H. Although, to his way of thinking, it was an unnecessary interruption, and he would have gladly cancelled the vacation if he hadn't promised Alice and Kate. When he had told Alice that they would go, it had been only because his conscience had for once asserted itself. He knew that his absences from home had been difficult for Alice, and it was his way of showing how much he appreciated her cooperation and understanding—and lack of nagging. The energy he poured out on Winton and the Miners' Bank was a good thing for Alice to see. For she had, at last, first-hand knowledge of how A.H. could disappear into long periods of silence, such as those which had occurred when he had been coming to Wilkes-Barre courting her. She had always believed, at the time, that he loved her sufficiently that his lengthy absences could not be due to his paying attention to another young lady, but she had thought him neglectful and ill-mannered. Then, too, she had been very annoyed because she could not control him and make him a servant to her every whim. But now, seeing the enormous mountain of work that he accomplished in a few months, and his drive, she realized how great his ability was. For the first time in all the years she had known him, she truly stood in awe of him.

The interruption that was Nantucket was really more beneficial to A.H. than anyone else. He saw, when he returned to Scranton, how well he had oiled the machinery of his father's empire. Of all W.W.'s enterprises, every single one had managed to survive in his absence. Returning from Nantucket with a refreshed, detached perspective, he was quick enough to observe and wise enough not to tamper. He and his father had built a fast-paced, high-living existence, but for all this it was so prudently administered that the day-to-day mechanics were nothing more than dull routine.

W.W.'s final salute to the year 1873, just before it ended, was to put $10,000 into quarter ownership of The Bristol House on Abington Road.

Things were indeed running smoothly. The excitement surrounding the revitalization of Winton had died down. The employees at the banks knew their jobs and openly showed their respect for their boss, W.W. And A.H. relaxed enough to pay attention to his wife for at least five minutes every day before wandering off. His unofficial watchdog role with the Poor Board became official once again when he was elected a director.

The cold winter months of 1874 melted into the past with the coming of the spring thaw; A.H. smiled more and more. Looking ahead, he could contemplate a pleasurable life. He and Alice would be celebrating their ninth anniversary, and Katie her third birthday. When their anniversary day came, A.H. impulsively planned a special treat. Closing his office early, at noon, he stopped first to purchase a dozen oyster plates. Carrying the package of plates, he next stopped at Byron's wholesale grocery for a small basket of clams, a round of cheese, and bread. When he reached home, he entered by way of the kitchen door.

"Bridget," he called softly.

"Oh, Mr. Winton," and Bridget, who had been with them from their honeymoon days, jumped in surprise at A.H.'s strange mode of entering.

"The weather is so delightful outside that I want you to set a table on the porch, and we'll have a picnic lunch. All the food is here. Bring a bottle of champagne."

Bridget had already started to unwrap the plates, "Do you want me to serve the clams on these?"

A.H. nodded, "You come and tell me when you have everything fixed up."

He found Alice reading to Kate; "How are my two most favorite ladies?" he asked.

"A.H., I didn't expect you home so early. I'll tell Bridget to prepare something right away."

But A.H. stopped her, "No, let me sit here a while with you. We can't let our anniversary go by without relaxing a little. After all, it isn't often I get a chance to see what you two are up to during the day."

Sensing something between her mother and father, Kate climbed possessively into her father's lap. She felt that she was first in her father's affections, and she wanted to keep it that way.

It was a perfect afternoon. The surprise anniversary lunch had the whole house and its occupants glowing in love and contentment for the rest of the day. As A.H. and Alice were retiring for the night, he kissed her with the strength and fervor of a man who knows he's rich enough to have anything he wants, but who realizes the best things are what he already has.

The happy glow of their ninth wedding anniversary stayed with A.H. for two weeks, which is saying a great deal about a couple who had been married for nine years. It might have stayed with him even longer if he hadn't settled down to read his copy of the *Scranton News-Letter*, a weekly journal. An article, "A Few Facts About the Poor Board," caught his eye. He read it quickly, and then called for Alice.

"What do you know about this?"

She came over and stood beside him, looking down at the paper, "Know about what?"

He gave it to her to read. Afterwards, she looked at him exasperatingly, "Now really, A.H., what would I know?"

"I thought you might have heard someone talking. Whoever wrote this has made it his business to learn every detail."

A.H. had reason to be upset. It was an article, in questionable taste, attacking the honesty of the Wintons; this was something that had never happened to them before. Whoever had written it showed that he was familiar with the Poor Board. The author had been careful to quote the Poor Board's history and trace its progress, from when it had administered solely to the indigent of Providence township, to its larger role as the welfare agency for the city of Scranton. The article concluded with the comment: "The affairs of the Poor Board seem to have been managed with honesty and economy, but it is a striking illustration of our municipal looseness, that a board can go on levying taxes when we are not certain that the board is legal, because they have never been re-elected every three years as the law requires." A listing of the expenses by the board followed, taken from the auditor's report. Of the nineteen entries, twelve were for either a service performed by a Winton or by the Second National Bank. This included the $12,000 balance of the Poor Board on deposit at that bank.

The closing paragraph continued: "This satisfactory condition of the Providence Poor Board insures us, with the judicious appointments of late made by Judge Harding, that the dear people's money is all safe and in good hands, and the officers of the Second National Bank and all their connections provided for." For his final facetious thought, the writer suggested that taxes be increased to make room for families yet to come under care of the board, and for the erection of imposing monuments to those who have passed away.

A.H.'s first reaction was of hurt pride. Having watched over the Poor Board from its Providence bankruptcy days, he regarded the $12,000 deposit as a singular achievement. A.H. mentioned the article to W.W., who had seen it, and was as confused as he was. On A.H.'s next trip to Wilkes-Barre, he asked Judge Harding, in view of the fact that his name had been included, what he knew about the article. His mentor, under whom he had first practiced law, had some definite ideas on the subject; "I wouldn't pay any attention to it," said he.

A.H. accepted Judge Harding's advice, in that he didn't pay any more attention to the article; he shared Harding's opinion. He also did not let it worry him, but he did not dismiss it from his mind. Somebody was too keenly interested in the Wintons and what they were doing; A.H. wanted to know why. He was not surprised that his family had been put under a microscope for analysis of their activities. He knew enough of human nature to know that anyone who controlled large sums of money was subject to attack. But the way in which the article had been written seemed, to him, to be more an attempt to provoke those mentioned into an emotional outburst, hoping thereby to trigger some shameful disclosure.

"But what would be the purpose of that?" mused A.H., "To discredit the Wintons? If the Wintons were discredited, it wouldn't affect their coal mine at Winton. What would it do, then?"

"Ah!" suddenly said A.H., audibly, "it would break their hold on Scranton. Or it would give a bad odor to Scranton's ability to manage its own affairs."

He fell back to musing again. Providence had lost its sovereignty because it apparently couldn't manage its own affairs. A.H. recalled the Constitutional revision, and how it had abolished the Mayor's Court at Scranton. Judge Harding had probably been more right than he realized, when he had said something was afoot. But it would not be a repetition of the bankruptcy commission; this time, A.H. would be prepared.

As the year of 1874 moved along, it was generally conceded that the Wintons were the richest family in the Wyoming Valley. Philadelphia inadvertently acknowledged this in the *Biographical Encyclopedia of Pennsylvania*, which was published in that city. This book described W.W. as the "largest owner of coal lands" in the valley. The editor of the book, Howe, further complimented W.W. by including a full-page, steel-engraved portrait of him in the book.

There was one Winton, however, who had his own opinion of everything that was going on—and at the first opportunity expressed it.

While A.H. was at his office one warm day in September, Bridget burst in on him, greatly agitated.

"Oh, Mr. Winton," she sobbed, "Miss Alice said for you to come quick! Hurry!"

Her message delivered, Bridget disappeared as quickly as she had come, leaving behind a confused A.H. He ran down the street after her, as fast as he could. All he could think of was that something had happened to Kate. To his relief, so much so that he stumbled and almost fell prostrate at the door to his house, little Katie greeted him, popping up from behind the veranda railing.

"Daddy!" she called, "Why are you running?"

Once inside, he found Alice and his sister-in-law Ella, Walter's wife, in each other's arms, both sobbing and crying. This time, A.H. did collapse, prostrated, on the sofa. He was fond of Ella, but not to the extent that he would make a spectacle of himself tearing along Lackawanna and Wyoming Avenues.

"Thank God you've come! It's Walter!" Alice broke off her sobbing to greet A.H.

A.H. croaked for Bridget to bring him something stronger than water.

"Walter!" he roared, "What the hell has he done now?"

"Shhh!" hissed Alice, "Please, Ella is here."

Fortunately, Bridget placed a tray with a bottle and a glass on the table beside A.H. Having fortified himself, he repeated an edited version of his question, in a much calmer tone.

"Ella can't find him. He's disappeared!"

"Oh, my God," exclaimed A.H., and rested his head on his hands.

The two women had quieted down in order to watch the pyrotechnic display by A.H.

"Ella, what happened?"

"When I came back, he wasn't there."

A.H. started to roar again, "How can I make any sense out of 'I came back and he wasn't there'?"

Ella broke out into elephantine sobs, and Alice shushed him again. A.H. devoted the next few minutes to emptying the bottle.

"Alice, please," he said, "see if you can get Ella to make some sense, or, if you know what happened, tell me."

Alice had been comforting Ella, "Shall I tell him?"

Ella nodded, daubing at her reddened eyes.

"Ella left two weeks ago with the children to visit her father in Peekskill. That was the last time she saw Walter. He went with her to the station, saw that she and the children were comfortably aboard, waited until the train left, waved good-by to them, and that was it. When she got back today, he wasn't there to meet them. She had to hire a cab to take them home, and when she arrived, the house was empty. She sent one of the children over to the store, but they said that they hadn't seen Mr. Winton for two weeks, and had assumed that he had accompanied his wife to Peekskill at the last minute," Alice finished her story and closed her mouth.

A.H. thanked her, "Thank God, succinctly put."

A.H. was known as a gifted orator and brilliant speaker, but whenever he got around his brother Walter, his vocabulary tended to be lumped into one descriptive category and limited in quantity.

At last, he stood up, "Alice, see if you can get Ella to control herself. I'll take a look around town and try to find Walter."

It was almost the dinner hour before A.H. got back. His tread was slow and heavy as he entered the house. He was so mad at Walter that the shame of Walter did not disturb him. He remembered Alice's old ploy of serving tea. He called Bridget.

"Bridget, will you please see that we have tea in the parlor immediately? And, Bridget," he whispered, "put a little brandy in the tea, will you?"

While he had been out searching, Alice had brought Ella's children over to play with Kate, and had taken Ella upstairs to her sitting room to rest. On her way down to the kitchen, she saw A.H. for the first time.

"Were you able to find out anything?"

"Yes. Get Ella, please; I'll tell you then."

Simultaneously, Bridget, with the tea, and a calmer Ella joined A.H. and Alice in the parlor. A.H. described his search in detail, luring Ella into relaxation and a feeling of security by his ramblings. Once he was sure of his audience, he concluded his recital.

"I finally located the stationmaster who had been on duty the day you departed. He remembered that he had seen Walter, back at the station, boarding a train for Carbondale and Honesdale shortly after seeing you and the children off.

"I rode the train to Honesdale. Fortunately, the same stationmaster was on duty there as on the day Walter arrived. He remembered everything very well because of what happened. He remembered a flashily dressed young lady with a suitcase waiting on the train platform all morning, until a train from Wilkes-Barre came in and a young man got off and joined her. Together, they waited for the first train to New York, which they boarded together."

"Oh, no," said Alice.

Large tears rolled down Ella's face.

"Were you able to find out the name of the woman?"

"Yes. Walter ran off with a Lou Wright from Honesdale."

Ella and the children spent the night with A.H. and Alice. A.H. decided that he had done enough running around for one day, and delayed telling his parents about Walter until the morrow.

The following evening, the family convened at W.W.'s and Catherine's. What to do about Walter was the sole topic of conversation. The family closed in around Ella, protecting her. They were a moral family, and Walter's behavior was really quite foreign to their way of thinking. Ella herself was the one who finally decided what to do.

"I have the children to think of," she said, "If I go back to my father, they may wonder how their father, Walter, will ever find them. There's also the store to think of. If I work there, it will give me something to do."

A.H. was the most vociferous. He was all for Ella filing divorce papers immediately, he was so disgusted with his brother. But Walter had always mesmerized Ella, and the attachment was too strong to break just because he was absent. Like a great cow in the midst of a rich and fertile green pasture, Ella chose to ignore all that life could offer, and instead settled down and uncomplainingly waited to be claimed by her master. Ella knew the family would let her do as she pleased because she was always on sure ground when she spoke of the children; they were her most prized possession. For many years, they had been the only grandchildren in the Winton family, and the grandparents, W.W. and Catherine, had lavished attention on them.

The most amazing thing about Walter's departure was that no one was at all amazed. Once the surprising fact that Walter had indeed gone was established, life continued on exactly as it had before. This was true even in Ella's case. She and Walter had been growing further and further apart, for almost three years prior to his unsuspected departure. In those three years, Ella and the children had had to establish a schedule independent of Walter's presence. Now, knowing that he would not suddenly pop up to interrupt them, they were almost relieved. No one had been dependent on Walter; thus, his going created no gap in the world he left behind—a sorry comment on any individual's existence.

But, perhaps, one should not be too harsh in their criticism of Walter. Maybe in his own way, Walter was pointing out the future for all the Wintons to follow. Life is never static; it is ever moving, always in flux. W.W. and his whole family had been working actively, in order to move from a subordinate valley settler status to the heady life of the tycoon and industrial magnate. This, they had finally achieved with their banks, their coal mine, the town of Winton, their real-estate enterprises and their mercantile stores. Were life static, there would have been nothing more for them, except to collect income; for their every venture was income producing, and no physical work was required of them at all.

But life is not static. After a period of time—two years, five years, eight years—there is always a change in the relationship existing between an individual and the object, be it person or thing, of his interests. Thus the Winton family would have to make a change, or it would be made for them; they would have to move with the future.

They had one choice to follow, and a possible second one. In the industrial growth that followed the Civil War, a fairly well established pattern had emerged. Once one had amassed great wealth, it was the custom to delegate authority to an agent and the possessor of that new wealth to migrate to a highly sophisticated urban center, usually New York City. The criterion of how well such people established themselves in their new locale, was the success with which they simultaneously managed cultural endeavors and financial manipulations, the survivor surviving because he knew never to outweigh finance over culture.

In other words, W.W., once the mine at Winton was established, once the banks were dull routine, and once the real estate business consisted of only rental collections, should have placed his affairs in the hands of a trusted general agent, not a member of his family, and departed from the Wyoming Valley, the fountain of his wealth. He should have moved his whole family to New York, and, once there, should have built or remodeled a number of houses. He should have installed his family in their own individually built houses along Fifth Avenue, preferably in the forties or fifties. As for his empire, W.W. lacked only one thing—a railroad. From his new base of operation, New York, by draining his money from its source back in the valley, he would be expected to successfully raid rivals' stocks of goodies for whatever he was lacking, always mindful that every $1,000 gained by supplying demand should be counterbalanced by a $1,200 expenditure, at least, on something nonproductive. For that was the ultimate—to have nothing, and neither to desire nor to spend one's own money on anything but culture; to buy only from the arts.

Unfortunately, that which was expected of W.W. had already been sampled by him and his family. They had been to New York; they had gotten rich while there. And in spite of all that, they had longed for their home, the Wyoming Valley.

The possible second choice open to W.W. would have been to invest himself with all the trappings of the *grande mysterieuse*—to remove himself and his family to a remote, but most beautiful, section of the valley, and erect a compound or living quarters, resembling an imaginary citadel at the top of Jack's Beanstalk, a marvel to endure forever, to say, "Here I am in a world apart, that only I may enter."

Well, by some strange quirk, or maybe because of that one facet in his personality—that facet universally common to mountain people, that facet that makes mountain people appear soft at the core—W.W. could not follow the second choice the world would expect of him, either. The Wintons loved their valley, the surrounding mountains, and their neighbors too much to draw apart and say, "Hey, everybody, look at me."

But life doesn't stand still; W.W. and his family had to move on. Perhaps Walter, in his own way a timeless philosopher, had been trying to say, "Come on, follow me from the valley out into the world. We don't have to play the game in New York; we can go anywhere." Edward Dolph had solved the same problem in his own way. He had also been saying, "Come follow me, my way"—meaning: how you do it is all important, not what you do. But W.W. was still too sharp a business man; he wasn't interested in investing his money in silver mines in Wisconsin, or logging and coal mining in Virginia. In his heart and his head, he belonged to the Wyoming Valley. To him, Edward Dolph had become a receptacle for money to change hands, money coming into the valley from coal and flowing out, through Dolph, to Virginia or Wisconsin or wherever would next excite his fancy.

Noteworthy is the fact that there was no interest in oil at this time. The first oil well, about two hundred and fifty direct-line miles west of the Wyoming Valley, and at approximately the same latitude, had been brought in fifteen years earlier at Titusville, Pennsylvania. And, as in the early days when only the blacksmith had known what to do with the anthracite coal, the only use for the oil was as fuel for illumination in kerosene lamps. It wasn't until the development of the gasoline engine and the automobile that oil took on deeper significance. Coal, as King of Energy, was to reign for another forty-four years until 1918, when a peak 177 million tons would be mined in the state of Pennsylvania alone.

Thus, none of the actions that were expected of W.W., in his new position of ceaseless wealth, appealed to him. He was not interested in changing his place of residence, and he wasn't interested in investing his money outside the valley. As he had told Isaac Dean and Edmund Heermans earlier on his return from New York, he was in a superior position because he was bringing new capital into the valley: he was not recirculating money already in the valley, and he definitely did not want to take money away from the valley.

Time would have to march on, though; it could not stand still. The Wintons, with all their wealth, or because of all their wealth, would have to have a purpose to living. Their basic aim, to feed and clothe themselves as comfortably as possible, was a problem of the past. A new goal would have to be found.

But before W.W. had found his adjusted *raison d'être*, the First National Bank of Carbondale, at the upper end of the valley, was robbed. And before the bank was robbed, the County Democrats held their nominating meeting in Scranton.

The County Democratic Committee's decision, to conduct their nominations at Scranton in September, 1874, did not concern A.H. Other than a busybody's curiosity concerning what was going on in his own bailiwick, A.H. would normally have paid no attention to the meeting at all. However, John B. Collings, the same John Collings who had accompanied his uncle to Russia, was A.H.'s brother-in-law and a Democrat, the latter affiliation inherited from his grandfather, Andrew Beaumont. Hearing that John was coming to Scranton, Alice invited her brother to stay with her and A.H. on Wyoming Avenue. John gladly accepted, and by his acceptance A.H. obtained an unexpected direct-line communication into the meeting. And what a meeting it turned out to be! Scranton air was apparently too heady for some of the Wilkes-Barre contingent, and, after a portion of the slate had been nominated for the November general election, a great fight broke out. A large group withdrew and returned to Wilkes-Barre; those who remained continued with the agenda before the meeting. John Collings was given the nod for county District Attorney, and Byron Winton's father-in-law Daniel Silkman was listed on the slate for county Sheriff.

Meanwhile, those who had gone back to Wilkes-Barre, also calling themselves the County Democratic Committee, convened themselves and nominated their own version of the Democratic ticket for the fall election. Thanks to his house guest, A.H. had a fascinating ringside description of all that went on. Afterwards, he told Alice that he would have to vote Democratic, since two members of his family were on the ticket. He helped John Collings campaign, and offered similar services to Daniel Silkman, but Byron sent word back that his father-in-law had decided to withdraw in favor of a Penn Kirkendall listed on Wilkes-Barre's version of the ticket.

This was the first time John Collings and A.H. worked together, although John had been a practicing lawyer in Wilkes-Barre for four years. The experience was so mutually satisfying that John announced he would like to join A.H. and move his law office to Scranton. This was a big change for him to make. By having his office in Scranton, John was essentially severing all connections with Wilkes-Barre, the town his grandfather Andrew Beaumont had been so devoted to. A.H. couldn't have been more pleased with John's decision. Frank Collins's peripatetic visits back to Scranton on legislative holidays had been too infrequent to enliven A.H.'s work hours. It was decided that definitely, win or lose, John Collings would join his brother-in-law after the election. John did lose to his competitor, a Mr. Farnham on the Wilkes-Barre version of the Democratic ticket. True to his word, though, John moved to Scranton and joined A.H., sharing his office and his home. Now there were two lawyers in the family, both practicing in Scranton.

After John arrived, things started to liven up. Whether action just naturally followed John Collings, or whether having some one in the office with him inspired A.H., one will never know. But after John's arrival, like Pandora's box, the forces of destiny swirled into a storm. On the Fourteenth of January in the following year, 1875, the First National Bank of Carbondale was robbed, as was noted above.

W.W. heard about the robbery, and the missing $7,000, within minutes after the wire came into the Western Union office in its rented basement location in the Second National Bank building. W.W. sent for A.H. immediately. Mr. H.S. Pierce, the bank's president, was a friend of the Wintons; A.H.'s first line of references on his business card named the First National Bank of Carbondale. An added motivation was the agreement between banks to help each other in time of emergencies. The federal government was also notified, it being one of their own banks that had been robbed. It, in turn, called on Robert A. Pinkerton, superintendent of the Pinkerton National Detective Agency, the detective agency started by his father. The Pinkertons had been handling much of the federal government's detective work. They had successfully forwarded information from behind the Confederate lines to the North during the Civil War. And six years earlier, the agency had begun to gather information about the Molly Maguires, a secret organization of oppressed Irish coal miners. The Molly Maguires were very active in Schuylkill County, Pennsylvania, at Mahanoy City and Mauch Chunk (now Jim Thorpe), coal-mining towns outside the Wyoming Valley and fifty miles due south on the Lehigh River.

Within hours, Superintendent Robert Pinkerton was in Carbondale and was introduced to A.H., who had come up from Scranton. The Pinkertons were scattered throughout the anthracite coal region because of their infiltration into the Molly Maguires. They viewed the wreckage and listened to James Stott, the bank's cashier. Mr. Stott described how he had been beaten and locked up by the thieves. Afterwards, the bank was searched for clues. It was A.H. who noticed a piece of unopened mail lying at the back of a counter. The letter was addressed to Mr. Stott. A.H. opened it:

Jan. 7, 1875

Mr. Stott,

Do not remain alone in the Bank while your assistants are at dinner. Keep this secret. There is danger hanging over you.

A friend

A.H. gave a great shout, "Look what we have here!"

Robert Pinkerton came over to A.H., and examined the letter and envelope closely. He called attention to the local Carbondale postmark and the proper form of the letter; the latter indicated that the writer had some education and was accustomed to composing letters.

With this lead, the robbers were apprehended just four days short of a month from the time they had taken the money. At the hearing, A.H. was counsel for the prosecution; that is, he represented the bank's interests. Edward Merrifield, a friend of A.H.'s, the son of another very early settler, represented the defendants. And when the hearing before Alderman Fuller was carried over to a second day, John Collings substituted for A.H.

The testimony and identification by Mr. Stott convicted the men, and they were sent to the county jail at Wilkes-Barre. The case had excited a great deal of interest among the valley residents because the testimony had brought out how the robbery had been hatched at a graveyard site, planned for the cold of winter when very few people would be about, and staged in broad daylight, at high noon, by thieves who were neighbors in the Wyoming Valley.

All through the spring months, after the capture of the thieves, A.H. basked in the celebrity's spotlight. Not only were the Wintons rich and important, but they were also famous, for one of them had helped the Pinkertons solve a case.

Before Robert Pinkerton left town, W.W. and A.H. asked for his help in trying to locate Walter Winton. No one had heard from him, and if it hadn't been for the station master at Honesdale remembering a man and a woman boarding a train for New York, no one would have had even the slightest idea where he might have gone.

Walter's restlessness had affected the family, and Alice was the first to react. Their financial worries were gone, her husband a celebrity; she felt the need to broaden her horizon. Eugene Heermans's return reinforced her feelings. His years of study at Bellevue Medical College and Hospital in New York City were over, and he and his wife Sarah had come back to Scranton. He was going to open his medical office at 10th and Scranton Avenue.

All the family gathered to welcome the new doctor home. He was the first M.D. in the large Heermans clan. They had lawyers—A.H., A.B. Dunning, and soon Arthur Dean—but no doctors. Eugene was Edmund's son, and the grandson of Mary Fellows Heermans and Philip Heermans. His other grandfather was Benjamine Slocum. A.H. had a soft spot for his cousin Eugene and his wife Sarah, because he remembered how he had counted on their wedding to bring Alice back to him from Wilkes-Barre.

At the family gathering, Alice was enchanted with the sophistication of Dr. and Mrs. Heermans. Their polished New York mannerisms seemed to be just the thing that she and A.H. lacked. A fleeting thought went across her mind: perhaps they should spend more time in New York. Another Heermans was at the party, too. This Henry Heermans, a younger edition of the original Henry Heermans, was also back from school, on summer vacation from Wesleyan University in Connecticut. Henry was very busy at the family gathering, promoting his college's participation in the intercollegiate races at Saratoga, New York, in July; he was representing Wesleyan on the Rowing Regatta Committee. Still admiring the New Yorkisms of Eugene and Sarah, Alice fell prey to Henry's suggestions.

"Cousin Alice," he said, "you'd like to come to Saratoga, wouldn't you? I can make all the arrangements for your stay, and get you the best seats at the crew races. Please say yes."

Alice wouldn't give him an answer one way or the other, but afterwards she told A.H. Saratoga was the queen of summer resorts, where the rich played all day and all night. It sparkled alluringly to Alice and A.H. in their new position of wealth, beckoning them. A.H. wondered about Nantucket, but Alice had an answer for that, too: the rowing regatta was in the middle of July, and they could go to Nantucket afterwards.

When they arrived in Saratoga, the famous spa was at its height. It was the second season for the Intercollegiate Racing Regatta, which almost rivaled the race track for betting and excitement. Henry had reserved rooms for them at the United States Hotel, still sparkling new from its reopening the year before; it had lain in ashes from a disastrous fire for almost nine years. A.H. and Alice arrived by train. They watched the intercollegiate sculling races on Saratoga Lake on July 13 and 14; they found time to rock in the rocking chairs on the piazza of the United States Hotel; they watched for a while the parade of carriages and people up and down Broadway; and they danced at the Regatta Ball in the ballroom of the United States Hotel on the evening of July 14. But on the morning of July 15,

A.H. and Alice thanked Henry for his considerate attentions to them while he had been so busy with committee arrangements, and departed Saratoga forever. They went back to Scranton and picked up Katie, and reached Nantucket a week before they were expected.

What was wrong? If anyone had a right to partake of Saratoga life, A.H. and Alice certainly did. They were wealthy, they were young, and Alice had the added refinement of a diplomatic background. It wasn't that they felt that they didn't belong; it was that they didn't want to belong. They loved the excitement, the flamboyant life style at Saratoga, but they had trees, mountains and lakes all year round in Scranton. They wanted something different; the expanse of the ocean, the inrushing waves, were a treat to them. They wanted something different for their vacation, not more of what they had already, even though it was on a scale so grand as to be almost unimaginable. Alice and A.H.'s first tentative step, then, to find another life style, came to a sudden stop. The cosmopolitan airs of Eugene and Sarah Heermans suddenly lost their magic. Alice and A.H. joined W.W. in their thinking; their energies would have to find another outlet, a new *raison d'être*, a new purpose for living, but it would be in the Wyoming Valley.

When A.H., Alice, and Kate came back from Nantucket, it was September. Fall was upon them, with all the activity that return from vacation time entails. It was time for A.H. to consider the fall and winter court schedule. Suddenly, he faced reality; the Mayor's Court would shortly be a thing of the past.

Pennsylvanians had long felt the need for reform in their state. In the general election of 1872, they gave authority for a revision of the State Constitution. One hundred thirty-two delegates, including A.B. Dunning, began the task at Harrisburg, the state capital, immediately after November 12, 1872. The most objectionable section of the existing constitution was the part that allowed for the enactment of special legislation. In practice, this had come to mean that almost any individual with enough influence or money or both could enact a law applicable only to where he lived. Rightly so, the main task of the constitutional convention was to do away with this special power of the legislature. In its place, the legislature would still be allowed to pass laws, only now the laws must apply universally, throughout all of Pennsylvania.

Before the revision was finished, the delegates moved their place of meeting from Harrisburg, the state capital, to Philadelphia, the state's largest city. In 1873, the following year, they completed their task. But man is very ingenious. Blocked from getting special legislation, he realized that he could word general bills so that they applied to only one specific situation. One such change, included into the constitutional revision, worked for the benefit of Wilkes-Barre and to the detriment of Scranton. It required that all judicial decisions, in order to be binding, must be determined at courthouses presided over by state or federal judges. Since all the courthouses were located at county seats, this invalidated any kind of courtroom held elsewhere. Unfortunately, Scranton's Mayor's Court turned out to be the only one affected.

The Mayor's Court could be considered to be one of the few remaining vestiges of the feudal system. It derived its power from the fact that a feudal lord of a manor, and similarly the mayor of a city, had the right to hear testimony and sit in judgment over those people belonging to his estate. Like the captain of a ship, who can perform valid marriages at sea, the mayor had the power to adjudicate within his district. Those members of the Luzerne County Bar who had their law offices in Scranton had been quick to make use of the mayor's special powers. From their point of view, it was a practical expedient; it saved considerable traveling expenses that would normally be incurred by all parties concerned, as well as the time that would be needed for one or more round trips to the county seat at Wilkes-Barre, especially on cases of relatively minor importance involving only Scranton residents.

The Mayor's Court had also been promised to those men who had voted for Scranton city status.

One of the lawyers most affected by the abolition of the Mayor's Court was A.H.; this was because of the nature of his practice. He worked with and for the people who were his neighbors. Boundary line disputes, imagined slanderous insults between friends, administration of decedents' estates, and collecting unpaid bills were his daily fare, and for these services his fees were modest. For the other part of his legal work, handling his father's affairs, the Mayor's Court was of no value anyway. For these he needed the services available at the county seat: the examination of deeds, the researching of titles, the mine inspectors' reports, etc. For this work A.H. was accustomed to going to the courthouse at Wilkes-Barre, but it had usually been at his own convenience. He contemplated his own list of cases for the fall session, and realized that after the Mayor's Court was disbanded, which it would be by law at the end of 1875, he would have to be in Wilkes-Barre all day, every single day court was in session. He was highly annoyed that he was going to be so inconvenienced.

John Collings didn't help matters either, "What are you going to do about your daily list?" he wanted to know.

He was referring to a daily listing of creditors' suits that A.H. published for the Scranton Board of Credit. The paper was nothing more than a list, of sheriff's sales in the upper end of the county, and of creditors who were pressing for their unpaid bills through the court each day. It was distributed among the merchants of Scranton, and served the purpose of alerting them as to who was running up impossible credit balances.

A.H. stared stonily back at his brother-in-law. He had no answer for his question at the moment.

John continued to ramble, "I don't know; maybe I ought to move back to Wilkes-Barre next year. We could divide up, and you could mail me instructions once a week or something like that."

A.H. hated to be discommoded. Writing weekly reports would be almost as odious as riding the train back and forth.

It was near election time, and Frank Collins stopped in. A.H. and John welcomed the return of the stranger. They discussed their problem with him, and asked him for a suggestion.

"I wish I could help you out. But I can't say that I agree with you. It's better to have the courts centralized."

The others allowed as how they would agree to the superiority of one permanent location, but that was all. Scranton was too big a city to be without a court.

"We're too big here in Scranton, and there's too much going on," complained A.H.

"I wish I could help you."

A.H. quickly bantered back, "Hope you remember your offer, Frank, when we come to you for help."

"I mean it, A.H. Wait 'til the time; you'll see."

A.H. carried the confusion of his thoughts home with him. As the Christmas season approached, Alice noticed that, before going to bed, he took to sitting for some time in the overstuffed lounge chair in the far corner of their bedroom. At first, she thought it was because he wanted to be entertained. While brushing her hair, she related, in minute detail, the activities of her day. A.H. watched the motion of her arm as she moved the brush back and forth, but obviously wasn't the least bit interested in what she was saying.

Finally, she turned to him one evening and asked, "What's disturbing you?"

"I'm going to have to go to Wilkes-Barre every time I have a case to be heard."

"Is that so terrible? You've been so glum this past week. I don't understand; you go to Wilkes-Barre all the time."

"Yes, but now I'll have to go every day, for the whole day, whenever court is in session."

"Oh, no wonder you're upset."

"I don't know, Alice. I get the feeling we're slowly being strangled here at this end of the valley."

"Isn't there anything you can do about it?"

"So far, I haven't thought of a thing."

A.H. fell silent. This time, Alice refrained from her idle chatter of previous evenings. She moved from the bench where she had been brushing her hair, and went over to the bed. She lounged across it at the end, waiting encouragingly for her husband to continue.

"It doesn't seem right to me. We're too big here—the iron works, the mills, the coal mines. We carry four newspapers. The largest individual tax assessments are at this end of the valley. I ought to know. Filer & Livey is one of them. Why must we now go so far to run our affairs? We don't know what's going on in Wilkes-Barre now; how is it going to be any different, once they start handling all our business as well?"

A.H. shrugged his shoulders, as if somehow by the gesture he could as easily dismiss the weight of his problem. He rose and came over to Alice, and pulled her under the covers.

"I think I'll put you in charge of the Solution Committee," he teased.

After that, it became a nightly ritual: A.H. ruminating from the chair, Alice listening, stretched out across the bed. If the truth were known, she became a little bored after a while. A.H. seemed to say the same thing over and over again. She had the feeling that he was going to rebel; but he never did.

At Christmas time, Alice received word from her sister Mary Collings Dillinger in Allentown that her husband was going to retire as prothonotary of Lehigh County. A.H. received an invitation to attend a farewell dinner that Jacob Dillinger was giving for members of the Lehigh County Bar. There was much discussion at the Winton house, but it was finally decided that they would all go down to Allentown on the twenty-ninth of December; the party was scheduled for the evening of January 1, 1876.

The merry party that rode the train included Alice and A.H., John Collings and Frank Collins. When they reached Allentown, there was quite a reunion, for Elizabeth Beaumont Collings was also there, helping her Dillinger grandchildren celebrate Christmas.

Almost every member of the Lehigh County Bar was expected at the dinner. Preparations began as soon as the new arrivals unpacked. Everyone took time off to welcome the new year, and then it was back to work. A.H. and Alice volunteered to arrange the buffet table on the day of the affair. They created a towering centerpiece of fresh fruit, and spread the serving dishes around it, as if composing a poem. A.H. insisted that everything be just so; he was a little apprehensive, afraid that the tension among the judges and lawyers would sour the festivities. Good food tastefully displayed, he knew, would make for a more congenial atmosphere.

At the dinner itself, the three Scranton lawyers insisted that they be seated unobtrusively at the end of the table. Other than Jacob Dillinger, their host, they knew very few of the attendees, and expected to be more observers than participants in the evening's activities. It wasn't long before the wine and the genial camaraderie of the guests awoke A.H. to a very interesting fact, one which he communicated to both John Collings and Frank Collins.

"How different this party would be, if it were being held in Luzerne County!"

Frank had noticed it too, "I keep waiting for the other faction to arrive."

For the rest of the evening, A.H. was quieter than he usually was at such affairs. Mentally, he formed a table of comparisons between the attitudes of the county bar of which he was a member and the one to which his brother-in-law belonged. He discussed some of his thoughts with Alice after the evening had come to an end and they were alone.

"There was no group sitting on one side watching the group on the other side. Just think, how much more could be accomplished in an air of cooperation, where everyone has respect for each other."

Alice wasn't sure that she understood his meaning, and said so.

"Jacob thanked the lawyers of the county for having never given him any trouble when he was scheduling cases. Can you imagine that happening in Luzerne? All the members of the bar here said that, if they thought he would reconsider, they would arrange for him to return to the prothonotary's office immediately; they hated to lose him. Can you imagine the Luzerne Bar speaking that way about their prothonotary? Almost every judge and lawyer in the county was here tonight; only five or so couldn't make it. Can you imagine a gathering in Luzerne, with similar attendance?" Clearly, A.H. had a lot to think about.

14

The year was now 1876. A.H. knew this well; he had just helped usher it in with a gala party in Allentown. Centennial year—the United States of America was 100 years old. The great centennial celebration would soon (in April) be opening in Philadelphia. But for some of the citizens of the hundred-year-old country, it was not a happy year. The economy had been sagging for almost three years; coal was bringing $1.70 instead of $2.00 or $2.25 a ton, and bankruptcy lists were growing longer.

Jacob Dillinger's farewell party should have been a little note of brightness within his circle of friends. But its effect on A.H. was to make him more gloomy than before, as he compared his lot in Luzeme County with that of his fellow lawyers in Lehigh County. Adding to his gloom was the fact that he was finally boarding the train for his daily ride to Wilkes-Barre and the courthouse. Now was the time—he finally erupted into action, for he had come to a decision at last.

He inserted an ad in the Scranton newspapers on the tenth of January:

> Notice is hereby Given that application will be made to the present session of the Legislature of Pennsylvania for the passage of an act, entitled, "An act to provide for holding session and providing, for the records of the courts of Quarter Session, Oyer and Terminer, Common Pleas and Orphans' Court, of the county of Luzerne, at the city of Scranton, and authorizing the County Commissioners to build a Court House and Jail thereat, the object of which being shown in said title
>
> A.H. Winton and others,
>
> Scranton, Jan. 10, 1876

For A.H., the wealth of the Wintons was as nothing, compared to the indignities of his surroundings. He lived on "black diamonds," and, while he did not expect to find a flawless one, he nevertheless wanted one that was first quality, not second-rate. If he had his way, the place where he lived was going to come as close to first quality as he could make it. The Wintons now had their *raison d'être.*

His notice was greeted by shocked surprise on all sides.

Silence. Silence for two days.

On the Thursday morning following the publication of his notice, as if by prearranged signal, everyone descended on A.H. in his office. W.W. was there; Isaac Dean, Edmund Heermans, Dr. Eugene Heermans, John Collings, and even A.B. Dunning had come in.

"What do you think you're doing?" they all shouted, almost simultaneously, at A.H.

A.H. would not be ruffled.

"Father, please," he appealed to W.W. first. One by one, he addressed each by name.

"It's perfectly obvious what I have in mind. Without a judge or a court, we are a judicial and political nonentity! For too many years, we have been the recipients of tyranny, by the other end of the county. Our men are very rarely elected to office. How many judges at Wilkes-Barre have lived their early lives north of Pittston? Every time we want redress, we might as well travel to Washington; we would know just about as much about what is going on. Since '72, our taxes have increased $30,000; yet who determines where the money is to be spent? Who collects the money and holds it on deposit for payment of bills? But it's our money that they've collected, because we're the ones paying the taxes. Do we ever get an accounting? The tax rolls show who has the ear of the assessor. Companies who do three and four times the business of others are rated only one class greater. To paraphrase an early patriot, in this our centennial year we have no representation, no consideration, and plenty of taxation."

The four older men and the two younger ones recognized the seriousness and strength of A.H.'s resolve to remedy the situation that Scranton, as a city, was drifting into. A.B. Dunning was the first to speak.

"I agree with everything you say, A.H. But I don't think that this is the way to go about it. You're right; but bringing in just a courthouse will not accomplish what you want."

"What will?" A.H. was belligerent.

"A new county. You'll have to push for a new county."

"Yes, yes," the others chorused, "that's what you want."

"A new county?" A..H. sat down abruptly, in his chair behind his desk. Momentarily off balance, he tried to reorganize his thinking along the path that those facing him were so encouragingly directing him to follow. The older generation, that of his father, pressed in on him. A.H. was the flag unfurled. the standard round which to rally. They were anxious to hoist their human banner and march to victory.

Years of inactive retirement fell from A.B. Dunning; he was once again his district's representative in Harrisburg. He had advocated a separation of counties even then. Now, he was passing his charge on to one who smelled of success, "It is the only way, A.H. For years, some of us have known that we should break away. I myself tried to form a new county for us, but the state senate beat me back. Times have changed since then. In those days, we knew it should be done; we knew that it would have to be done, sometime. Then, we were trying to plan for the future. But now, the future is upon us. Now, it is a matter of necessity. I promise you that you'll get the support of the people. The voters will be behind you."

"I don't know," answered A.H., subdued. Then he added, "I wasn't planning to go that far."

"Think about it, A.H." interjected W.W., "You've come this far. You've already admitted the need for action, by your request for a courthouse. But just a courthouse is a lukewarm remedy. You know how easily lukewarm water can turn cold. With the same amount of effort, we can break free. I'm behind you."

Shortly afterwards, the meeting disbanded. All these men were master gamesters. Just because they were plying their wiles on one of their own, they could not risk being any less cautious. They were quick to recognize the signs that they had their customer almost sold.

After they departed, A.H. went down to Wilkes-Barre for the afternoon. He poked and peered through the routine of the court and county schedules. The temptation to have the same thing going on in Scranton, by right, was tantalizing. He held back from making a commitment, though; he was still very uncertain. When he had told his relatives earlier that he hadn't planned to go so far as to completely sever from Luzerne County, he had implied all his reservations; he was not agitating for the sake of making trouble, and he did not want to take maximum measures if minimum ones would do.

It was late, past the supper hour, when he got back home. Indecision had made him irritable, tired, and cold. Alice had heard about the morning meeting in his office from her brother John; she saw that A.H. had some food, and then left him, going to take care of Katie. She was coming from the nightly bedtime ritual with their daughter, when she heard a noise in their bedroom. Peering in, she saw that A.H. had pulled the lounge chair over in front of the fireplace. He was sunk deep in the cushions, the fire poker in one hand and a mug of hot rum in the other. He was staring intently at the blazing coals.

"Are you going to bed now?" she called from the doorway.

It was sometime before A.H. answered her, "Soon."

"Yes, I think I'll retire early, too," Alice bustled off to inform the rest of the household that she wouldn't be staying up. When she came back, A.H. was just as she had observed him earlier. Quietly, without disturbing him, she prepared for bed.

"John tells me that you had quite a session with your father and uncles today."

"I don't know what to do, Alice. They seem to think that nothing will be satisfactory, unless we break off from Wilkes-Barre. I hate to start a fight when there isn't one," A.H. paused, "The situation is getting more intolerable, though, every year," pausing again, "I just don't know what to do."

The only light in the room was from the warming fire burning on its grate. Alice had stretched herself out on the bed on her back, looking up at the movement of shadows on the ceiling.

"I remember," she said, "you once told me, a long time ago, when we were first thinking about getting married, that if I didn't respect you, our union would destroy us both. Do you think Wilkes-Barre respects Scranton for what she is?

"It seems to me, that when a couple cannot abide each other, they're better off divorced. Isn't that what you yourself have often said?"

A.H. didn't answer her, but he did pull himself forward, to the edge of the chair. For a minute or two, he poked the fire. Then he rose, came over to the bed, and looked down at Alice.

"Oh, Alice," he said, "you are my love." His voice was soft and relaxed. His burden had been cast off. Now, the future beckoned invitingly. "You have arranged all my ethics and values into one neat little pile. With a few words, you have cleansed me of any stain of ulterior motives, of covetousness. You have shown me, oh ever so clearly, my duty." A spark flashed in his eyes. "Do you think there will be any objection if I propose you for the new county's first judge?"

Then he fell on her, almost as if she were a goddess. This time, he loved her as if he worshipped her. And as if the love that he poured out to her was the greatest single offering that he had to give.

The morning light was only hazy shadows when he arose. His mind, clear at last, now faced the task of accomplishing what had to be done. Once started, he was not going to turn back. His great mind went to work immediately. The force and energy that he had expended in setting up Winton was like an exercise, compared to his intensity and concentration now. But then his task was more difficult, now. When he had composed his request for the erection of a courthouse at Scranton, he had been petitioning the state legislature for a special variance to an existing law. His task now was to prepare a request for the enactment of a general law under which Scranton would qualify. Instead of creating an exception to a law, he had to create the law itself. And so, finally, the little acorn of many years ago was stretching its branches into a mighty oak.

On that first morning of his commitment to a new county for the upper end of the Wyoming Valley, he worked quickly and easily. His first thoughts flowed onto the paper, without need of correction. What he proposed was to have a large number of voters who lived in the area within the proposed county's boundaries petition the state to erect a new county because it would be to their best interests, and also for the convenience of the petitioners. Neither the Luzerne-to-be nor the new county was to be less than 400 square miles in size nor have less than 20,000 inhabitants, and the boundary line dividing Luzerne into two counties would be more than ten miles from the county seat at Wilkes-Barre. This part, A.H. wrote quickly. For his first rough draft, he had inserted the name Luzerne in specifically, because it freed his mind from the all-comprehensive legal phraseology of "whits, wherefores, and said parties, etc." When he read back to himself out loud what he had written, substituting "the original county" for "Luzerne," he saw that it would meet the requirement of a general bill, and was satisfied.

Most of his time he spent poring over a map of the valley. What he wanted to do was to divide the existing Luzerne County neatly in half. He finally decided that to draw the boundary line just above Pittston would meet all the requirements. A.H. was now ready to leave for Harrisburg.

But before he could go, he had to attend a meeting of the directors of the Providence Poor Board, and see John Collings elected counsel for the board. He also had to congratulate his mother Catherine Winton on her election as president of The Home of the Friendless, basically Scranton's orphanage. But most importantly, he had to have a meeting with his father, Isaac Dean, and A.B. Dunning.

He read them the bill as he had written it. When he had finished reading, he said, "I'm ready to leave for Harrisburg. If the legislature approves, then we'll be able to go out and get the voters' signatures. But we can't do it alone. Do you think we'll get any help?"

W.W. was enthusiastic, "I'm sure we'll have plenty of people behind us. This is also the time, I think, to get an answer to that question you raised a while back."

"About Scranton City?"

"Yes: whether the Scrantons and Throop were fooled the same way we were when we merged Hyde Park and Providence into the city. If they were, they're going to want to push this thing through as much as we do."

A.B. Dunning had his thought to add, "You're well acquainted with Edward Merrifield, aren't you, A.H.? Speak to him. I'm sure he'll want to be in the vanguard of our effort."

"Why Edward Merrifield? Because he's a lawyer?"

"No, because I don't think his father is well enough to carry the fight. I hear he's quite ill."

"I'm sorry, Uncle Abram, but I don't understand why you're so insistent about the Merrifields."

"When William Merrifield was in Harrisburg in '46, he put up quite a defense to save us, that is the anthracite coal regions, from extra heavy taxation. He brought the Scrantons in when he sold them his ground for their ironworks. He's always had the interest of this area at heart. I'm sure the son will turn out to be your strongest supporter and ablest worker."

"All right. I'll speak to Edward when I get back."

"I'll go around and see the good Doctor [Throop] while you're in Harrisburg, A.H.," said W.W., "Pierce and Sanderson, I think, will join us right away."

W.W. was calling on old friendships, asking for a show of allegiance. He did not doubt that he would get it. Pierce was the head of the First National Bank of Carbondale, and George Sanderson had given W.W. his first opening into banking, when he had appreciated the deposits in his bank of W.W.'s large New York store profits.

So, the initial plans of the protagonists were well laid; they were determined to march to victory, to let nothing stand in their way.

But what of the antagonists? Were there any antagonists?

Were the proponents of the new county going to meet adversaries who would try to stop them? And if so, at what cost? If, indeed, there were to be adversaries, would the order go out that the Scranton drive for a new county was to be stopped at all costs?

As it turned out, there were adversaries—not always the same, not a tightly knit secret organization, but just some people who felt that there should not be a new county for Scranton. Some of the people were attracted to the antagonists' cause because of a personal grudge against some or all of the Wintons. Others joined because, whatever the Wintons were for, they were against. These people generally resided in the Scranton area, but usually had their actions directed from Wilkes-Barre.

Wilkes-Barre, you see, was absolutely, adamantly dead set against the county being broken into two. She was the county seat of Luzerne County, and Luzerne County was the Wyoming Valley from one end to the other.

The power that Wilkes-Barre had was from her jurisdiction over coal mines, railroads, iron foundries, factories, and the tax money they paid into the county coffers. Remember, at this time, the last quarter of the nineteenth century, the Wyoming Valley was fueling the nation. Coal left the area for all over the world. Even San Diegans in faraway California knew to watch for the spontaneous combustion of the blacksmith coal from Pennsylvania. Many railroads' iron rails were forged at Scranton. And the D.L.&W.'s order, just at the time A.H. was leaving for Harrisburg, to convert their track to narrow gauge, meant that extra revenues of two and a half million dollars would be pouring into the valley, for at least 13,000 coal cars alone would have to be remodeled. And over all this industrial activity sat the politicians at the county seat in Wilkes-Barre.

Then finally, there were those descendants of the early Pennsylvania settlers at Wilkes-Barre who just weren't going to stand for the breaking away of the upstart Connecticut progeny at Scranton.

Were the enthusiastic new county proponents going to have a fight on their hands? Oh, yes indeed; the answer was definitely yes. But the fighting was going to be complex and sophisticated. No one could afford to soil his image before the eyes of the electoral public, especially when all the men who resisted the new county had hopes of public service, right up to the highest office in the land. The enemy camp was very astute, and one absolutely dared not underestimate them.

A.H. was well received at Harrisburg; Frank Collins opened every door for him. His petition was entered into the schedule. A.H. spent his time lobbying for the new county. When it came up for its first reading in the House, there was much discussion. The bill, after being amended and revised, was scheduled to be read, that is heard again, on March 18.

A.H.'s team of workers had been busy at home. Everyone who W.W. thought would support the new county, did so enthusiastically; he did not meet a negative reaction anywhere. He was so encouraged that he called on his banking friends in Pittston and Wilkes-Barre; they, too, told W.W. that they thought it was a good idea. They said that they would not stand in the way of the new county.

Back in Harrisburg, A.H. listened intently from his gallery seat while the House was in session on March 18. He was pleasantly surprised at the second reading of the new county bill; his basic thoughts had been preserved. The legislative body had decided to set the number of electoral signatures required to petition for a new county at 1,500 voters. They had kept his requirements of 400 square miles and 20,000 inhabitants. But the boundary lines they put under the authority of a five-man commission, who were to survey the territory under question before fixing the boundary. The additions to A.H.'s original proposal dealt with the specifics regarding the filing of the commissioners' report, the advertising of the bill, the organization of the courts, and the procedure for electing county officers. The biggest change was that the location of the county seat would have to be designated at the time the petition was filed.

Hurriedly, suddenly, it was all over. The roll was called, the vote tallied. At its evening session, House bill #138 was passed.

A.H. was jubilant! He was jubilant because the new county would soon be a reality. A.H. and Frank Collins spent an enjoyable remainder of the evening, celebrating.

"I'll be heading back to Scranton now," A.H. told Frank, "We'll have to set up the mechanics to get the voters' signatures on the petition."

Frank replied, "I think you're safe enough in starting that now. The new county bill has been passed by the House, and they're the larger, more difficult body to get something through, like this bill. I can't see the Senate objecting when the House has approved. Anyway, it will keep you busy while you're waiting for the bill to come up in the Senate." Frank showed, with his last remark, that he understood A.H. pretty well.

"No, I'm not anticipating any trouble with the Senate."

"What makes you so sure?"

"I've heard from father, and he tells me that he's talked with some of the Wilkes-Barre boys, and they're not planning to put up any opposition."

"I'll keep my ear to the ground, just in case," offered Frank.

"Thanks. Anyway, I'll be back before it comes up in the Senate."

Jubilant, weary, driven by nervous energy to get started on the rest of the campaign, A.H. returned home to Scranton. His father and the others gave him a hero's welcome. Powerful men that they were, their eyes were moist as A.H. described the details of the bill's passage.

The gods of true rewards for honest labors were smiling down on the new county advocates. There was not a cloud in the sky.

A.H. had been back from Harrisburg only a few days when there was a knock at the front door of his home on Wyoming Avenue. It was slightly before eight in the morning; he and John Collings were still at the breakfast table. Bridget came into the dining room, and handed A.H. a folded piece of paper. He opened the note and read it quickly.

"John, this is from George Winans."

"You mean that crazy inventor who has an office down from us on Lackawanna? What has he done—blown himself up?"

"No, it's much more serious than that. He says he was arrested last night, and wants me to help him. Come on; I think we had both better go."

The two brothers-in-law almost ran from the house. A.H. was so impolite as to blast from just inside the door, "Alice, we're leaving!" on the odd chance she would hear; the shout was mainly for his self-justification, were he accused later of not telling her that he was going.

They found poor Mr. Winans so upset that they couldn't make any sense of the situation from their client's description; John had better luck talking to the U.S. Marshal.

"A U.S. Secret Service agent from Washington has charged him with a plot to defraud the U.S. Government by printing counterfeit U.S. Bonds and Treasury Notes."

"You're kidding?"

"No, I'm serious," said John between fits of laughter, "they think he's the head of a large counterfeit ring."

A.H. and John were stupefied. George Winans was well known in Scranton and was generally well liked—even by John, who had the newcomer's objectivity when first introduced to one of Scranton's more colorful citizens.

A.H. replied, "No wonder I can't make any sense out of what he is saying."

He went back to George Winans, "All right, I think we can straighten it out, Mr. Winans."

"Oh, I hope so, Mr. Winton. Please do hurry, we don't have much time."

"When's your hearing?"

"In about twenty minutes. I think they told me nine o'clock."

A.H. withdrew to consult with John again. "The hearing's in twenty minutes," he hissed. "There's something funny about this."

"Do you want me to go into the hearing?"

"No, we'll go together. Draw the prosecution's witness out, first. Let's see if we can find what's behind this, before we start talking."

The hearing was convened by the United States commissioner for the district. On testimony, a complicated plot was described by the Secret Service agent. He had posed as a counterfeiter, and through the introduction of another man, met George Winans, and arranged to buy from him a galvanic battery and other special materials required in the reproduction process developed by Winans. He concluded that Mr. Winans had offered to show him the process and supply him with paper (Mr. Winans should have talked with Xerox), and that Winans had promised to find three responsible parties in Scranton who would accept the counterfeit bonds and notes made by the disguised undercover agent.

George Winans emphatically denied the last charge, of arranging to pass the forged papers. As for knowing that he was dealing with a counterfeiter, Winans said that it was not his duty to see what use a buyer was going to put goods just purchased. And as for the process itself, he said that he had never made a secret of the matter, but on the contrary, had shown his work around the city freely and with pride at his success. He had developed the process to use in the reproduction of art prints. He added that he had tried several times to sell the process to the government.

At this point, A.H. reminded the U.S. commissioner in charge of the hearing that Mr. Winans and his process had been before the courts earlier and that his process had not been considered fraudulent at that time.

The Secret Service agent, however, was not through; he had more to add. "When I arrested Mr. Winans last night, our men in Philadelphia were simultaneously arresting his brother and another man. In their room, a battery and all the other equipment were discovered, as well as paper with the lattice work, such as is found on bonds, already printed on it."

"I have a question of the witness," called A.H., "If you were already watching the counterfeiters in Philadelphia, what alerted you to George Winans here in Scranton?"

"Information was received at the Secret Service Division in Washington, and I was sent out to investigate."

John made the summation for the defense, pointing out that at no time had Mr. Winans actually passed counterfeit papers, "Nor is a man responsible for his brother's actions. As far as his process goes, in granting his patent the courts have never considered the process illegal."

But after all was said, the commissioner ordered George Winans held for $6,000 bail, and scheduled his trial for the third Thursday in June at the District Court in Williamsport, Pa.

A.H. and John were stunned that George Winans should be bound over for trial.

"I don't like it," A.H. told John, "There's something behind it."

"Do you think it was leading up to someone else? Whoever started this was trying to catch somebody else? The people, perhaps, whom Winans was supposed to get to accept the forgeries?"

A.H. gave John's questions thought, "Possibly, particularly if they were trying to incriminate a banker," And A.H. thought of W.W. and the Second National Bank.

The day had begun early, and turned out to be a long and busy one. Besides helping Winans to arrange bail, there was a trip to Wilkes-Barre and consultations with clients. It was late when A.H. finally fell into bed. He hadn't been there long when a loud and persistent banging on the front door of his home awakened him. Alice heard it, too.

"Do you hear the knocking, A.H.?" she asked, frightened, "What do you think it's about?"

"I don't know. I'll go down and see," A.H. struck a match and held it over the face of his pocket watch, "It's a quarter to two," he said.

Downstairs, he opened the door to face one of the Poor Board's perpetual recipients.

"Mr. Winton, come quick, the bank's on fire!"

"Pat, are you sure? The Second National?"

"Yes sir, Mr. Winton. The alarm just came in over to Crystal."

"Thank you, Pat," A.H. handed the well-meaning fellow a gold coin, "Pat, you know where my father lives in Providence?"

"Do you want me to go over and tell him?"

"Would you, please?"

The man was gone before A.H. had the door shut. He ran back upstairs, and told Alice about the fire as he threw on some clothes. When he reached Lackawanna Avenue, he saw the Crystal, Nay Aug, Neptune, and Franklin fire engines clustered together. The Mayor of Scranton, Robert McKune, first president of the Crystal Hose Fire Company, and A.H.'s fellow Sir Knight in the Coeur de Lion Commandry, was assisting the companies pack their new fabric and rubber hose.

He saw A.H. approach, and called out to him, "You're lucky, A.H. Tell your father he had the 'luck of the Irish' riding with him."

"The fire?" cried back A.H.

"Don't worry, it's out. Western Union's night operator saved the building for you. He saw a strange light over the back door, took a quick look, and sounded the alarm."

"Thank God! It's Tom O'Brien, Western Union's night man; is he all right? What about the damage?"

"I'm telling you, your father has 'the luck of the Irish.' I don't think he's going to be able to point to enough damage to get even one cent out of the insurance companies." By now, the fire trucks were packed and ready to return to their houses. "Come on, I'll show you where it started."

The two men walked towards the rear of the building, but a cry and a great shout stopped them.

"The Opera House! The Opera House!"

Turning, A.H. and Robert McKune saw enormous red and yellow flames leap from the windows of the building across Lackawanna Avenue, opposite the Second National Bank building. There was pandemonium until the four fire companies succeeded in maneuvering their engines to the other side and unpacking their just-packed gear. This time, A.H. as well as every other available man, pitched in. By then, W.W. had arrived and added his help.

"Pat told me it was the bank building that was burning," W.W. shouted to A.H.

"It was. I haven't seen it yet, but Bob McKune tells me there's no damage."

There was no more time for conversation. One wall after another of the Opera House collapsed. At 3:00 A.M., the firemen admitted that they couldn't save the Opera House, and turned their attention to the surrounding area. They worked to keep the adjoining buildings from catching on fire. They were hampered by the cold and the snow still on the ground from the last storm. Their only blessing was that they didn't have the high winds that had been blowing on the previous day. In the bitter cold of the night, when the temperature is always at its lowest, the water they poured on the flames turned to ice, and hung from parts of the building in huge icicles. It was a holocaust.

As soon as the morning light was bright enough, W.W. and A.H. crossed back over the street to the bank. Carefully, they inspected the outside of the building, and then the basement inside; there was no mistaking the signs—someone had deliberately started a fire by breaking a window into an empty room adjoining the Western Union office in the basement. Shreds of cotton and hay still marked the trajectory they had followed after having been thrown into the room through the broken window. The heavy, lighted torch that had been thrown in after them still lay, charred but in one piece, on the bank's cement floor. Outside on Railroad Alley, the barrels of kerosene were still lined up as the arsonist had placed them, pressed tightly against the bank's back wall in one row, starting from each side of the broken window. Beads of perspiration stood out on W.W.'s forehead as he viewed the evidence. Afterwards, they rejoined Mayor McKune, and described their observations in detail.

He listened, repeatedly nodding his head in agreement. When they had finished describing the bank's back wall, he said, "Follow me."

He took them towards the front of the Opera House, which faced the bank across the street, and pointed downward. In the snow, preserved under a clear ice coating from the firepumps' water, were the footprints of the incendiarist. W.W. and A.H. stared down at the incriminating footprints, wishing that they knew to whom the prints belonged. Their eyes ranged over the pile of smoldering ashes and rubble that had been the Opera House, and the part of its first floor rented to the Boston Store. They shared a common thought: but for the night operator, Tom O'Brien, in the basement office that W.W. had inveigled Western Union to rent in his bank building, the beautiful, elegant Second National would be a similar ruined hulk.

"I'm calling a joint meeting of the Council tonight," Mayor McKune said. "Try to come."

But before they could get to the meeting, the fire alarm sounded again. This time, it was a barrel of rags and a bundle of half-burned firewood at the top of the cellar stairs in the storeroom of a building adjoining the post office. Crystal Hose was the first fire company to arrive; it extinguished the fire in time to retrieve the incriminating evidence of an arsonist at work again. Had the fire had a chance to burn, the entire post-office block would have been gone in two hours.

The City Joint Council, consisting of the Select and Common Councils, convened a little later. Mayor McKune described the number and seriousness of the fires that had been plaguing the city in the past week.

"It's as if somebody wanted to destroy the whole city of Scranton," he remarked, "as if they wanted Scranton to go up in flames."

The council responded to the seriousness of the fires and the frightening effect that they were having on the citizens. They authorized the mayor to offer a $5,000 reward for the conviction of the arsonist.

Almost a week elapsed. The Opera House and Second National Bank fires and George Winans had become a thing of the past—a strange week, after all the excitement, for it was a week that was peaceful and quiet, ordinary. But it was only a week. After the week of calm, A.H. heard that J.C. Coon had been charged with embezzlement. The man was a Scranton neighbor and a friend of the Wintons. The arrest and charge against him were very upsetting, particularly at this time; Coon had promised A.H. invaluable help in reaching the voters during the final push for the new county. He was editor of the *Sunday Morning Free Press*, one of Scranton's best newspapers and one with a large reading public. He was for the new county, and he had promised to give as much coverage in his paper as he could.

A.H. went around immediately to see his friend, Joe Coon, and find out if the rumor of the embezzlement charge was true. He found a white-faced and confused man.

"There's been a hearing," Coon told A.H., "I think it was the morning after the Opera House burned down. No, wait; that was when I was served with the papers."

"I was charged with being an accessory to embezzling the license money of the county for 1875 while acting in my capacity as county auditor."

"And had you?"

"A.H., believe me, no. They said I had taken between $6,000 and $7,000."

"When's the trial?"

"I don't know. They told me that the court calendar was pretty full, and it might be a while before they could schedule my case."

A.H. frowned at that. He had not been aware that the court calendar was so full, especially for a case as serious as this one seemed to be.

Because Coon was so depressed, he strove for heartiness, "I'll look into it, and see what I can find out." He tried to be reassuring.

After he left Coon, he stopped in to see his father at the bank.

"What do you think about what's happened to Coon?"

W.W. professed ignorance. A.H. informed him.

W.W. commented, "That's too bad. He promised us a lot of publicity in his paper for the new county petition."

"There's something funny about it. He's been served with the charge. He's had his hearing. But no one will give him a date for his trial. It's very odd to leave a man in limbo like that. Whether he comes to trial tomorrow, or five years from now, he should still know the date for his trial. I think I'll poke around and see what's going on. Maybe you had better keep your ears open, too."

No matter what avenue of approach he used, A.H. could not learn anything more than what Coon had told him. Whoever was asked knew nothing. As far as he could find out, the case was not listed on any court calendar. While he was in Wilkes-Barre, A.H. did have luck, though, from another source. The three general auditors for the county, of which Coon was one, had finished their audit for 1875, and were ready to post a copy for public inspection. A.H. asked to see the report, thinking that there might be some reference to the discrepancies in the License Department. To his surprise, he found that the auditors had been heavily critical, and very openly critical, of various county office-holders. He saw immediately that the criticisms would almost guarantee the electoral public voting for the new county. But nothing pointed to irregularities in the License Department.

A.H. read their statement quickly. For one thing, the auditors had not authorized payment of $6,000 on an $11,000 bill from a New York engraving firm for printing maps of Luzerne County. They had also objected to $1,200 charged for courthouse alterations that had not been legally authorized. But the most damaging charge by the three auditors was that a total of $19,500, money collected from tax, had been paid out by the county commissioners for unauthorized bills. The auditors had written, "We find the commissioners practiced fraud, bribery, and malfeasance in office by compromising the credit of the county through a vile system, etc."

No wonder a warrant had been sworn out for J.C. Coon!

In haste, A.H. returned to Scranton, and went immediately to see Coon.

"Why didn't you tell me about your findings as county auditor?"

"I couldn't, until we finished and the report passed into public knowledge. But that was one reason why I had promised to help your new county drive with the newspaper. I knew the report could positively affect the new county vote."

A.H. was very excited, "Yes, your report is the greatest support that we could have to convince the voters that we need to break off and erect our own county!"

But with his recent legal troubles, Coon's hopes would not be raised now; he was too pessimistic to yield to A.H.'s enthusiasm. He was a newspaperman, and he had just had a sample of what blowing the whistle and bringing down a house of cards was going to mean: what kind of trouble it was going to bring him. However, he had never conceived that he would be attacked by outright lies. Any charge based on fact did not concern him, because, while he was not perfect, he had nothing in his past worth worrying about. He said as much to A.H.

"The public will support you," responded A.H., "When the voters read that the auditor who reports on irregularities in the county is arrested for embezzlement, instead of the county trying to correct the wrongs, they will be behind you, and they won't be able to vote for the new county fast enough."

"They'll get me before we get the new county," replied Coon.

A.H. left Coon and went over to the *Scranton Republican* office, Joe Scranton's newspaper. He talked with Joe Scranton at great length, telling him about the auditors' report. Joe decided to publish the report *in toto*, as a supplement to his paper. They both agreed that the report should not be buried; it had to be brought to the attention of the electoral public. A.H. left him, full of confidence. But, a couple of days later, he began to have some doubts, and not because of Coon's pessimistic attitude. John Collings had picked up the rumor that it had been a clerk in the auditor general's office at Harrisburg who had noticed the discrepancy in the license fee money forwarded to Harrisburg by Coon. A.H. didn't like to hear of anything coming out of Harrisburg until the Senate had given their approval to House Bill #138.

A.H. and his family were at dinner, the evening that John had come home with the latest Harrisburg rumor on Coon. As they were discussing it, Byron Winton, A.H.'s younger brother, came in.

Alice was glad to see her brother-in-law, "Byron, how nice! What a pleasant surprise! We don't often see you. How is Frances?"

"Frances and the children are fine, Alice. Thank you," Byron appeared awkward and ill at ease.

His unexpected entry into the dining room had brightened those at the table; but the new arrival's lackluster conversation soon dampened all talk. After a prolonged silence, Alice excused herself and left the room. But even after she had gone, Byron seemed no more prone to conversation than he had before. A.H. poured some brandy, and offered it around. Quite some time passed in silence, as the three men savored their drinks.

Finally, impatient with his brother, A.H. questioned him, "What's troubling you, Byron?"

Byron didn't answer.

John Collings interpreted the silence as if directed at him. He started to rise, "I think I'll leave you two, if you don't mind. I just remembered—"

This time, Byron did indicate a desire, "No, John, it's all right. You should hear this anyway."

A.H. and John waited patiently.

A.H. said, "Well?"

"Daniel Silkman and I were served with warrants for our arrest this afternoon."

Everybody in the room was silent.

"They released us on our own recognizance, because we gave them our word that we would be here for the hearing."

Kindly, patiently, the older child's concern for the younger brother, A.H. spoke, "Why, Byron?"

"Forgery."

A.H. and John looked at each other. Were Byron and his father-in-law two of the three men Winans was accused of conspiring with to receive the forged bonds and treasury notes? Byron was his father W.W.'s vice-president at the Second National. Were the forged papers to go into the assets of the Second National?

"Forgery of what?" A.H. wasn't sure whether he could bear to hear the answer, so sure was he as to what he was going to hear.

"An obligation note from George—"

At the word "George," A.H. groaned, and slumped back in his chair.

Byron stopped, and looked questioningly at John Collings, wondering what was ailing his brother. John, on the other hand, was in better shape; he was only married into the family—it wasn't his flesh and blood.

John completed Byron's sentence for him, "Winans?"

Now Byron was more puzzled than before, "Winans? George Winans? The fellow with that crazy process of his that he's always talking about?" He looked from A.H. to John.

"Byron, George who?" A.H. had recovered enough to realize that there was still some hope.

"I was just going to tell you—George Washington Kirkendall."

"Kirkendall? The county sheriff s brother? How did you get involved with him?"

"We didn't; he came to us. Remember the election two years ago, John, when you ran for district attorney? My father-in-law was up for sheriff. And then some of the delegates bolted and went back to Wilkes-Barre. Remember, they put Farnham against you, John? And they put William Penn Kirkendall on their version of the Democratic ticket, after the committee had already put my father-in-law Daniel Silkman up for sheriff. Shortly afterwards, Penn Kirkendall's brother George contacted me, and asked me to speak to my father-in-law. I was to ask him whether he would consent to withdraw his name from the Democratic ticket so that just Kirkendall's name would appear. If he would, George Kirkendall would give Daniel Silkman $4,000, as a sort of remuneration.

"Well, my father-in-law and I talked it over, and we couldn't see any harm in the arrangement. We thought that, in the interest of party harmony and of presenting a united front to the voters, it was as good a way as any to solve the double ticket problem. So my father-in-law agreed to withdraw, and George gave him $2,000 plus a promissory note for $2,000 more, to be paid after the election.

"A year and a half has gone by, and the Kirkendalls still haven't paid the other $2,000 they promised. So my father-in-law and I went down to Wilkes-Barre a couple of days ago, and demanded very firmly that George pay up what he had promised.

"He said that it would take him two days to get the money together. Well, you see what he did; in the two days he swore out a false complaint, saying that we were trying to blackmail him with a promissory note which we had fabricated."

A.H. swore softly and profusely for quite a while. When he had run out of expletives, he asked to see the note.

"I don't have it with me. My father-in-law has it."

A.H. went to look for Alice, "We're going over to Daniel Silkman's house for a while; I don't know when we will get back. I'll tell you everything later." He gave her a passing kiss.

On the way to Daniel Silkman's home, A.H. reviewed the events of the three weeks since he had returned from Harrisburg—the fires around Scranton and at the Second National bank, Joe Coon's trouble, George Winans' "forgery," and now Byron and Daniel Silkman. And when he talked to Daniel Silkman and Byron, while studying the note, he reflected the change in his thinking. He was no longer the optimistic, encouraging defense counsel which he had been with George Winans; nor did he speak of the arrest in terms of a trifling annoyance, as he had to J.C. Coon. In fact, he went so far as to say that he believed they would be bound over for trial. He was convinced that Byron and Daniel Silkman would have to stand trial for forgery.

By now, A.H. was getting very worried about the health of the new county bill at Harrisburg. If passage of the bill were to be automatic, as he had firmly believed it would be when he left Harrisburg, why then the sudden avalanche of false charges against his friends and incendiary attacks on the city and the family bank? He was convinced that bringing charges against his brother and Daniel Silkman was not only an attempt to discredit a member of the Winton family, but also a gambit to reach him and embroil him, hopefully, in a perjury charge, thereby providing the method by which he could be sent to jail—his fate for his work on the new county bill.

A.H. had Daniel Silkman give his version of the events leading up to the exchange of the $2,000 and the I.O.U. There was no difference from what Byron had related.

"I will be frank with you," said A.H., addressing Byron and Daniel Silkman. John Collings listened attentively, too. "I am sure that you will be held for trial. In fact, I'm planning to ask that your case be brought to trial immediately.

"As far as what you did, I can't see how they can prove any wrongdoing. Essentially, you agreed to settle a difference of opinion—not even a fight, just a difference of opinion—for money. That is a perfectly legal and acceptable method.

"But I will tell you what is really worrying me. I think that this was a God-given opportunity, so to speak, for some men who want to oppose our bid for a new county. If that is what is really behind the charge against you, we will have to proceed very cautiously. I have the feeling that the Kirkendalls, and others, would be only too happy if we lost our self-control and accused them of wrongdoing or crookedness in office. That, we will not do. And we must be very careful in what we say, so as in no way to intimate such thoughts. Do you understand me?"

John Collings had been listening, as avidly as the two defendants, to A.H.'s instructions. They all murmured their understanding of the situation.

"John," A.H. said, turning to face John Collings, "I think the best thing to do is to ask at the hearing for a speedy trial. Once we have that set, then, I think, we should file our countercharge, bringing suit for breach of contract, specifically for nonpayment of debt."

John's face glowed with pleasure at A.H.'s maneuvering.

A.H. continued, "It's going to be difficult to handle this bunch. If they can take the very evidence that is against them, and turn it around and make it work for them, you can see how clever they can be. There is no way of proving who is lying. Their claim, that the note is a forgery, explains the similarity between the writing in the note and their own handwriting. But if we prove that they made part payment on a debt, the forgery will be unimportant.

"Now, Byron, you tell me that George Kirkendall made out a bank draft for $2,000 and had his man cash it? And Daniel, when you got the $2,000 in cash, you deposited it in your account?" Now it was John's turn. "John, I think our best tactic is to trace that $2,000 out of Kirkendall's account and into Daniel's. I know Father can help there; I'll speak to him. Once we do that, it will be easy to show that the note for the remaining $2,000 is valid, and not a forgery. In the meantime, John, you prepare the nonpayment of debt charge."

It was very late when A.H. and John returned home. A.H. had been on the run for three weeks now, and was beginning to feel the strain. He looked back on his busy days at Harrisburg, almost as if it had been a relaxed vacation time.

Alice was awake when A.H. came to bed. "Is it anything serious with Byron?" she wanted to know.

He told her what had happened. In his exhausted state, deep depression took over. "I know that all this activity has something to do with the new county. Yet, when I left Harrisburg, everything was assured. It was to be only a matter of time before the bill would be passed into law. And when I got back here, father assured me he had the promise of everybody at Wilkes-Barre that they would not go against the bill. They've either changed their minds, or else they lied to father from the beginning."

"But, A.H., how can sending Byron and Daniel, and Coons, and Winans off to jail stop the new county bill?"

"Ah, that's just it. They haven't gone yet. Neither is the whole city of Scranton lying in ashes; only one building is, at the moment. If we turn back, nothing more will come of any of these charges."

"Then how can you go on? You can't be the instrument by which destruction comes to others."

"How can I stop it, Alice? I'm not the only one who wants a new county for Scranton. These men and others, starting with Uncle Abram and also Grandpop, wanted a new county long before I came to the conclusion it was the only way to go. No, it's a fight, now. And a general never concedes a battle because he is afraid just one soldier may lose his life. No, the battle has to be fought. You just pray to God that each soldier has in himself a survival instinct strong enough to bring him out on top."

A.H. clenched his hands into powerful fists. He unclenched them, and then clenched them again quickly into fists. This he did several times.

"The hardest part, Alice, is that I can't talk about what I know. I can't say in public what I'm telling you. You see, Alice, I have them figured out. The only way that they could come up with these charges so quickly, is if they were actually involved themselves. The forgery charge that they accused Byron and Daniel Silkman of showed me that. They knew to file the charges because they were the ones doing the scheming. Otherwise, it would take months to unearth the Winans counterfeit bonds, Coons dipping into the license money, and an extra two or four thousand in Silkman's account. No, they knew what was going on because they were doing it themselves—not Byron, nor Winans, nor Joe Coon. It's like the man who cries, "There's a wolf in the closet!" and it turns out to be true—because he put the wolf there in the first place.

"I've got to keep my mouth closed, and never let anyone know that I know. They would be only too glad to arrest me, on any charge."

With that, A.H. fell into a sound sleep, to prepare for the battle.

The next day, he saw W.W. and told him about Byron, Daniel Silkman, and the forgery charge. He explained what he wanted: a record of the withdrawal and the subsequent deposit. W.W. said that he thought he could get it; he didn't anticipate any difficulty. W.W. was glad to see A.H., for reasons of his own. He was just getting ready to leave for Winton.

"Come with me, A.H.; George Filer wants to show me something."

Starting in February, the mine operators at the northern end of the Wyoming Valley had suspended operations. The winter had been an exceptionally cold one in the valley, but elsewhere, outside the valley, the winter had been the reverse, very mild; coal had remained unsold at its deposit yards. Consequently, everyone concerned with mining had suspended operations until the supply on hand was sufficiently diminished. George Filer had taken advantage of the inactivity to engage in some work on his own. He had sent word to W.W. that he wanted to see him at Winton before the mines returned to normal operations.

It was like a ghost town when W.W. and A.H. reached Winton. George was in the company office, enjoying a cup of coffee, when they arrived. He was glad to see both father and son.

"A.H., this is wonderful. I wasn't expecting to get you, too." He offered both of them coffee from the agate pot, "You better take some; we're going to have to go in pretty far. It's going to take a while."

A.H. poured some for his father and himself, and they gulped down the hot brew as quickly as they could. They were anxious to see what George Filer had been up to. They walked over to the mine entrance and rode a coal car in. George took them almost seventy-five feet down, and then out a branch tunnel for about half a mile. They stopped and got out where the tunnel's dug out area ended.

"You see this?" George waved his torch over the wall. "See? The vein has petered out here." He pointed to traces of coal in the matrix. "But now look here." He raised his torch slightly and pointed to traces of coal again, but this coal was slightly removed from the other. "When the men who were working this end came and told me that the vein was running thin, I let it go by. But since the shutdown, with plenty of time on my hands, I thought I'd come down and take a look-see for myself. What do you think, W.W.,.A.H.?"

W.W. answered for both of them, "We're here to listen, George. Go ahead."

"Well, when I first took a look, I thought the same as the men, that the vein had petered out. Now take a close look, and tell me if you notice anything about these two traces."

The two men studied them, but admitted they couldn't.

"W.W., it looks to me as though this lower deposit is at the end of the vein we've been working. See how the coal is sort of thrust into the matrix, the same direction we've been working from? But I don't know, when I look at this deposit up here," and he raised his torch about twelve inches higher, the flame making the little flecks of coal sparkle in the light, like the black diamonds they were, "I get the feeling that the thrust into the matrix up here is from the opposite direction."

A.H. and W.W. could sense an undertone of excitement in Filer's words.

"What are you telling us, George?" asked W.W.

"I think we've had unbelievable luck, and exposed the spot where two large deposits have ended back to back. I think, W.W., we ought to sink another shaft, maybe about a mile from here, over towards Archbald."

"All right, go ahead."

Then it was back out of the mine, and back to Scranton, for W.W. and A.H.

Everything went just about as A.H. had predicted it would go with Byron and his father-in-law. The defense insisted on a quick trial, going to court April 18. But this time, A.H. was prepared. He knew what to expect, and he was going to fight it through. While in court, they were very careful not to hurl any charges of unethical conduct or malfeasance in office at Sheriff Kirkendall; that was not the question at issue. They spoke only to and about the doings of George Kirkendall, the sheriff's brother. As the trial progressed, A.H. could tell that their strategy was taking effect. When he and John Collings pressed for payment of the second half of the debt, they put on a very convincing show. W.W. had not let his sons down. A.H. was able to trace the money, from the time George Kirkendall had written the check, to the time Daniel Silkman had deposited the cash. At the conclusion of the trial, Kirkendall was ordered to pay the remaining $2,000 to Daniel Silkman, and Byron and his father-in-law were cleared of the criminal charge of forgery.

There was no doubt that A.H. had successfully fended off the attack on his brother and Daniel Silkman—but at great cost. The real outcome of the proceedings was to alert the antagonists of the new county bill that, when aroused, A.H. could fight back, and what was more, fight successfully.

On the twenty-fifth, shortly after the trial, Frank Collins came into Scranton on the evening train from Harrisburg. He wanted to talk to A.H., but found Alice and Katie the only ones home on Wyoming Avenue.

"A.H. and John are over at the Valley House, watching the billiard match," she told Frank.

"What match is this?" Frank wanted to know.

"A Mr. Shaw here in Scranton challenged anyone in the county to play him a game of billiards for the championship of the county. A.H. got very involved in it when a Mr. Brandt from Wilkes-Barre accepted the challenge. A.H. is looking on the match as an allegorical display to show which end of the valley is superior.

"I think he has been spending his free time the past few days, although he doesn't really have any free time at all, talking up the match as a contest between the two cities, sort of like the days of old when two kings would fight each other, instead of their armies, to decide the fate of their kingdoms."

Frank laughed at her description, "I wish I could stay and talk with you longer, Alice, but I have to get back to Harrisburg. So if you'll excuse me, I'll see if I can find A.H. at the Valley House."

Alice's quick retort reached Frank as he was running down the steps, "You're not fooling me, Frank Collins, you want to go over and watch the match yourself."

The Lackawanna Valley House was under new management and had been recently redecorated. What had started out as an advertising scheme to publicize the new image of the hotel and its six Griffith's Standard American Bevel Billiard Tables, had turned into a contest between two cities, with their reputations at stake. When Frank arrived, the duelists had been playing for over an hour. It was the twenty-first inning, and Shaw, Scranton, was in the lead. They were playing an American four-ball version of the French Carom, which had been sweeping the U.S. in recent years.

Frank moved to a spot where he could watch the play. He did not try to locate A.H. He did not want to disturb the tension and excitement in the room. Shortly before 11 p.m., Shaw, or Scranton as A.H. would have it, went out on the thirty-third inning with 1002 points. Brandt, Wilkes-Barre, barely made it to 650 points. Frank couldn't be happier to see the match end in Shaw's victory. He had to find A.H. and give him the news. It would be easier to talk to him in the first flush of Shaw's, that is Scranton's win. A.H. was so enthusiastic over the match and its outcome that he showed no surprise when Frank finally found him.

"Frank, you're here because you heard about the match?"

Frank dodged, "I wanted to talk to you, and this seemed like the perfect time."

He drew A.H. towards the lobby of the hotel. Before he could maneuver him to an isolated corner, W.W., Isaac Dean, John Collings, Arthur Dean, Dr. Eugene Heermans, Byron, and Thomas Livey had found them. Everyone expressed a desire for a thirst-quencher, and wanted to go across the lobby to the bar.

Frank stopped them, "You're all here; I might as well tell you now. In a surprise move, the Senate called for House Bill #138, and voted it down. The new county bill has been killed."

The jocularity, the pleasure of their evening, faded instantly. But A.H. would not be downed. He had been expecting this, especially since he had caught on to the series of troubles that had appeared to plague him. Before the eyes of his family, he metamorphized into the leader.

"I'm not through," he said, "I'm going to fight. I'm going to fight, and we're going to get a new county." This time, there was no indecisiveness, no uncertainty, no introspection; A.H. had grown larger than life-size before the opposition. He knew the gauntlet had been thrown in his face, and he showed no hesitation in picking it up.

The men moved out of the lobby, off to one corner of the veranda. They clustered together and spoke in whispers; they wanted no one to hear them.

A.H. continued speaking, "I'm not quitting. After what has happened this past month, I'm more convinced than ever; we have got to break off and run this end of the valley ourselves."

"How are you going to do it? You can't put the same bill through Harrisburg again—not for a while, anyway."

"I don't care about the bill. We'll write another one; I'm not worried about that. The only thing that's important now is to break off and get on our own."

Nods of approval greeted A.H.'s call to arms.

At this point, Arthur Dean, Isaac Dean's son, stepped forward from the back edge of the circle. He was the same age as Byron Winton, but because he was still unmarried and had not yet taken his bar exam, he had been treated more casually by the other, more settled members of the family.

Arthur Dean now spoke up; he was going to take his place among his relatives. "Has everyone heard about J.C. Coon and the county audit?" he asked.

A.H. started to dismiss him peremptorily, but Arthur Dean persisted.

"And the auditors that the court appointed?" Arthur Dean succeeded in making his presence felt.

"What court-appointed auditors, Arthur?" and A.H. yielded.

"Monday a week ago, a petition from a hundred taxable inhabitants of Luzerne County asked the court to appoint new auditors to reaudit the county's financial statement."

A.H. tried to think, "Last Monday? Where was I? I didn't hear about it." Then he remembered—and he swore, "Son-of-a-bitch." It was the day before Byron and Daniel Silkman's trial, and he had been busy consulting with them. The opposition had put one over on him, "What happened? Were new auditors appointed?"

"Oh yes; somebody had dug up a county law from 1842, that said that the courts could appoint auditors in 'certain cases'—and this was deemed a 'certain case.' "

"Well, that does it," commented A.H., "J.C. Coon is finished now. He won't stand a chance. They'll find him guilty of something, or they'll make the embezzlement charge stick," A.H. encompassed all the men around him with his next remarks, "You can see what we're up against. Any attempt at reform will achieve nothing. They'll find a legal ruling for everything we try. We're going to have to work at this new county bill until we get it, and that's all there is to it.

"I think now's as good a time as any to start. If we get enough people behind us clamoring for a new county, Harrisburg will have to legislate one through regardless. I suggest that we all adjourn to the bar and each one of us start talking the new county up to a friend."

And so the great campaign began. In the beginning, the men were very careful and selective as to whom they contacted. They had had a sampling of what they were up against. They realized that they could not make mistakes or treat the campaign for the new county as a joke. For if they did, it was not inconceivable that they would end up viewing their world from behind bars.

Their objective, as they fanned out to begin the push anew, was to generate a public outcry against injustices in the county. If all the voters at the upper end of the valley demanded separation, there would be little that a small handful of men could do to stop it. It would take time to accomplish this because the demand would have to come naturally. But A.H., and everyone close to him dedicated to the erection of a new county, had all the time necessary. They were men who had no other interests.

For a while, all was quiet. A.H.'s new county bill had been defeated at Harrisburg. The reauditing of the county books would calm ruffled feelings; A.H. was not expecting much to be accomplished by the reaudit. And as far as the opponents of the new county were concerned, the upstarts had been smartly spanked and sent back to their corner of the valley. On the surface, life returned to routine.

One day, to brighten the monotony and because he had reason, W.W. hosted an impromptu luncheon at the Valley House. He left the bank with Byron, and together the two of them stopped at the law office and picked up A.H. and John Collings. After they had been shown to their table in the dining room of the Valley House, W.W. ordered Moet. When their glasses had been filled, he raised his:

"To Winton!"

"Hear, hear, to Winton!"

"And now, I have an announcement. George Filer has sunk a new shaft, and tells that the vein is of superior quality, and runs as much as ten feet thick!"

It is always a pleasant time when one hears how one has just become very much richer. The woes and the cares of the new county struggle were forgotten for a while; the men relaxed and enjoyed their meal. It had been some time since they had sat down together and talked of something other than the new county effort. W.W. enjoyed the luncheon most of all. As a father, his pride in his two sons before him was unparalleled. Then his glance rested briefly on his daughter-in-law's brother; in that second, a flood of memories filled his mind, and he was carried off to the almost forgotten days when the arrival of John Collings's grandfather Andrew Beaumont, for a visit with his Razorville constituents, was a cause for celebration at Heermans's White Tavern. Just as quickly, the memory evaporated, and W.W. was back in the present, sitting at the table in the Valley House. He was sure of the future; there would be a new county for Scranton. And celebrating the discovery of a new and vast coal deposit was something that did not often happen.

15

A.H. and Alice spent the summer months of the centennial year, 1876, in relatively idle pleasure. At the beginning of June, they traveled to Philadelphia for the reunion of the Knights Templar, in commemoration of the one-hundredth anniversary of American Independence. They were part of a large group of Sir Knights and their ladies who departed from Scranton early on Tuesday morning, May 30. They traveled aboard the L & S (Lehigh and Southern) Railroad because they had been able to get a group rate even lower than the excursion fare. The only explanation that comes to mind for this strange quirk of men of wealth is that, for them, any trip outside the valley was justifiable if it was reasonably enough priced. For they certainly traveled in comfort. The Coeur de Lion Commandry engaged the services of a first-rate seventeen piece band to accompany them both to and from Philadelphia.

By mutual agreement, both the Commandry and Sir Knight Winton avoided the past error of appointing A.H. treasurer for the trip; this time a committee was named to handle the finances. The latter promised that the cost of the four-day trip, with the band, would not exceed $20.00 per person. The Knights from Scranton were to be lodged at the Old Temple, on Chestnut Street in the heart of the city.

On the first of June, in full Templar uniform under the banner of their Commandry, the Coeur de Lions joined with the other Knights Templar of Pennsylvania in a grand march down Chestnut Street to Independence Hall. After the ceremony of speeches and dedications, the Knights and their ladies were transported to Fairmount Park, the site of the Centennial Exposition. There, they and their ladies promenaded under the glass roof of Horticultural Hall, one of the two most popular buildings at the exposition. As they strolled the paths among the semitropical plants, some fifty feet tall, a band performed in concert. In the evening, they returned to the center of Philadelphia for a grand reception and dancing at the American Academy of Music on South Broad Street—now one of Philadelphia's historic buildings, The Academy of Music. By Friday evening, the Sir Knights and their ladies were back in Scranton.

A.H. resumed lobbying for the new county. The mine operators had suspended operations again, this time throughout the entire valley. There was general unrest about, which worked to A.H.'s benefit; he found receptive ears for his cause. He and his father worked the hardest and the longest, each one going to the men he knew best. A.H. finally followed A.B. Dunning's advice, and sought out fellow lawyer Edward Merrifield. Merrifield, however, was dubious.

"I'm not sure, A.H.; my father is not well. And now that I'm the only child living, I devote my free time to looking after my mother and handling my father's affairs."

"Well, if you change your mind, let me know. We could use you in the campaign for the new county. Your name is much respected here, and I would be glad to have you."

It was now the middle of June, and the passion and activity that had bared itself in the spring months following A.H.'s trip to Harrisburg had become a thing of the past. There were men who felt it to be their duty, and rightly so, to resist any breakup of Luzerne County territory, and had acted accordingly. But they were not just deliberately intolerant or blind to the needs of the people in the county; they fought to preserve what was. For a while, they thought they had succeeded. Then the wisdom and strength of A.H.'s campaign began to manifest itself. While he, his father, and their relatives had been careful, nevertheless rumors of what they were advocating—a separation from Luzerne County because of its incompetence and corruption, and the tyranny of the money grabbers of the courthouse ring—surfaced from time to time.

Like the mole who tunnels underground, A.H.'s first efforts went unnoticed. But after the mole has worked a virgin lawn for a while, there is a suspicion of ridges here and there, compounded ofttimes, because confused by his maze of tunnels, he will get careless and burrow too close to the surface. Then, at last, his existence cannot go unnoticed. By then, however, he has so weakened the structure of the surface that a careless heavy tread will collapse the smooth appearance of the lawn. Thus, eventually the campaign by A.H. and his followers, to get dissatisfied voters to call for a county partition, leaked out and was heard by its opponents. They had nothing definite to go on, just rumors and rumblings, but it was enough to alarm them; they moved quickly to placate the electoral public.

The court-appointed auditing committee, from which A.H. hoped little and expected nothing, amazingly substantiated the findings of J.C. Coon and his original audit committee. Starting the last week of June, one by one the county commissioners, the county treasurer, and some of their clerks were arrested, found guilty, and sentenced. Unfortunately, Coon was not to escape unscathed; he would have to pay the price for having "blown the whistle" on the corruption at the county seat. On June 29, he, too, was arrested for embezzlement, convicted and sentenced to the county jail.

As A.H. had informed Alice, once a general goes into battle and the war machine has been put into motion, the entire military cannot then suddenly come to a halt and disband for the sake of one life. The sacrifice of one, for the good of all, is accepted. For the more than twelve inconsistencies that Coon cited in the auditor's report, he was going to have to sacrifice his freedom. Such is the way that battles are fought and won. Coon provided the first great *cause célèbre*, the first tangible reason why the northern end of Luzerne County wanted to break off, and for this he would go to jail. There was nothing that A.H. and the others at Scranton could do to help him. They were not powerful enough, yet.

No sooner had Coon been sentenced than it was time to celebrate the Fourth of July. For the Centennial July Fourth, the celebration at Carbondale, at the uppermost end of the valley, was the same as elsewhere: lots of parades, lots of speeches, lots of picnics, fireworks galore, plenty of pistol-shooting into the air if firecrackers were lacking, and lots and lots of intoxicating spirits. At dusk, the population settled into subdued clusters of patriotic Americans, enjoying the last moments of an emotion-satisfying day. There was one man, however—Thomas Campbell—who had been celebrating the one-hundredth Fourth of July with all the enthusiasm he could muster and who had yet to find his friends.

He went first in search of one particular friend—Bernie NcNulty. He finally found him, relaxing with others on Mr. Foy's front porch. They were hotly discussing who was the father of the country; McNulty, irritatingly loud, insisted that whoever the father was, he was an Irishman. Tom Campbell couldn't care less, and soon devoted his attention to one of Mr. Foy's pretty girls, who was also the object of Bernie McNulty's interest.

McNulty was quick enough to apply physical force when he requested Tom Campbell to leave the porch. From the bottom of the steps, Tom turned and yelled at his one-time friend, "By Christ! I will put a bullet through your head!"

He pulled the pistol that he had been firing to celebrate the Fourth from his pocket, and shot McNulty, killing him.

So, in one minute, poor Tom Campbell, who had been young and free and single, although somewhat intoxicated, over-celebrated the Fourth of July, and in that minute, found himself a murderer. His friend lay dead, and he was on his way to jail. In disbelief and shock, he called for the aid of another friend, lawyer Montgomery Flanigan.

Mont Flanigan answered the call immediately. He tried to get Tom Campbell released, but had no luck. Tom was to stay in jail until all the hot heads had gotten cooler. Mont Flanigan promised his friend that he would stand by him. There, the matter stood.

A.H. had much better luck celebrating the Fourth. For him and his family, it was a pleasant social interlude, a day when people were unashamed to show their pride in being American. When the day came to a close, the Wintons started to pack for their annual pilgrimage to Nantucket.

There at Nantucket, on the western sands of the limitless Atlantic Ocean, A.H. collapsed. The roar and roll of the unending waves were a force too strong to be conquered; so by the water's edge he rested from all that had happened to him, from all that he had had to do in recent weeks. He forgot that he had a home in the valley of the mountains. He forgot the names of the days, he forgot the numbers to the hours; and most importantly, he forgot his duties, his obligations, and his loyalties. He needed rest, rest from what had happened in the past; and then he needed rest, rest to strengthen him for the future.

While A.H., Alice and Katie were lounging on the sand at Nantucket, and Tom Campbell was cooped up in the jail at Wilkes-Barre, Luzerne County was in turmoil and upheaval. A.H.'s attack with the new county bill had been like the bad sting of a bee, and while it had the courthouse crowd reeling, they were nevertheless still on their feet. But the flood from the auditors' report they could not withstand. All summer long, the purge continued; it was the only action that the men at Wilkes-Barre could take to stave off the inevitable downfall. They went about their task with a heavy heart. The year 1876 was a presidential election year; the voter had to be placated. But for all their scurrying around to save as much of their political power as possible, they also had time to plan reprisals against those they thought responsible for their discomfort. In addition to the strictly political men, there was also that restless sea of conservatives who were the opponents of the new county. They joined forces to settle their score with the Wintons. The Wintons had to be dealt with. Coon had paid his price for having opened up the present administration and exposed it to the light. The Wintons had aided Coon, had taken Coon's work and blazoned it across the county; and the Wintons had demanded partition of the county. The Wintons had to be dealt with. It was not going to be easy; they had seen how Byron had been snatched away to victory, instead of incarcerated in shame. But in the end, they knew that they would have obliterated the Wintons for good.

The first problem, first because it was the easiest to solve, was Frank Collins. He had an excellent reputation, he was loyal to his party, and his father had been respected as a judge in Wilkes-Barre. But he was a friend of A.H.'s. The problem of what to do with Frank Collins was solved quite easily; they would remove him. They removed him by placing his name on the Democratic ticket for the November election. They would get him away, by sending him to Washington as the U.S. congressman from the Eleventh Congressional District.

Concerning A.H. himself, for the present, they planned nothing. They had not yet found a way to get through to him. They had made a trial test of the timber of this man, long before he had brought up the issue of another county. When in '74 the Wintons had emerged as a potential money power in the valley, a trial balloon had been raised over the Providence Poor Board to see what kind of people the Wintons were. The article in the *Scranton News-Letter* had been to gauge their measure. There had never been a response of any kind to the insinuations, raised in the letter, that the Wintons were profiting by $11,000 from the welfare money. By his silence, A.H. had shown that he could not be easily baited, nor would he play the buffoon knowingly.

They next turned to W.W. Here, they thought, there was a weakness. Surely, somewhere in his banks there must be an Achilles' heel. So, it was about this time that remarks were heard in the valley questioning the financial soundness of the Second National Bank. It was easy to give credibility to their intimations, for the economy was quite depressed all over the U.S. But that, by itself, would not be enough; there had to be something else. The lowering of the Democrats' own standing in the county provided the solution.

With the purge at the courthouse starting in June, the Democrats, who were in power, now had a bad odor. They realized that it was possible, in a wave of reform, for them all to be swept from office. They directed their energies toward preventing this. Their reasoning, and the methods that they subsequently adopted, were highly sophisticated.

Until the auditors' report, there had never been any question in the valley as to which political party held the edge. That had been one of A.H.'s loudest cries when he started the new county campaign. The Democrats held the majority, and had for years. The Democrats now reasoned that it was possible that there would be a reaction to the auditors' report, and, if there were to be a reform, then the voters would turn away from their habitual voting patterns and cast their votes elsewhere. They would take their votes to only one place: the Republican pocket. Something then, somehow, would have to be done to divide the defecting Democrats. They turned their eyes towards a third party with which to split the voting power. Hopes ran high; perhaps all would not be lost. If the disgruntled voters could be divided between two other parties, there was even a chance that the plurality could be in the Democratic column after all. They eyed two minor parties appraisingly: the Independent, or Greenback, and the Temperance. The Independent, they quickly rejected as unsuitable for their purposes; it was strongly pro-labor and too close to their own Democratic philosophy. It would not accomplish what they were hoping for.

They turned to view the Temperance party—here was just the thing. The only trouble was that it rarely drew more than a hundred or so votes in an election. If they could find a man who was well known, well liked, and very close to the Republicans in his philosophy, they could almost hear the voters rush from the Democratic and Republican factions to the Temperance. Handled just right, it could leave the Democrats, in spite of their bad odor, with the winning ticket. W.W., they decided, was just the man to make it work for them.

It would take some doing, they knew; but, if successful, they would remain in power, and as a bonus, W.W. would probably talk himself into a libel charge or be caught buying votes, or suborning perjury as he campaigned. Thus, like Coon, W.W. would then be taken care of. They would be watching to see that he was repaid in full for his part in agitating for the new county. They would have to proceed cautiously in their scheme, to finesse; the Temperance people made their bid on the basis of honesty and forthrightness. They were smart enough to realize that the Temperance people would not traffic in deals and bribes. Their best avenue of approach, they decided, was by using suggestions appropriately placed and correctly timed.

They thought it would work, because they had sized up W.W. and decided that if he had any weakness, it was his vanity. W.W. was not vain, but his vanity would allow him to accept the nomination, because he would be pleased and flattered that others had recognized his most sterling attributes.

Everything came to pass as they had painstakingly plotted. While A.H. was at Nantucket, the Temperance party announced that they were going to nominate W.W. for congressman to Washington, representing the Twelfth Congressional District.

W.W. was flattered and pleased. He had never run for any public office, and he had never sought public office. To be asked when he hadn't been aware that he was even being considered, he regarded as an honor which he could not refuse.

When A.H. returned from Nantucket, the valley was once again its usual bustling self. The mines had resumed operations, the DL&W was busy converting to the narrow gauge track, men were at work, and politics were uppermost in everyone's mind; people were wondering what, if anything, would happen to the courthouse power-grabbers in the November election. W.W. told A.H. of his nomination. A.H. was surprised, and questioned the wisdom of running on the Temperance ticket.

"This could be a ruse to split the Republican ticket, Father."

But his father appeared to have only rosy plans, "If I win, A.H., you and Alice and Kate—dear little Kate—she especially must come and visit her grandparents in Washington."

"Father, I'm serious. Somebody could be using you; have you considered that possibility?"

"And have you considered how much power I would have, A.H., if I were a congressman? Think of what I could accomplish for the new county."

A.H. was impatient with his father. "No wonder you never went into politics. I don't think you understand a thing about it."

W.W. drew in his ruffled feathers and stared at his son, "Now just a minute—don't talk to your father like that. I'm perfectly well aware of what I'm doing. I was asked, because some people around here recognize me for the good man that I am; I was pleased to accept the honor they had bestowed on me, because I think it will put me in a position to help the new county bill."

"I'm sorry, father; I don't agree. Somehow, you were asked because the people who will vote for you will be the kind who would ordinarily vote Republican. As far as I can see, your purpose in the election is to split the reform vote, thereby throwing the plurality to a third group, namely the Democrats." A.H.'s tone was very final. By this time, he was so annoyed by his father's lack of perceptiveness in things political that he was almost mad at him.

W.W. toyed with his watch fob before looking up at his son; there was a sly, triumphant look on his face. "Very nicely put, son. Very nice indeed—except for one thing. For your theory to work, just so many and only so many votes, within a very narrow range, must split from the Democratic and Republican parties, over to the Temperance, to make both the Temperate and Republican candidates lose to the Democratic one.

"From where I'm standing, all that is necessary is to take enough votes from the Democratic party to make either the Temperance or Republican candidate win. You see, my aim, in taking office, is the new county. Surely you must know that if I had wanted to go to Washington that badly, I would have been there long before now. Be honest, A.H.; what would your mother and I do there now?

"We want the new county very badly. If I am elected, I will be in a position to accomplish this. If the Republicans win, they will do the same, because they have been behind us clamoring for a new county, too. Either way, we will get what we want."

"Father, I apologize. I did you a great disservice when I criticized you."

"No, A.H., you just forgot that you are not the only one who can do things."

A.H. mused, "I don't know, Father; I think it would be great if you did win. You—in Congress from the Twelfth District. Frank Collins—in Congress beside you, from the Eleventh District. Everybody back in Scranton would be expecting you two to do an awful lot for them."

"I hope Frank Collins wins. He's been a great help in the past. He's a fine boy; I like him very much. If the Republicans do sweep the county, though, he'll be out."

At the time that W.W. and A.H. were holding this discussion, the Republican County Committee and its delegates had not yet met to nominate their candidates. In early September, just as they were ready to convene their meeting, W.W. spoke to several of the committee members, to make sure that they would continue to support the new county bill, if elected to power. To his very great surprise and dismay, they no longer showed any interest in splitting Luzerne County.

The Republicans had appraised the courthouse purging correctly, as a remedy to stop, hopefully, the swing of voters away from the Democratic party. After many years as a minority, they saw that opportunity was at last going to put them into the driver's seat. Suddenly, they lost all interest in reducing by half the territory they would control. Now that the Republicans thought there was a chance that they would have a county to run, they weren't interested in creating another county.

Gravely alarmed, W.W. reported this to A.H.; it was a wrinkle they had not been expecting. On analysis, though, it should not have been that much of a surprise. Most of the Republicans that W.W. and A.H. had worked with were from Scranton's First and Second Wards, the old Providence and Hyde Park areas. But those Republicans were not all of the Republicans in Luzerne County. There was a large number of Republicans at Wilkes-Barre and throughout the rest of the county to be considered. Now that they were going to come into power, they saw no necessity for a county division.

A.H. and W.W. decided upon a bold but somewhat questionable move because, to them, the creation of a new county for Scranton was all-important. At the actual meeting of the Republicans at Washington Hall, where A.H. had his office and across from the Second National Bank building, W.W. arrived at the "eleventh hour" and asked them to place his name on their ballot, as Congressman from the Twelfth district. If they did so, he would withdraw his name from the Temperance ticket. His fellow Republicans, with whom he had been affiliated until the Temperance party had sought him, were so shocked at his seemingly cavalier behavior that they almost booed him from the floor.

Now, A.H. and W.W. were truly upset. A Temperance ticket had yet to carry an election. The way things stood now, a win by either the Republicans or Democrats meant that nothing would be done to advance the cause for a new county. One last hope remained to them, which they decided to pursue. W.W. went down to Wilkes-Barre and called on his old acquaintance, Col. Hendrick

Wright. Shortly after the Temperance Party had nominated W.W. for Congress, his Democratic opponent had passed away. Col. Wright had stepped in and filled the vacancy; for now at the age of sixty-eight, he was the elder statesman of the Wilkes-Barre and Luzerne County Democrats. W.W. went to him, to find out whether he would throw all his power and influence behind the drive for the new county at the next session of the Harrisburg legislature, in return for being elected to the U.S. House of Representatives in spite of a Republican county victory.

It was no idle gift that W.W. had to offer. In the past, he and A.H. had thrown their weight behind Frank Collins, so that Frank had often carried a Republican section for his lone Democratic office. They needed only to pass the word that the support for Frank Collins was also to include Hendrick Wright, this time.

The promise was given. On election day—this was the election in which Rutherford B. Hayes was eventually to be declared President by Congress's Electoral Commission—the Republicans swept the local Luzerne County offices. W.W. received only ninety-one votes on the Temperance ticket. By a comfortable majority, both Frank Collins and Hendrick Wright, on the Democratic ticket, were sent to the U.S. House of Representatives. In their first dabbling in politics, W.W. and A.H. had certainly maneuvered, and power-played, and double-dealt in the style of the worst of them; but they didn't care, for they would soon have what they wanted: new county status for the upper half of the Wyoming Valley was as good as accomplished.

The Republicans were in office at last, and they lost no time in righting the wrongs that they had been unjustly burdened with in the past. In Scranton, Democrat F.A. Beamish was charged with embezzlement, and his trial was set for December 15. The annoyance with Mr. Beamish stemmed from the days when he had been secretary, and a director, of Scranton's School Board, Fourth District. A.H. knew Frank Beamish very well; they had served together on the Providence Poor Board. Beamish was the owner of the *Sunday Morning Free Press*, of which J.C. Coon had been the editor. He was a Democrat; in fact, he was more or less the head of the Democrats in Scranton. He was a natural leader, a shrewd politician, charming, and had a jovial personality.

The annoyance in Scranton with Beamish had started in 1872, the time when A.H. and W.W. had been busy setting up the town of Winton and its coal mine. The cause of the annoyance emanated from Harrisburg. At a general assembly of the Legislature in Harrisburg, there was a law passed which imposed upon the secretary of the School Board of the Fourth District of the city of Scranton the additional duties of receiver of school taxes for that District. In other words, Beamish was to collect the school taxes instead of the tax collector. This law had come into effect when the Legislature had the power to pass "special laws," and before the state's Constitutional revision.

The Republicans hadn't liked the special powers of Mr. Beamish, and at their next election had turned half of the School Board members into Republicans. It was quite some time before the School Board could meet and carry out its duties, for every time the members assembled, violent disagreement erupted and the meeting was broken off. At last they did manage to complete a meeting, but immediately afterwards the Republicans set up their own version of the Fourth District's School Board. This created two school boards, both collecting taxes from the citizens; it also made for a great deal of confusion and double-paid or unpaid taxes in some cases.

The case was carried to the state supreme court, and the second (Republican) board was ruled illegal. Beamish lost his school board post in the next election, and all appeared to be forgotten. However, the Republicans had managed to get hold of some of his record books, and in December of '75 a charge of forgery was brought against him. His trial was postponed, and probably would have been postponed indefinitely, if the Republicans hadn't come into power at the court house in the November '76 election. On December 15, Beamish was speedily brought to trial and convicted of forgery.

Other than clearing out those Democrats who had plundered Scranton, A.H. was uninterested in the Beamish case, although he had always suspected Beamish as being the author of the article attacking the Poor Board and the Wintons which had appeared in the *Scranton News-Letter* in '74. However, there was one who was very upset—Col. Hendrick Wright was greatly disturbed at his friend Beamish's sorry fate. The Democrats, as a whole, were also upset about their most popular member being attacked.

A.H. should have been disturbed at the outcome of Beamish's trial—not because he was for Beamish, but because of the effect that the conviction had on Col. Wright. A.H. was too young at the time and W.W. never knew about it, but Col. Wright had given his promise once before—to Andrew Beaumont, to help elect Samuel Collings to the U.S. Congress. Shortly thereafter he had changed his mind, and Samuel Collings had lost the election. In the Collings election, there had been no provocation, such as a Beamish, to make Wright change his mind. Now, resenting the attack on his friend Beamish, would Beamish's conviction be enough to make him feel that he had justification for reneging on his promise to W.W.?

Christmas was fast approaching. Tom Campbell, the luckless young man from Carbondale, was still sitting in jail for killing his friend on the Fourth of July. His lawyer, Mont Flanigan, was still trying to obtain his release. And Stephen Tunstall, the father of Ella Tunstall Winton, had just arrived in Scranton to find out why his daughter and her family would not be visiting him in Peekskill for Christmas. Of all the things A.H. could have paid attention to at this time, he devoted his energies to Mr. Tunstall, a very irate father-in-law.

Ella and her father arrived at A.H.'s office early, the morning after Mr. Tunstall reached Scranton. In a few short words, he expressed disgust with his daughter's in-laws and criticized their handling of Walter's disappearance.

"What have you done to bring him back?" he shouted at A.H.

A.H. bristled back, ready to defend his brother, solely because of Mr. Tunstall's attitude. With A.H.'s own low personal opinion of Walter, A.H.'s annoyance with Mr. Tunstall's belligerent attitude was so great that he would go so far as to actually defend Walter.

"Mr. Tunstall, we have tried. I assure you, it was as upsetting to his parents as it was to his wife. My father engaged the services of detectives, but while we have reports of closing in on him from time to time, so far he has always managed to elude them."

"Shameful! It's shameful the way you have allowed my daughter to live here."

A.H. glared at Ella. It was up to her to tell her father that she had wanted to remain alone in Scranton, hoping that Walter would return. "How typical," he thought, "not to tell her father and let him think that we had forced her to remain here unbefriended."

"It was Ella's decision, Mr. Tunstall. We have worried about her, but she insisted that she was all right."

"Humph; I wouldn't even know now if I hadn't come down to take her back with me for Christmas." But the father was not that easily duped, or else he was more familiar with the foibles of the Tunstall women than anyone realized, for he turned to Ella and said, "Ella, is that why you wrote last Christmas, saying that you were too busy with the store and parties in Scranton to come to Peekskill for a visit? Because you didn't want me to know that that son-of-a-bitch you prefer for a husband had left you?"

Ella's little sniffle and somewhat shifting glance gave him his answer.

"What would you like me to do, Mr. Tunstall?"

"Well, I'm taking Ella back with me. That's one thing I'm certain of. Now you put an ad in the paper for that boy and the woman he ran off with. Then we're going to get my little girl divorced and forget that we ever came to this hell-hole valley."

Ella broke into sobs, and A.H. bowed to a wise decision.

A.H. and Mr. Tunstall were now thinking alike. He arranged for an ad in the local papers. For the first notice, Mr. Tunstall expressed his feelings, just about as well as anyone could in print, by the postscript he appended to the advertisement:

> *Information Wanted* of the whereabouts of one Lou Wright, alias Mrs. Foster, alias Mrs. Walter Winton. Last heard from in one of the western states. Then gave her name as Mrs. Walter Winton.
>
> address Stephen Tunstall, Scranton, Pa.
>
> P.S. No reward will be given.

The following day, Mr. Tunstall relented slightly and altered his ad to read:

> Five Cents Reward
>
> for one Lou Wright, a woman of questionable character, alias Miss Foster, alias Mrs. Walter W. Winton
>
> Stephen Tunstall

A week later, just before he and Ella and his grandchildren were ready to leave for Peekskill, Mr. Tunstall got downright generous—maybe because of the Christmas spirit or maybe because he was going to see the last of Scranton:

> $25.00 Reward
> for any information that will lead to the whereabouts of Mrs. Lou Foster, a lewd woman, representing herself to be the wife of Walter W. Winton.
> Stephen Tunstall.

Except for Alice's single comment, Ella passed unnoticed from the Scranton scene, "A.H., I really miss Ella. I know you didn't approve of her. But, after all, her only crime was that she loved a Winton too much for her own good," Alice paused and looked archly at A.H., "You know, you could say that of me, too."

"Never," he replied, wrapping his arms around her and burrowing his face where the neckline of her dress dipped the lowest.

"Oh? And where is there a difference?"

"Because you haven't loved me enough yet for it to be too much—for today, anyway."

After Ella departed, it was time to celebrate Christmas—time to ring in the new year of 1877. And what a year it was going to be! A.H. counted the days until the state legislature reconvened and the new county became a fact. All the while, poor Tom Campbell was still sitting in jail, Mont Flanigan was still trying to get him released, and F.A. Beamish was waiting on an appeal. A.H. also breathed a sigh of relief and relaxed; it would be a couple of weeks before he would have to ride the train to Wilkes-Barre every time he had a case to try in court.

There was a feverish excitement to everything he did over the holidays. The snow appeared more white to him, the Christmas tree was bigger, the presents more thoughtful, friends more friendly, social occasions more pleasant, all because it would soon be time for the state legislature to reconvene. Humming busily as he worked, A.H. prepared a fresh draft of the new county bill. He made it as simple as he could; he wanted to remove as many grounds for objection as possible. This time, he asked for a separation on the basis of population alone. He asked for an act to provide for the division of counties containing a population of 150,000 or more and the erection of a new county therefrom.

Shortly after the new year, A.H., with his head held high, smiling and laughing, full of hopes and the promise of the new life to come, departed for Harrisburg; at the same time, Frank Collins left to take his seat in the U.S. House of Representatives in Washington.

"It won't be long now. I'll be back soon," A.H. said jubilantly, kissing Alice and Kate farewell.

The new version of the new county bill was introduced to the Legislature on January 19. Almost before A.H. could find a seat in the gallery, it had been struck down. Again, separate county status for Scranton was vetoed. It happened so quickly that A.H. couldn't believe that it had happened. Tight-lipped, white-faced, in a frenzy of anger, he rode the train back to Scranton.

Something terrible happened to A.H. on that ride home. He rode almost the entire distance without saying a word, even to the conductor; he didn't trust himself to speak. This plummet to the depths of defeat had wracked him so much, mentally, that it almost had a debilitating physical effect on his body. He was now thirty-nine years old; he had been practicing law for seventeen years. Together, he and his father were two of the most influential men in the valley. The money and natural resources at their command were a vast storehouse. Railroads and their robber-baron overlords courted them because the right to transport coal, from the mine to the factory, could make a railroad or break it. He was no child, and he had not set out on his campaign for a new county for Scranton because it would make him richer or more powerful. He had come from a family, and he had married into a family, where each man's actions in the valley were to be undertaken for the good of all. Many who were supposed to look after the valley, who were supposed to have the interests of the Wyoming Valley uppermost, had fallen prey to bribery, deceit, the misapplication of public monies. It was an easy habit to fall into, to have no regard for money, when the attentions of the rest of the world were being showered on the valley, and had been since the start of the Civil War, because of its coal—when the courting of favors by railroad owners, by international financiers, by exploiters, was a common everyday occurrence—when the corporate taxes coming into the county at Wilkes-Barre from one company's stock alone could run as high as a half-million dollars per annum. He realized that he was standing alone.

A change came over A.H. as the train rolled northeastward. He became totally self-sufficient, dependent unto himself and on no one else. He had risen to lead when family and friends had pressed for the new county. Now, out of the ashes of a devastating, unexpected defeat, a new phoenix rose to fly higher, stronger than before.

When A.H. reached Wyoming Avenue, he was just as white-faced, lips pressed, and in a frenzy of suppressed anger as intense as when he had boarded the train at Harrisburg. Alice ran to greet him in alarm, wondering why he had returned so early. But seeing him, she fell back and uttered no sound at all, not even one of welcome. Instead, she fed him and waited for him to speak; she remained silent.

At last, he spoke, "There's to be no new county."

"What happened?"

"They wouldn't even consider it;" for a very brief, fleeting moment the giant of a leader almost cracked, almost sobbed. But in him there was an ability that no one could withstand. He did not take destiny by the neck and shape it; he followed his destiny, "I haven't decided what to do yet. I want to tell Father and the others first." A.H. left immediately afterwards to find W.W.

As soon as W.W. heard, he knew, as A.H. knew, that they had been double-crossed. For a while, they discussed the avenues of approach still left open to them. But in the end, they came to the conclusion that there was no longer going to be any interest in erecting a new county.

"I wish the Republicans would not be so short-sighted," sighed W.W., "They should have enough sense to know that they won't be in office forever. They should use this time now to prepare for the day when they turn everything over to the Democrats. When the Democrats once get in again, it will be too late to do anything about a new county."

A.H. agreed completely.

They made plans to notify the other interested men, "If they haven't already heard," W.W. added, wryly.

They were a small group now. A.H., W.W., and only a few of their relatives and friends were still interested in separating from Wilkes-Barre. Of the group, A.H. was the one who yielded least to defeat. A few days later, he returned to W.W.

"I want you to back me in whatever I do."

W.W. looked interested. There was a change in his son; W.W. couldn't quite define it, but his perceptiveness told him it was there, "What are you going to do?"

"I don't want to say yet; I don't want anyone to know. Just tell me whether you will promise to support me."

W.W. was somewhat hesitant about a blind promise, even though it was to his son. In the end, he did agree to stand behind A.H., whatever he was up to.

A.H. next cancelled what appointments he could; the rest, he turned over to John Collings, "I'm going to have to be in Winton the next few days, John. You can handle whatever comes into the office, I know."

John looked questioningly at A.H., but did not press for an explanation. Lawyer Winton was not going to reveal anything he didn't want to.

To Alice, A.H. said, "I'm going to be spending most of the daytime at Winton for a week or two. If you need anything, John will take care of it."

Alice was puzzled, "But isn't it too cold to spend all day at the mine? Is there trouble with George [Filer] or Tom [Livey]? Don't you have to be in Wilkes-Barre for court?"

"Alice, please don't ask me so many questions. I have some work to do. I just wanted you to know where I would be."

Out of the ashes of defeat, a phoenix had risen to conceive a plan so daring, so bold, so imaginative, that he was afraid to say one word about it to anyone, for fear something would slip out and he would be blocked. A.H. was smart enough to realize that if he told no one, not one word, failure could come only from the natural occurrence of events, not by any one or two people conspiring or reneging on their word, as had just happened.

At Winton, A.H. visited the residents, family by family. He extolled the progress they had made, the cleanness and neatness of the village even though it was a coal community, and gave them a short lesson in American government. When he left, he departed smiling and with their support.

Adjacent to Winton on the southwest boundary, separated by the D & H coal lands, was another community—Jessup. At Jessup, A.H. repeated his actions at Winton—he visited the families, talked with them at length, and departed smiling and with their support.

Soon application was filed, and on February 24, 1877, the borough of Winton was proclaimed. Winton and Jessup were the principal communities of the new borough. This was a month after A.H. had returned from his dismal trip to Harrisburg. Then one month later, on March 23, the ordinances of the new borough were passed into law. To accomplish all this had not been without cost. W.W. sold fourteen acres of his 2,235, including the second of his two breakers, to the Wurts tract. But as he was always of an optimistic turn of mind, he had not grumbled too much; the generally depressed state of the nation's economy made him just as happy to pick up a large sum of cash.

A.H. wanted no one to suspect his intentions. So cautious was he that he was not adverse to throwing in protective coloration where he thought it would help the most. The Winton Borough seal was designed as a picture of William Penn, with the words "Borough of Winton" underneath. Privately, A.H. thought of him as the "Little New England Pilgrim Man." But to anyone stumbling by chance on his activities in that section of Luzerne County, the words would automatically be dismissed, and hopefully the activity, too, when seen under the symbol of Philadelphia's William Penn. Never think for a moment that A.H. was not aware of what went on in the valley or what the motivating forces were.

A.H.'s next move was to Harrisburg. He reached there early in April, and submitted a rather odd bill, which was passed and proclaimed into law on April 18. The law provided, through the courts, for the erection of boroughs out of territory that was presently included in cities of the third class. It was an odd bill, in the sense that it had no meaning, or did not seem to have one to the politicians who heard of it. There were only a few cities in the state—Scranton, Wilkes-Barre, Allentown, Bethlehem, Harrisburg, Lancaster, Reading, and Erie—that might be affected. These cities were all happy as they were; whoever heard of a city downgrading, dismembering itself? A.H. succeeded because he threw out the bait that a dismembered Scranton would enhance Wilkes-Barre; his strange petition quickly became law. But in A.H.'s grand scheme, it was another vital, necessary link. As soon as the law was signed, A.H. wired W.W. to go ahead with their preparations; for A.H. had revealed his plan to his father at the time the fourteen acres were sold at Winton.

This time, when A.H. returned to Scranton, he was a jubilant, assured, smiling conqueror. From the train station, he first went home and picked up Alice and Kate. Together, they stopped at the office for John Collings, and finally across the street at the Second National Bank for W.W. A noisy procession of two carriages, they clattered over to the old Providence area and W.W.'s home. For the rest of the day, family and friends alike squeezed into W.W.'s spacious house. The laughter and sounds of exhilarating success filled the air. Everywhere, everyone was celebrating. A.H. was the toast of Providence, and it was his hour. The partying lasted far into the night.

When A.H. awoke the morning after the celebration, as the clock was ticking past twelve noon, his head almost burst from his shoulders. He moaned and groaned under a gargantuan hangover.

Alice could not help but take advantage of him and tease him, "You should have seen yourself last night. Would you like me to tell you *everything* you did?," emphasizing the "everything."

With an effort, A.H. cracked open one eye and regarded her suspiciously, "No, thank you," he said, somewhat prissily.

"Ah, but you should have seen yourself, leading the parade, jumping from one fire engine to another. How do you do it? You must teach me the trick."

"Spare me the details, Alice; I don't believe a word you're saying," which was true, because A.H. could remember very little of what had actually transpired the previous evening after the celebrations had gotten underway.

His eye fell upon the *Scranton Times*, which had been tossed on top of the bed's coverlet, "Is there anything about yesterday evening in the paper? I think I can safely take their version over yours."

A.H. reached for the newspaper, lying near the foot of the bed. His too large head throbbed unbearably, and he fell back among the pillows.

Pityingly, Alice offered to read to him the newspaper story:

> Last evening was a joyful one in the borough of Providence. When the news arrived that the Governor had signed the Providence bill, the rejoicings of the people knew no bounds.
>
> A huge bonfire was built on Rockwell's hill, amidst the discordant shrieks of the gongs, and ringing of the bells, the firing of cannons and other firearms, and the glare of the rockets that flew skyward: the people of Providence laid themselves out for a jubilee. Everyone seemed to feel just right. The old fogies who have lived here for many years grasped each other's hands on the street and while tears of joy welled up in their eyes, they spoke of the prospective good times in store for the old borough.
>
> The Franklin Fire Company of Hyde Park came up and brought their steamer with them. The Liberty boys met them and escorted them to their rooms where a pleasant time was spent in a genuine, old fashioned firemen's reunion.
>
> The Providence people appreciated the kindness and fraternal feeling manifested by the Franklin Company in coming over to visit them, and they hope the day is not far distant when the Liberty boys will have an opportunity of returning the compliment under similar exceedingly pleasant circumstances.
>
> Liberty is pleasant under all circumstances, and the people of Providence felt the force of the word more last night than they have for the last ten years.
>
> Good-bye, Scranton; you have been anything but a tender nurse to us; however we shall try in the future to paddle alone without your motherly care.
>
> We bid you a last, a long adieu.

A happy smile spread over A.H.'s face, as he thought of the past evening and its significance.

Alice saw the smile and commented, "Are you pleased?"

"Yes, very. Now if you'll excuse me, I'll dress. I've got to get everyone circulating the petitions. It's important that we move as quickly as possible," He started to get out of bed, felt the throbbing in his head, groaned, but persisted anyway. There was too much to do, and no time to delay.

"Have breakfast first, A.H.; although in your case, I think it will be low tea. Besides, I think John took the papers this morning when he left. He was going to see your father, and together they were going to get everything started."

Relieved, A.H. took his time dressing, and Alice's prediction of breakfast after three came true. As he sat in solitary splendor in the dining room, he obviously enjoyed the food, savoring every bite. It was the first time that he had enjoyed eating anything at all in the past three months. A last cup of coffee had just been poured when John Collings returned home.

"Well, A.H., I see you finally made it up! Tsk, tsk, here we've been out working hard since seven-thirty this morning, and you've been lolly-gagging around," He leered, in comic distortion towards Alice, "Letting yourself be distracted by earthly pleasures when there's work to be done! Aren't you ashamed of yourself?"

A.H. put his hands to his head; the coffee had not cleared his head enough to withstand John's exuberance. However, he was not going to let John down him completely, "And what are you doing here—sneaking off for a rest when you're supposed to be out working? Tsk, tsk, yourself."

"I thought you might want to see this," and he handed a late-edition paper to A.H., "Note the last paragraph."

A.H. tried to read, but the small type persisted in blurring. He, in turn, handed the newspaper over to Alice to read:

> As a result of the Providence bill, which legalizes the dismemberment of cities of the third class that have been formed from boroughs, we notice that petitions are circulating freely in various sections of this city, praying the courts to appoint commissions for the purpose of setting them aside into separate and distinct boroughs. The Hyde Park people, anxious to emulate the example of Providence, are taking the preliminary steps towards being set apart, and in the old Eighth and Ninth Wards, petitions are circulating, and being numerously signed, for the same purpose. We understand that Shanty Hill is also astir, so that the movement is simultaneous throughout the city, of course there will be small nooks and out of the way places that will be discarded entirely by the several new boroughs, and we may expect to see some streets and alleys left out in the cold in this way, with no corporate or municipal organization to cling to. They will be much in the condition of the man without a country.

> The breaking up of a mighty iceberg makes a considerable stir even in mid-ocean, but it is nothing to the general scattering that may be expected to follow upon the smashing up of the city. The greatness of our mayor will be gone; the golden dream of our city controller, the anticipation of the city treasurer upon the consolidation of the different school districts, and even the city surveyor will pass into oblivion and his sewer schemes into smithereens. The city fathers, Common and Select, together with their imposing arrays of standing and sitting committees, will bid farewell to all their greatness, and enter anew on a race for fame and fortune as burgesses of the new boroughs.
>
> Our police force, principally, will cling to the old Eighth and Ninth Wards, where Squire Schoonmaker will fill up his spare hours perusing the history of the sewer system and holding court, when he is not studying up the Turko-Russian War, and there will be a new deal all around. Of course, our local historians will not be slow to avail themselves of the opportunity for making new books, and we may expect volumes on the rise and fall of Scranton—or a city for ten years.
>
> Truly, the people of Providence are powerful, to make their influence felt so extensively and so thoroughly, and who shall dare prophesy that Razorville, with its sharp citizens and its multitudinous plans, may not yet aspire to becoming the state capital.

When Alice finished, A.H. remarked only, "We're not planning to go that far," referring to the comment concerning the state capital.

Exactly what was it that A.H. had done?

And what was his grand scheme?

What he had done, essentially, was to redraw the map of the Wyoming Valley before anyone realized it was being redrawn. This he did in only ninety days, from that day in January when the new county bill had been rejected in Harrisburg, to the day in April when Providence and, hopefully, Hyde Park had the right to break off from Scranton and return to their independent identity.

And the grand scheme—the grand plan that was worthy of the phoenix who had risen out of the January ashes of total defeat?

A.H. planned to create a new county without the aid of anyone, except the people living in the area encompassed by the county's boundary. By the plan he had conceived, Scranton, Wilkes-Barre, and all their government leaders were no longer necessary for the erection of a new county. To accomplish this, he had gone first to Winton and Jessup, and convinced them to incorporate into a borough, a necessary structure for the lodging of a county seat. Next, he had gone to the state legislature, who gave him the means to withdraw Providence and Hyde Park from Scranton. He wanted Providence and Hyde Park for two reasons: first, their total population would give the necessary strength to vote in a new county; second, he had a sentimental attachment for his home area. Providence and Hyde Park had been the center of his early life, and the residents were either Heermans or other early settlers strongly in favor of the new county. He would rather take Providence with him than leave it behind.

For the new county built in this fashion, he was intending to draw the county boundary line along the Lackawanna River down through the city of Scranton, including Providence and Hyde Park on one side and excluding what was left of Scranton on the other. He would have to use Winton as the county seat, in order to make sure that it was far enough removed from the new county line. Hopefully, his new county would include all of the Wyoming Valley northeast of Scranton, taking in Carbondale at the end. That A.H. would succeed, there was little doubt. He had already made Winton a borough; he had already legislated Providence and Hyde Park to the point where they could divorce themselves from Scranton city and return to their old borough status. As far as proclaiming a new county was concerned, the governor would be forced to do it if enough inhabitants clamored for it and demanded it.

All the while, hapless Tom Campbell was sitting in the jail at Wilkes-Barre; Mont Flanigan, his lawyer, had yet to gain his release.

At this point, A.H. was satisfied, and relaxed. It would take a while to accumulate the necessary number of signatures on his petitions, but he was not worried. He knew that they would come: Providence already had the required minimum for separation from Scranton. A.H. had everything to his liking, and acted accordingly.

Part of his success among the voting citizens could be attributed to the restlessness of the times. Economically, people were anxious to change their impoverished lot. At such a point, the people can be more easily induced to follow any course opened to them, if they think they will be the better for it. A.H.'s timing was just right for the reactivation of the old boroughs of Providence and Hyde Park.

But what of the antagonists? To be truthful, at this point they felt more like the abused hero than the opposition. They considered themselves so ill-treated as to fear for their future. A.H. had jockeyed them into an unbelievable position. He held the whole deck of cards in his hand, and considering the way he was playing, there was no way they could be dealt in. He had also united Democrats and Republicans against a common enemy. That ever-moving conglomeration of men opposed to A.H.'s plans expanded into a massive body. Something had to be done, and done quickly, to prevent the division of Scranton and then Luzerne County. Another chapter in the battle for possession of the Wyoming Valley was being fought. At the moment, it looked as if the men from Connecticut were going to have the right to allocate the territory as they pleased.

There was only one school of thought, from the antagonists' point of view, as to how to handle the situation. No one voiced a hope for conciliation or a compromise. The modern day extension of Razorville had to be destroyed; W.W.'s banks became the prime target.

As for A.H., suddenly he was the most interesting and sought after man in the Wyoming Valley. He was now an acknowledged leader and a public figure.

He relaxed in the limelight and enjoyed it. His personality—speaking well in public, his courteous manner, his cheery, genial nature, enjoying the ladies, socializing with men of all interests—was put into service. Late spring was a very busy time for A.H. He and W.W., with John Collings, Isaac Dean, and Dr. Eugene Heermans, spearheaded the activities. Arthur Dean, Isaac's son, passed his bar examination in time to join the ranks at Scranton. It was quite a formidable array of lawyers; A.H., John Collings, Arthur Dean, and Frank Collins when he was home. It was not an uncommon occurrence for an unwary stranger who had wandered into Scranton and run afoul of the law to find himself defended by A.H. and prosecuted by John Collings or by some other combination of the four.

A.H. was enjoying the popularity—and he was popular: demand for his services as a lawyer had suddenly increased; he was asked to address various organization meetings; and the socially minded, as well as those politically interested, were anxious to hear his opinions. Nevertheless, he found it all very fatiguing. His fear of talking, and giving voice to some of his thoughts about what he knew of the underhanded dealings going on in Luzerne County, had almost reached the point of becoming a phobia with him.

On one particular evening, he returned home from a meeting with prospective Hyde Park Council members particularly frustrated and exhausted. There had been at least a dozen times during the meeting when he had wanted to speak out and tell them of the infamy practiced on them by some of their local administrators. He was even more depressed when he realized that it was also his twelfth wedding anniversary. Entering, he found Alice entertaining his cousin Dr. Eugene Heermans. From the look on her face, he assumed that Eugene had been treating her to one of his more lengthy medical dissertations. He soon found, however, that such was not the case.

From where he was sitting, Eugene called out to him without greeting, "A.H., I have been cuckolded! I want redress!"

Alice rose hastily to leave the room, but Eugene's cold tone stopped her, "It's not necessary for you to leave, Alice. In fact, I think you should know. You see Sarah almost daily; you have a right to know what she has done."

Alice hesitated, and looked questioningly at A.H.

"If it's all right with Eugene, stay, Alice. You've often said that you wanted to be with me when I was working on a case."

She seated herself on an uncomfortable chair near the door.

A.H. returned to Eugene, "What happened? Are you sure you're not exaggerating?"

"I am not," he replied frostily. It was plain to see that Eugene's anger was bottled inside him like a virulent bacteria stoppered in a test tube.

Watching, Alice wondered how long it would be before Eugene exploded.

"Eugene, I think we should have a drink before we go into your problem. You look as though you could use one, and I know I certainly can."

"I'll tell Bridget," Alice said, jumping from her chair.

Eugene waited in silence until she returned with a decanter and glasses on a tray.

"No wonder she looked so glum when I came in," thought A.H., "Eugene is anything but the pleasant guest."

After A.H. had poured and served the whiskey, Eugene talked.

"I want that woman out of my house. I want to get rid of her, and I want to get rid of her right now—immediately."

"Well, I don't know, Eugene. It usually takes a little time. After all, Sarah's been your wife for quite a few years."

"Don't tell me she's my wife. Remind her."

Very patiently, A.H. asked, "All right, Eugene, what did Sarah do that was so terrible?"

"She was engaged in the sex act with another man—on my sofa, in my parlor, in my house—when I came home this afternoon from the office."

Nothing disturbed the silence in the room.

Finally, Alice spoke, "Oh, how awful for you, Eugene."

Righteous wrath accepted the few words of comfort.

"Be that as it may, you're going to need more than that to get rid of her," advised A.H.

"My God, A.H., how much is a man supposed to take? What do you want me to do? Invite the neighborhood in?"

"It would help. No, all joking aside, Eugene, Sarah is going to have to admit that she was wrong, or she'll have to ask for a divorce, or you're going to have to have proof of what went on. Right now, it's your word against hers."

"Don't you believe me?" Eugene was on the verge of screaming.

Alice interrupted to speak soothingly, "It's not that, Eugene. Of course, we believe you. We know you too well to think you could be lying. What A.H. means is that there has to be some tangible proof that Sarah committed adultery, something that people who don't even know you can see, and see how you have been abused."

The medical mind was as sharp as the legal mind, "How do you mean, she has to admit she was wrong?"

"Oh, to say so in public or something like that."

From Eugene's general demeanor as he remained quiet and thoughtful, both A.H. and Alice saw that the idea appealed to him. "You mean like a signed confession?"

"Yes, that would be one way."

Eugene digressed slightly from his main attack, "You know, Lizzie Adele is not nine yet. Suppose she had come into the parlor and had seen her mother just as I did?"

Two sympathetic faces stared solemnly back at him. In spite of his tragic circumstances, Dr. Eugene Heermans still had that air of sophistication about him that he and Sarah had acquired during their stay in New York City for his medical education.

"If I bring Sarah to the office tomorrow, A.H., would you attend to it for me?"

"Well, I'd like to talk to her first. I think…" A.H.'s voice floated into silence at the look of impatience on his cousin's face.

"I am not interested in Sarah or anything she has to say."

Now A.H. was getting a little snappy, too, "I'll handle it, Eugene, but I have to talk to Sarah. I can't do anything until I can show just cause for you to put her aside as a final action. I don't ask you how to treat me; don't tell me how to practice law for you."

"Thank you, A.H.; that's all I wanted to know. While I descend from Benjamine Slocum through my mother, we do share a Heermans great-grandfather in common, and I should have known that your blood would be as outraged as mine over this degrading episode."

It was several days before A.H. could talk to Sarah. She pleaded excuses every time he called at the house. He finally recommended that she retain her own counsel; Eugene would tolerate no more delay. Agreement was reached at last, and Sarah and her lawyer met A.H. at his office, early on May 23.

"I'm going to read your statement to you, Sarah. Then, you take a look at it. If it is not correct in any way, tell Mr. Wells. Together, we will correct it. When you are satisfied with the way it is written, I'll ask you to sign it."

> To whom it may concern:
>
> I hereby acknowledge that I, Sarah F. Heermans, wife of Eugene A. Heermans, of the city of Scranton and the State of Pennsylvania have had unlawful carnal communication and cohabitation with S.C. Stewart, in the parlor of my husband's residence on Scranton Avenue several distinct times within the last two months. I further acknowledge that he gave me a ring. I also acknowledge that this confession is made and signed by me of my own free will and accord, and with the understanding that articles of separation to be drawn and signed by myself and husband: and further that no legal proceedings are to be begun or prosecuted against the said S.C. Stewart on account of the above adultery.
>
> Witness my hand this twenty-third day of May, 1877.

With almost a flourish, Sarah signed her name to the bottom of the paper.

A.H. walked her and Tom Wells to the door, then watched them leave. As they walked away down Lackawanna Avenue, disgust showed on his face. Perhaps it was the way Sarah Finch Heermans was holding her head, or the lightness of her step, but he felt no remorse for her.

Alice wanted to know when he came home how things had gone with Sarah. He couldn't tell her his impression that Sarah was without scruples. Without elucidating, he said, "It didn't take long."

"Where do you think she will go?"

"She didn't say."

Like Walter Winton, Sarah Heermans faded from their existence, but Eugene's marital problem preyed on A.H. He and Alice had always enjoyed an evening with Sarah and Eugene. Now, arbitrarily, such times were to be no more. He locked the memory of her flaunting manner in a recess of his mind, never to be mentioned. He wished that he could talk openly about her lack of contrition; somehow it would be a more human reaction when putting aside a dear friend's faithless wife. But he managed to restrain himself, cataloging Sarah's Confession of Sin with all the other things that he saw and knew about Scranton and Wilkes-Barre but dared not speak about. He had seen, in libel suits, more than one respectable citizen brought to his knees in court for uttering far less then the least that could cross his lips.

A day later, still in a reflective, lost-soul kind of mood, A.H. stopped in the large assembly room of Washington Hall after closing up his office for the day. The room had been hired by an out-of-town group and he was curious to see what was going on. Inside the hall, his eyes fell first upon the mayor of Scranton, Robert H. McKune, who was standing at the rear. A.H. moved over towards him and joined him.

He greeted the mayor with a "Ho, ho, what brings you here? I certainly never expected to see you at a meeting like this."

"I might say the same for you. I always heard that the cows at Providence delivered one-hundred-proof milk, and all you Providence babies were weaned on 'good ol' healthy likker'!"

"Oh, now I know why you're here," came A.H.'s quick rejoinder, "you think you'll get an extra vote. Bob, you go anywhere for a vote, don't you? Now with me, I'm just here out of curiosity."

"Well, if you're so curious, go down and take a seat."

"I intend to. And you're coming with me."

A.H. and Mayor McKune moved from the back wall down the aisle nearest them to within five rows of the stage before they found seats. The hall was filled and noisy, awaiting the first speaker. A good deal of laughter and light banter could be heard in the audience. It promised to be a dramatic and emotional time, and the audience was savoring the anticipation. The newly formed Scranton Temperance Union, sponsoring the meeting, was hoping to do some missionary work and increase the number of pledge card signers.

Temperance, in the United States, was never a popular cause; but it always had devoted adherents. Since the first Massachusetts license law was passed in 1651, the temperance movement had always been alive; it never disappeared entirely. It next popped up in York, Maine, in 1690, when the first prohibition law in America went into effect. Another important advance for the cause came in 1789, when the first temperance society was formed at Litchfield, Connecticut. With all its ups and downs, temperance persisted. It surged to the foreground again in 1826, when the Constitution of the American Society for the Promotion of Temperance was drafted at Boston. Essentially, then, Temperance was a New England philosophy.

An Irish priest, Father Mathew, toured the U.S. in 1849, speaking mainly to Irish Catholics. In his wake, he left numerous Father Mathew Temperance Societies; Scranton had one that was quite active. However, the meeting that A.H. and Mayor McKune were attending was the work of another group, which had sprung up in November of the preceding year, 1876. It was directed by Francis Murphy, and had started in Pittsburgh, Pennsylvania, spreading quickly over neighboring states.

The Prohibition political party was something else again. It had grown out of the temperance societies, when their delegates had met at Chicago in 1869. The aim of that meeting had been to obtain federal legislation prohibiting the manufacturing, transporting, and selling of alcoholic beverages. The delegates had wanted one or both of the major political parties, the Republicans or Democrats, to bring the Temperance Party into their own party, in the relationship of a special task force. But when both parties ignored such an idea, the Chicago convention group had felt themselves forced into nominating their own candidates, which they had done starting in 1872. It was this political party, derived from the temperance societies, that had put W.W.'s name in nomination for the fall of '76 election.

The temperance societies, however, adhered strictly to their missionary work: to retrieve the morally deprived from drunkenness, gambling, and general lawlessness, to a new life of health and family. The local temperance societies varied from place to place; some wanted total abstinence, prohibiting drink of any kind, whereas others were more moderate or temperate in their thinking, allowing wine and beer.

This was A.H.'s first attendance at a temperance meeting. Suddenly, since President Hayes had taken his oath of office a few months earlier at Washington, temperance was a burning question and Temperance meetings were springing up everywhere—for the First Lady, Lucy Hayes, or "Lemonade Lucy" as she was nicknamed, had startled Washington society by serving no alcoholic beverages at White House functions. In a matter of months, temperance had come very much into vogue.

A.H. really had no idea what to expect from this new group of Murphy Blue Ribbon wearers. So, he and Mayor McKune settled back in their chairs, waiting to be amused, or to be entertained, or, at the very least, definitely to observe. At last, a small militant band of five musicians came from the back of the hall. They were followed, in procession, by the three speakers and, lastly, by the ushers with their broad blue sashes, each carrying his allotment of pledge cards. The procession had begun at the rear of the hall and had marched, quasi-military style, down the same aisle that A.H. and Mayor McKune had used while seeking their seats. The procession moved past A.H. and McKune and continued on to the stage. The audience seemed to know what to expect, and had broken lustily into song at the sound of the familiar, at least to them, hymn. "Yield not to temptation, for yielding is sin; Each vict'ry will help you some other to win…"

Over and over again the verses and chorus were repeated, until the sound of the singing voices had reached a feverish pitch. A.H. sat quietly listening, taking it all in. But he soon found himself hearing the words of the hymn as if they had been written for him: "Be thoughtful and earnest, kind hearted and true." Had he ever felt otherwise about his valley? "Fight manfully onward, dark passions subdue. Shun evil companions. To him that o'ercometh..."—it was as if A.H. were hearing the last ten years of his life described: "Fight manfully onward" for a new county, and he had overcome defeat with the Scranton dismemberment bill—"Each victory will help you some other to win." His victory on Winton borough and then Providence would help him to win the victory for a new county. He was no longer an uninterested spectator but an avid listener.

The first speaker gave a brief history of the struggles and trials of the society and the Temperance movement as a whole. Again A.H. was amazed; it was from Connecticut. It was a Connecticut philosophy, being extolled in Pennsylvania's Wyoming Valley! For the second speaker, A.H. could have cared less. It was the speaker's personal account of how he had been "saved"; A.H. had heard enough stories daily in his law office to give this one no more credence than he did to some that crossed his threshold. But the third speaker—that was a different matter. He strummed and stroked the English language as A.H. had never heard it done. Of course, A.H. knew that the object was to work everyone up to the emotional climax of signing their Temperance pledge cards. But that was of secondary importance, compared to what and how the man was talking.

Listening to him, A.H. felt a great burst of relief from within. He saw within his grasp a way to talk—to talk at last and unburden himself of all the unsaid things that he had been wanting to say for at least seven years and didn't dare. If he were on the stage speaking, he could call everyone to help in the fight against the crookedness of the money-grabbers in the valley, against the corruption at the Wilkes-Barre courthouse. He could speak of the devilish way in which they worked—of the deceit they practiced on the citizens. He could tell of the double-cross, the reneging on promises; he could describe the hurt look in a husband's eye at his wife's unfaithfulness, and more. And no one would ever know whom he was talking about, no one could ever hurl libel charges at him; and he might actually awake his complacent neighbors to action. His inhibitions and frustrations fell from him, as easily as a cloak after losing its single neck button. When the usher stood at the end of his row and passed the pledge cards, A.H. reached eagerly for one and signed it.

Beside him, Mayor Robert McKune affixed his name to another Temperance pledge card. They were both blue-ribbon wearers now.

16

All the phantasms implied in a midsummer's dream progressed on their inevitable course, as the days of June moved towards the summer solstice.

There were those people who had decided that A.H. could do whatever he wanted to with the valley; they were impressed with the power he held—they joined him, they flattered him, and they offered him no resistance. But there were others who believed that the only way to control him was to fight him and stop his grand plan. They were the ones who could find no break in his defenses, nothing that they could accuse him of, in order to remove him from Scranton. They were the ones who realized that the only way to get to A.H. was through W.W.—the ones who recognized that the banks, the Second National and the Miner's Savings of Providence, would be the vulnerable spot and the key to A.H.'s defeat.

All the while, poor Tom Campbell was still sitting in the county jail, and Mont Flanigan wasn't having any luck releasing him.

In a contest for supremacy or control, very, very rarely will an adversary risk attacking his opponent directly, usually because the outcome is dubious; only superior ability decides the winner. The preferred tactic is to wait for an opening in the hunted's defenses, especially if there is the expectation that an opening will occur by chance. If there is no such luck, then a seemingly chance occurrence has to be contrived or manufactured. The advantages to this *modus operandi*, including the artificial "chance," lies in the fact that the attacker and his strategy are more easily disguised. In the first week of June, there came just such an opportunity.

The Scranton Trust Company and Savings Bank was considered one of the city's most reliable banks. Information was forwarded to Scranton and Wilkes-Barre from New York City that two directors of the Scranton Trust Company and Savings Bank had invested heavily in Wall Street stocks. Just as Jay Gould has not been above manipulating the gold market, using the unknowing President Grant in 1869, neither were those opposed to A.H. and the new county above using the Wall Street information to their advantage.

There were many ties between New York's financial center and the coal region that was the Wyoming Valley. Samuel Sloan, the president of the D L & W, the railroad that had built the Winton Branch to carry out the coal from Winton, summered near J.P. Morgan, and in 1868 had gotten to know the young financier very well. Later, in a fight between the Erie Railroad's Jay Gould and the D & H Canal Company, for possession of the Albany and Susquehanna (A & S), a small, 142-mile long New York railroad, Sloan had sent the A & S men to J.P. Morgan for help. After Morgan had won control of the A & S away from Gould, he had turned around and leased the 142 miles of the A & S track to the D & H on a ninety-nine year lease.

Jay Gould had also risen to his position of power through the auspices of men in the Wyoming Valley. The Erie's contract to build a railroad across New York State had brought the company to the the Scranton brothers and Scranton, to obtain iron rails. The Scrantons' ability to manufacture and deliver the rails ahead of schedule, thereby enabling Gould to finish the railroad ahead of time, had laid a basis for tying the Erie to the Valley, a tie which became even stronger when Gould became Erie's president.

The D L & W was essentially a Wyoming Valley railroad. George Scranton was looked upon as its father, and while Samuel Sloan spent very little time in the valley, the legacy left from history, and the 1851 opening of its first section of track in the valley, was too strong a tie to discount interest on Wall Street in the doings of people who lived in the Wyoming Valley.

It was not unusual then to see a robber-baron financier on the streets of Scranton, hurrying to a meeting with colliery owners. Nor was it unusual to hear about it on Wall Street whenever there was a substantial cash investment originating from Scranton or Wilkes-Barre. Runners could command a high price for their services whenever they could bring information to an investor that his rival was accumulating stock in a certain company, or, instead of accumulating, had stopped and was ridding himself of it. And in New York, stock manipulations were a common occurrence in the days before the regulatory Securities and Exchange Commission began operating in 1934.

A.H.'s opponents saw an opportunity when the news arrived telling of the two bank directors' heavy speculation. Word was passed back to New York that it would be a great help if the stocks which the two men held were to turn downward rather than upward—at least for a while. The speculating directors of the Scranton Trust Company and Savings Bank were Mr. Sutphin and Mr. Hunt; that W.W. had not speculated made no difference at all, although W.W. was also on the bank's Board of Directors. In fact, for the conspirators' purposes it was really better that W.W. wasn't directly involved on Wall Street, because it camouflaged the manufactured "chance occurrence." By June 2, the stocks did exactly as planned; they fell sharply and quickly in value. A.E. Hunt suffered a loss of $150,000; J.H. Sutphin lost $80,000.

There was nothing wrong in what Hunt and Sutphin had done; they were certainly within their rights in drawing from their own personal funds to invest in the stock market. But, as if by magic, on June 2, the same day the stocks were at their lowest, the rumor started to circulate in the valley that directors of the Scranton Trust Company and Savings Bank were insolvent, that they had used money on deposit at the bank for their wild Wall Street speculations, and that the

Scranton Trust Company and Savings Bank was itself insolvent. The rumor needed only a day and a half to accomplish what it had been intended to do.

Before the bank opened its doors for business on the morning of June 4, there was a long line of depositors who were waiting outside on Wyoming Avenue to withdraw their money. It was a run on the bank, and the directors and officers feared a panic. Those at the head of the bank realized that they had to meet the demand in order to prevent a bank panic. Once word of a panic got out, it was possible that all the banks in the valley would be subjected to ruinous mass withdrawals. To meet the situation, the Scranton Trust Company and Savings Bank needed cash, a large amount of it, and needed it in a hurry. Of all the men on the board of directors, not one had enough cash at his finger tips to make up the quantity needed immediately—except W.W.

W.W. reacted as had been hoped and predicted on the basis of his character. Because he was a director of the bank, he advanced, without hesitation, whatever monies were needed to meet the demands of the agitated depositors. To do this—to secure the soundness of the Scranton Trust Company and Savings Bank—because he felt a responsibility and because he was a director, W.W. withdrew the needed cash from his own Second National Bank reserves, of which he was the president and, with Isaac Dean, the owner.

When A.H. returned from a morning court session at Wilkes-Barre, to meet W.W. at the Wyoming Valley House for a previously arranged lunch, W.W. lost no time, but immediately described the morning's activities at the Scranton Trust Company and Savings Bank. To help, A.H. reminded W.W. of the clause in the depositor's contract, that the withdrawal of any sum over $25 was subject to so many days' advance notice. After lunch, starting that afternoon, the cashiers willingly paid out the $25 to anyone who asked, but adhered strictly to the contract, in that a depositor must make a request several days in advance if he wished to withdraw a larger sum. Very fortunately, the change made by the bank in the afternoon to what it was legally responsible for, was accepted without objection; it was generally known that everybody who had asked had been given their money in the morning. The $25 limit had its effect; by the morning of the following day, the newspapers were all reporting the bank as sound and as safe as everyone had always believed it to be.

The reputation of the Scranton Trust Company and Savings Bank was firmly reestablished. The judgment and action on the part of the bank's officers had proved the wisest course. Had they handled the rumor in any other fashion, it would most likely have been disastrous. For had they put a limit of $25 on the withdrawals from the time the bank first opened in the morning of June 4, a new, more devastating rumor would most certainly have spread—that the bank was able to pay out only $25, regardless of the amount on deposit. This would definitely have indicated a shortage of cash. To limit the sum in the afternoon was the right move; calm and reason had a chance to take over.

In retrospect, after all the flurry, no harm had been done to anyone, except W.W. To calm the depositors of the bank of which he was a director, W.W. had jeopardized the banks of which he was the owner. He was the one who had provided the resources whereby the Scranton Trust Company and Savings Bank was able to meet its obligations. But it had been at the expense of his own Second National Bank and Miner's Savings Bank of Providence—even though W.W. had personally come through as the dependable and reliable financier, rendering temporary aid on a moment's notice in an emergency situation.

The Second National and the Miner's Savings had been left in a weakened position, for now they were low in actual cash on hand. If the money which W.W. had advanced in the emergency had been repaid immediately, as it should have been, there would have been nothing more to it. And if all the directors of the Scranton Trust Company and Savings Bank had been equally friendly to W.W., and if all the depositors who had been in such a hurry to withdraw had been as quick to redeposit, all would have been well and no harm would have come to W.W. because of his unquestioning, generous support.

On the days following the "incident at the bank," as it was referred to, the Wintons devoted their time to planning how to win the support of the electoral public. With his Temperance Pledge Card in his pocket and Mayor McKune beside him, A.H. toured all over the northern end of the county, speaking. A meeting advertising Mayor McKune and A.H. Winton was sure of drawing a full crowd. They were very much in demand.

Almost all of Providence had followed A.H. down the temperance path. As a result of the Murphy campaign, during which A.H. and Mayor McKune had signed their pledge cards, two thousand Providence residents had also signed. Together, they formed the Providence Temperance Union, and immediately began to make plans for a grand Fourth of July celebration, conscious that everyone was watching to see what the city seceders were doing. Catherine Winton, to help her son and her husband, brought those interested in the Home for the Friendless along, to plan an outing that would supplement A.H.'s campaign.

As the summer sun hung at its 23.6 degrees north declination before starting its southward progression into winter, the entire cast of valley actors converged, as for a midsummer night's dream, and came on stage all at once. The luckless Tom Campbell was really in trouble; he had been brought to trial and sentenced to hang on the gallows. Beamish had been sentenced to the penitentiary at Philadelphia, to the delight of the Republicans in control. A.H., his family, and friends were campaigning—some for dismemberment of Scranton, to the dislike of both Republicans and Democrats; some for temperance, to the dislike of the drinking crowd. And the Democrats were battling to save their lovable Irishman, Beamish, plus whatever prestige was remaining to them.

Into the midst of all this, Mont Flanigan raised his voice in outraged protest, and succeeded in being the loudest of all participants. He bellowed in the direction of A.H., who heard his roar for help and took time to listen.

St Luke's Episcopal Church, on Wyoming Avenue, was just a short distance away from A.H.'s home at Wyoming and Mulberry. This particular year, the sixth annual conference of the Central Pennsylvania Diocese of the Episcopal Church, with the Right Reverend Bishop Howe presiding, was to be held there, starting June 13. A.H. and Alice had been asked to serve as hosts for some of the out-of-town clergy. A.H. was interested in the meetings and spent most of his time at St. Luke's, where they were being held. One of the main questions before the body was a cathedral for the Central Pennsylvania Diocese. From the wording in an earlier report, it had been assumed that the city of Reading would be the location for the cathedral. But because of the strong objections to Reading, voiced by the rector of St. Luke's of Scranton, the host church, a cathedral was authorized, but the site was left open—to be determined later. A.H. was keenly interested in the question of the cathedral site; he had hopes for Scranton.

While he was closeted inside St. Luke's Church, the Scranton newspapers outside were busy publishing articles describing the crookedness of Lawyer A.H. Winton. The various articles accused him of writing a fraudulent contract for the sale of property in Scranton between a store-owner and the renter of the store. He was accused of forging the signature of the seller and also of filing a spurious deed at the courthouse in Wilkes-Barre. In one article, the author had written, "Winton's act could not fail to put him in the penitentiary and strike his name forever from the roll of attorneys."

When A.H. emerged from the Episcopal convention and read the attacks, he was livid. After he had calmed down enough to reread the articles a little more objectively, the closing paragraph of one showed him what the attack was really all about, and what had prompted it. This particular article made a great point of devoting the entirety of its lengthy prose to the sole subject of A.H. and a description of his crookedness in minute detail. Then suddenly, in the last paragraph, the article ended on an unrelated note: "The handwriting on the walls of our prosperity needs no interpreter. Municipally dismembered; financially on the breakers; morally bankrupt, the Scranton of other year is as really departed as the spirits of our dead."

In regard to the accusations leveled at him, A.H. was quick to notify the papers that, in an editorial capacity, they were liable by the laws of the Commonwealth for libel. In a tone that they dared not refuse, he requested the editors and owners of the newspapers to accompany him on a trip to Wilkes-Barre immediately. Once at Wilkes-Barre, A.H. directed their efforts as they researched for the true facts about the incident which they had so glibly thrown to the reading public. The results of their findings appeared a few days later: "We sincerely regret the publication of the libelous article, which after diligent inquiry concerning all the facts in the case, we have ascertained to be a tissue of falsehoods in every particular, as far as it relates to the legal profession, and circulated to do some of our best friends harm."

These articles were the one and only attempt ever made to attack A.H. directly. The article in the *Scranton News Letter* in '74, which made veiled references to Winton nepotism on the Poor Board, had been just that: oblique slurs on the family as a whole. This was the first open attack directed exclusively at A.H. He settled the issue so speedily and arbitrarily that there was never a repeated attempt.

Mont Flanigan was wandering around the corridors of the Wilkes-Barre courthouse, looking for help for his friend Tom Campbell, on the day the outraged A.H. and his entourage of newspapermen arrived. He hung unobtrusively around the group, making it his business to know what they were about. He followed them, observing their progress and reactions, as A.H. prodded them in their research. A couple of days later, Mont Flanigan showed up in Scranton at A.H.'s office, just as A.H. was preparing to close for the day. Mont Flanigan had liked A.H.'s style at the county courthouse, and had been impressed with the way in which A.H. had handled the newspapermen. He had decided that A.H. was just the one to help him with Tom Campbell.

Entering the office, Mont Flanigan asked, "Winton, could I have a word with you?"

Making a great show of looking at his pocket watch, A.H. replied, "I was just getting ready to leave."

"I won't be long, but I would like you to hear my story. I really could stand the help of someone honest like yourself."

A.H. returned to his chair behind his desk, indicating the chair opposite to Mont Flanigan; Mont sat down and started to talk. A.H. did not look at his watch again until three hours had passed.

The first part of Mont Flanigan's tale was a description of Tom Campbell and what had happened to him. The second part was a brief recital of Mont's efforts to get Tom Campbell released. This had included several trips to Harrisburg as well as Wilkes-Barre, and the laying out of some cash. Mont now realized that, in every case, he had been led along and the offers of assistance had all been false. Realizing that he had been duped, Mont was now very indignant. He recited several other cases to A.H. in which crimes of a nature similar to Tom Campbell's had been passed off with a sentence of no more than two years. Considering the efforts he had made, the injustice had him boiling—boiling enough that he was prepared to let off some steam in the direction which would do his tormenters the most harm. For the third part of his talk with A.H., Mont opened his memory and told A.H. of the whos and hows of almost every dirty deal practiced in Luzerne County.

He talked because he resented being given the runaround, because he thought the shabby treatment of Tom Campbell was very unfair. His years of service to those in power in Luzerne County made him a walking encyclopedia on every dirty deal perpetrated. He could talk because he had been present as an observer at almost every one, although he had never actually dirtied his hands doing the misdeeds.

He told A.H. that in the fall election of '74, when John Collings had run for district attorney on the official Democratic ticket and Aleck Farnham on the spurious Wilkes-Barre Democratic ticket, John Collings had legally been elected by a majority of seven hundred votes—that the ballot returns had been fixed six or seven times to make Farnham come out the winner.

Mont Flanigan described to A.H. how the ballot boxes had been stolen by masked men, in Scranton's Twelfth Ward and also in the Seventh, Sixth, and

Third Wards—and that ballots had been physically stolen out of the box from Archbald and forgeries substituted.

In every instance, money had changed hands.

A.H. interrupted Mont in his recital only once, and that inadvertently, when he heard that many of the deals, the altering of the election returns, and the payoffs had taken place in upstairs rooms at The Bristol House, the hotel W.W. was part owner of.

There was no doubt that Mont Flanigan knew the secrets of Luzerne County and wanted to talk.

He knew that Dr. Throop had paid $600 to be counted the winner in an election which Dr. Cressler had legally won. He described the scene in detail to A.H.: how Dr. Throop was still not the winner after the ballots had been fixed the first time; how Throop himself had counted the number of necessary extra votes and asked for 160 more, which he got for an additional $600. At this point in his revelations, Mont gave way to laughter. Dr. Throop had miscounted; and after the ballots had been manipulated again, he was still short the necessary number to make him the winner. "And then he wanted all his money back! As if they would give it!" laughed Mont.

Mont had many other names to mention, both Democrats and Republicans. As he told A.H., he had been in on their secret meetings, and he had seen more than the county clerks thought he could understand.

Mont Flanigan concluded his revelations, "They may arrest me, but they won't be able to make it stick. I'll demand an investigation, and that they won't be able to stand. I know of two cases where men were sent to jail for two years for what Tom Campbell did. There was no malice or forethought on Tom's part. That shooting was a spontaneous action which grew out of drinking too much intoxicating liquor. He doesn't have to be sentenced to the gallows."

By Mont's standards, rearranging ballots was one thing, but to deliberately take a life in payment for an accident was as base a crime as any.

"What crosses my mind as you talk, Mont," questioned A.H., "is this: for every fellow bribed, there has to be another one doing the bribing," which was A.H.'s way of saying that there had to be someone behind the scenes directing the others.

Mont caught the drift of A.H.'s thinking immediately, "Yes, and I know their names, too."

"I wonder if they realize that bribing a public official is a crime? I think we could contend that the members of the election boards are public officers. There could be a lot of arrests for this offense, I think."

"I knew I was right coming to you, Winton. You help me get Tom Campbell out from under the gallows, and I'll open up with everything I know, even if it gets me disbarred."

"I think we can get everything we want, Mont, and it won't cost you a thing."

For another half hour, the meeting between the two lawyers continued. This time, A.H. was doing the talking and Mont Flanigan the listening. A.H. had a very simple plan of attack in mind. Whatever they did, he wanted to make sure that they did not exchange the power of their knowledge for a charge of blackmail. The next day, both Mont and A.H. traveled to Wilkes-Barre. Mont went to the courthouse and requested that John Collings be appointed his assistant, to take testimony in Carbondale from the witnesses to the Campbell shooting. While Mont was in the county courthouse, A.H. went to the office of the *Sunday Morning News*. He promised them a good story if they would agree to publish it. A few days later, a headline in the *Sunday Morning News* proclaimed:

Mont Squeals!
He Tells What He Knows About
Luzerne County Crookedness

Not everything was in the article, only a sampling of how big the iceberg could be. But all those that had been guilty over the years knew what would follow if Mont told everything he knew. True, most of his information dealt with the Democrats, and they were out of office; however, he knew some things about the Republicans as well.

After the article was published, all hell broke loose!

Although up to that time both Republicans and Democrats had been annoyed at A.H. and his governmental maneuvering, they had been angry but not without hope of stopping him. They had come to the conclusion that, at the most, he would succeed in breaking off only a small portion of the county and its population. But with him and Mont Flanigan working together, it was possible that Mont's revelations would drive everyone in Luzerne County, both Republican and Democratic voters, into the arms of the waiting A.H. In such a mood, it was conceivable that throughout the entire county, many, many people would vote to join A.H., in effect neutralizing Luzerne County and making Winton the new county seat.

A.H. was enjoying the reaction immensely. From the moment when he had first thought of publicly associating John Collings's name with Montgomery Flanigan, he knew that the political men of both parties in the county would understand who was backing Mont. He had planned the timing of the first news article so that some idea, of how much Flanigan was prepared to talk, would leak out at the same time. As open reactions, there were only a few protestations and expressions of shocked surprise. There were no outright denials, and no charges of libel were filed against Mont Flanigan; however, there was quite a flurry of unpublicized meetings among the county's political men, regardless of party affiliation. These meetings were small and very private. Something would happen soon, A.H. knew. He relaxed and waited, filling in the time with Alice and his mother, who, as the newly elected president of the Home for the Friendless (the orphanage), had made plans for an excursion, outing and picnic aboard the D & H's gravity railroad. He also helped the Providence Temperance Society make its plans for the Fourth of July celebration in Providence. A.H. was smart enough to know that if all the political powers saw him unconcernedly proceeding with his plans for pulling Providence and Hyde Park into another new county, it would give him greater bargaining strength.

The trip planned by the Home for the Friendless was scheduled for the second of July. But before then, on the thirtieth of June, A.H. had been called into a meeting with the Republican and Democratic leaders of the county. It was a lengthy session, and no one left until all were satisfied that they were going to come out with what each one had wanted going into the meeting.

For A.H., it was the biggest achievement of all; both Republicans and Democrats would stand behind him in the drive to legislate new county status for Scranton and the upper end of Luzerne County. In return, he would drop his plans for dismembering Scranton and reducing the city to a borough. Also, he and every prominent man in the county would earnestly petition for a pardon for Frank Beamish, so that he might return to Scranton and resume his life there. And in return, Tom Campbell was to be saved from the gallows. And in return, nothing more was to be said by Montgomery Flanigan or A.H. on the subject of the political secrets of the county. And in return J.C. Coon was to be released. The "and in returns" went on a while longer; there were still a few small annoyances to be cleared up, but that was the purpose of the joint meeting. If A.H. would stop his plans, everyone else would support him in his desire for a courthouse at Scranton and a new county for the upper end of the Wyoming Valley. A.H. came out of the meeting smiling, the happiest of them all. He had the promises of Dr. Throop and Joe Scranton to actively work with him for the new county. He also had another promise from Hendrick Wright, that nothing would be put in the path of the new county to hinder its formation or to otherwise prevent it, this time.

As far as the promises and offers of help were concerned, A.H. had enough experience by now to know that with Mont Flanigan in the background, there would be little thought of reneging or backing down; for at any moment Mont could start talking again. Also, A.H. was not discarding his arrangements to erect a new county with its seat at Winton; he was holding them in reserve until the larger planned county, including all of Scranton, had become a fact. At the end of the meeting, A.H. announced that all were invited to the Providence Temperance Society's celebration on the Fourth of July. He made a point of calling attention to the menu: a New England picnic supper. He wanted to test the temper of the promise-makers. When several men said they were planning to attend, A.H. had a genuine hope that, this time, the new county bill would go through.

So, at the height of mid-summer, all the players in the great Wyoming Valley had come on stage at once and intermingled, pushing and shoving, not knowing what would happen—until Mont's voice, like a great clap of thunder, had sent everyone scurrying, seeking companionship and safety, leaving the scene of their restless ambitions serene and peaceful.

On July 2, A.H., Alice, and Kate, along with W.W., Catherine, and three hundred other friends of the Home for the Friendless, boarded the D & H's gravity train for an excursion to Shepherd's Crook. In April, the D & H had started to carry passengers on its gravity track for the first time since opening in 1829. Attention and every convenience was provided for the picnickers as they headed for Shepherd's Crook, a point beyond Carbondale where the track doubled back on itself, providing one of the most scenic views along the Gravity Railroad. The way-stations, head-houses, and engine-houses along the road were decorated, with flags flying and fresh picked flowers arranged by the railroad men in honor of the excursionists. At the last minute, because the weather was damp, the itinerary was altered so that the picnic would take place at Waymart, the next community east of Carbondale. The power and influence of the Wintons was very much in evidence when the three hundred ebullient pleasure-seekers suddenly swooped down, without warning, on the quiet, rural town of Waymart. The good citizens welcomed them gladly. Their well-kept front lawns were converted immediately into picnic grounds, to accommodate the friends of The Home for the Friendless; afterwards, the band which had accompanied the group assembled on the porch of one of the houses, and played for dancing. The picnic trip to Waymart, however, was only a prelude to the festivities planned for two days later, the 101st natal day of the nation.

The 101st Anniversary Celebration of American Independence had new meaning to those planning the day. In one way or another, the people of Providence knew they would have their independence in a new county before the 102nd Fourth of July. W.W., Mayor McKune, and former Mayor William Monies were among the sixty-four officers of the day. They were responsible for seeing that the program moved on time and that order was kept. When the day dawned on Wednesday, it was cloudy and spitting light bits of rain; but in spite of the overcast sky, people poured into the town square at Providence, jubilant and enthusiastic.

The celebration began at sunrise, with a musketry salute to every state and territory in the union. At 9:30 in the morning, the church bells in Providence were rung, calling everyone to assemble on the Providence public square near Winton's fountain—the name had been given to the public water fountain after W.W. had opened the Miner's Savings Bank, only a few feet away. At 10:30, the program officially opened with a prayer. Then the Welsh Glee Club sang "Old Hundred" in Welsh; the Methodist Choir, the Crystal Cornet Band, and the Band of Hope also performed. This was to be the greatest Fourth of July ever, and the excited spirits of the people made it so.

From the town square, the crowd, with the marshals directing, formed a line to march to Providence Grove, a five-minute walk away on the south side of Providence Heights. In the line of marchers, A.H. was among the first; he was to be a speaker when they reassembled at the grove. At the last minute, just as the band was striking up its marching tune, Kate, now six, ran forward to pull at her father's hand. A.H. looked down at the happy, smiling face that he treasured; he did not have the heart to send her back to her mother. So together, hand in hand, they marched proudly in the American spirit. For Kate, that day and that moment of march were to remain with her the rest of her adult life. She was never more proud of her father than on that July Fourth. Children are very sensitive to the moods and feelings of their parents, and A.H.'s wild, carefree joy, as he treasured the agreements of the combined political meeting a week earlier, carried Kate on a peak of happiness.

A large, in fact the largest, American flag in the Wyoming Valley—a U.S. Regulation Garrison size, purchased in New York for the occasion—was flying from a specially built pole at the center of the picnic site. From its place on Providence Heights, it fluttered over the valley; a thousand people had kept it in view as they marched from the square to the grove. When everyone had reassembled, a prayer was again offered; then A.H. came forward to stand at the front and center of the platform, especially built for the occasion. The crowd before him stood silently as he began, "We hold these truths to be self-evident, that all men are created equal, that they are endowed by their Creator with certain unalienable rights; that among these rights are Life, Liberty, and the pursuit of Happiness. That to secure these rights, Governments are instituted among Men, deriving their just powers from the consent of the governed." A.H. meant every word as he recited the Declaration of Independence; he believed every word, and he conveyed this belief to his listening audience. He spoke in full oratorical manner, giving the instrument of independence meaning and energy more perfect than those listening had ever heard before. It was A.H.'s most shining hour.

When he had finished, the Methodist choir led everyone in singing "The Star Spangled Banner." As the voices paused before the closing line, they could hear the high "F" of the "free" reverberate across the valley. Tears filled the eyes of many, so intense was the patriotic emotion on that day.

The main speaker followed A.H. The Reverend H. Wheeler from Kingston delivered an address on national topics and civic affairs, making no special reference to the temperance topic—noteworthy because the celebrations for the day were under the auspices of the Providence Temperance Society. The typical New England meal, including Yankee beans, etc., was served for a modest fee, and then all was quiet again as the people settled back to hear the after-dinner speaker. He, unfortunately, proved to be the only thing to mar a perfect day. He delivered a heavy, earnest, and methodical diatribe against "devil rum." Afterwards, the entire audience was ready to indict him "guilty in the first degree—of all cussedness." But for emotion in the American spirit and pride in the American life, there was never a day like it.

Immediately after the Fourth, the A.H. Wintons, as per custom, again left for Nantucket, Massachusetts. This time, however, A.H. was not interested in going; too much had been happening around home for him to suddenly disappear. But he had promised Alice, and he knew that Kate wouldn't understand if they didn't go. So for the first time with reluctance, he shepherded his family aboard the train. In past years, he had gone because he wanted to please Alice and do something for her, because it was a welcome change from the mountains and the cold winters, and because it gave him an opportunity for a much needed rest. But this time, it was only because he had promised.

17

Scranton dozed lazily under the hot summer sun; she was waiting for her leader to return from his vacation—for that was what A.H. had become. After reciting the Declaration of Independence on July Fourth, he was the acknowledged leader who would lead the northern end of Luzerne County to independent government in only a matter of months. Mayor Robert McKune particularly missed his friend. He and A.H. had had a fine time, wandering up and down the valley speaking at temperance meetings. Even the newspapers in Wilkes-Barre had commented that the mayor of Scranton and A.H. Winton were Blue-Ribbon wearers.

In the heat of the summer days, the mayor took to daydreaming at his desk, particularly when the temperature reached over ninety degrees. Scranton was quiet; people went on summer picnics outside the mountain wall. He spent most of his time making plans for the fall election, the new county, and all the administrative work that would go into setting up the new county's government. Outside, the ordinary hum of living surrounded him.

On July 18, the comfort and security of the lazy summer days were suddenly interrupted by the staccato taps of the telegraph in Western Union's basement office in the Second National Bank building. Only a few short bursts when it started, by midday its clatter continued without pause. W.W. was among the earliest to know; it didn't take the news long to spread. The newspapers also were quick to pick up the transmissions. Discontented workers at the Pennsylvania Railroad's depot in Pittsburgh had gone on strike and turned into a murderous mob, which was now out of control. Each time additional news was tapped into Scranton, the information told of an escalating nightmare.

In Pittsburgh, a wall of fire three miles long was destroying the railroad's Union Depot, the roundhouse, and the company's stores. The damage was estimated at six million dollars. The telegraph, in its basement office at Scranton, didn't cease its tapping of clicks and clacks for a week. The strike had spread from Pittsburgh eastward, along the Pennsylvania's main line to Johnstown, Altoona, Harrisburg, and Reading. The Pittsburgh militia had been unable to contain the rioting; a militia unit sent out from Philadelphia was laughed at and derogated as the "Philadelphia Kid-Glove Sunday Soldiers;" it was fired on, shot at, and besieged until it too ran for cover. Before the end of July, 10,000 state and federal troops were on duty, guarding the railroad's property over the short distance of thirty or so miles from Pittsburgh east.

Western Pennsylvania was not the only place having trouble. Just before Pittsburgh burst into flames, in Baltimore, Maryland and West Virginia the same scene had been repeated, although not with as much property damage as at Pittsburgh. Everywhere, the citizenry fell before the advancing mobs, and the military was moved in to try to restore order. Then, segments of the Erie and New York Central railroads were struck. Suddenly, the unrest erupted in the Wyoming Valley, at Wilkes-Barre. When employees there refused to work on the railroads and turned into a raging mob, Wilkes-Barre's mayor came before them, reading a prayer for peace in a loud voice, the sheriff standing beside him in fright. The governor of Pennsylvania dispatched more troops, this time to restore order in Wilkes-Barre.

What was happening? It was the climactic fulcrum, the turning point to five or more years of the country's economic downslide. It was also notice that the dominance of the economic philosophy that had prevailed throughout the buildup of the industrial age had at last come to an end. The blue-collar working classes had finally faced the fact that economic advance from labor to management was going to apply to only a very, very limited number within their ranks; that they were not going to be satisfied with the concept of a cohesive labor force, which remained content with contributing its allotted share towards the good of the overall social structure, and nothing more.

This was the message that the railroad strikers, and the factory workers who joined them, were sending to the privileged percentage of the country's population. To their immediate employers, they were protesting another of a series of pay cuts. In the depressed times of the middle '70s, their wages were already at subsistence level; they could not tolerate another reduction in their earnings.

As the telegraph tapped out its information and the news was picked up and printed in the papers, the people in Scranton were fearful that it might happen there also. Mayor McKune was particularly concerned; the ultimate responsibility and decision would rest with him if trouble should develop. He did not know, nor did anyone else, whether there actually would be trouble in Scranton. Luzerne County, especially the upper end, had always been free of agitation and trouble- makers. Even the Molly Maguires, who roamed the lower Schuylkill County coal regions, agitating and plotting, had never been able to make any kind of headway in Luzerne County.

Fully aware of what was happening at Wilkes-Barre and elsewhere in the state, Mayor McKune finally decided to send out an appeal to his friends for aid. It was a poor time; many of these men were out of the city, like A.H. But in the last week of July, as an emergency measure, Mayor McKune deputized fifty men as special policemen, with the authority to enforce the law in case trouble should arise in Scranton. These men were the Mayor's friends, and they were A.H.'s friends; they included Bill Scranton, George Throop, and Edward Fuller, who, with Byron Winton, was a son-in-law of Daniel Silkman. They were all men who lived their lives for the good of Scranton. After the posse had been deputized, they dispersed, almost forgetting their oath, for the date was now July 31 and all reports indicated that the strike, on a nationwide basis, was in ruins. Scranton breathed a sigh of relief; apparently it was going to escape conflict.

At the far end of Washington Avenue, a street parallel to Wyoming Avenue but the only one to cross Lackawanna and run under the railroad tracks, a large group of workers met at the Scranton Silk Works on the morning of August 1. By voice vote, they passed a resolution to go in a body to stop operations in the various machine shops in the city. Unlike strikers elsewhere in Pennsylvania, they were not interested in the railroads, although it was always believed afterwards that the instigator who had worded the resolution was from outside Luzerne County. Shortly before noon, the workers, thinking only emotionally, marched to the nearby Lackawanna Iron and Coal Company, the Scrantons' original factory. There, the mob from the Silk Works forcibly entered the foundry and attacked the workers, beating them, bruising them, and driving them from the building. With their easy success at the foundry, the mob now became riotous and entered another machine shop close by, where they repeated their attack. Having finished there, yelling and screaming, brandishing clubs, sticks, and a few pistols, they came back out onto Washington Avenue, into the blazing hot sun that is high noon. Their tempers flared with excitement; they wanted resistance; they were hoping for a fight; they desired destruction and bloodshed.

The mob attacks Mayor McKune, at right in dark suit with hat.

A cry went up, "Let's go for Bill Scranton! We'll have his blood! Let's go for Lackawanna Avenue! To the company's stores! We'll gut 'em!"

Like rampaging buffalo on the western plains, they surged up Washington Avenue past the D L & W building towards Lackawanna Avenue, blind instinct directing them, the lust for destruction and violence their power.

Mayor McKune, in his hot office on Lackawanna, just past Washington Avenue, heard the distant roar of the unruly mob through the open windows behind him. Alert for almost two weeks for just such a sound, he rushed from the building, running down Washington Avenue towards the mob, to take a stand in the center of Washington Avenue facing the rioters.

To an aide, he shouted, "Go back up to Lackawanna and round up as many of the posse as you can! Hurry!"

To speak as he just had was natural to the mayor. He had traveled to California and worked the gold camps in 1849, and in 1850 he had taken an active part in San Francisco politics. He had survived by the Code of the West—so different from the civilized law of the East. Scranton was fortunate to have Robert McKune standing for her in the middle of Washington Avenue, alone and unarmed at high noon, facing an angry mob.

The mob came up to him, still shouting, "Let's go for Bill Scranton! Let's go for Lackawanna Avenue!"

Alone, unarmed, he waited for them to come. For a moment, the wild crowd hesitated; then the front ranks rushed him. They attacked him and beat him. Twice, he fell to the ground. The second time he fell, the ruffians paused to see whether he was going to get up again. Two of his aides and a priest ran from the sidewalk and dragged him back out of the line of march.

"Let's go for Bill Scranton! We'll have his blood! Let's go for Lackawanna Avenue! To the company stores! We'll gut 'em!" The refrain echoed in rote; the marchers surged past the bleeding mayor.

"Hurry!" the Hon. Robert McKune whispered, "Get me up there. To Lackawanna Avenue, hurry!"

Half supporting him, half dragging him, McKune's two aides ran in the shadow of the buildings on the edge of the mob. As they neared Lackawanna Avenue, they could see the "Blue-blood Vigilantes," as the Mayor's special police force was later called, forming in the broad space where Washington Avenue crossed Lackawanna. Throwing off his supporters, Mayor McKune ran before the mob to join his posse. A rioter snapped his fist out and punched the mayor as he ran by, breaking his jaw.

Forty-seven had been able to answer the Mayor's call, that August 1 at high noon, to do battle on the streets of Scranton, to help preserve the public peace; forty-seven stood behind the mayor of Scranton to save the commerce and property of the city that was life to them. The courage of the men was as great as the mountains of black diamonds they loved. They stood there, strong and hard, hard as the black diamonds they lived on.

This time, the rioters did not hesitate, but started to stone the posse, to throw rocks, to throw clubs; a shot rang out from the mob, wounding one of the posse.

"Fire!" ordered Mayor McKune.

Patrick Langan fell dead.

Under the Mayor's cool gaze, not one of the "Blue-blood Know-Nothing Warriors and Braves," as the posse was nicknamed, altered their line of defense. Sun glinted off their raised pistols. Blood flowed out from the ebbing life onto the hot road.

With the shooting, reason returned. The wild crowd backed off, not exactly turning and running, but retreating, to melt into the cool shadows between the buildings. Now the intersection of Washington and Lackawanna held only a bleeding, lifeless, prostrate form, a battered mayor with his hand at his face, and forty-seven statues forming a formidable barrier. High noon—and the mob had been routed, never to return. Far off in the distance, blurred shadows of running figures flitted under the summer sun.

Mayor McKune was not aware that they had routed the mob and that it would never appear again. He knew that they had met the emergency and, for the moment, there was safety. He feared for the future; he knew what had happened at Pittsburgh. He dispatched one of his aides to Western Union's office in the Second National Bank, to send a telegram to the Governor of Pennsylvania: "In God's name, come and save the city."

Governor Hartranft wired back, "I am with you."

The next day, members of the First Pennsylvania Volunteers, State Militia, and eight companies of the Thirteenth Infantry, Regular Army, marched into Scranton, and the city was put under military occupation.

A.H. first learned of the trouble at home when he read a description of it, two days later, in a local Nantucket newspaper. He wired W.W. for details. The comforting reply came that all was quiet and the army had arrived and was in control. Satisfied, A.H. was about to leave the telegraph office when he had a second thought. Returning to the clerk, he sent another wire to his father, asking him to find out how they could best prepare themselves in Scranton should another such situation arise.

A.H. was in no hurry to leave Nantucket unless it became imperative. This was diametrically opposed to his feelings when he had first arrived. At that time, he had felt very much like the water skier who, after losing his grasp on the tow line, paddles gently in the water, still feeling the swift rush over the water in his muscles, but is now stationary, watching and waiting as the motorboat rushes on without him, the tow line snapping briskly over the waves from the boat's wake—he knows the motorboat will cut a wide swath and circle back to pick him up again, but the sensation, of fast motion while stationary, suspends him in nowhere.

A.H.'s first few days at Nantucket had been very much like the downed skier; he was paddling idly while his companions in Scranton were still plummeting on. It was too much for A.H., and, in desperation, he achieved what no other transient summer tourist has: he managed to involve himself in local Nantucket affairs. He made his presence known to the Nantucket Temperance Society, and before long he was addressing their meetings. Again, his ability as a public speaker enthralled his audiences, and they couldn't praise him enough; they insisted that he speak before a larger Massachusetts Temperance convention in the fall. A.H. preferred to remain on the island until the beginning of September, as usual, because of his speaking commitments. If W.W. had told him that there was trouble in Scranton, he would have returned. But with the assurance from W.W. that all was calm, he kept to his original schedule.

When W.W. received his son's return wire, he liked the idea suggested and took it up with the recuperating Mayor McKune and the visiting military. On August 14, the Scranton City Guard was formally organized, and the fourth floor of the Second National Bank building became their first headquarters and armory. As men returned to Scranton from summer pleasures with their families, the number of generals seeking to join the guard was almost too many; for a while, it looked as if the Scranton Guard would have at least 265 generals and no noncommissioned officers at all. But before long, many graciously stepped down to serve in the ranks as privates and corporals. H.M. Boies became the commanding Major, and it was finally settled that under him there would be a battalion of 264 men, evenly divided among four companies: Companies A, B, C, and D of the Thirteenth Pennsylvania Regiment.

Urgency and necessity inspired the Scranton City Guard in their drilling. They knew that they were fortunate to have the Regular Army on hand, and took advantage of its presence by having the officers train them. They made no secret of what they were doing; in fact, they preferred to have it known that in the future anyone conspiring to do harm to the citizens and property of Scranton would have a professional fighting machine to reckon with.

Things military were now the theme. Scranton and its environs were very obviously under military occupation. The First Regiment of the State Troops was camped in Providence, and the Thirteenth Infantry of the U.S. Army, in Scranton. The latter patrolled the city streets, while the native Pennsylvanians were dispatched to the coal mines in the area, overseeing the miners.

One hot August summer day passed into the next. While the sun was just as hot as it had been at the end of July, there was a knowing coolness in the air. Long before the last day of August, a yellow or red-yellow branchlet high up on a tree would already have waved a greeting to passersby, reminding them that the season was changing. Perhaps the little change of color spotted here and there among the trees was enough to soften men's tempers for the coming cooler season. One day passed into the next, without incident. Soon, soldiers on the street became an excuse for exchanging pleasantries, and by the third of September, when the A.H. Wintons returned home from Nantucket, a festive air presided over the city. The anger, hate and fear of the high noon of August 1 could now be recorded into history as just that: a hot passion of only a few hours' duration.

In the early evening of September 4, glad of an excuse, the Thirteenth Infantry Regimental Band paraded down Wyoming Avenue to Mulberry. There in the broad avenue, they stopped and turned to face the residence of Mr. and Mrs. A.H. Winton. In concert, they serenaded A.H. and Alice, to welcome them home. Scranton's leader had returned to his city; the business of independence could now begin.

At the first sounds of the music, A.H. came to the door. On looking out, he called to Alice. She came and joined him; together, they stood silently on the veranda with the most loving and kindest of expressions on their faces, acknowledging the honor intended in the welcome. Afterwards, they invited the performers in for refreshments.

Why was the army band, who had not yet met A.H., so anxious to honor him? Not because of the riot; many cities all across the nation, including San Francisco, who had had trouble with segments of her Chinese population, had had riots—worse riots and heavier damages than those at Scranton. It was because the course of events after the riot clearly demonstrated to the inhabitants of the upper end of Luzerne County that if left alone to handle their own affairs, they could manage very, very well. Not only manage very well, but, in all likelihood, better than anywhere else, particularly Wilkes-Barre. It was a general acknowledgment of the need for a new county.

In the uprising and unrest that filled the United States from the sixteenth of July on, Scranton had been the only place which contained its rioters without outside aid. It could not be said that the presence of the military had put a stop to the unruly mob. The army had come to the aid of Pittsburgh, Baltimore, and Wilkes-Barre, to name a few; and in every instance, the angry, uncontrollable strikers had not been overawed, fighting the military with as much expertise as they had manhandled the populace. On the other hand, Scranton men, by themselves, had been able to disperse the mob; Scranton men, by themselves, had limited property damage to only a few hundred dollars; Scranton men, by themselves, had lost only one life.

They were proud of their capabilities—strengths which they never knew they had. It was then that Scranton men bethought themselves of the one among them, who alone had been urgently pleading with them to assert their right to govern themselves, because he alone had been conscious of their ability, their humanity, and the destiny that could be theirs if they were allowed to persevere by themselves. In the aftermath of the confrontation with the rioters, A.H., who up to now had stood alone advocating a new county, and who had planned and plotted alone for a new county, now had the entire population, regardless of political affiliation, regardless of working status, regardless of social outlook, behind him. And so they had come to thank him for having recognized them for what they could be, and for wanting it for them, long before they had recognized it themselves.

The army had been ordered to march into Scranton and to occupy it; but somehow, as things are wont to be among mountain people, the order was turned around and it was the army who was occupied. The soldiers were quickly pronounced a genial lot, honest in their duties and more than polite at social occasions. They were entertained everywhere; morning, noon, and night were filled with lunches, dinners, parties, dances, and hops. Scranton's fall social season had a sparkle and a zest never before experienced. The Providence Temperance Society, rich from the money collected at their New England supper, which had been served during the Fourth of July Celebration they had sponsored, rented a large building on the town square, near W.W.'s Miners' Savings Bank of Providence, and fixed it up as a social hall. It was expected that many of the young people would mingle with the bivouacked soldiers in wholesome frivolity.

As if there weren't enough going on in the last two weeks of September, A.H. received a letter from the Prohibition Party's nominating convention at Harrisburg, asking him to run for judge of the State Supreme Court on the Prohibition ticket in the November election; Catherine Winton met Starkey, the artist; six-year old Kate May began school at St. Cecilia's Academy, neighboring the Wintons on Wyoming Avenue; and Alice welcomed A.H. home one evening with the oddest look on her face.

A.H. reacted much the same as his father had a year earlier when he received the letter from the Prohibition party. He was flattered and pleased. However, he put it aside and did not reply right away; he wanted to think it over before committing himself. He did not keep the nomination a secret; he let everyone know, broadcasting to friends and acquaintances that he had been asked to run for state supreme court judge. But other than that, he let the matter rest temporarily; as far as committing himself, he had something else more important to occupy his thoughts. The county Democrats were having their meeting to nominate candidates for the November election. He had accumulated enough experience in the past year to realize that in the political arena one could never be idle and assume that all was well. He wanted to see whether the promises and bargains made in the last week of June were going to be adhered to.

A.H. attended the convention at Wilkes-Barre, and, for the most part, remained in the visitors' section, outside the railing that defined the delegates' area. But on those occasions when he suspected extraordinary activity during a vote call, he would vault the railing and take his place among the delegates as an observer. The first time that he jumped the railing, a convention policeman tried to stop him. A.H. spoke to him in a courteous and dignified manner, informing the lord of the baton, night stick, and star that his action was allowed. The policeman must have caught the eye of someone from the June meeting, for he tipped his hat and bowed, allowing A.H. to continue unimpeded among the voting delegates. For A.H., the moment was like an insurance policy coming due; it indicated that the June promise-makers were standing behind their word, so far.

George Starkey, the artist, was Scranton's resident sculptor. He had built himself a chapel-like studio, with cathedral ceiling and mellow-wood interior, shadowing the Lackawanna River, on the Providence side near 7th Street. He was an industrious sculptor, and had just finished a plaster bust of the late Judge John Conyngham of Wilkes-Barre, Hendrick Wright's old friend and law mentor, and also a memorial statue of Gertie Tripp. No one in the Winton family ever knew what gave Catherine the idea—W.W. always swore he was innocent of his wife's plans—but somehow she and Starkey met and an idea blossomed.

One day, accompanied by her daughter and daughters-in-law, she found her way down to Starkey's cozy nook overlooking the river. They were a serious group as they approached his studio; this was their first venture as patrons of the arts. Catherine had a specific commission in mind: she wanted him to sculpt a bust of W.W., to form part of an elaborate fountain in Providence's town square, transforming the old drinking fountain into a thing of aesthetic beauty. Catherine became Starkey's favored patroness. When he heard what she wanted, he suggested that it be executed in Carrara marble, and then mumbled something that sounded like a thousand dollars. Then he waited. When he heard no demurral, he was convinced that the muse of inspiration had indeed come to reward him. All that fall, he hardly dared let Catherine out of his sight. When he could not have W.W. in person as a model, he would call on Catherine, to come and describe a bone structure, or see whether she got the feeling of a twinkle when she looked at the unseeing eyes carved in the cold marble. As his final tribute to his wonderful patron, he planned an exhibition in his studio, with a gala opening to display much of his work, including W.W.'s bust, prior to sending it out to adorn the water fountain in Providence's town square.

Alice, however, had something of another nature to occupy her thoughts; an almost unfamiliar feeling told her that another Winton would be joining the family in a few months. That day, A.H. returned home to be greeted in the hallway by the oddest looking Alice he had ever seen.

"Alice? Is there something wrong?" he inquired immediately.

"No, not really."

He pecked a kiss on her cheek, in the manner of the absent-minded but dutiful husband, "Something must be disturbing you. What is it?" A.H. was disturbed enough to persist.

"Nothing, really."

He stood, waiting; he knew there was more to come.

Alice stood motionless, too. At last, the pressure of his silent presence brought her large, luminous eyes to meet his, "I think we're going to have a baby, again."

Alice and A.H. were halfway through their twelfth year of married life. A.H. had long ago reached the conclusion that Kate May would probably be their only heir. Besides, they were settled parents now, long past the stage of romping on the floor after a toddler.

There was a moment of awkward silence; then A.H. embraced her, "Well," he teased, "how did all this come about?"

"Oh!" Alice shoved him away, "Come and get your dinner," she snapped.

The meal was a rather silent affair. John Collings was dining elsewhere; the parents were busy, each with his own thoughts, so little Katie did most of the chattering.

After dinner, Alice spoke, "I've been thinking. There is so much going on now and so much planned. I hate terribly to be out of it all. Would you mind if John went down and got Julia to stay with us for a while?"

Julia Collings was another of Alice's sisters and was still at home in Wilkes-Barre with their mother, Elizabeth Beaumont Collings. A.H. had been thinking much the same thing—not about Julia, but of the poor timing for a baby's arrival.

"It's fine with me," he replied, "Maybe we can find her a husband among the soldiers while we're at it."

Alice glared at her husband and called him gross, mainly because he had been male enough to verbalize a secret thought that she had been treasuring from when she had first considered asking Julia to come to Scranton and share the burden of their entertaining.

A week later, Julia arrived.

The rioting mob may have quietly melted away at high noon on August 1 from the intersection of Washington and Lackawanna Avenues, but all they had done was not to melt away as easily. For the remainder of the summer, that is while the heat of the day was still intense enough to make men's tempers flare quickly and illogically as on that day, the riot and the men who had participated in it were ignored, as if nothing had ever happened. All parties concerned were wary; who could tell whether or not there would be another flareup? But when the nights turned cold and the days of September turned dark at an early hour as a reminder to prepare for cold winter snows, the fear of another uprising passed away. It was then that the superintendents quickly passed the word among the laboring force in the upper end of the valley, among the miners and the factory workers, that the outcome of any issue would hang on the law.

For law is at the base of civilized society. Once man raises himself above savage, animalistic behavior, he has order; to maintain order, he must have law. The law, to be the true expression of civilized man, has to come from man as a group, and not by direction of any one individual. It is only then that there are just laws. The rioters were soon told that they would have to turn to the law if they ever wanted to have satisfaction for their grievances.

Reprisals and recriminations were relatively mild for the riot, now two months in the past. The D L & W learned that fifty of its employees had been among the rioters and discharged them immediately. On the other hand, President Dickson of the D & H Canal Company gave instructions that nobody was to be discharged for being in the strike nor for being a member of a society, that is a union, provided they were not guilty of breaking the law. And if a foreman discharged a man, he had to tell him the cause and give him a hearing.

The greatest crime that the rioters were accused of, and that by their fellow citizens and not in a court of law, was of striking down civil authority; this they had done when they had knocked Mayor McKune to the street. The strikers were told to turn to the law and to the ballot box to correct the wrongs.

This they did. Patsey Mahon went before an alderman and charged W.W., Scranton, and sixteen other members of the Blue-blood Vigilantes, out of the forty-seven who had answered the Mayor's call, because they had had guns on August 1, with the voluntary manslaughter of Patrick Langan. Trial date was set for the last week in November; there the matter rested until then.

A.H. took almost a month to make up his mind about what he wanted to do with his nomination for state supreme court judge. Finally, in a quiet moment a little over a month later, he penned his reply:

Scranton, Oct. 16, 1877.
Hon. James Black, Chairman and I. Newton Pierce, Secretary,
Prohibition State Committee &c.

Gentlemen:

I am in receipt of yours of the 13th ultimo, officially informing me that the Prohibition Reform Party Convention, which met on the 12th of September, 1877, unanimously placed me in nomination as their candidate for the high office of Judge of the Supreme Court of Pennsylvania.

Assuring you of my gratitude for the unexpected and entirely unsolicited honor and high expression of confidence, after mature deliberation and a careful perusal of your accompanying resolutions, which, all must admit, are axioms self-evident as Scriptural truths, I deem it my duty to accept the nomination and permit the use of my name in behalf of a political question which must soon be a policy in the State and nation.

Now that the old problem of slavery no longer vexes our national councils, and polygamy seems to be on the wane; amidst the upheaval of party politics with the platforms of glittering generalities and with apparent change or reversal of sides, so that the war of parties seems to be only a battle waged between the ins and outs for party spoils, it does seem that your platform and policy present something reliable and tangible upon which all good men may unite for the greatest good.

By your action that majority of the well-meaning and honest-thinking people of our Commonwealth who carried the Local Option Law in forty-one of our sixty-six counties and thereby cast a halo of protection about themselves, will have an opportunity now to administer a merited rebuke to those time-serving politicians who swept away the will of the majority, and re-established the baneful License System, so anomalous that we almost wonder why pure-minded Judges do not resign rather than become the tools of a monstrously iniquitous code which compels them in one breath to throw an air of sanctity around some vile den, and in another breath to pass sentence upon the miserable victim made wretched at a poisonous fountain of their own indirect creation.

When will a State cease to gather lucre for its treasury which is revenue from the wrecks and ruin of its own people; sustaining evil by law; and legally plundering its citizens by systematic rules akin to such as are now in vogue in one of our great States? If women, the chief sufferer, whose counsel might always be taken with profit, could give the deciding answer all would be well.

Let our people answer now, and be assured that they are not throwing away their votes while they are sowing the seeds for future harvests, and exhibiting a power that shall hereafter make them respected by their creatures.

"There is a tide in the affairs of men,
Which, taken at its flood, leads on to fortune"

May we not hope that the Murphy men may now prove themselves "true blues"; and that all the members of the Father Mathews', the Good Templars and various other kindred Associations; all anxious fathers and brothers; all men whom noble, loving women can properly influence, and all local optionists, in short, all who love their fellow-men, may forthwith unite against a gigantic evil. By thus showing the almighty power of the free ballot in the hands of an offended, thwarted and long suffering people, they will gather a golden harvest next November, even if my nomination should not be the choice of my fellow-citizens.

Thanking you personally for your kind expressions of esteem, I remain
Very respectfully yours &C.,

A.H. Winton

In this fashion did A.H. campaign. His letter of acceptance was printed in various newspapers throughout the state, but other than that and a biographical sketch of his life also printed from time to time, he did nothing more. As one newspaper reporter observed very shrewdly, "If Winton gets elected he will make a good Judge, and if he gets defeated he won't mourn."

At this point, it was a wonder that A.H. knew what he was doing, much less able to accomplish anything. He was running his life in at least eight channels simultaneously, each demanding an enormous amount of energy and concentration: the drive for a new county was his underlying interest; his fingers were always on the pulse of the political parties and the execution of public offices; he had his own political career seeking election for state supreme court judge to think about; he was involved in the affairs of the Scranton City Guard and the military defense of the city; he was still overseeing W.W.'s financial empire; he had his private law practice and all that entailed, including trips to Wilkes-Barre when court was in session; there was his great demand and popularity as a public speaker, especially on temperance; lastly, he had an active social life of dinners and hops, the tempo now increased because of the soldiers' presence in the city. There were days when it seemed to Alice that she saw her husband only because he was one of the guests at a dinner or evening gathering which she was hosting, with Julia, at home. It was an existence as tumultuous and riotous as the colors of the autumn surrounding him. With no effort, he strode from one to the other, winning more acclaim and praise each time.

The same day that A.H. penned his reply accepting the Prohibition nomination, he joined with Edward Merrifield, Fred Gunster, Charles Welles, R.W. Archbald, S.B. Price, L. Ammerman, Fred Fuller, and F.L. Hitchcock, to form a scientific law club devoted to their mutual improvement in the legal profession. They were to read original papers on various legal subjects weekly and discuss them. The men elected A.H. as their first president. After the meeting, A.H. had a lengthy talk with Edward Merrifield.

It was the first time he had seen him in almost a year, since he had gone to him after his return from the Knights Templar Centennial trip to Philadelphia, and had asked him to help in the drive for a new county. In the intervening year, the senior Merrifield, the William Merrifield who had sold the Scranton brothers their first piece of land at Slocum Flats, had passed away.

Edward initiated the conversation with A.H., "I have often thought of what you asked me to do, A.H. I would have liked to have helped you then, but my father's condition made it impossible to take on any more than I was doing."

"I was sorry about that, Ed; I could have used your help. Who knows—maybe we would have had our new county by now. But that's all in the past; it was a long time ago."

"Well, what I wanted to speak to you about is that if you're still interested, I'd like to come out and work with you on the new county now. With my father's passing, I'm free of that responsibility. And I'll have the time."

A.H. didn't much care at this point; he felt that the new county for Scranton was pretty definite, especially because he was intending to keep a close watch on the promise-makers, right up to the last minute. But underneath, down deep in him, the desire for the right to self-determination was so overpowering that he could not, because of his own integrity, turn a deaf ear to any offer.

"I would rather have you at this late date, Ed, than not at all. Thank you for your offer."

The two men shook hands warmly.

The next time that the two men greeted each other formally was a little over a week later, when Governor John Hartranft, the governor of Pennsylvania, and his military staff arrived in Scranton to inspect the Scranton City Guard. It was quite a day of military pomp and pageantry. At ten o'clock in the morning, the Scranton City Guard mustered on its parade ground at Adams and Spruce Streets. Before the distinguished in the reviewing stand, it executed the battalion drill with such expertise and proficiency that it won the loud praises of all present; to have accomplished so much in so short a time was truly remarkable. Afterwards, the Lackawanna Valley House, which had been closed for several months due to lack of business, was opened especially to serve lunch to the Governor's party.

There were five speakers at the luncheon: Governor Hartranft; Mayor McKune, who was just barely able to talk; the Commander of the Scranton City Guard, Maj. Boies; A.H.; and George Sanderson, president of Scranton's Select City Council and W.W.'s old banking friend from the early 1860's. The speeches were all much the same—praise and congratulations for the governor, for the Scranton City Guard and for the men attending.

A.H., however, had to digress slightly and make reference to the subject dearest to his heart, "I am proud of Luzerne, of its length and breadth, but I would like to see it cut in twain."

George Sanderson, who followed A.H., would not be outdone, and accordingly departed from generalities to say how much he loved Scranton, "I love the city as my own child and expect great things from it."

The remarks of these two last speakers were heard with some surprise by those in the Governor's party. Outside of Luzerne County, there was no knowledge of the agreements reached at the June promise-making meeting. Without checking at Wilkes-Barre first, word was eventually carried back to interested political men elsewhere in the state, that there were some in Scranton agitating for a partition of Luzerne County.

From the luncheon, a carriage-line procession of the entire party moved northwest on Lackawanna Avenue, across the bridge towards Providence, where the encamped militia had assembled its members from their duties in the surrounding mines, for inspection by the governor. The governor's visit to Scranton was pronounced a huge success, mainly because all the ingredients for a magnificent wrangle had been mixed into one pot, but in the mingling of Scranton men, men from Wilkes-Barre and from Harrisburg, Republicans, Democrats, Temperance, Labor, Regular Army, Militia, and City Guard, it had developed into one enormous love feast.

Nothing marred the Governor's visit—no threat of violence, no fear that there would be trouble. Scranton was more peaceful than anyone realized. The rest of the nation was still clearing away the debris from the various uprisings across the country. Chicago had had to deputize an extra force of 5,000 men during the July rioting; Baltimore and Pittsburgh had much damage to rebuild. But Scranton showed all the signs of having returned to its usual peaceful existence. This was reinforced and made self-evident the following day.

The morning after the governor's inspection, at about seven in the morning, fire broke out once again in the Second National Bank building. This time, the flames appeared at a third floor window after the fire's furnace-like heat had caused the window panes to shatter. After the previous fire, W.W. had turned over a portion of the third floor to a janitor and his family; this was his way of safeguarding the building during closing hours. The janitor was outside sweeping the pavement when the windows broke; he looked up and saw masses of billowing smoke and streaks of red flame darting in and out of the windows. First, he sounded the alarm and then ran up the stairs to save his family. Very fortunately, they were safe, since the fire had been restricted to two rooms, due to the fireproof properties of the building.

The fire companies answered the call and quickly extinguished the blaze. Among the firemen, the Nay Aug Company had been wetting the roof from its position on Penn Street, while stationed in Railroad Alley was Franklin Hose Company. With the fire out, all the companies were reeling in their hose, except Nay Aug, which was still directing water alongside the bank building, drenching the roof and testing the height to which their engine could throw a perpendicular stream.

Some of the water, after rising so high, descended, and in its descent wet the Franklin boys as they were reeling in their hose at their position in the alley. The immediate thought of Franklin Company firemen was that the wetting was done intentionally; they began to fire stones, tin cans, and whatever other missiles were readily available, at the Nay Augs. This made the Nay Aug firemen very mad—so mad that they did turn their hose and deliberately directed the stream on the Franklins, sweeping the alley and driving the Franklins around a corner of the building. Everything was set for a first-class fight; more rocks were on hand and one man had drawn a knife, but just then the chief of police arrived. He stopped the fight and arrested the knife-wielder, who, it turned out, was a bystander and didn't belong to any fire company at all. Nothing more came of the rumpus; the temperament of the city now being so even that it remained undisturbed and unaffected by the firemen's fight.

The cause of the fire was generally believed to have been the janitor's children playing in the empty rooms with matches. As for damage, there was almost none; the articles in the charred rooms had been of no value, if one did not count a bag of potatoes, a bundle of new brooms, and a couple of city ballot boxes.

City ballot boxes? A carefully staged surprise had been discovered. After Mont Flanigan had shown A.H. how some of the ballot stealing was done, by use of double ballot boxes, they had removed the bogus boxes from their cache, which was known to Mont—thereby leaving for the future perpetrators of adjusted election totals the unpleasant necessity of having to hand in the legal ballot boxes.

As a result of the fire, two decisions were made whose importance was far greater than any actual damage to the bank building. One was to move the Scranton City Guard into a separate building of its own—an armory. W.W. was not anxious to have his beautiful bank erupt skyward, propelled by pounds of gunpowder. To aid the Guard in their relocation, both he and A.H. contributed large sums towards the building of the armory. The other decision came about because the firemen's fight had remained just that: a firemen's fight—albeit it may have been the first time firemen fought each other. The military occupation of the city was no longer deemed necessary; new orders called for moving the army of occupation out after election day, November 6.

Later in the day, as late as when dusk is first turning into early dark, the fifty men who had been fired by the D L & W Railroad for their participation in the riot on August 1, conducted a torchlight parade and meeting outside the city limits. After the railroad company had discharged them, the fifty had worked hard, forming the nucleus of a new political faction in the valley. And later, when the rioters had been told that if they wanted reform, they could get it by resorting to legal maneuvers and the ballot box. The men had been intelligent enough to recognize the advice for the constructive wisdom that it was, and not a placebo sent out to placate them. They had turned to the law; Patsey Mahon had charged seventeen of the mayor's "vigilantes" with murder. Now, with the November elections approaching, they were about to pursue the other avenue open to them: the ballot box.

The miners were asked to bring their lamps, to turn the meeting into a torchlight gathering. There was a large attendance by members of the laboring force, numbering several thousand, for word of the mass meeting had spread among the workers throughout all of the Wyoming Valley. They were peaceful and orderly at the torchlight gathering—no more rioting; they could get all they wanted, and have greater strength and power, if they stuck together at the polls.

One of the men, to whom most of the credit should go for the orderly behavior at the night meeting, was Terence Powderly. He was the antithesis of A.H. in many ways. He had worked hard among the laboring force almost all his life, mainly in the machine shops. His education, he got as he could, a good bit of it at night. But in several important areas, Terence Powderly and A.H. were evenly matched. They had both been born in the valley, Powderly at the northern end, in Carbondale. They both had high intellectual creativity, and inborn in them was a great sense of responsibility for their fellow man; on A.H.'s part, he defined fellow men as those who lived in the valley, whereas Terence Powderly considered as his fellow men those who like him strived to better their lot while remaining within the laboring ranks. At the moment, the two would be looking after the same men—laborers who lived in the Wyoming Valley. Terence Powderly also espoused the temperance cause. Should these two men meet, it would be possible for them to work together harmoniously.

Powderly knew how to talk and hold his listeners' attention. He had served as president of the Machinists and Blacksmiths National Union. He also had the experience to know the power that could come from controlling legislation. A man with principle, he charged his listeners to go about getting their wants—reform, and change—openly and peacefully through their power as the voting public. He promised them success if they did so.

The October 25 torchlight mass meeting was as much a direct outgrowth of the August lst rumble as was the establishment of the Scranton City Guard. The northern end of Luzerne County now had a structure and frame on which to build into the future a history peculiarly its own, although at the moment no one was paying much attention to this aspect. The mass meeting was noticed by the rest of the citizenry only insofar as to observe that it did not turn into another riot. Seeing that it remained peaceful, the encamped soldiers, the politicians, and even A.H. ignored the emerging labor group, and turned instead to preparations for the November election.

A.H.'s remark on the occasion of the governor's visit, of hoping to see Luzerne cut in twain, attracted far more attention than the laborers' torchlight parade. It circulated from Harrisburg to Philadelphia, and returned to Luzerne County in a most disconcerting way. Outside of the county, no one had a true assessment of Mont Flanigan's and A.H.'s power. The June promise-makers were still adhering to their resolves, but they saw no reason why they should broadcast them about; there was always the outside possibility that they would not be called on to fulfil their side of the bargain. So, they followed the policy of silence except when absolutely necessary. Unaware of the promises, men at Harrisburg and elsewhere in the state, including Philadelphia with its strong

Wilkes-Barre ties, moved to counteract A.H.'s brash comment before more came of it. In their urgency, they seized on the first thing available: the financial situation of the city of Scranton.

After the Republicans had taken over in the preceding election, they had been careful to avoid pitfalls such as Joe Coon had noted when he had been a member of the county auditing committee. The new auditors, for fiscal 1876, were so confused by the past erratic and erased ledger entries that they had resorted to the courts to clear up the matter. In a strictly legal maneuver to give the auditors a base line from which to start, the County of Luzerne became plaintiff, the auditors defendants, and the court was to make the decision as to which date and accompanying totals the auditors were to use to begin their audit. Anxious inquiries from outside the valley hurriedly learned of the case before Judge Handley. He was made the beneficiary of highly learned accountants' analyses, as accounting was not his forte; and once technically informed, he was in a position to pronounce wiser judgment.

Thus came his surprise decision. He announced that the president of Scranton's Select Council, George Sanderson, the same banker who had befriended W.W. in the early 1860s, had illegally sold $44,000 of unauthorized Scranton city bonds to a Philadelphia financial house. Newspapers in Philadelphia and elsewhere outside the valley were quick to make the most of the judge's decision; this, incidentally, was not what the auditors had gone into court for. They were well aware that many names in public life had the reputation of questionable activities attached to them, but, of all the names, Sanderson's would certainly not be among the first.

The newspapers were quick to point out the doubtful reliability of Scranton. Their comments implied that Scranton could not exist on her own, for who could have faith in her finances? If the city's word was to be as good as her bonds, then the city was too untrustworthy, and headed for bankruptcy. That Coon and Beamish, both former city officials, were in jail, was appended to every article, further creating the impression that Scranton was unreliable, emphasizing the spurious character of the people and their city. Their aim was to destroy the reputation of Scranton, so that if she did try to break away, she could not survive because no one would underwrite her money needs.

Taken aback by this surprise move, A.H. and Mont Flanigan called a hasty consultation. They reminded the others that Beamish had not yet received his pardon. This matter was quickly cleared up; but it showed A.H. that he could not relax his vigil until the new county was an accomplished fact. It also alerted him to the fact that he would probably run into opposition from outside Luzerne when the time came for the new county bill's passage at Harrisburg. He devoted considerable time to mulling countermeasures over in his mind.

Ten days after Judge Handley came out with his surprise decision, the electoral public went to the polls. It proved to be one of the quietest November election days on record; remember, the Republicans and Democrats were on their best behavior. The votes were tallied in stunned shock. The intelligent laboring masses of Luzerne County had gone to the ballot box and had put their own men into the five county offices up for election; for the first time, the Reformed Labor party, which became nationally known the following year as the Greenback-Labor party, elected men to public office from their own ranks. It was a triumph for the rioters of August 1, who had been told to resort to the law and the ballot box and not destroy property when they had objections and grievances. It was also a victory for Terence Powderly, for he had guided his fellow workers. The winning campaign had been conducted on a party treasury of only $300.

The Temperance party hadn't done too badly, either. A.H. collected 470 votes within Luzerne County, five times as many as had his father the year before. Of all the Temperance candidates for various offices, A.H. was the most popular; he pulled more than twice as many votes as anyone else listed on the Temperance ticket. The official election tally also put the Democrats as much out of the running as the Temperance movement; it was the Republicans who had lost out to the Labor challenger.

For the most part, the reaction to the election results was shocked surprise. It was the first time in the valley that "somebody else" had come into public office. One of the five contested positions had been that of additional law judge. To the Labor winner of that post, the losers directed most of their anger—for he had won over the incumbent Judge, a direct descendant of the Mrs. Dana who had preserved her husband's record books of land ownership before fleeing the valley at the time of the Wyoming Massacre.

Instead of taking their defeat philosophically, as men should always take defeat after a fair battle, the more ardent of the old-line politicans cast about for means to overthrow the declared will of the people; the winner, W.H. Stanton, had had a three-thousand plurality over Judge Edmund Dana. They at first thought of crying illegal votes, but, thanks to the efforts of A.H. and Mont Flanigan, this had been one of the most honest elections in Luzerne for quite some time; there was no way to alter three thousand ballots. They next thought to remedy the situation by the tried and true method used in the past whenever something had not pleased them; they would go to Harrisburg at its next session in January, and procure the repeal of the law that created the office of additional law judges. That repealing the law would also throw out additional law judges all over the state was inconsequential; they would at least unseat the upstart, which was where their interest lay. But that idea met with resistance, too; a cry was arising for more judges, not less. Over much grumbling, Judge Stanton took his place on the bench at Wilkes-Barre.

The army, both federal and state troops, moved out on the day following the elections; Scranton's military occupation was ended. The departure was quite a love feast of farewells, half the population coming to the station to see the soldiers off. At one o'clock in the afternoon, to songs and cheers, the trains slowly pulled out in a northeasterly direction from the D & H station, heading first for Carbondale, where they would be hooked onto Erie Railroad engines, and then west, eventually arriving at Baton Rouge, Louisiana.

The following week to the day, Wednesday the fourteenth, on Adams Street between Linden and Mulberry—two blocks away from A.H.'s house—the Scranton City Guard, in full parade uniform, marched from their temporary headquarters in the Second National Bank building. The Masons, also in full dress, marched from their Temple on Lackawanna Avenue. The ceremony of the laying of the permanent armory's cornerstone got underway sharply at 2:30. After the presentation of colors, the Scranton City Guard's regimental flag, consisting of the coat of arms of the Commonwealth of Pennsylvania on a blue field with "Scranton City Guard" underneath, was presented by the Ladies of Scranton. Then, in formal ceremony, the Masons were called upon to plumb and mortar in the building's cornerstone—another bright day in the social life of this mountain coal town that was fueling and heating the nation.

Now there were but two weeks left in November, the month that had brought labor into power—a first, anywhere; that had seen the peaceful departure of military might; the foundation of the outward symbol of local military power—all were direct outgrowths of those few hot hours under the August sun at the intersection of Washington and Lackawanna Avenues. There remained one more item on the November agenda before it could be said that the riot of August 1 had truly completed its course. But before *finis* could be written, on Thanksgiving night, Company D of the Scranton City Guard entertained their ladies and friends at their first annual hop in their temporary armory headquarters in the Second National Bank building.

The last week of November was reserved for Patsey Mahon's charge against Bill Scranton and the sixteen other blue-bloods, who had been indicted for manslaughter.

Judge Garrick Harding, under whom A.H. had first begun his practice of law, was the presiding judge. The testimony was dichotomous; defense witnesses were consistent and believable in their descriptions of the riot and shooting on August 1, and those for the prosecution were similarly consistent and believable in their descriptions of the incident. However, the two believable descriptions were in no way consistent with each other; each side had its own version. It was placed in the hands of the jury to determine who was telling the truth.

In his charge to the jury, Judge Harding said, "Gentlemen, I will say at the outset, that if the facts and circumstances have been truthfully detailed by the Commonwealth, then the defendants named in this indictment may be convicted of voluntary manslaughter.

"People may assemble together to the number of three, or of thousands, and peaceably discuss the difficulties surrounding them; they may march with music and banners through the streets of our towns and cities, and no person has a right to interfere with, or molest them, so long as they do not disturb the public peace, nor violate individual rights. More than that, though their march be tumultuous, their conduct riotous within the meaning of the penal law, thus rendering them liable to arrest, prosecution, conviction and punishment, still, they are not to be attacked and slain by armed men, with impunity. If they are, the offenders, no matter who they may be, nor what their importance, nor what their standing, social or otherwise, become liable to arrest, trial and conviction, either of murder of the first degree, or of murder of the second degree, or of voluntary manslaughter, as the circumstances may warrant. To be more explicit: if that mass of people designated by most of the witnesses as the mob, came up Washington Avenue on the morning referred to, in the manner described by the several witnesses examined on the part of the Commonwealth, and as they turned into Lackawanna Avenue, they were fired upon by the defendants, then, even though the slain man and his associates were engaged in what might be termed a riot, there was no justification for that killing. Because according to this testimony, the riot, if riot it was, was of the mildest conceivable type, it could not therefore have required murderous force to suppress it.

"But, gentlemen, we have had two sworn descriptions of the manner of conduct of that multitude, or mob, as it has been called, on that day. Which of the descriptions is the correct one? This is the great fact to be determined, and the determination of it is solely for you. It would be idle to deny that there is a wide, even irreconcilable, conflict between the testimony on the part of the Commonwealth, and that on the part of the defense. It is your province, no matter what may be the views of the Court, or the views of the counsel in the case, to believe, of the witnesses, whom you will. You should, however, examine with care all the testimony presented on the one side and the other; you should weigh it in just balance; you should find according to your convictions of the truth.

"What is the answer of the defendants? It is, that on the first of August last, a large body of men came together within the limits of the city of Scranton, ostensibly for the purpose of discussing the difficulties, real or imaginary, that surrounded them, but really for the purpose of organizing in force with a view to stop every industry connected with mining or manufacturing in and about that city; that, being thus convened, they resolved to go in a body and drive from employment every person engaged about the machine shops and other places of labor belonging to the two great companies of that vicinity; that this resolution, passed in the midst of uproar and confusion, they proceeded at once to carry out; that violence, bloodshed and terror marked their path; that, meeting with no adequate resistance, they rushed on beyond the shops towards the chief avenue of the city, proclaiming as they went the further purpose of robbery and murder; that they struck down the mayor, who, in obedience to the mandates of official duty, had bravely interposed himself in their path; that they overthrew the civil law outright; that thereupon, the defendants committed the act here charged against them as a high crime.

"At this point, gentlemen, more particularly for your own instruction, but incidentally for the hundreds of laboring men within reach of my voice, I will state the law governing their rights. Laboring men, no matter in what capacity, have the right to demand what to them seems a fair compensation for their work, and if that compensation is not accorded, they have the right to strike: in other words, to quit work; again, any laborer who is willing to work for a compensation satisfactory to himself, even though it be less than that demanded by his associates of the same class, has the right to work. And, as the law will compel no man to work for a price not agreed upon by himself, so the law will not permit any man, or body of men, to enforce the idleness of others who are willing to work for a price that suits them. Such is the rule wherever civilization extends; and will be the rule as long as civilization lasts.

"It is not strange, however, that laboring men should mistake their rights in this particular; it is not strange cunning, wicked, dangerous demagogues should lead them astray; it has been so in times past, it is so in times present—demagogues swarm amongst them like bees—and so it will continue, most likely down to the end of time.

"The history of strikes is but a harrowing story of the sufferings of the laboring classes. Betrayed through evil advisers into violations of the law, they have languished and died in prisons, and their burial places have been in prison yards; their children, orphaned, have grown up to early vagabondism and crime.

"And yet, the teachings of experience seem to go unheeded. The demagogue is as powerful today as ever. But the wheel of civilization and good government move on, nevertheless; it will move on till the latest day. The striker, grown into a rioter, may achieve a temporary triumph, but its duration can scarcely be of a day. Law and order are characteristics of our institutions, and no person on earth can supplant them. True enough any law may be changed, but never by violence. The redress for bad laws is the ballot-box; the redress for unsatisfactory officials is likewise the ballot-box—we have recently had an example of the latter in our midst. I may say, however, that no matter who are our officials, the law as it stands will be enforced. It may be changed, as I have indicated; but by the bludgeon, never.

"Again, gentlemen, when an actual riot is at hand, when its more dangerous form has been put on, and life and property are threatened, more decisive measures may be adopted. Citizens may, of their own authority, lawfully endeavor to suppress it; they may arm themselves, and whatever they honestly and reasonably do in their efforts to suppress it, will be supported and justified by the law. A riotous mob is the most dangerous thing on the face of the earth. Of all animals under the sun, men running mad are the worst in their fury.

"Now, gentlemen, what was the real condition of affairs, at Scranton, on the morning of the first of August last? You must find an answer to this, from the testimony alone, from no other sources. The showing on the part of the Commonwealth was full, clear, and to the point. If you are satisfied of its correctness, beyond a reasonable doubt, then, I have already instructed you as to your duty in the premises. If, on the other hand, the testimony adduced for the defense leads you to view the occurrences of that morning in a different light; or, in other words, if that testimony raises in your minds a reasonable doubt of the guilt of the accused, that is to say, a doubt springing from a fair and full consideration of the testimony on both sides, then all the defendants named in the indictment are entitled to an acquittal.

"Gentlemen, the credibility of the witnesses, the defendant's witnesses, I mean, who gave the history of that day's occurrences, as thus briefly stated, is for you. If you are satisfied that it is the true history, the city of Scranton was fortunate in having for her chief officer on that day Robert H. McKune, one of the few mayors of the cities of Pennsylvania who, in the almost general troubles of the time, manfully stood up for law and order; if it is the true history, the city of Scranton was fortunate that the mayor's posse was composed of just such men as W.W., Scranton, Lewis Bortree and their associates; if it is the true history, these defendents, I repeat, are entitled to a general finding of not guilty. The case is now with you."

What was so unusual about Judge Harding's instructions to the jury?

Nothing, really.

What was so unusual, then?

Everything!

There was nothing unusual in what Judge Harding charged his jury with. A dedicated judge, a dedicated lawyer, will treat the law as supreme. He will not hold anybody as being above the law; he will use the law to see that no one is treated unfairly. Judge Harding was only stating the law as embodied in the Constitution of the United States. What was so unusual was that he dared to do it.

The year was almost 1878 when Judge Harding spoke to his jury, instructing them. It was the age of wealth, power, privilege, robber barons, plunderers, accumulations of vast industrial empires, the time when the laboring masses could be publicly called "voting cattle" and no objecting voice would dare to protest. It was the period when Henry Ward Beecher, rector of the Plymouth church in Brooklyn, New York, the recognized exponent of the prevailing social philosophy among the upper classes—for the lower classes didn't matter—could say, "God has intended the Great to be Great and the little to be little…I do not say that a dollar is enough to support a workingman, but it is enough to support a man!…Not enough to support a man and five children if a man would insist on smoking and drinking beer…But the man who cannot live on bread and water is not fit to live," and be applauded for what he has said. He was applauded by Big Business, the only people who counted: the same kind of men who formed Mayor McKune's posse; the Mayor's Vigilantes were not laborers in the factories.

For Judge Harding to say that workers had the right to strike, that the "great" should be punished if deserving of it when in a conflict with laboring men, was, for 1877, a very daring and courageous and unusual thing to say—as courageous as Mayor McKune was when, unarmed, he faced the raging mob. And for Judge Harding to require his jury to decide whether the accused should be set free from any sentence for their alleged crime, whether they had in truth not committed any crime at all but should actually be applauded for doing the right thing, was also the action of a very unusual man and public servant. For Judge Harding, the well-being of the Wyoming Valley was all-important; for him, its well-being was by the law. What a friend A.H. had in his early law mentor; but then they were two alike, and each had respect for the other.

Before leaving the issue of the August 1 riot, the Scranton City Guard, the November victory of the Labor party, and the trial of the Mayor's shooting posse, there is but one question that remains to be answered.

Why was one shot sufficient to disperse the rioters, and why were the ensuing events accepted so calmly? For one thing, there was the caliber of the men involved: Mayor McKune and his posse, who were fearless as they faced a danger never before experienced by any of them except the mayor. Then, there was Judge Harding, who dared to show his understanding of and love for law and order, in the face of public opinion to the contrary. There was also the fact that these rioters were unlike many of the troubled working class across the nation; as A.H. had told Governor Hartranft when the governor had come to Scranton to review his new Guard unit, "Nobody ever heard of Scranton men making a row."

The working men in the Wyoming Valley were unlike their counterparts elsewhere in the nation, mainly because of their living conditions. There were very few slum tenement housing sections in the valley; elsewhere, five floors to a building usually meant as many families, a living arrangement common in the large coastal cities such as New York, Philadelphia, and San Francisco, and in cities along the big waterways, as Chicago and Pittsburgh. In the Wyoming Valley, many of the houses, even of the lowest-paid workers, were neat single frame dwellings. At the worst, their houses would be semidetached or in short rows. Even the fifty houses that W.W. had built at Winton were free-standing. The living standard matched the shelter comforts; it was not unusual to hear of mine owners, such as William Connell, paying from his own pocket a teacher's salary to provide elementary schooling for his breaker boys in the evening. In other words, Wyoming Valley was driven by enlightened self-interest. For those who lived in the valley, the pioneering days were too close to be forgotten; their social conscience directed survival by mutual help.

That there was a working class in the first place, was never questioned—and never would be until scientific technology advanced enough to devise other methods for producing and marketing for the world's needs. Yet today, ironically, the same worker cries in anger because technology is at last able to free him from his menial, rote tasks. But in 1877, it was the fate of the working class to be; that is, to exist for such tasks. Valley people accepted the fact that there had to be a working class, but they unconsciously demanded that it be a self-improving lot. Then there was the valley itself.

For those who lived in the valley, there was no other place to go. Many people, especially the immigrants shipped by train directly from their ocean crossing, found crossing the mountain barrier a harrowing experience, particularly through Cobb's Gap, the light, thin rail winding its way at the base of the mountains to look up at sheer walls of "black diamond" earth, rising majestically to tower two thousand feet over their heads as they crawled puffingly along the frail and delicate railroad tracks—so much so that once sanctuary was reached in the valley, there was no impetus to brave the forbidding passage in an outward direction.

So since there was no place to run off to, as in the port cities which restless wanderers leave for "that other town where things will be better," they dared not destroy. They had to make their lives work, whatever happened; it was their last chance. The shot that was fired, the bullet that killed Patrick Langan, was not what had stopped the rioters. It was that one of the valley was lying dead by the hand of another of the valley. The code within the mountain walls forbade preying on those who, like themselves, were contained within the valley.

When the jury returned from its deliberation, they knew the intent of the mob, the intent of the posse; like someone you love who is hysterical and only by a sharp, hard slap can you calm them, they knew there was never a reason to accuse the defendants in the first place; they said, "Not Guilty."

18

Three weeks before Christmas, Alice handed A.H. a letter at the breakfast table.

"Here is a rather unusual letter; it came in the mail yesterday."

A.H. glanced at it, "Lt. Steever?"

"Yes, from Lt. Steever. He says he will be passing through Scranton on his Christmas leave and would like to stop and see us."

"Which was he, Alice? I can't seem to recall."

"I have difficulty myself. There were so many here at one time or another."

Husband and wife locked gazes briefly.

"Julia?"

"Oh, A.H., you are an incurable romantic. How can you say so quickly that this Lt. Steever is coming to see Julia?"

"Because I think my little *hausfrau* is a little too plump right now to excite a young man into coming all this distance."

"I'll write him and tell him we'll be glad to see him, then?"

"See what Julia has to say, first."

Christmas night, A.H. and Alice entertained in honor of Julia Beaumont Collings at a grand masquerade hop in their palatial residence, an affair which was enjoyed by the elite of the city—thus the party was described by a *Times* reporter. It was the same house at Wyoming and Mulberry, but suddenly it had become a palatial residence. By the time the dancing had ended, a glowing Julia had promised to answer Lt. Edgar Steever's letters from West Point, where he would be assuming his new duties as a mathematics instructor.

Time was now growing short; only a few days remained before the legislature reconvened at Harrisburg. This time, the new county bill had to go through. There was but one more detail for A.H. to attend to before he could devote all his energies to the partitioning of Luzerne County. Under the aegis of a concerned citizens' meeting held in the Father Mathew Temperance Hall, he helped in the wording of several resolutions that were later published in the city newspapers. One in particular marked his concern for W.W. and the Second National Bank:

> Resolved, That managers and directors of savings institutions, by their disregard of law in exacting illegal rates of interests and hiding money that

> belongs to creditors, have done much to cripple and destroy the industries of our country, and in our opinion usurers are a greater evil in the community than thieves.

Note that W.W. had not yet been reimbursed for the aid he had rendered the Scranton Trust Company and Savings Bank on their day of near panic, June 4—support freely given, but to the disadvantage of the Second National Bank.

A.H. closed out the year 1877 while attending a meeting of the Scranton Bar. He was chosen chairman of the group to consider ways and means to assist in the passage of the new county bill at Harrisburg. Edward Merrifield, John Ranck, Burns, and Hitchock joined his committee. Also present were the area's three members to the state's House of Representatives, the Honorables Kiersted, Ackerley, and Jones. It was at this meeting that the name "Lackawanna" was first mentioned for the new county.

Then it was the next year. A.H. stepped over the midnight into 1878 with fantastic energy in reserve, his brilliant mind pruned and pared to be at its best. He would be celebrating his fortieth birthday this year; he had the strength and ability of a hundred men, and he was restless to achieve the greatest prize of all: a new county and a courthouse for Scranton. Vibrant, powerful, alive, he was everywhere. His temperance speeches were so popular that he was addressing the various ethnic groups in the valley—those for people of German descent, the Irish at their Father Mathew Hall—as well as the Providence Temperance Society. But every engagement, every dinner was subject to interruption by a call from Harrisburg; once the new bill was submitted to the state legislature, he wanted to be free of any other entanglement.

The New Year began at a fast pace, and full of high spirits. John Collings was part of a group of Scranton men who put on a New Year's show at the Forest House—Scranton's first hotel now that the Valley House was closed. John was billed as a "Dashing Serio-Comic Singer." Lewis Bortree, so recently freed of Patsey Mahon's manslaughter charge, was the stage manager. There was Bob Reaves, "the Great Flat-Foot Dancer," and C.V. McKinney, who would sing a piece of his own composition entitled "Sing Something, Carl." William Storrs was advertised as the juggler whose feats of balancing plates had astonished the world. After the local vaudeville performance, there was the new armory building to open, and somewhere, sometime, there would be a triumphant ride from Harrisburg to Scranton.

But A.H. was not to have life as easy, or as free of distractions, as he wished. On the fourth of January, the courts at Wilkes-Barre appointed him chairman of a committee to revise the rules of the court. So keyed up and tensed for action was A.H. that he plunged into this first task at hand like a fury on a rampage. When the committee was finally ready to submit their recommendations a month later, most of the suggested revisions were results of A.H.'s effort.

The judges had facetiously suggested, at the start, that one of the new rules should forbid members of the bar appearing in court while intoxicated. Had that been included, it would have made the paper livelier reading, for the suggestions were mainly ones defining court procedures: the time for filing cases and their listing on the court calendar. With an eye to the future, it was recommended that a separate list be kept of all Luzerne County lawyers who lived north of Pittston.

In the meantime, the Honorables Kiersted, Ackerly, and Jones had departed for the state capitol. In their hands were copies of this year's version of the bill for a new county—this time, the work of the Scranton Bar Committee, with suggestions from local merchants; not of A.H. alone. Anxiously, A.H. waited to hear from them. Finally word came; they had submitted the petition, and it had been listed as House Bill #50. When it would come up, they couldn't say.

In the last week of January, A.H. was called to Wilkes-Barre to handle the Pauli case for the Commonwealth. F.S. Pauli was a Scranton landlord accused of altering the lease he had with a tenant, specifically by inserting words into the lease permitting him to remove sections of porch from the leased store and building on Lackawanna Avenue. The case was Greenback-Labor Judge William Stanton's first major trial after taking his seat on the bench at Wilkes-Barre. While in court, A.H. observed the new judge with critical eyes, knowing the insults and barbs that had been thrown at Stanton's competency at the time of his election. He could find neither errors nor omissions on the judge's part; instead, he was impressed with the way Judge Stanton controlled the proceedings.

At the end of the two-day trial, the jury returned a guilty verdict, but, as counsel for the defense made an immediate appeal, sentencing was temporarily postponed. After the trial, A.H. was approached by D.M. Runk, also a Scranton lawyer, and asked whether he would consent to taking Mr. Runk's son, John, into his office and allow him to read law under A.H. It was a sure sign of success and esteem in the legal field; A.H. was only too glad to take young John Runk under his tutelage.

During this same last week of January, the political factions in Scranton, both Republican and Democrat, started to worry about the Scranton city elections, which were to take place in the beginning of February. They were disturbed because they were not sure what to expect after the surprising Greenback-Labor victory in the county in November—so much so, in fact, that as the first of February and city election time approached, they proposed, since it was generally known that the new county bill was under consideration at Harrisburg, postponing Scranton city elections until Scranton was actually in its new county environment. But the Greenback-Labor men were growing more confident daily and protested loudly, claiming that their candidates were the first honest ones in Scranton's history. They also intimated that if the old parties, the Republicans and Democrats, were successful in their move to push back city elections, thereby continuing the present regime one year longer, then it would be many years before anybody had the privilege of attending a Lackawanna County court.

On this point, a deep rift opened between A.H. and his brother-in-law John Collings. John had been almost as busy about the city as A.H. had. He had been part of the select group under lawyer Simrell that had staged the "comique" New Year's Day production at the Forest House. When others had feared a labor takeover in Scranton city politics, John Collings became an important part of the movement to extend the elected office holders', including the mayor's, terms of office for a year. In fact, he was one of the three who made up a specially appointed political commission which issued a statement declaring that the next city elections should be in 1879 instead of 1878.

When A.H. heard of labor's threat to withdraw their support for a new county because of the controversy about when the next city elections should be held, he was upset beyond words. In the tense days that were to be his environrnent until the new county issue was settled one way or another, John Collings's actions took on the appearance of the greatest treachery and betrayal conceivable. So upset was A.H. that he disassociated himself from his brother-in-law, to the point where the two men went their separate ways—other than for formal greetings of the "Good morning, John, how are you?" variety and nothing more, when in each other's presence.

In the midst of all this personal and political turmoil, time was taken out for a gala event—much to W.W.'s relief, too. At last, W.W. was able to breathe a sigh of relaxation. The battalion of Scranton City Guard was scheduled to move out of the Second National Bank building, and into its new home, on the last day of January. Racing around, into everything, with the energy and force of someone possessed, A.H., although not officially on the committee, helped with the decorations for the Armory's gala opening. Governor Hartranft was expected, and the Committee of Arrangements was planning for a thousand guests.

Up from his Third Street store in Philadelphia came Eugene Scheible with $8,000 worth of flags and bunting. The flag of every nation and every state was suspended from the armory's rafters; and, like the Norman castles of the twelfth century, those draped from the walls gave warmth to the room, despite the nadir of winter's passage over the valley. Any space that dared show itself bare was immediately filled with red, white, and blue streamers. The special platform for the distinguished speakers was carpeted, and a balustrade was formed around it by a line of upright Springfield rifles with bayonets fixed.

Late in the afternoon, two days before the gala opening of the armory, W.W. sent word to A.H. that he wanted to see him. A.H. hurried around to the bank.

"I have great news, A.H.; Halstead has been in to see me. And he has offered me 439 acres that he owns."

Halstead and W.W. had last done business when they had negotiated the sale of the four hundred Hollenback acres at Winton. Now he had come to W.W., this time offering him four hundred of his own acres.

"Congratulations, Father! What does George Filer think of it?"

"As rich in coal as the rest."

W.W.'s holdings, with this new purchase from Halstead, would be increased to a total of 2,674 acres of prime coal land. All that remained was for A.H. to draw up the agreement of sale—and this he did promptly. The Winton wealth was now greater than ever.

For the night of the Armory opening, the winter blustered and stormed until it had almost filled up the valley with snow. Trains bringing guests from Wilkes-Barre and Kingston were delayed for half an hour; the governor never came. But once inside, eight hundred party-goers broke free of their icicles and applauded loudly when A.H. rose from his chair on the speakers' platform and came forward on the carpeting to open with Byron's "There was a sound of revelry by night." He called the Armory "not an armory but a Temple to Law and Order"; he then formally presented the building to the battalion. A.H. was followed by Mayor McKune and Dr. Logan, the battalion chaplain and rector of Scranton's First Presbyterian Church, and then by Captain Tom Paine of the Wyoming Artillerists. After that, dancing was ordered, the first of a monthly series of such dances.

With the armory opening, the distribution of rewards for the August 1 riot was now complete. For the strikers, it was being named to the honors list of politicians and public officials; for the defenders of the city on that hot day, a new club house and parties—a strange honors list. Was it indicative of decadence and weakness that the old order had given way to the new? Think not that thought; the pioneers were still leading. They were always to build up their community; the installation of the battalion was another advancement in their march toward civilized living. The Armory was another jewel to glitter in their crown, carved from a wilderness—all the more enjoyed, in spite of the fact that they had to be forcibly reminded, because of the ease of, and results from, correcting an oversight.

According to all reports gathered from Harrisburg and relayed back to Scranton, everything was proceeding smoothly and according to plan. The Wilkes-Barre faction and their friends throughout the state, the Republicans and Democrats of Luzerne County—all were living up to their promises of the previous June. No opposition from Harrisburg had been heard to the new county bill, although it had not yet come up for a vote. But a canvass of the legislators indicated that no one was opposed enough to block its passage. Now, other terms of the June promise-makers' meeting had to be met. A concentrated effort was begun to have the governor of Pennsylvania, Governor Hartranft, pardon Frank Beamish. To accomplish this, the Hon. A.B. Dunning, A.H.'s uncle, was named a prison commissioner from Luzerne County, to work with the county commissioners on the County Board of Pardons.

Then, suddenly, Scranton had its own problem—one of the first magnitude. City elections, held at the beginning of February, despite the urgings of the politicians, brought an end to the Hon. Robert H. McKune's tenure as mayor of Scranton. Terence Powderly, the Greenback-Labor nominee, who was originally from Carbondale, was swept into office by a 531 vote plurality. A.H. and his family and friends literally went into shock. Not to have Robert McKune at their side was unthinkable—that at the very moment when the new county would need the help and guidance of her ablest men, the burgeoning county would be stripped of the experience and advice of the one most qualified.

The fears of the last week of January had materialized. Those in power had correctly assessed that if any change were made in the city political picture, it would be Robert McKune who would go. He was the very essence, the personification, of all that labor was trying to free from its back. Mayor McKune was the symbol of resistance; he was the one who had ordered, "Fire!" To save face, to prove to themselves that their riot had not been in vain, that they had accomplished something by their hour of unrest, Mayor McKune had to go.

The arrival of Terence Powderly on the scene was very disconcerting to A.H., dedicated to the cause of a new county. Powderly was an unknown element to further complicate A.H.'s efforts in the drive for the new county. A.H. was predisposed towards Powderly, but only in the sense that, in the past, A.H. had received some of the greatest loyalties from among the Irish political men. A.H. had been so impressed with Frank Collins that he had never wavered in his support of him. And he was well aware he had much to thank Montgomery Flanigan for. But Terence Powderly—he might be something else again.

A.H. had always mingled with men of all backgrounds. But those who were of immigrant extraction rather than pioneer had always been like Mont Flanigan, who had risen from being an impoverished, industrial laborer to acquire the education and fluidity of the intellectual and wealthy. A.H. had always moved over and made room for one who was moving from one class to another. But here was Powderly, who required everyone to accept him, not as one who had climbed his way from rags to riches, as had many of the wealthiest robber-barons, but as a working man who gloried in what he had always been.

For Terence Powderly, after winning the election, it was an experience, too, to be suddenly thrust among the city's most elite men. He was a brilliant administrator—he suffered no inferiority on that score—but because of the drive for the new county, he had to open his life to equal intimacy with men of the very class he was leading his Labor party to destroy.

The election was over. So be it; Terence Powderly was the mayor-elect. Heartsick, in despair and anguish, the friends of Robert McKune honored him at a dinner, ostensibly for his years of service, but most of all for his bravery in the face of the mob. Testimonials from all over the county poured in, to give the Hon. Robert McKune a trunk full of mementos. What else could be done? As mayor of Scranton, the will of the people had chosen Terence Powderly, unknown, inexperienced, in Scranton's most critical hour. And Robert McKune, for his one hour of valiant glory, had his reward: he was to be dismissed as if in disgrace.

At this point, Frank Beamish's pardon came through and on February 24 he was released from the penitentiary. Terence Powderly was going to be the mayor, the Greenback-Labor party was now an important factor in Scranton, Republicans and Democrats were in confusion in the city; and just that quickly, the climate at Harrisburg changed. For somewhere down in the dark and jealous bowels of Wilkes-Barre, a fury and a rage still festered. With Beamish back in Luzerne County, some of the promise-makers, as of old, could now afford to renege. The Democrats were out of office, and had very little to lose anyway. And as for the Republicans, some of them began to have a change of heart, now that the time was actually at hand to cut up Luzerne County.

Alarmed, A.H. gathered his army of workers about him. It was decided to maintain a lobbying force at the state capital. A.H., Robert McKune, Edward

Merrifield, Fred Gunster, George Sanderson, Dr. Throop, Joe Scranton, E.N. Willard, F.L. Hitchcock, J.E. Barrett, Lewis Pughe, H.S. Pierce, Corydon Wells, U.G. Schoonmaker, and John H. Powell rotated, traveling back and forth between Scranton and Harrisburg. Unexpectedly, House Bill #50 was called up for consideration by the House of Representatives early in March. It was read and sent back to committee for rewording and then brought back to the floor for its second reading. At this point, James Kiersted, one of Scranton's two representatives to Harrisburg, sent word from the House Chambers that opposition to House Bill #50 was snowballing at an alarming rate.

Hastily, at two o'clock on Saturday afternoon, the sixteenth of March, A.H., W.W., Fred and Joe Gunster, Victor Koch (owner of the Scranton House Hotel), Edward Merrifield, George Sanderson, E.N. Willard, Dr. Benj. Throop, F.L. Hitchcock, James Kiersted's brother George, Alexander Hay, U.L. Schoonover, Mayor-elect Terence Powderly, and the outgoing Mayor Robert McKune met in Scranton. They were serious men; the hour of trial was at hand. They knew that the time was now if the new county bill were ever to pass, at least in their lifetime. It was a very formal meeting, each man taking his turn and speaking correctly and stiffly, but there was no doubt that they knew what they were about.

Addressing the group first, Edward Merrifield proposed that Dr. Throop chair the meeting. Then he said, "We've heard from George Kiersted that opposition is mounting. We've got to raise money, now, to see this thing through. I'm not talking about money to buy the legislators, I mean money to cover our expenses going to and from Harrisburg. Joe Scranton should be reimbursed for all the newspapers he's sent down there explaining our position.

"George tells us that Wilkes-Barre has violated her pledges to us, and is fighting the bill fiercely. It's necessary to meet this fight with fight; the sinews of war are wanted now, if they ever are.

"I haven't charged a penny for my services, and I don't intend to, but we can't ask that of everyone. There are others, I know, who cannot afford to give their time, in addition to paying their own traveling expenses. We can't ask them to do that."

Fred Hitchcock spoke up, "Yes, that's right. Wilkes-Barre has completely faced about; they're determined to kill the bill. And all our people still think everything is safe. They're lapsing into apathy. We've got a Carbondale faction to fight, too. There's an impression about that a large part of the county doesn't want the bill. I don't think Jones is truthfully representing his constituents on the floor of the House. I know he thinks he's being honest, but nevertheless he's misrepresenting his district on this question." Turning to the newcomer of the group, Hitchcock continued, "Mr. Powderly, would you go to Harrisburg and represent the interests of the very important labor element of this community?"

Before Terence Powderly could respond, Robert McKune's voice was heard. "I don't think that's the right approach, Hitchcock. Not that labor can't be powerful, but I think we have to look elsewhere to correct our troubles. In the Senate, Senator Wadhams is representing the Wilkes-Barre faction and is working hard against the bill. And the trouble is, Wadhams has a lot of social influence among the other senators.

"Now I know our Senator Seamans is working hard to counteract Wadhams in the Senate. He deserves a lot of credit for his real and untiring effort.

"I'm sure we'll be successful if we don't have opposition that is bitter. The way the bill was read on its second reading makes it free from any tangling alliances with other measures. All who understand our claims admit they're just. No, I think the best way is for every man here in Scranton who has a personal friend in the House or Senate should go down at once to see him."

"It's now or never. Work now is necessary," Fred Gunster's was the next opinion to be heard, "A week hence is too late. The bill ought to pass the House Tuesday, if it's going to pass at all. If work ceases now, the bill will fall. We should concentrate all our energies on getting a full House on Tuesday. I know we have the sympathy of every unprejudiced legislator there, but we must have them all there to get the 101 votes necessary.

"It requires money to send men to see that this legitimate work is done, and those men must go now—today if possible."

"I've heard from my brother," replied George Kiersted, "Since the second reading, the enemies of the bill are fighting it tooth and nail. Something must be done. He tells me all our friends are being worked on by the opponents to the bill. They've got to be counteracted. I don't want to throw any cold water on your enthusiasm, but I think I should warn you that trick and fraud are being used. The bill stands a chance of failing."

"On my last turn at Harrisburg, all of us from Scranton met with some Carbondale people. They promised to withdraw all opposition if Scranton would promise to pay the expense of the county buildings. We told them we would; we guaranteed it. Then they wanted the guarantee incorporated in the bill. But we couldn't do that. It would have made the bill unconstitutional. When we told them that, they said they would fight the bill, and they did!" Robert McKune became more agitated as he described the heated sessions that he and the other Scranton men had had with the gentlemen from Carbondale, "We asked them what guarantee they would accept from us, that they would not be asked to contribute to the county buildings? And all they kept saying was, 'We will oppose you in every honorable way until the bill includes a clause requiring Scranton to erect the county buildings.'"

"All right, McKune, but right now our fight is not with Carbondale," George Kiersted and Robert McKune glared at each other.

Fred Hitchcock quickly brought the meeting away from personalities and back to the issue at hand, "Let me remind you, gentlemen, if the bill fails now, no man at this meeting will live to see the county divided. The benefits of a new county to Scranton are inestimable, and sacrifices ought to be made."

For the first time, Mayor-elect Powderly spoke up, "I've been all through Jones's district, Carbondale area. I tell you, that district will poll a large majority in favor of a new county.

"I'll tell you why I say that so strongly. Both in Archbald and Carbondale, I've talked with men who said their names were on petitions remonstrating against a new county, and not one of those men had ever signed to such a thing or even given their consent. I favor Mr. McKune; I think we can accomplish the most by piling up petitions with our friends in the Senate, the same way Wilkes-Barre is flooding them with negative orders."

A.H. watched Powderly sharply as he spoke. The whole future direction of the new county, if there was to be one, would hang on this man who would be occupying the mayor's office in a few days. A.H. wondered what Powderly was up to. Was he trying to placate the retiring Robert McKune, to unctuously pour oil over troubled waters, or was he agreeing with McKune because he could wield his own oar equally as well as the others, and was convinced that more could be done at Harrisburg by talking directly with the legislators on a personal basis?

Dr. Throop was the next to speak. He agreed wholeheartedly with Terence Powderly, "I know for a fact Senator Seamans does not have one petition for the new county. He has complained of that to me. Yet Wadhams has them piling up daily."

At this, A.H. pointed out that there was no money to cover even the expense of printing a petition head, "Everyone says they want a new county. They're all telling me how important it is to have a new county. But not one has backed up his wishes with cash. That's where you tell the sincerity. Scranton's Board of Trade stingily gave $200. All the merchants say, 'Let the lawyers pay.' Well, we've been paying and we are paying now, until we are bled dry. We've already furnished three-quarters of the money."

"A.H., $500 will see us through for now," Fred Hitchcock roughly estimated.

"All right. Then get Fred Gunster on the four o'clock train for Harrisburg. Everybody down there has told me, 'Send Gunster down, he knows how to fight these fellows.' Mr. Gunster has got to go and he must have his expenses paid."

"Yes, A.H., I'll second that," and George Sanderson at last had something to say, "The whole Pittsburgh delegation nabbed me one day. 'Send Gunster down—best man you ever had here,' they said."

U.L. Schoonover drew $50 from his pocket, "All right, I'll start it off with $50, but not one cent more. I've already given more than any of you here."

The others silently dropped their share into the passed hat and the money was raised for Fred Gunster on the spot.

"If it's all right with you, gentlemen," said Dr. Throop in his capacity as chairman, "I'll bring this meeting to a close. But before I do, I'll appoint Mayor McKune, Mayor-elect Powderly, Joe Gunster and Alexander Hay to a committee of four to solicit further subscriptions. If there's no objection, meeting adjourned."

The men rose, and formally, as if bidding farewell to Columbus on his first voyage, shook hands with Fred Gunster and wished him good luck. Fred left immediately and hurried to the depot; he was just in time for the train for Harrisburg.

A.H. left just as hurriedly; he was hoping to catch Joe Scranton at *The Scranton Republican* office. He was in time.

"Is it too late to fix up a special paper for Monday?" he wanted to know. He could think of no other way, on such short notice, to achieve the same effect as petitions would have.

"What do you have in mind, A.H.?"

"We just held an emergency session; we've decided that we've got to go all out now, or it's going to be never. The papers you've been sending down, Joe, are about the only thing the legislators can put in their hands and study. I think that if we could get an issue to them stating all the reasons for our cause, it could be a big help and play a decisive part in influencing them."

"You want to get this to them in Harrisburg Monday?"

"I can take the papers with me on the train; delivery will be no problem. Can you run off a special edition?"

Joe Scranton took so long deliberating his answer that A.H. was almost ready to shake it out of him. Finally, A.H. said, "What's the matter, Joe? You're not going to turn us down at the last minute, are you? Not after all the help you've given us up to now?"

"Noooo; it isn't that. I just don't see how I can get everything written and set in time. I didn't think anything was coming up this weekend, so I let everybody go early. A couple have gone fishing—no way of getting them back."

"I'll do it. I'll write and you set and print it. We've got to get this issue to them Monday."

A.H. settled himself at the first available desk, and his pencil was curling and spiraling across the cheap newsprint even before he was fully seated in the oak swivel chair before the desk. He had worked intently for half an hour before he remembered Alice. Calling, he commandeered the boy who was helping Joe Scranton and sent a note home to Alice telling her where he was and what he was doing. He said nothing about when to expect him home. A.H.'s mind poured out and poured out, like a gushing wide-mouth pitcher, all the thoughts which he had been storing in his mind since he had first undertaken the new county cause. He went from one item to another without any hesitation or chewing the end of his pencil as if waiting for inspiration.

Most of the copy which he generated was in the form of short thoughts, designed to fill two-or-three-line spaces between news articles. He thought these "fillers" would make the most effective presentation; they would be scattered throughout the paper instead of all contained within one lengthy article. He advanced every conceivable reason he could think of that might possibly influence the legislators with vote power at Harrisburg:

> Away with county pride as to Luzerne. Divide us up or let all the counties go back into the original three.

Over ten thousand civil actions are started each year in Luzerne Courts. Only five hundred and seventy are set down for trial in her eight regular courts. When will justice be reached at this rate?

Large counties invite crime. Many of our merchants decline to prosecute offenders in court so far away. Doctors refuse to attend in cases where they are likely to be taken away as witnesses.

The only opposition to our new county comes from selfish men at the county seat, who desire us to continue to pay tribute at their Mecca, and from those in Carbondale who desire a small county of their own, with that city as county seat.

The merchant and business men of Scranton demand that the court records affecting their debtors and their titles shall be in their midst.

Give us a new county and don't make us run from twenty or thirty miles to look at the records.

Let the Honorable Gentlemen at Harrisburg compare the court figures of Luzerne with those of their own counties. In 1877 there were 10,806 actions brought in the Common Pleas; 3,309 executions filed, 1,412 cases on the argument list, 750 cases on the trial list, 547 sheriff sales of real estate, 977 criminal cases docketed, 3,050 deeds, mortgages &c. recorded, and 244 letters of administration granted. Verily, our courts, with four judges, running all the while can never relieve the hotch-potch. We should have more courts, more judges, or more counties.

By a division of Luzerne County, her people will be rid of the gross burdens imposed by the salary bill, which has become intolerable and virtually denies justice to her poor suitors.

A new county will not hurt Wilkes-Barre. Easton continued prosperous after Wayne, Pike, Monroe, Schuylkill, Carbon, and Lehigh left old Northampton. Williamsport held her own after large and populous counties were taken from Lycoming.

A Luzerne County defendant may go around the world four or five times before his case is reached.

The merchants of Philadelphia, from whom our people buy, demand that they shall not be stopped from collecting their just claims by reason of an overburdened court. As it now is they must wait from three to four years for collection. Let the Philadelphia members consult the interests of their constituents in this behalf and vote for the new county bill.

With this one in particular, A.H. hoped to provide, that is suggest the reason for, the Philadelphia legislators with a good reason, and a valid excuse, for casting affirmative votes. This was in case they should be criticized by their party colleagues for going against party interests in Wilkes-Barre.

> If we had hourly balloon trains running to and from our county seat, and a network of telephone communication with the court records, still our people would not be happy and would want their records at their doors. Even these would not lessen the distance when the sheriff taxes his costs under the hated salary bill.
>
> See the opinions of President Judge Harding, and Judge Rhone and others. The written opinions of the four judges of Luzerne, Hon. T.H.B. Lewis, ex-Senator Stark, Prothonotary A.P. Barber, and Mayor Loomis of Wilkes-Barre, all of whom are in a position to know, far outweigh the interested views and selfish motives of parties at the county seat.

For his longest piece, A.H. recopied a letter he had E.N. Willard write for just such a purpose:

> An Open Letter to Hon. Charles A. Miner, Scranton, March 18, 1878.
> Hon. Charles A. Miner, House of Representatives, Harrisburg, Pa.
> (Representing Luzerne County from Wilkes-Barre area.):
> Dear Sir:
>
> You and I are Republicans. As such we have worked together in the county of Luzerne since 1861. As a Republican I now address you on the subject of House Bill No. 50. While I don't expect you to vote for the bill on its final passage, I do expect you to treat this subject fairly. After the bill had passed its second reading, I was not a little surprised to hear that you had determined to kill it on third reading. This I am satisfied you will not do, if you will stop and consider the case on its merits, for you know that the measure is just and right, and at this time you will do our people a great wrong by any action on your part that would deprive them of court facilities at home. You know that it is cruel to drag seventy thousand people twenty to thirty miles from their homes to your town of Wilkes-Barre in order to try their cases. You know that this bill is not asked for by a few men for any particular or selfish purpose; but on the contrary, you know that it is the unanimous prayer of a populous and wealthy portion of Luzerne County, and you have no right, by any act of yours, to deprive these people of the privileges asked for in this bill.
>
> And now, Mr. Miner, allow me to call your attention to a few facts. When we went to Harrisburg in the early part of the session with this bill, you met us frankly with your amendment relative to the adjustment of indebtedness, and you told us that if your amendment was accepted by us

your objections to the bill would be removed, though you could not vote for it. Your amendment was accepted in good faith, we took you at your word, and relied upon it, and we have worked faithfully for the passage of the bill, ever sincere, and now we are told that you propose to prevent its final passage.

I am not unmindful of your power of the Republican party at Wilkes-Barre, but I beg of you, when you appeal to your Republican friends in the House to defeat it, to remember that there are good and tried Republicans in the proposed new county who have stood by you and your political friends at Wilkes-Barre for years, and we ask you to consider our feelings and our condition before you deprive us of our rights.

We consulted with a large number of the leading members of the bar, with the business men and the property holders of your own town before asking for the passage of this bill, and they told us to "go on." You know, Mr. Miner, that a large number of your own people assured us that they had no objection to the proposed division of the county, and you gave us to distinctly understand that you would have none if your amendment was accepted, and I cannot believe we have been deceived. The vote tomorrow will show. If we are to be disappointed in the profession of your people and your own position let us know it at once, and hereafter we will know where we stand. We have fought this fight for thirty years, and we propose to fight it for thirty more if necessary. In other words, so long as we are deprived of our rights so long we propose to press our cause, and we do not propose to be discouraged because we are weak and you are strong.

Respectfully, E.N. Willard

House Bill No. 50 affects only Luzerne County, therefore let her own people decide by their votes as to a division that is just.

But the strongest reason that he could think of, the thought A.H. had uppermost in his mind, he saved for last:

We have failed yet to see a good reason advanced against the division of this county. In fact we have seen no reasons at all.

It was almost daylight Sunday morning before the papers were ready. Tired and exhausted, A.H. hurried home to freshen up and change his clothes before leaving. He would take the noon train for Harrisburg and get the copies of the special edition of the *Scranton Republican* placed on the desks of the legislators so that they would be waiting for them when they arrived for their morning session. He had done all that he could think to do. Would it be enough? Would he get the new county this time?

A.H. reached Harrisburg at suppertime Sunday, exhausted. He had dozed fitfully, never really sleeping, on the train. Once in the state capital, he turned his bundle of papers over to the others—Fred Gunster, etc.—and went to bed, sleeping soundly until ten on Monday morning. After he woke, he ate lightly and hurried over to the capitol building. He found the rest of the Scranton delegation in the hall. Robert McKune advised him of the situation.

"They've decided to go into a night session tonight, A.H. We've been told there are forty-two bills to consider for a first reading. Tomorrow the bills that are up for their final passage will be heard. No. 50 is fourth on the list tomorrow, so I've been told."

"Has there been any change in people's allegiances, or anyone coming out strongly for or against the bill?" A.H. wanted to know.

"Miner says he will definitely go against us. And Lewis is trying to recover for the help that he gave you last year on the Providence separation bill. He intimates he's going to go against the new county, too."

"That's only two. All we need to pass is 101. How do we stand on the total?"

Robert McKune didn't need to think or count. The group had been revising their totals so frequently that almost any number he came out with would do, "We can't tell. Wadhams comes in from the Senate every now and then and talks to a couple of the House members. Whether he's able to change their vote or not, we can't tell. We do know that every member on the floor has been getting a barrage of telegrams from Wilkes-Barre decrying the bill."

"Did they get the newspapers?"

"Waiting for them when they got in. Kiersted and Ackerly read one of your little 'bon mots' out loud from time to time."

All afternoon and early evening the men from Scranton worked hard and diligently; not once did they yield to physical discomfort. They talked to every legislator who showed his face outside the chamber doors. The evening session was lengthy and tiring. Everyone knew of the conflict coming up on the new county bill the following day; it was a hotly contested issue. The legislators were anxious to get as much done Monday evening as they could. They were well aware of the importance of the bills coming up for final consideration on Tuesday. The Scranton delegation, working hard as a unified, homogeneous group, stayed with the session until it broke up. Quietly, softly, but very, very persuasively, they talked with as many as they could, as the members of the House were departing. Finally, just before eleven, they returned to their lodgings. The morrow would see the culmination of their labors; then they would have the answer as to how successful their campaign had been.

By this time, the name of the proposed new county was "Lackawanna County" in all but a legal sense. The men from the upper end of Luzerne County had, on more than one occasion, identified themselves with that part of the Wyoming Valley where the Lackawanna River flows, and some of the state Senators and Representatives had informally referred to them as "the Lackawanna men." In their tense waiting, the hour of truth at hand, "Lackawanna" had fallen more and more frequently and naturally from their lips. Soon, it had become "Lackawanna County." What a beautiful sounding tone it had when it reached their ears!

The hour was almost midnight. Off in the distance, the Scranton men, in their hotel, could hear the chug of a train. A.H. stared pensively out the window. He had been here, in Harrisburg, so many times. He had been disappointed before; how could it happen again? Surely, the new county must come into being somehow. What more could they do, he wondered. He looked at the men around him; a feeling of belonging overwhelmed him as never before. He was deeply moved by the emotional commitment his compatriots were showing to the new county cause. He had stood alone for so long that he couldn't quite believe they were working with him, wanting what he wanted for Scranton—no, for Lackawanna County, now.

Movement in the street below, shadows of people walking by the window of the hotel, distracted him from his own well of emotional involvements. In the distance, the departing train could be heard as it left the town. Sharply his mind focused; who would come into Harrisburg at midnight? He went downstairs, pausing on the steps just long enough to recognize Peter Jennings and John McNeish, two residents of Wilkes-Barre. Quietly he returned upstairs and woke Robert McKune.

"Bob, wake up!" he whispered, "Do you hear me? Jennings and McNeish have just come in from Wilkes-Barre!"

"What the hell are they up to?"

"I don't know. I just saw them come in."

Quickly, A.H. and Robert McKune roused the others. Downstairs in the lobby, there was a confrontation.

"Get out of our way, Merrifield!" Jennings said brusquely, "Touch us and we'll swear out a warrant for your arrest. Isn't that right, John?"

John McNeish moved in closer to his companion. "What's the matter with you Scranton boys—nervous you're not going to get your new little county? Wait and see; wait 'til we get through with you."

With that, the two left the lobby and went back out into the night. After their departure, there was no sleep for the advocates of the new county bill. For Wilkes-Barre to send a delegation such as Jennings and McNeish, at this hour of the night, spelled trouble and disappointment. In this frame of mind, the time ticked on towards morning. Because of the interlude with Jennings and his partner, they were awake when the 3:00 A.M. train came in, also. The three o'clock brought Jadwin from Carbondale. The opposition to the new county bill was still rallying even at the last minute.

Now the lobbying and pressuring began in earnest. As soon as it was light, A.H. and the others converged on the eating places and streets leading to the capitol building, anywhere they had hopes of finding a legislator. Their pleas for a new county could be heard from one end of the state capital to the other. As for the legislators so earnestly petitioned, not one spoke his true thoughts. There was no idea, no indication how the vote would go.

The morning session of the House of Representatives lasted until two in the afternoon; the members covered the first three bills on their schedule. Then they adjourned until three. Everyone from Scranton, including A.H., was seated in the visitors' gallery when the afternoon session began. Tension clung as like a magnet to everything and everyone; yet no audible reference was made to the pending bill. The House had been thorough and overmeticulous in its consideration of the three bills in the morning. It was as if the members of the House of Representatives were themselves afraid to proceed, afraid to see just how they were going to divide on the new county issue—how they were going to show where they stood.

As soon as the bill number and the title of the proposed act was announced, the chamber and the gallery above grew absolutely soundless. Only the clerk's voice rippled the atmosphere. When he had finished, Charles Miner desired recognition.

"I want only to say that I am distinctly and unalterably opposed to this bill," his voice rang out, "However, I will not delay the proceedings with my remarks. I have, instead, inscribed them here in this report, which I submit for the Congressional record." With that, Charles Miner handed the papers to the reporter at his desk and resumed his seat. Then it was S.S. Jones from Carbondale who desired recognition. Intensely, and slightly hysterically, he came out against the bill; his speech was not long, either. He was followed immediately by Mr. Judge from Pittston. The theme was the same: a brief, rapid fire attack on Scranton and the new county.

Then, for a few moments, the House was quiet. Into the silence the clerk's voice boomed; the roll call had began at last: "Ackerly?" "Aye!" "Agnew?" "Nay!" "Alexander?" "Aye!" "Andre?" "Aye!" "Bachman?" "Aye!" "Bakeoven?" "Aye!" "Black?" "Nay!" —and so on it went. Never one sound other than a name followed immediately by "aye" or "nay," until the pattern had been repeated 171 times. Then again there was silence while the vote was tallied. Of course by this time, A.H. knew the answer, as did the others in the gallery; they had been recording votes along with the clerk. Still, the terrible silence in the huge room—there was neither discussion nor demonstration. The victorious side was as quiet as the loser; both friend and foe had been watching the progress of the bill in mute suspense. There at last, chalked on the board, was official confirmation for all to see: 151 votes for the new county! Never had an issue been contested so fiercely and passed by such a wide margin. Only twenty were recorded against House Bill #50. Quietly, the Scranton delegation left their seats in the gallery and filtered out into the corridor. The prize of their freedom was so near, so real, that they were trembling.

There were only a few odds and ends to take care of before returning to Scranton for a brief respite. Now that House Bill #50 had passed in the House of Representatives, it would have to go over to the Senate. At the fastest, a week would intervene, possibly two, before the bill would come up there. The general opinion was that the Senate would pass the bill easily and quickly because of the wide margin recorded for it in the House. But A.H. had traveled this road once before; he was taking nothing for granted. The Scranton men discussed their plan of attack and decided to maintain a small permanent lobby in Harrisburg at all times. A.H. was the first to leave, however, to return briefly to Scranton; he had finally remembered Alice, W.W. and the rest of the family.

It was just as well that he went home. Senator Wadhams, from the Wilkes-Barre district, was back in Wilkes-Barre by Friday. At the moment, he was all-powerful; any and all moves to kill the new county bill in the Senate would have to come from him. He had returned to Wilkes-Barre for last minute instructions; he would also go to Philadelphia before returning to Harrisburg. Indirectly, A.H. heard that Wilkes-Barre would come out in favor of the new county bill in the Senate, provided something could be arranged about the courts.

At first, A.H. was confused. A new county would also mean new courts; this had been his strongest motivation, propelling him to drive for a new county in the first place, so that Scranton would have her own courts. It took some heavy thinking on his part, but he finally figured out what was behind the feeler. Once he did, he went to Joe Scranton and arranged to have him publish a reply in the *Scranton Republican.* A.H.'s reply to the feeler from Wilkes-Barre was in the form of an open letter:

> To the Editor of the *Republican*:
>
> It would seem that at last the people of Wilkes-Barre have concluded to take a sensible view of the new county question. The only wonder is why they did not do so before. It may be a little strange that the idea of harmony among brethren never struck the editor of the *Record* till after the vote in the House on the New County bill, but perhaps this may be set down in the language of the tract peddler as a remarkable conversion late in life.
>
> There are some who question the good faith of this proposition by Wilkes-Barre to offer no opposition, but rather her assistance in case we agree to amend the bill so as to divide the Judicial district as well as the county, but I am disposed to think her people sincere because I can easily see the strong motive they have to a division such as they propose. While their proposed amendment will doubtless placate them, it can in no way hurt the people of Lackawanna county. Whether the district be divided or not, Judge Handley and Judge Stanton would doubtless be the ones who would hold our courts, and if it would please Luzerne to have Judge Harding reelected, with Palmer as Additional Law Judge of the Luzerne district, certainly the people of Lackawanna would not complain.
>
> Besides this, the amendment would give our Orphan's Court facilities at home, a matter that might be left in some doubt as the bill is at present. If those in charge of the new county bill at Harrisburg are satisfied that sending it back to the House for concurrence in the amendment will not endanger its final success, I would say by all means let us meet the Wilkes-Barre people in the spirit of harmony they seem to manifest, and let us have a bill that will be mutually satisfactory to all concerned.
>
> So long as we obtain the substantial relief we seek there is no use quarreling over trifles. If a mutual agreement is arrived at there will be no after contests in the courts of law with all the incident vexations, delays and

uncertainties. I cordially agree with your suggestion that harmony is the best policy, for we can certainly accomplish more by all heartily pulling in the same direction than by working against each other. Let us have peace.

A.H. then signed it simply, "A Scranton Lawyer."

Now, what was this all about? In their last minute attempt to disconcert and to wreak any amount of havoc if possible, those interested at Wilkes-Barre had raised the question of how the court system was to be divided between the old and new counties. The aim was twofold: first, to harass the new county people, and hopefully get House Bill #50 mired down in a long legal wrangle so that its final passage could be delayed, forever. And second, if the division of Luzerne could not be stopped, then as a final gesture the men from the upper end of the valley were to get out and take their "undesirables" with them. Judge William Stanton had came into the county court in the November election on the Greenback-Labor ticket. From the moment his winning votes had been tallied, he had been resented and unwanted on the bench at Wilkes-Barre. So, in desperation, Wilkes-Barre was telling Scranton she would help her to go, provided she took her "trash" with her.

A.H. was in a state of near collapse at the thought that the new county bill might be returned to the state House of Representatives because of a question over which county was to get what judge. However, he had too much integrity to agree to anything just to accomplish the end he desired so passionately. He was not concerned about Stanton as a judge; there was a precedent for removing "bad" judges, if need be. In fact, at the very time the new county bill was going through the House of Representatives, the citizens of Wayne and Pike counties, two counties adjoining Luzerne, were petitioning the legislators at Harrisburg for the removal of their president judge because of his gross inefficiency. Therefore, when A.H. wrote that he could easily see the strong motive behind Wilkes-Barre's questioning of which county got what judge, and that they would be known for the kind of people they were showing themselves to be, he meant it. He was not alarmed or ashamed to have a Greenback-Labor man as a judge in his precious new county; also, he had seen Stanton in court, and had found him to be more than competent at the time of the Pauli case.

A.H.'s openness—heresy to some—in the matter of empathy for labor could be traced to his own personal philosophy. In the 1870's, the leading social philosophies, the guides of the nation's social consciences, were represented by two men: The Rev. Henry Ward Beecher and Col. Robert Ingersoll. Of the two, A.H. had aligned himself under Ingersoll's banner; so much so, that when Beecher had addressed an audience in Scranton on February 11 of this same year, 1878, he had ignored the lecture. What was it that appealed to him about Robert Ingersoll? Because of the inherent truths in many of Ingersoll's homilies, such as: "Man should live for man, and not for the aristocracy of the air"; "It seems to me even an infinite God has no right to compel by force or fear the meanest of mankind to accept a dogma abhorrent to his mind." And even though Ingersoll often said, "Preserve my pocketbook from lawyers," the lawyer in A.H.

wholeheartedly responded to "Whoever denies to another the right to think, denies it to himself."

And Terence Powderly knew it. At this point, Terence Powderly was forever bound to A.H. The full portent of A.H.'s published open letter was not lost on Mayor-elect Powderly. The weeks of intensive collaboration with some of Scranton's wealthiest men were to influence him all the rest of his life. Up to this time, Terence Powderly had interacted with management. He had dealt with robber-barons before; since 1872, when he was first elected president of the Machinists and Blacksmiths Union, he had been no stranger to men of power and wealth and education. But in his dealings with the upper end of the economic scale, he had interacted with the men, but he had never worked with them. There is quite a difference between interacting with adversaries and working with colleagues. Now, just as he was about to assume his first public office, he was forced into the position of actually working with the elite. He had to cooperate with them; he had to solicit funds for a cause initiated by them; he had to join with the moneyed class and help them achieve one of their goals. Terence Powderly did not hesitate nor hold back, for he had met A.H. on the most intimate of terms and he was forever to feel his influence, so much so that he patterned his life after him—because there was no one like A.H.

Of the small group striving for the new county goal, A.H., by himself and through his father, was the wealthiest, the most grand of the group. He embodied everything labor wanted to overcome: financial power, labor employer, influential beyond words through family and friends. Terence Powderly should have turned from him in hate. Instead, he found A.H. so remarkable, so honest, with such a high set of values, that he adopted him as his model. When he read A.H.'s open letter in the *Scranton Republican*, including his remark that to have William Stanton, a labor man, could in no way hurt the people of Lackawanna County, a bond of respect and admiration was forged greater than any chain link of iron.

Terence Powderly communicated his feelings of respect and cooperation to the men below him, and domino-like, the fall was to the benefit of the managing class of Scranton's industry. In later years, Terence Powderly was to suffer for it. At times he was accused of being too idealistic, criticized because he would not lead his workers to strike, because he seemed content to improve their lot through education and cooperation instead of violence. But he could not help it; he could not think otherwise. He had seen how even the highest, the very antithesis of labor, would struggle and strain and fear for something which they wanted very badly and needed in order to overcome their own oppression. He saw first-hand how the elite could work and plan and, more importantly, succeed in overthrowing the yoke of tyranny. For that was what A.H. had often called the suppression and taxation by the ring at the courthouse in Wilkes-Barre: "tyrannical overlords"—the very words that Terence Powderly and his committee often used to describe their oppressors. So, at the most crucial time in the history of the fight for a new county, labor fell silently in behind the new county advocates.

The silent majority—no one yet had any idea of their true power; they were not too sure themselves. There had been some indication in the elections that had put Stanton into the judgeship and Powderly into the mayor's office, but there had been no real display of that power yet. It was all too new.

The silent majority that was labor, all across the state, knew that Powderly and the laboring class at the mines and iron works in Luzerne County were behind the men who wanted to split the county. Any member of the legislature at Harrisburg felt the unseen pressure of votes at home that would or would not return them to the next session. Why would there be any objection to what a small minority of the state's population wanted to do about their right to self-government?

Senator Wadhams had been back in Wilkes-Barre only a few days after the new county bill had been passed by the House when he asked for a meeting with a few of the new county advocates at the bar office in Wilkes-Barre. There, it was formally agreed that there would be no objection to the new county bill in the state Senate if the new county would agree to take the two judges, Handley and Stanton.

Fortunately, but in this specific case unfortunately, a democracy is for all voices, and A.H.'s was not the only one to speak on the question of judges and judicial districts in erecting a new county. Consideration of House Bill #50 by the Senate was delayed a week, while the legal aspects of amending the bill to include reference to a new judicial district were studied. At this, A.H.'s nerves were ready to break, like his father's while waiting for Halstead's decision at the time of the critical Hollenback purchase for Winton; A.H. turned his mind to other matters.

Very exciting matters, too. On April 2, William O. Wilson, agent, journeyed from Scranton to the Supreme Court Chamber in the courthouse at Wilkes-Barre. There, he presented a demonstration of Prof. Alexander Bell's speaking telephone for The Bell Telephone Company, by whom he was authorized to lease telephones and magneto coils. The telephone had finally been perfected to a degree such that it was now readily available for public, private, social, or business communication at the lease rate of $20 per annum for each station (telephone). Three days later, on April 5, A.H. had one installed in his office, and he and Alice entertained there, in Washington Hall, at a "telephone concert."

Their guests were Catherine and W.W., Mr. and Mrs. R.J. Matthews, Mrs. William R. Storrs, Mrs. A. Hendrick, Mrs. G.W. Bushnell, Miss Belle Lucas, Miss E. Howell, Miss Hattie Storrs, the Messrs. Samuel Newhouse, J.M.C. Ranck, W.H. Gearhart and Master Storrs. For the concert, Mr. Wilson ran a line from his residence to A.H.'s office. There in his home, his three brothers, a sister, and Joseph Harper sang quartets, duets, and solos over the open telephone, as well as sending the sound of instrumental music. The audience was treated to "Sweet By and By" and other, similar songs. Afterwards, A.H., like the Lackawanna Iron and Coal Company, had one of the early phones in Scranton.

With the passage of each day, as the time approached for the Senate at Harrisburg to consider the new county bill, in direct ratio A.H.'s degree and intensity of nervous disorder increased to the point where he was almost physically ill. Remember—he had traveled this road once before, two years earlier. And it had been now, at the state Senate, that he had been turned back and lost his first bid for a new county. Memories of that experience were his constant companion in these early days of April, 1878. Despite the optimism of his cadre of workers, resulting from the wide margin of the bill's passage in the House, A.H. drove them to work harder and harder. In '76 he had been just as optimistic as they were, only to suffer defeat in the Senate. He didn't want that to happen again. Past experience was solely responsible for his concern.

Late Monday, at the beginning of the second week in April, Senator Seamans sent word to Scranton that the new county bill had been introduced and would probably come up for its second reading near the end of the week. Wednesday and Thursday mornings, Scranton emptied herself of her chief citizens; they poured down on the state capital like a blanket of silencing snow, to field all objections and to make the world appear as they would have it. There was reason for worry, too; in the twelfth hour, some Republicans of Luzerne County had named Henry Hoyt, a Wilkes-Barre resident who was going to run for governor on the Republican ticket in the forthcoming fall elections, as being the one most opposed to the division of Luzerne—thereby implying that a gubernatorial candidate had much influence throughout the state and could, and would, stop the bill.

On this trip to Harrisburg, A.H. was planning to take his protege John Runk; A.H. and John Collings were still not doing much talking. A.H. also thought that it would be a worthwhile experience for Runk, especially if he were to practice law in Scranton. At the very last minute, when A.H. was ready to leave and had gone to Alice to say good-bye, he came upon her packing, with Bridget's help, a small trunk.

"Alice, what are you doing?" he wanted to know in amazement—amazement, because he feared he knew already what she was doing.

"I'm going to Harrisburg."

He stared at her, speechless. She was now quite large; they were both constantly being reminded that the baby's arrival was very, very imminent.

"Are you out of your mind?" he wanted to know, "You can't go like this. It just isn't done!"

"I'm going, A.H.," Alice pursed her lips and moved determinedly among the few clothes still lying on the bed.

A.H. looked to Bridget for support, but saw that she was very carefully ignoring husband and wife; he realized that he was going to get no help from her. At that, A.H. stiffened perceptibly and said, somewhat imperiously, "It's too dangerous. I can't worry about you and the baby, and attend to any emergency that may come up. You should not be traveling at this time."

Alice came over to him and smiled tenderly, "I'm sorry; I suppose you're right. But this time, I'm going with you anyway, What happens at Harrisburg means as much to me as it does to you. Besides, I feel fine. I'll be all right. Please don't worry about me," Alice gave him another smile and finished her packing, shutting the lid of the trunk with a smart clap. Obviously, both Mr. and Mrs. A.H. Winton would be arriving in Harrisburg.

House Bill #50 came up for its second reading in the Senate on Friday, April 12. Alice remained in their hotel room, leaving A.H. free to wander, John Runk his faithful shadow. The two men secured excellent seats in the visitors' gallery, some time before the bill was introduced. From where they were sitting, they could observe Wilkes-Barre's Senator Wadhams bustling about. Once the bill was read by the clerk, time was taken to detail the terms of the proportioning of Luzerne County's indebtedness between the new county and the old county. That settled, the amendment to create a separate judicial district was introduced and refused; the judicial question was set aside for consideration as a separate bill.

Once the question of the courts was out of the way, the roll was called for the new county bill. Opposition ceased; the bill passed. Without fuss or fanfare, in a matter of minutes, A.H. had the right to plan for Lackawanna County.

Now that it had finally been accomplished, A.H. withdrew from the world around him, remaining motionless in his seat—going into an existence of his own, with all the ramifications of an independent county and its courts flooding in on him. No one else could fully understand what it meant to him—how deeply he was moved. At this first moment of success, even he could not have put into words all the emotions and thoughts coursing through him. It was left to John Runk to think of Alice. Taking one of his calling cards from his card case, he wrote on the reverse: "Mrs. Winton—New County Bill passed second reading in the Senate today." He left A.H. long enough to go out in the corridor and summon a messenger boy to deliver the note to the waiting Alice.

Success at last? Not quite. There was still much to be done before proclaiming Lackawanna County.

For one thing, the question of the Judicial District remained to be settled. This Senator Seamans, who represented the Scranton area, obligingly did a week later in the Senate. When the roll was called, the Senate quickly approved the creation of the Forty-Fifth Judicial District. All that remained was to send the bill over to the House for their approval; hopefully, it would be called before they adjourned for the summer recess.

19

Wilkes-Barre had still not given up entirely. Once approved by the House and the Senate, House Bill #50 had to go to the Governor for his signature. At this point, some dissidents raised the question of the constitutionality of the new county bill. Time was lost while the state's attorney-general gave the bill a thorough examination before pronouncing it, in his opinion, constitutionally sound.

Immediately after the passage of the new county bill by the Senate, A.H. hurried Alice out of Harrisburg and back home to Scranton. If fatherhood was to be his lot again, he wanted it to be in his own new county. The delay caused by the constitutionality study of the bill, by the state executive branch, did not disturb him. In fact, he welcomed it, if only because he would prefer to have all questions anticipated now, so that a charge of corrupt or illegal actions could not destroy the new county some time hence, after it had been set up and was functioning.

He had carefully gone over the bill himself, and doubted that the Attorney-General would find anything objectionable. There were also other reasons for his hurrying back to Scranton, although none so urgent as Alice. The real work of erecting a new county now had to begin. For, as passed by the House and Senate, the new county bill was technically only the authorization, by the legislative branch of the Commonwealth of Pennsylvania to the governor of the Commonwealth, to appoint a three-man commission to look into the matter and recommend whether or not there should be a new county. Finally, on Wednesday, April 17, shortly before noon, Governor Hartranft signed the bill, thereby creating the special commission to conduct the study on the question of a new county from the upper end of Luzerne. Whether or not a new county would be recommended was entirely up to the will of the inhabitants of the area that would constitute the new county; this they would show the commission by a special vote. Much remained yet to be done, then, before proclaiming Lackawanna County.

Fortunately for A.H., he got Alice back to Scranton safely, still in good health. Then he had to hurry down to Wilkes-Barre; the Pauli landlord-forged-lease case was up for retrial. This time, it was very obvious that the whole purpose of the trial was to prove the unfitness of Greenback-Labor Judge Stanton, which Philadelphia newspapers had been proclaiming since his election the previous November. Openly, money and influence were brought to bear, hopefully to warp the actions of the court, thereby demonstrating Judge Stanton incapable of performing his "sacred duties." A.H., as counsel for the Commonwealth, was at the center of the storm.

To seek a retrial, lawyer Daniel Dougherty came up from Philadelphia—he would handle the defense of F. Pauli. After a three-hour discourse by Dougherty in Pauli's defense, Judge Stanton proceeded to read his opinion from a paper before him. The jury had found Pauli guilty, there was no reason for a retrial; would Pauli please step forward for sentencing, requested Judge Stanton. At this, the district attorney of Luzerne County mutinied and refused to execute the proper procedure in sentencing. His eyes leaping from the flushed face of Judge Stanton to the flushed face of District Attorney Rice to the flushed face of Philadelphia lawyer Dougherty, A.H. was aghast at the courtroom histrionics.

Judge Stanton did not get a chance to sentence Pauli until Tuesday of the following week. Over the weekend, and for days afterwards, he was subject to vilification of every kind by Philadelphia newspapers. When the headlines finally went so far as to scream for Stanton's impeachment, and the newspapers printed instructions how to go about it as well, A.H., a man of Connecticut heritage defiant of Philadelphia opinion, telegraphed an open letter to the *Philadelphia Public Ledger:*

> Scranton, May 3, 1878
> Mr. Editor:
>
> I read your editorial of yesterday in relation to the Pauli case. It both pained and surprised me to find your journal, always so reliable and truthful, adopting the tissue of falsehoods about Judge Stanton's actions in the case. I have read all the reports about the case sent to the Philadelphia and other papers, together with their editorial remarks, and as one of the counsel for the Commonwealth in the case, I must say that the Judge is one of the most maligned of men, and his action in the case has been most maliciously misrepresented. The Judge's enemies, whom he defeated last fall, are fighting that battle over again, and are whipping him over the shoulders of the Pauli case.
>
> The facts in the case, when you come to fully understand them, will convince you that you have been grossly deceived. The argument for a new trial was first made on the thirtieth of March, by two counsel on each side, each side occupying two hours, and the judge reserved his decision until the eighth of April. On that day counsel for Pauli appeared and urged the Court, before delivering its opinion, which was then prepared, and which the Judge was about to read, to grant a further extension of time until the twentieth of April, to hear Daniel Dougherty, of Philadelphia, for the defense. Mr. Dougherty failing to put in an appearance on the appointed day, the time was further extended to the twenty-seventh of April, when he came and argued for his client, Mr. Pauli, at length, consuming three and a half hours in the delivery of his speech.

Mr. Dougherty having made no new points, having said nothing that had not been already said by other counsel in their lengthy arguments of the case, and as a consequence produced no reasons that had not already been produced why a new trial should be granted, the counsel for the Commonwealth arose and said they were ready to respond to the argument of Mr. Dougherty, if there was anything in it that the Court thought was new, or that need be further discussed. The Judge said that he had closely followed Mr. Dougherty's argument throughout, and had disposed of his points as they were raised so that it was only taking useless time to keep the case hanging in court from week to week under dramatic colorings; that as Mr. Dougherty had not made any point that had not been fully argued before, he considered that it was now his duty to dispose of the case.

The Judge then said that he had now lying before him an opinion which he had prepared when he came there on the eighth of April, to deliver, which covered the arguments made before that; he would file that opinion and dispose of the case. The day was in the regular term of the Court of the Quarter Sessions. It cannot be truthfully said that the case was not fairly tried, fully and extensively argued and considered; as the defendant had more courtesies extended to him than any defendant has had before our Court since its establishment, and the more the journals of the State let the light of truth into the case the more will Judge Stanton be vindicated and his enemies confounded. It was not Judge Stanton's fault that the jury believed the testimony pointing conclusively to Pauli's guilt.

A.H. Winton—of Counsel for Commonwealth

When A.H.'s letter appeared in the *Ledger*, Philadelphians asked, "Who is he, this A.H. Winton? Who is he that dares to say that a Greenback-Labor Judge must be vindicated?" And when the answer came back that he was the same A.H. Winton who was carving Luzerne into Lackawanna County, A.H.'s fate was sealed.

In addition, A.H. was defending labor in the age when the imperious robber-baron aristocrats ruled. The Wintons, therefore, had to go.

John Collings was as busy in court as A.H. was during early May, but for other reasons. Eventually, someday, the two brothers-in-law would have to make up, but, for the present, their relations were distinctly growing more distant; everything they did seemed to emphasize their chasm of separation, making it deeper. While A.H. was before Judge Stanton on the much publicized Pauli case, John Collings had reason to seek out Judge Stanton, too. He wanted him to issue a writ of habeas corpus to release three young ladies whom Mayor Powderly was holding following a raid on a disorderly house, a house of prostitution. John enjoyed having the writ delivered to him at his office in his own name, but identified as A.H. Winton's office, which of course they were sharing.

Elsbeth Beaumont Collings Winton entered the world of Wyoming and Mulberry Avenues early in the morning, just as Scranton was awakening, in time to be a thirteenth wedding anniversary present for her parents, being born two days before on the seventh of May, 1878. Outside the house, the clear light was glinting down through the tender, delicate green that was particular to the first early promise of spring trees. Inside, A.H. was speaking softly to Alice. For this birth, only a part of him was as exuberant as when they were first married; there was another part to him now. His love for his wife, in the way of any hero of an enduring epic ballad, had grown, but the passions of youth were now channeled, for the time being, into the new world that was coming into the valley.

"You are all I ever want," he told Alice, "and now I have two little chicks. I'm very lucky, do you know that?"

"You told me in the beginning that I had to work with you or else I would destroy you. You are everything to me, too, A.H. If I didn't have you, it would be the same as if I were alone." She gave him a relaxed smile of pure love.

A.H. leaned over and kissed her. This moment of tenderness, in the first hours of promise at the beginning of day in springtime, was a cool island of repose in the hectic life that had been the pattern of their recent daily living. They kissed again. It was far in the past when they had last taken the time for the luxury of thinking only of each other. Lazily, A.H. sat with Alice a while longer, holding her hand, until she drifted into sleep. He wished for no other life. He thought back, more than thirteen years, to his eager letter to Mr. Smith, imploring him to call him to Washington. He would never have seen Lackawanna County, had he gone. His eyes rested briefly on Alice. She was his real strength, he knew. Rising to leave, he bent over her and lightly brushed his lips across his sleeping wife's; as he did so, the memory of the time when his lips had first touched her, back in the vestibule of the Collings home in Wilkes-Barre, darted forward into his consciousness from his storehouse of accessible material. He had never forgotten a moment of his association with Alice Collings.

The beauty of early May, and all the promises that spring makes, then ripened into full-blown culmination as the days turned closer to the month of June. A grand celebration was planned by the Veterans' Association for Memorial Day, May 30. A.H. was asked to be the speaker in the afternoon after the parade had reached the soldiers' graves in Forest Hill cemetery. Arriving concurrently with the invitation for Memorial Day in Scranton was an invitation from the Wyoming Centennial Committee.

For the Wyoming Valley, the year 1878 was to be the occasion for an even bigger celebration than the Centennial of 1876. Or rather, for the people in the Wyoming Valley, July 4, 1878 was their date for commemorating the nation's 100th Birthday. The centennial of the Wyoming Massacre was to be marked with as much pageantry as possible. A monument, dedicated to the brave defenders at the time of the holocaust, would be unveiled at Forty Fort, the site of the battle, on the Fourth of July. Mr. and Mrs. A.H. Winton, since Mrs. Winton was a direct descendant of Elisha Blackman and Eleazer Blackman, were invited to sit on the speakers' platform. A.H. accepted both invitations, the one for Memorial Day and the one for the Fourth of July, and then sent off a letter to Frank Collins in Washington.

A.H. described the progress of the new county to Frank, and then asked him to make his contribution towards the erection of Lackawanna County. Gladly, in the last week of May Frank Collins introduced, into the House of Representatives, a bill calling for Congress to create a new district court centered at Scranton. For sixty years, since the early days of the nation, in spite of the tremendous growth and increase in population, the federal government had never correspondingly increased the number of judicial districts. The entire state of Pennsylvania was still divided into two judicial districts, with one court and accompanying records in Philadelphia and the other court and its records at Pittsburgh. A.H. knew that the state would eventually be opened up, because the growing population all across the country would force redistricting of the courts. Luzerne County in Pennsylvania alone had grown from 20,000 inhabitants in 1818 to 160,765 in 1878. He wanted Scranton to be among the first to benefit from the additional districts.

Frank Collins sent word back, confirming his action on the measure. The Scranton Bar Association met and appointed a committee, consisting of A.H., Fred Gunster, Edward Merrifield, George Sanderson, R. Archbald and E. Dimmick, to work with Frank on the Federal court question.

A.H. was not the only one in his family who was invited to participate in dedication ceremonies. John Collings joined Col. William Monies, mayor of Scranton in 1869, as a speaker at the ceremony inaugurating a new stop on the Lehigh and Southern Railroad, "Slocum Flats" in Scranton's Eleventh Ward area. Eventually, the brother-in-law would again be a friend, but not yet.

The baby Elsbeth, or Elsie as her father called her, was growing as healthily and happily as Kate had. Anxious to return to a social life again, Alice looked forward to the Memorial Day exercises joyfully. With all the activities of the past months, and those in store for the near future, she was happy to be a full-time participant once again. Everybody was going all out for the Memorial Day remembrance. Mayor Powderly issued a request that all the business houses close for the afternoon of May 30, to show respect for the honored dead.

For the actual observance, the day's program called for the veterans of the Civil War to parade through Scranton before going to the final resting place of their dead comrades. Alice worked with other Scranton ladies to make the floral arrangements that would be placed on the soldiers' graves. In the evening, the Scranton High School, now nearing the end of its second year of existence, would entertain with songs and poems in the Academy of Music, long since relocated and rebuilt on Wyoming Avenue near Linden after its disastrous fire.

The plans were many and great, and there was much excitement in anticipation of the big event. But man proposes and God disposes; when Memorial Day finally arrived, torrents of rain arrived, too. The parade, scheduled to start at one in the afternoon, was first ordered cancelled, but the order was then changed; it was postponed until two o'clock. It wasn't until 2:15 that the actual marching began; by this time, many marchers were missing, including the Scranton City Guard. A.H.'s speech, planned for the ceremony at Forest Hill Cemetery, was moved to the evening at the Academy of Music.

He spoke brilliantly and beautifully, paying tribute to the Civil War soldier and the promise to care for their families made to them as they marched away. He looked down from the stage at his family: his wife sitting with his mother and father. He was proud of them, of his city, of his county-to-be, and of his country; he had no quarrel with life.

Memorial Day was Thursday. On Friday, W.W. posted a piece of paper at the front of the Second National Bank building:

> Circumstances compel us to suspend business for the present.
> Scranton, May 31, 1878 W.W. Winton
> President

Having done that, he walked over to A.H.'s office and went in to see him.

A.H. looked up pleasantly at his father's entrance. He was still basking in the excitement of the Memorial Day observances. His father's visit at the early morning hour was unusual, but as he greeted his father, A.H. thought only that he looked slightly grim.

"I've closed the bank," said W.W., sitting down.

"I'm sorry, father; I didn't quite get that. You said something about the bank?"

"Yes. I said it's closed. I can't open. There's no money."

This time, A.H. heard, for he screamed, "My God! What happened?"

"I don't know, A.H. I truly don't know. There just isn't enough money."

Wounded, confused, uncomprehending, the two Winton men, W.W. and A.H., battled their uncertainties that awful Friday morning in the privacy of A.H.'s office. When they appeared in public, they would have to show sureness and calm composure. Meanwhile, outside, in front of the Second National Bank, very little attention was paid to the shut doors and attached note. There was no crowd of curious or of trapped depositors wondering what was going on.

They had succeeded at last, that everchanging sea of faceless men who said the Wintons had to go—who disliked the Wintons because they were too wealthy, who disliked the Wintons because they were too powerful—because the Wintons had shown Dr. Throop to be an inept bungler at fixing votes, because they had supported Joe Coon in the auditor's report that had chased the Democrats out of power, because A.H. supported labor men—but mainly because A.H., supported by W.W., had carved Luzerne into two and taken the rich taxes of the collieries and factories away from Wilkes-Barre.

There were many reasons, then, why the Wintons had to be punished. Joe Coon had been punished; he had gone to jail. When the Republicans had come to power in the county, Frank Beamish had had to pay. But of all the many reasons why the Wintons had to be punished, mostly it was because of Lackawanna County. They had to be gotten rid of; and finally, at last, the day had come when they were indeed destroyed, and in the best possible way: in shame and disgrace. To have removed them any other way would have made them heroes and martyrs.

There was still another reason why the Wintons had to be removed—why it had to be at this moment. Lackawanna County would soon be an actuality; those around A.H. knew that he was the one responsible for their being a Lackawanna County in the first place, that it had been his vision and his dream to carve up the valley, and his genius in divorcing Providence from Scranton, and associating with Mont Flanigan, that had made Lackawanna possible. So that when the new county was finally erected, the greatest of political and historical prestige did not fall to A.H.; in the disbursing of the fruits from his labor, he had to be removed. Yet still unexpressed was also the fear that he could be the new county's first judge; and all knew that he would make a good judge, who would be above reproach. What more effective way was there to remove him than to disgrace him in the eyes of all?

As truly as if they had stood before the Indians, A.H. and W.W. gave up their lives in a Wyoming Valley massacre that involved two men only. A hundred years later, and the battle for territory ownership was still being fought between those from Connecticut and those from Pennsylvania. And with the erection of Lackawanna County, those of Connecticut heritage at last would have a portion of the valley that they could call their own.

The Wintons' financial empire had been attacked from all sides. The slowest and most subtle had been the rumors constantly circulated and recirculated around the valley that the Second National was unsafe—not a sound bank. There was the tardiness in repaying W.W.'s aid at the time of the panic of the Scranton Trust Company and Savings Bank. But with the beginning of 1878, the pace of this destructive campaign was stepped up and made more direct. It was a very simple technique: those who owed money to W.W. or the bank, in the form of large commercial loans, would be slow to repay, while those who had large sums on deposit were extra quick to withdraw. The first thing that brought A.H. to alert, suspicious attention, was that as he and his father went over the finances of the bank, he noticed that no large financial or commercial depositor would be caught with his money tied up when the Second National suspended; they had all cleared out their monies on deposit before the first of April.

W.W. and A.H. walked back to the bank. As they approached, they were struck by the lack of excitement. The pavement in front of the building was devoid of angry depositors, or even curious calamity-watchers. Remembrance of the long line outside The Scranton Trust Company and Savings Bank a year earlier flashed through their minds. What was going on, they wondered, that there was no interest in a bank closing? Why was there no excitement? W.W. unlocked the door and he and A.H. entered; turning, he locked it again behind them. The two men walked straight back to the cashier's cage to look at the books. A.H. studied the ledgers for a while. What he found was very depressing indeed; cash on hand was less than ten percent of the total amount credited to depositors' accounts. The Second National Bank was indeed in a very precarious position. W.W. left A.H. to go downstairs to send a telegram to the Treasury Department at Washington, notifying them that he was closing a national bank.

After W.W. had returned and they had worked for a while analyzing the financial sheets, A.H. and W.W. began to look a little brighter. Neither one was ever a fool; they were both astute, sharp men. The lack of an angry crowd outside, the calm acceptance of the bank's closing, and the lack of large commercial and financial depositors told them the story that the bank's insolvency was a contrived and not a natural happening. When they had arrived at that conclusion, they sat back, relaxing for a minute. They reviewed the immediate past events.

"Ten percent cash on hand, Father, is not healthy. But in view of the type of depositor you have—small miners, factory workers, serving girls, waitresses, and farmers—it need not have necessarily brought you to this point. Most of the activity in accounts of that type would be one of deposit rather than voluminous check writing."

"Precisely, A.H. In the depressed times of the past few years, I saw nothing that led me to suspect a shortage like this. Instead, I felt we were quite sound, that we were continually building."

"Drew? What has he had to say?"

"The bank examiner? He audited the books in November, and pronounced us as healthy as any national bank in the country."

"But you knew last night; didn't you, Father? When you were sitting in the audience and I was up on the stage at the Academy of Music, you knew then that you were going to close today." A.H. looked reproachfully at his father. They had always worked together as a team. He would expect to share this with W.W. as much as he had the planning and acquiring of Winton.

"I couldn't, A.H.; I couldn't spoil it for you." The father of a tough lot of boys softened perceptibly into a sentimental parent.

A.H. responded to the parental pride. His voice was kinder when he spoke, "How long have you known, Father?"

"Only three days, A.H.—when I got notice from New York that I would have to settle for $15,000 on the first of June."

W.W. was referring to the twice-monthly clearing house procedure. On the first and fifteenth of every month, checks written on one bank but cashed at another were sent to a central location, a banking clearing-house. There, they would be sorted and forwarded to the bank drawn on, with a statement of how much was due for reimbursement of the banks which had cashed the checks, or drafts. In the case of the Second National Bank of Scranton, checks totalling $15,000 had been cashed by various New York banks; these checks had been written by people who had accounts at the Second National Bank in Scranton, but were payable to New Yorkers.

A.H. commented on the obvious: "At least we know what we're up against, Father. When your depositors are mainly laborers and the little fellows, it is no accident that $15,000 worth of cashed checks show up in New York. The coal miner at Winton doesn't do his shopping in New York, nor does he buy $15,000 worth of trinkets."

W.W. clapped his hand to his forehead. "I should have known!" he exclaimed.

"Should have known what?"

"When I got the statement of how much was due in New York on the first, I went down to Pittston and Wilkes-Barre and asked the banks there to lend me enough to tide me over. I thought it was strange when they refused."

"Refused you?"

"Yes; I was stunned. I remember now—I even offered them a mortgage on some coal land to carry the $15,000."

"And they wouldn't help you, even then?"

"No."

Knowing that they had a fight on their hands, and that the Second National Bank's failure was not due to his father's bungling, A.H. set his shoulders and really looked the part of one going forth to do battle.

"I think, then, Father, that this has been planned for some time. It's obvious, now, what has been going on. These few new accounts here, plus these old accounts, all with large deposits from the sale of real-estate or securities from the stock market," at which A.H. was jabbing his finger at a name here and there in the ledger, "when matched up with these other people who came to you asking for large commercial loans, almost without exception within one or two days after each large deposit," and A.H. jabbed his finger at other names, "combined to drain you dry. Look; see here, here, and here," he was pointing excitedly now, "the large depositor, in every instance, the day after you had to settle with a clearing house, wrote a check or two removing almost all of his balance with you. He cleared out with his money, leaving you with no cash and a loan backed by nothing except your working man's savings deposit, although at the time you granted the loan, there was plenty of cash in the bank.

"Let me see; how long has this been going on?" A.H. hastily thumbed back through the sheets. After reading for a minute, he closed the book and looked at his father, "A concentrated attack, Father, from the beginning of the year."

W.W. spoke up, "And not helped any by Halstead's invitation to buy from him—I had to take money out of reserve for that. Nor helped by the D & H's failure to pay its coal rents—I was squeezed and had to take out another $10,000 to pay Moss." W.W. was referring to a time in February when he had been short of cash because of a drop in his own income due to the lack of D & H rents, and a man from whom he was buying land had refused to delay settlement.

Somehow, even though they realized that the Second National Bank might never open again, the two men felt much, much better knowing that the sorry state of affairs had not come about through their own incompetence.

A.H. spoke, expressing another as yet unsaid thought, "I don't see, Father, how you could have prevented this. The only way to have protected yourself would have been to have stopped issuing loans. Once you did that, you would be as good as finished anyway. The life blood of a bank—its profits—comes from loans. Once it got out that you weren't going to issue loans, you would have been in trouble anyway."

W.W. nodded his head, agreeing, "Well, we'll wait for Drew, the examiner. I don't see that there's anything else we can do."

In this statement W.W. was more than right; there wasn't a thing that could be done. The deposits, the loans, the withdrawals—all were perfectly legal. The most that could ever be done was to talk about the rotten luck, of the timing of the events as they had occurred. However, for the perpetrators, and now for W.W. and A.H., the true story behind the closing of the Second National Bank would be no mystery.

It was unbelievable, but absolutely no fuss was made over the closing of the bank. So little attention was paid to the shutting of its doors that it was as if it hadn't happened at all. When W.P. Drew, the federal government bank examiner, arrived the next day, he brought word of additional perfidy, thereby revealing, unconsciously, added scope and depth to the scheme to ruin the Wintons through their Second National Bank. For he brought with him, from New York, a cancelled $5,000 check from the Fourth National Bank, drawn on W.W.'s private account there. It was a valid check; W.W. remembered writing it as soon as he saw it. But that it had been cashed so soon was a surprise. He had written it with the understanding that it would be held until W.W. redeemed it, or if it had to be cashed, that the payee would first notify W.W.

Not only did Drew have the check, but he knew how it had come to the Fourth National Bank of New York. After the Memorial Day exercises at the Academy of Music at which A.H. had spoken, the cashier of the Merchants' and Mechanics' Bank of Scranton had taken the midnight train out of Scranton for New York. He had W.W.'s $5,000 check with him, which W.W. had made payable to the Merchants' and Mechanics' Bank of Scranton. Arriving in New York early in the morning, the cashier had gone directly to the Fourth National Bank of New York and waited until they opened, at which time he presented W.W.'s check, payable to the Merchants' and Mechanics' Bank of Scranton and drawn on W.W.'s account at the Fourth National Bank. W.W. had the account in New York for deposit of coal royalties, and his draft to the Scranton bank had been due to an emergency one day when he had found his own Second National in need of immediate cash.

W.W. and A.H. realized the importance of the timing on the cashing of the check, which Drew, the examiner, had been given by the Fourth National Bank of New York—that the midnight ride and the cashing of W.W.'s check in New York had all taken place before W.W. had posted the notice suspending operations of the Second National Bank. Obviously, bankers in the Wyoming Valley knew what W.W. would be forced to do on the thirty-first of May, before he had done it. Father and son became very sober; this was a very serious matter.

Drew, the bank examiner, closeted himself with the bank ledgers, and sometimes with W.W., as soon as he arrived. After reviewing the ledgers again—after all, Drew had been looking at them regularly for a period of seven years—he issued a statement declaring the assets of the Second National Bank more than ample to cover its liabilities. He also authorized the bank to go into voluntary liquidation and authorized the existing management, namely W.W. and his staff of workers, to handle it. He saw no reason at all for bringing in a receiver; in fact, he was decidedly against it, as being an unnecessary expense. Joe Scranton was particularly kind to W.W.; he reported Drew's full statement in the *Scranton Republican*, closing the article with a few words of his own: "Whatever one may think of Mr. Winton's career as a banker, he will receive personally the kindliest sympathy for the great misfortunes of his later years."

Once Drew had determined that the bank's assets more than covered the amount of its indebtedness, W.W. again mentioned mortgaging some of his coal lands. None of the Wintons really wanted to lose the Second National Bank, and raising needed cash through mortgages was certainly an acceptable method. On this, Drew concurred, and after informing Washington, sent W.W. back to Pittston and Wilkes-Barre. This time, W.W. was successful, mainly because of gubernatorial candidate Henry Hoyt.

President Rutherford Hayes and the Republican party, of which he was the standard-bearer, were not anxious to have one, or possibly a series of national bank closings vex their administration in Washington. Luzerne County Republicans were soon given to know that if they wanted national Republican support throughout the state for their gubernatorial nominee in the fall, they should assist the troubled national bank in Scranton as much as possible. In the middle of June, W.W. made out a mortgage agreement and received an initial installment of $8,000. The picture didn't look as grim now and, buoyed, W.W. began to have hopes of a brighter future. At this point, he made a fatal mistake.

To encourage confidence in the Second National Bank, and to redeem some of his tarnished image before the public, W.W. announced that there would be plenty of money to cover the depositors, that there had been no wrongdoing on the part of the management of the Second National Bank, and that the payments to the depositors would begin. If he had closed his mouth at this point, the Wintons might have gotten by; but unfortunately W.W. added that he thought that after the depositors of the Second National Bank were satisfied, since the funds were more than ample, he would reopen as a private house. From this statement, the adversaries realized that the Wintons had not yet been crushed, and immediately set out to finish them off.

While his father was talking, A.H. was beside himself with worry. In addition to the bank failing, the new county bill was meeting with one frustrating obstacle after another. The three commissioners, appointed by the governor to make a report on the question of a new county, had arrived and were going over the boundary lines. First, a suit was filed, from Wilkes-Barre again, asserting that the new county bill was generally unconstitutional and in conflict with the judicial district. Next, suit was brought against the three commissioners, stating that their actions were improper. One thing after another was brought up; unfortunately, whether ridiculous or not, each charge, once filed, had to be investigated and answered.

Dr. Eugene Heermans also picked this time to seek out his cousin's aid, adding one more distraction to A.H.'s troubled thoughts, "A.H., that woman is troubling me again."

"What has Sarah done now?" A.H. knew exactly whom Eugene meant when he said "that woman." It was also the most gentle of the many titles Eugene had for his estranged wife.

"She's come back, and demands custody of Lizzie Adele!"

A.H. raised his eyebrows in surprise, "She does? Any reason given for wanting her?"

"'Mother Love,' she says. She just wants to make more trouble."

"Don't worry, Eugene. I'll handle it. Leave it to me; she won't bother you or Lizzie Adele again."

"Thank you, A.H."

A.H. made a mental note to speak to Sarah and inform her that there was no way that her claim for custody of the child could be supported.

With all that was going on, A.H., however, could not afford to forget that the time was fast approaching for what should have been one of the most joyous occasions of his life. Only fifteen families were to be honored at the centennial celebration commemorating the Wyoming Massacre; of these, two families no longer had any living descendants. The people were honored, not because they were the first settlers in the valley, but because they were among the first settlers who had fought against and survived the attack by the English, Tories and Indians on July 3 and 4 of 1778. Courtesy of Alice and her Blackman grandparents, both A.H. and Alice would be counted among the distinguished guests on July 4, when the battle monument was to be dedicated at Forty Fort.

Temporarily shelving his problems, A.H. and his family, including W.W., Catherine, Byron and Frances, and Elnorah and Thomas Livey, climbed aboard the special excursion train which left Scranton for Forty Fort in time for the procession and opening exercises, starting at 8:00 A.M. on the Fourth of July. It was a very elegant group that assembled at Forty Fort to lead the way to the battle monument site; those at the front of the march were quite conscious of their distinguished ancestors. In almost every instance, the present-day descendants continued to play important roles in valley affairs. For the first time since January, John Collings and A.H. forgot their differences enough to relax in each other's company. While John was also directly descended from the Blackmans, the attention of the crowd was directed towards Alice and her husband. Because of his new county fight and the disgrace of the family banking failure, A.H. was probably the most interesting person in the line of march.

One of the fifteen families honored were the Blackmans, represented by Alice and her brothers and sisters, with A.H. accompanying them. Col. Zebulon Butler's family included a couple of Butler grandsons and an in-law, Hendrick Wright. Judge Garrick Harding was there, representing ancestor Elisha Harding. Captain William McKerachan and Samuel Carey were the only two families honored which had no descendants, but the Inman family was well represented, as was Anderson Dana by many progeny including Judge Dana, who had lost to Labor Judge William Stanton in the past November elections. James Nesbitt's family, Col. Palmer Ransom, Capt. Lazarus Stewart, Col. John Jenkins, Col. Dennison, Luke Sweetland, John Abbott, and Col. Mathias Hollenback all had descendants present. For the first time in peace, Pennsylvania and Connecticut settlers, through their offspring, stood together side by side in happiness and harmony, if only for one day. While the festivities were at their highest point, a group of Onondaga Indians, who had floated down to Forty Fort by ark, arrived and were welcomed; the sentiment was expressed afterwards that perhaps they had enjoyed the celebration more than anyone else. The place associated with the bitterness of the fight of a hundred years ago was now the scene of a joyful reunion. At nine in the evening, a salute of thirteen guns signaled the end of the festivities.

But, perhaps, something more permanent was accomplished in the general good feelings and harmony on the day that the Wyoming Massacre monument was dedicated. Five days later, opposition to the new county ceased, so much so that on July 9 Gov. Hartranft ordered a special election on the new county question, to take place August 13. If the voting public did not reject it, then the new county would be a fact.

The question of whether or not there would be a new county was now up to the voters. With this in mind, A.H. sought out the largest block of voters in the upper end of Luzerne County. On July 16, A.H. attended a county Greenback-Labor meeting; the men were gathering to start work on their slate for the '78 fall elections. Time was given to A.H. He addressed the group from the floor, and also spoke directly to some of the party's most powerful men from Carbondale, urgently pleading for the new county. By the time he left the meeting, the men had responded; he carried back with him a copy of a resolution they had passed: that the Greenback-Labor Reform party of the Twentieth Senatorial District, being the largest in square area and third largest in population in the state, did officially endorse and recommend a yes vote on August 13 for the new county. W.W.'s years of high interest rates for the "little" depositors in his banks, and A.H.'s outspoken support of Judge Stanton and respect for Mayor Powderly, accomplished what none of Winton's friends in Scranton could have. Honest respect and consideration for every man who was a valley resident, regardless of his station in life, had brought in a priceless dividend: the support of the working man for whatever the Wintons wanted to do, the support of the working man for their new county.

With the support of labor in his pocket, a very strange thing came over A.H.—strange in that he had never been working towards it as one of his goals, strange in that he had it as a beneficial side effect, as an unexpected reward, and not as a main desire—he became the most powerful man in the valley. Labor, as a unified block, could legislate whatever it wanted, because it was the majority, provided the men stuck together. If A.H. had enough influence to get labor to step in behind him, then there was nothing that A.H. couldn't do.

That assemblage of political tricksters and gamesmen who were A.H.'s friends and acquaintances, his associates and neighbors, took alarm as soon as he told them that labor would back the new county. Immediately, the rest of the installments due W.W. on his mortgage note ceased; consequently, his Miner's Savings Bank was next caught without funds, and W.W. had to close it. Now

W.W. was in the added predicament of not being able to repay depositors. As for A.H., he was to be stopped another way.

Lackawanna Co.

Why Every Citizen Should Vote for it.

It will reduce the county-tax from 7 to five mill, thus a saving of $2 on a $1,000.

The competition for the county-seat will be so great between the different localities that the public buildings will be offered free, hence there will be no building-tax. Offers have already been made and the people are to decide by vote where the county-seat shall be located. The next election in November is the time when the question is to be settled.

Even if the buildings had to be built by tax

it does not necessitate a greater levy than the present county rate. The valuation of the district is $10,500,000, raising a tax of $76,300, or $32,000 more than is necessary for the expenses of the county. Mr. Woolsey offers to build a fire-proof building for $42,408, so that it would be more than

PAID FOR IN TWO YEARS.

In case of the establishment of the new

County all power and authority of all the OFFICERS of the old county, except the judges, ceases, hence the power of the Commissioners TO COLLECT THE PRESENT YEARS' TAX-LEVY WILL BE GONE and THERE WILL BE A SAVING TO THE TAXPAYERS OF THE DISTRICT OF 75,000 DOLLARS.

It will cause an expenditure in this valley

$1,500,000 annually, that is now TAKEN OUT OF IT. EVERY MAN, WOMAN and CHILD will be BENEFITTED thereby.

There is NO organized opposition except

that which comes from WILKESBARRE OFFICE-HOLDERS. They are trying to corrupt the people by the USE OF MONEY. LOOK OUT FOR THEM and the LYING CIRCULARS that they have put in their hands. VOTE TO SUSTAIN YOUR OWN SECTION.

By order of the New County Executive Committee.
E. MERRIFIELD Chairman.

Handbill distributed July/August 1878, requesting votes for new county

Washington Hall, where he had his office across from the Second National Bank on Lackawanna Avenue, became the headquarters of the final campaign for the new county. A general meeting, open to all interested citizens, was held there the evening of July 19. It was an historic event in that it was the first time that the leading men of Scranton came together to talk and work for the common good without regard to party affiliations. Until the governor proclaimed Lackawanna County, the Republicans, Democrats, Greenback-Laborers, and Prohibitionists were setting aside their separate ideologies and party interests.

To call the meeting to order, Edward Merrifield rose and nominated Fred Gunster to assume the chair for this first meeting on the nineteenth of July. Afterwards, both Merrifield and A.H. spoke strongly for an affirmative vote on the new county. As the meeting was about to adjourn, Fred Gunster appointed a nominating committee to recommend a slate of names for an official New County Executive Committee, presenting the slate for approval at the next meeting. He announced the next meeting for the following evening, July 20.

The meeting on July 20 was not a long one. A.H. was called on to address the group; passionately and fervently he extolled the rewards that would be theirs if the upper end of the Wyoming Valley constituted its own separate county. While he spoke, the nominating committee caucused in an adjoining room. When he had finished, they returned and presented their slate for election. Twenty-five men were named to the permanent New County Executive Committee—such men as A.B. Dunning, Col. William Monies, Terence Powderly, and Frank Beamish. For chairman of the new county committee, the nominating committee put forth the name of Edward Merrifield. A.H.'s name was not read at all; he had been left out, ignored. At what should have been his moment of greatest triumph, he had his moment of greatest pain.

Fred Gunster installed the new committee, and then stepped down. The permanent committee then installed Merrifield as their chairman. Only then was there a motion to have alternate members of the committee, in case someone could not attend; W.W. was one of the three alternates elected. For the remainder of the brief meeting, the assembled men spent their time peering covertly at A.H. Everyone was very conscious of him, watching how he was taking the slight: most were hoping for an emotional outburst, some public display that would forever disgrace him. However, A.H. was of the stuff heroes were made of; he was a giant among giants. They should have known that he would behave heroically, that he could handle himself. While every man there knew how he felt, not one saw any telltale sign—nor would they ever.

After the meeting broke up, A.H. bade "good-night" to W.W. and walked slowly home. He was deep in thought; he had much to think about. Alice was awake when he came in; she had been anxiously awaiting news of the meeting and the progress towards Lackawanna County. After all, she, Kate, and the baby Elsie were foregoing their annual trip to Nantucket, for the sake of the new county. A.H. undressed, saying almost nothing, and then settled himself in the overstuffed lounge chair in the bedroom, before reporting the results of the meeting to her. For the first time when disturbed by a problem, A.H. did not seek the nearness of his wife.

When he had finished his brief description of the evening, Alice started to speak out forcibly, decrying the infamy of the men; but in the dark she lost contact with A.H. She wasn't sure whether he was still in the chair or had gone elsewhere in the house. She was confused, because her husband's presence seemed to have left the room. So she lay back, silent, waiting for a sign from him, until sleep finally, involuntarily, overcame her.

A.H. was still in the chair physically, but lost so deep in thought that it was no accident that Alice could not feel the presence of his personality.

His mind was reviewing, over and over again, the portent of the meeting. What did they think he was going to do, that they feared him so much—so much that they had to remove him so thoroughly? Didn't they realize that his only interest was the new county? If he had wanted political power, he would have had it long before now. With his father and the Heermans clan, they could have long since become a political dynasty in the valley that no one could match, had they wanted it to be so.

A.H. spent very little time dwelling on or questioning their stupidity, their misinterpretation of his motives. Instead, he turned inward and delved more and more deeply into himself—when Alice hadn't been sure whether or not he had left the room, it was because he had turned introspective. The question that he had to answer, that was all important, was what did he really want for himself? One part, he answered very quickly: he did not want to be counted out—that, he knew. Of that, he was very sure; he was not going to let them ignore him.

But what else did he want? He was behind Mayor Terence Powderly because he admired him. It was beginning to look as if the new mayor, by the end of his first year in office, would have saved the city of Scranton $100,000 in public funds. He was for Mayor Powderly because the mayor had shown that he had the interests of the people he governed at heart. He was not for him, or against him, because he was Labor.

What about Judge Stanton, then? Why had he supported him? He had come to the judge's defense because he had been there. He had seen at the trial that the judge had in no way administered his official duties illegally or incompetently. He could not stand by and see a man slaughtered by means of untruths.

His mind drifted to the Second National Bank; he still hadn't absorbed the fact that it was over. Banking had been a part of his life ever since he and his family had returned to Providence from New York City. But it was his father's bank. Perhaps Byron's—Byron had worked with W.W. as vice-president. If there were to be a bank in the family again, it would not be because of him, he knew; he was lawyer Winton, not banker Winton.

A.H. tried to see himself in public office; the picture was extraordinarily fuzzy. A.H. knew himself well enough to know his likes and dislikes. He liked freedom; he scheduled his law practice to his convenience, as much as he could. As a public figure, he would be tied down to time and place. He wondered: would he have accepted the nomination for supreme court judge as readily, had it been offered to him on the Republican ticket instead of the Prohibition? Alice crossed his mind; he enjoyed coming home early on occasion to surprise her, to spend a relaxed hour before dinner with her and Kate—now with both his daughters. Most likely he would have to give all that up, were he in public office.

There was something else about himself that A.H. was hesitant to admit—he knew he was overly moralistic at times; he knew he had always pursed his lips at Walter's escapades; he knew he would not have been attracted to the Prohibition party otherwise. Briefly, A.H. returned to full consciousness, to shudder. He had remembered, from Francis Murphy's visit to Scranton in March, the tediousness of Murphy's moral diatribes at meetings specially arranged for him as the founder of the Blue-Ribbon wearers; it had almost been enough to drive him to a life of debauchery.

A.H. slipped back into the depths of introversion, to where he had left off. As a lawyer, he would not have to make changes in his personality; in the glare of public office, however, he would have to become someone else. What did he want, then? He knew the answer: he had everything he wanted, thank God. He wanted only Lackawanna County and a courthouse in Scranton; that was all he lacked. After he had Lackawanna County, he would return to what he was.

Thus did A.H. arrive at the same conclusion that another outstanding hero of the next century was to express in his autobiography, *The Seven Pillars of Wisdom*: that rebels or creative geniuses who could successfully lead a revolt for new authority were, of necessity, bad administrators. The prophetic personality that could carry the fight for a new county through to victory was not the same type of personality that could endure as the peaceful civil servant with his conservative, deliberate methods; the successful revolutionary was not of the solidity upon which a new government must rest. And in fact that was what A.H. was: he had led a revolt against existing authority, as represented by the occupation rule from the Luzerne County seat at Wilkes-Barre.

But as for the stick that would wield the authority in the new county, A.H. was definitely determined to have his hand on it—and not at the bottom, either. He was not going to let them get away with counting him out.

He closed his eyes but briefly—or so he thought. He opened them to see light in the room; it was morning. He jerked forward in the chair, at a loss; he couldn't remember when he had ever sat up all night in a chair. For the first time, he and Alice had slept apart in the same room. He went over to the bed and lay down beside her, throwing his arm across her.

"Did you miss me?" he whispered in her ear.

"Oh, A.H., I was so worried about you. I don't want you to be unhappy. That was so mean of them to leave your name off the committee. How could they do such a thing?"

He kissed her, allowing his passion to be satisfied for the time being, "Don't worry. It won't happen again. I'm going to take care of it this morning."

Alice opened her eyes wide and turned her head to look at him directly, "What are you going to do?"

His hand caressed her as he got up. He chuckled, "I'll tell you later."

And he left her to dress. He wanted to pay an early visit to the *Plain Dealer* newspaper office. He was not going to let the insult of the New County Executive Committee go unanswered: he couldn't, if he wanted Scranton to continue to be his home and if he wanted to remain one of the city's prominent residents.

After A.H. left the house, he first detoured by his office before finding his way to the newspaper office; he had something he wanted the paper to print for him. Later, when the paper came out, Scrantonians were astonished to read Sarah F. Heermans's confession of sin in bold, black type.

What exactly had A.H. done and what did he hope to accomplish by taking Sarah Heermans's signed statement and releasing it for publication? The obvious explanation was that he had promised Cousin Eugene that he would silence Sarah forever, from trying to spread false rumors in order to gain custody of their child. But, very subtly, A.H. had much more in mind when he had the "Confession" published in the *Plain Dealer*. For the article had been prefaced with the editorial comment that, in view of the gossip, and attempts to malign the innocent, and the grievous pain caused to the honest, the following was a true description of the separation. What A.H. did was to indulge, very neatly, in a case of highly refined blackmail by extension, for which he could not be accused of anything.

Sarah had been attempting to destroy Dr. Eugene Heermans's reputation by untruths. Her "Confessions," being her own statement, clearly showed where the blame for the divorce lay; its release could cause no more embarrassment to Eugene than the malicious lies which his former wife had already spread about. As Eugene's lawyer, Eugene had thanked A.H. for his promise to silence Sarah, which A.H. had now done. But by implication, A.H. was really issuing a warning to those who would deal him out in the new county planning—who felt that he was expendable, now that the politicians could see, as a sure thing, success in the erection of Lackawanna County.

What A.H. was really saying, was that to all who did not keep the true facts in mind as to who had worked for the new county, he would not hesitate to extract, from his files or his memory, anything that he knew about his political associates, regardless of how embarrassing it might be, and hold it up for public viewing. They would have to count him in, or else he would count them out of Scranton, and thereby, in their absence, he would fall heir to everything that they were trying so hard to keep from him.

Actually, A.H. had no other recourse than this. For the only choice left to him, other than the intimidation he adopted, was to destroy the new county effort entirely. This other alternative would involve going back to Labor and cancelling their vote for Lackawanna County. This he could do, but in doing so, he would kill forever his heart's desire. No matter how far he was pushed, he could never go so far as to stop the new county movement. His associates realized this, and they felt that they could discard him as they pleased. Therefore, he had to have some leverage that would bring them back in line. If they did not fear the demise of the new county effort, what then would they fear? So, through implication,

A.H. got the message across that things hitherto left unsaid—the midnight raids in the past on Scranton's bawdy houses and the arraignment of the girls and the names of their gentlemen customers, gentlemen whom A.H. addressed by first name; the number of out of town cancellations on checks to supposedly married maidens visiting for a few months in a remote village that had cleared through accounts in W.W.'s banks; the treatment for medical disorders best left unmentioned—would now become part of public record.

What a magnificent beast A.H. was! Wounded, brought to his knees, he was still strong enough and powerful enough to hold his attackers at bay. They fell before the ingenuity of his defense. Their hands faltered when it came to the killing thrust; they could not execute. They took him back into their midst. By unspoken agreement, it was understood that A.H. was to continue to play out his role in the history of Lackawanna County.

Although A.H. had power over the others, they wanted him to know that they had a checkrein, too. On July 25, four days after "The Confession of Sin" appeared, Fred Gunster and R. Archbald joined with others to lead 150 depositors of the Second National Bank in a mass meeting, to learn from the Wintons when they would get their money back. Three days after this meeting, at a July 28 meeting of the New County Executive Committee, A.H. was named as one of the team of speakers who would travel throughout the proposed new county area, speaking for a yes vote. Both sides showed that they understood each other very well.

The time between the twenty-eighth of July and the day of the actual voting in August was occupied with nothing but speeches and talks. Even John Collings joined in helping to speak of the many advantages to be gained by being in their own separate county. The goal was to have so large an affirmative vote that the new county would have to be proclaimed by popular demand. The Scranton Board of Trade supported the election day, too; it requested all business houses to close in the afternoon of August 13, so that all energies could be devoted to visiting the polling places. The new county had to be voted in.

Then on August 6, Joe Scranton, who had been so helpful with his newspaper throughout the entire new county campaign, almost wrecked the whole project, turning it into one glorious free-for-all. He published a special new county edition of the *Scranton Journal*; in it, he denounced "the *Scranton Times* under its true Colors" and stated that its owner, Aaron Chase, afraid of losing his post as mine inspector's clerk and afraid of losing a share of Wilkes-Barre money, had brought the *Times* out, as could be predicted, against the new county.

Aaron Chase was not one to let an attack like this go by, and returned the compliment on August 11, just two days before the new county vote was to take place. Through another of his papers published from the *Times* office, the *True Labor Advocate*, he accused Joe Scranton's brother Bill of murder at the time of the August 1 riot, and expressed the opinion that Bill Scranton should either be in the penitentiary or executed. He also accused Bill Scranton of conspiring to erect a new county with the intention of controlling the courts for his own unlawful purposes.

Although the new county was only hours away, Bill Scranton hastened to the Luzerne County Court, sued Aaron Chase for libel and had him arrested. Chase was brought before Judge Stanton, the "unwanted" Greenback-Labor judge. Judge Stanton set a ridiculously low bail and deferred the case until the question of the new county was answered, stating that it would be better to bring the case to trial in Lackawanna County if there were to be one.

Then, at last, the great day had come. It was now Tuesday, August 13, 1878; and that great mass, the inheritors of the earth, the people, were finally going to have their chance to say what they thought about a new county for the upper end of Luzerne. In all, 11,701 men—this was almost a half-century before women had the right to vote—turned out on the hot Tuesday that was the thirteenth day in August of 1878.

Temporary headquarters were set up at the Forest House, at the corner of Wyoming and Spruce, to receive the election returns. As the morning progressed, it became more and more obvious that the voters had gone to the polls early and in enthusiastic support of the idea of living in a county called Lackawanna. With the increasing plurality, enthusiasm mounted and people gathered. Every time a telegram was received from a country district, its totals were read out loud to the waiting crowd; cheer after cheer greeted each such announcement.

The voters had turned out early, and for the new county—for Lackawanna County. By evening, the results were conclusive. The New County Executive Committee assembled at Washington Hall. The vote was announced: over nine thousand for Lackawanna County and less than two thousand against the new county. Scranton erupted into her streets in joy; tar barrels were lined up along the roads and set ablaze. Cannons boomed all evening. At 9:30, the factory gongs and every bell in the city blew and rang and rang, for twenty minutes. A.H. had his new county at last.

But it was Edward Merrifield who came forward to the edge of the stage at Washington Hall and accepted the cheers and acclaim of the assembled people. It was the chairman of the New County Executive Committee who received congratulations for the work that he and his committee had done. Behind him, all the remaining twenty-five committee members spread out across the stage and acknowledged the shouts of acclaim, smiling and waving back to the crowd. There were a few others at the back of the stage too, behind the committee. Oh, yes; there in the movement of the victors, jubilant as they responded to the cheers of the audience, as they shifted about with their hands above their heads in triumph, one could catch a glimpse of A.H. Winton.

A.H.'s moment of greatest glory was his moment of greatest ignominy.

When A.H. finally returned home, he found Alice with a sleeping Kate beside her, swaying slightly in the suspended swing by the dark corner of the veranda.

"Hello, A.H.," she called to him in a whisper, "It's so exciting. Kate and I have been watching all the celebrations."

He crossed the porch floor to her and rested one hand on the swing's chain, looking down at his wife and daughter, "Did you hear the bells and gongs, Alice—pealing out the good news?"

"Oh, yes; that was what brought us out. Kate wanted to know why they were ringing," Alice looked up at her husband eagerly, "Are you happy?" she asked.

"I'm pleased, Alice—very pleased."

"Only pleased? Are you never satisfied?"

"When I'm with you. Then, I am happy. When I am with you here, at Wyoming and Mulberry, then I'm the happiest. Besides, we don't have our courthouse yet."

"Ugh, always the law. Just think instead how happy everybody is tonight. Oh, it was thrilling to be here when the bells were ringing and the barrels were flaring, outlining the streets.

"I think this day must have been better than that Fourth of July, so long ago. When our grandparents declared independence then, they didn't know what was going to happen to them afterwards. They still had a fight to live through and win. But we've already had our fight. We don't have to worry about what is going to happen next. Now we can celebrate our future."

"Now we can have our future. That's right; it's our future now."

A.H. gathered Kate up and carried her upstairs to bed. Later, he made love to Alice with the joyous exuberance of youth. The summer night, the excitement, their love—he was happiest when he was with Alice. For some reason, his thoughts went back to the summer before they were married. He remembered the afternoons of summer picnics; he had yearned so much to make love to her then, he almost had pain. Those frustrations had long since gone—maybe that was why he thought of that time now. The frustrations of daily pilgrimages and taxing tithes to Wilkes-Barre were gone now, too. A.H. felt so free, as if life were only to enjoy. In many ways, it was the most beautiful time he and Alice ever had together.

The balloting had taken place on Tuesday. On Thursday the 15th, the three commissioners met at noon to formally receive the votes cast; however, it wasn't until three in the afternoon that all the slips of paper from all over the territory were placed in their hands. The official tally was 9,615 votes for Lackawanna County and 1,986 against it; the "ayes" carried the question. The Commissioners filed a report of their findings with the Governor of the Commonwealth of Pennsylvania. On August 21, at noon, Governor Hartranft proclaimed Lackawanna County.

20

The very first business of the new county was to install a judge. Three days later, on August 24, Judge Benjamine Bentley, who had served as president judge in Lycoming County at Williamsport, was appointed by the governor to be Lackawanna County's first judge. Judge Bentley had more or less retired to the area and had been living just outside Scranton for a few years. He was affiliated with the Greenback-Labor party; everyone was pleased with the choice. Whether or not he would continue as judge after the new county was on its feet, would be up to the voters. It had been agreed that, in order to start Lackawanna County functioning, the governor of the Commonwealth would arbitrarily appoint men for every position. These officials would remain in their respective offices until the first general election; thereafter, the duly elected nominees would then assume the titles and duties of Lackawanna County's elective posts for full term.

On Saturday, a large crowd gathered at the Wyoming Valley House to watch Harold Leach, the youngest member of the Scranton Bar, administer the oath of office to Judge Bentley. There was as yet no county bar association. The audience remained afterwards for most of the afternoon, watching the bond-posting. It was a lively affair. F.H. Hitchcock, who had worked at Harrisburg with A.H., was named Prothonotary. Col. William Monies, Scranton city's early mayor, got the treasurer's job, and Fred Gunster became the new county's district attorney. Of Lackawanna County's three commissioners, one was from Scranton: Dennis Tierney. The other two, H.L. Gaige and Horace Barrett, were from opposite ends of the county—Moscow and Schultzville. For each of these office-holders, a bond had to be posted for the amount that his position was supposedly worth—that is, for the amount of money that, it was estimated, would come under his control. This was the age of no professional bondsmen, and it was up to each appointee to find, from among his friends, those who would be willing to cover any losses he might accidentally, or deliberately, cause the county. After much scurrying to and fro, the necessary funds were posted, and the first day's business of Lackawanna County ended.

The county commissioners, after looking at the Second National Bank building, selected Ira Tripp's building at Wyoming Avenue and Linden Street for the first county courthouse. It was plainly apparent on entering the building that it was unfit for its new purpose, and there was much grumbling about the commissioners' choice. Eventually, the courthouse moved to Washington Hall, and the county rented office space on the second and third floors of the Second National Bank building across the street, but on September 3, 1878, the birth of the Lackawanna County Courts took place at Wyoming and Linden. Judge Bentley took his seat on the bench at 10:15 A.M.

The Hon. W.G. Ward stepped forward and said, "Gentlemen of the Bar, and citizens of Lackawanna County, you are well aware of the purpose for which we are assembled here today. I now have the honor of introducing to you the Hon. Benjamine S. Bentley, President Judge of Lackawanna County." Judge Bentley would automatically become the president judge, as he was the first judge sworn in; hence, he would always be the longest sitting on the bench.

Judge Bentley acknowledged Ward's introduction and made a short speech himself, "Gentlemen and fellow citizens, I have but a word to say. I deeply appreciate the honor conferred upon me in being called upon to open the first court held in Lackawanna County. I desire to do full and equal justice to all and, God helping me, I shall do it. This is a new organization and so far has gone on harmoniously.

"The officers have received their commissions and they will be read." Turning to Prothonotary Fred Hitchcock, Judge Bentley continued, "Perhaps it would be as well to read the action of the county commissioners in regard to temporary place for county seat and for holding court."

This Fred Hitchcock did, announcing that the county commissioners had selected the city of Scranton as the proper place for the county seat and that Ira Tripp's building would remain the county courthouse until January 1, 1879.

Judge Bentley formally opened court, and on a motion from one of the lawyers in the crowd, swore in the first member of the Lackawanna County Bar, Alfred Darte, who after some discussion had been determined to be the oldest attorney. After Judge Bentley swore in Mr. Darte, he facetiously remarked that, as the only member of the bar, it was solely up to Mr. Darte to move for the admission of the other lawyers—that is, if he saw fit. Darte played along with the judge and said that he thought he would keep all the legal practice to himself.

After this bit of by-play, it was suggested that a list of Luzerne County Bar members living in Lackawanna County be made out and those lawyers be sworn in collectively, *in globo*. While the list was being prepared, Alfred Darte proposed Fred Gunster's name, and the Hon. W.G. Ward, who had just introduced Judge Bentley to the group, proposed E.N. Willard's name. These two men became the second and third members of the Lackawanna County Bar. After this, the list of names was read, and lawyers Alfred Hand, R.W. Archbald, H.H. Coston, P.R. Weitzel, E.B. Sturges, Daniel Hannah, Edward Merrifield, F.E. Loomis, Corydon Wells, L.M. Bonnell, Harold Leach, C. DuPont Breck, F.S. Porter, J.J. Post, Charles Welles, D.W. Connelly, Edward Dimmick, A.H. Winton, M.J. Wilson, C. Smith, W.H. Gearhart, J.H. Campbell, H.M. Edwards, C.R. Pitcher, George Sanderson, George Sanderson, Jr., and T.F. Welles were sworn in as members of the new Lackawanna County Bar.

Others were administered the oath of membership, Frank Collins and A.H.'s brother-in-law John Collings coming in, too. Then it was A.H.'s turn. He proposed that Isaac Dean's son Arthur Dean, Alex Farnham, G.M. Lewis, S.J. Strouse, and W.W. Lathrop, all Wilkes-Barre lawyers, also be admitted to practice before Lackawanna County courts. Afterwards, various court clerks were installed and Edward Merrifield read the list of court terms and their dates. At this point, the first session of the new court was adjourned.

This was on the third of September. Three days later, on the sixth of September, a Friday, Aaron Chase, as a petitioner residing in Scranton, journeyed to Wilkes-Barre and formally filed suit at the Luzerne County Courthouse, asking that Judges Harding, Handley, Stanton and Rhone of the Eleventh Judicial District appoint judges to sit on the bench in the Lackawanna County Courts!

Had Chase taken leave of his senses? It would seem so. For he said that he needed to go into court, and could not because there was no judge to hear his case (in Lackawanna County).

No, Chase had not taken leave of his senses. Probably, this was the most altruistic moment of his career. Aaron Chase was performing the service of test-citizen, needed to clarify the Constitution of the Commonwealth of Pennsylvania.

In March and April, when House Bill #50 had been going through the General Assembly at Harrisburg, adversaries of the new county proposition had pointed to the provision in the state constitution that scheduled the creation of judicial districts every ten years, after a census. Hoping to stop the formation of Lackawanna County, they had advanced the claim that even if the new county bill were passed, it would not have its own court district until after the 1880 Census was tallied.

"Not so" had been the answering argument; proponents for the new county had pointed to the text of the state constitution itself: "Whenever a county shall contain 40,000 inhabitants, it shall constitute a separate judicial district, and shall elect one judge learned in the law." It was mainly because of the confusion that then arose as to how to interpret the state constitution, that the amendment to Bill #50, calling for the creation of a new judicial district simultaneously with a new county, had been removed.

The men of Lackawanna, however, wanted their own courts as much as they wanted their own county. So in the middle of April, after the new county bill had been approved by the Senate, Senator Seamans had introduced a separate bill creating the Forty-fifth (Lackawanna) Judicial District. Passed immediately by the Senate, it waited for House approval—the mounting concern over interpretation of the state constitution being the main cause for delay. Near the end of May, since no solution seemed imminent, Bill #168 was approved, empowering a judge, whether in a separate judicial district or not.

The popular vote of August 13 made Lackawanna County a fact. The governor, using Bill #168 as a guideline, commissioned President Judge Bentley; for the new county and her officers needed a judge to function. Bentley, therefore, was a valid judge. But whether he was a judge of a valid district or not remained for the courts to clear up. In other words, his actions were legally correct, but whether they had any force or not remained to be determined. And for this, Aaron Chase stepped forward.

Whether Chase was acting from ulterior, selfish reasons or not will probably never be known. But as a court cannot decide anything without a case in point (before it), Chase actually performed a public service for the whole state by filing his suit.

The judges at Wilkes-Barre, of the Eleventh Judicial District, were well acquainted with the basic point under question: interpretation of the State Constitution. (Lackawanna County was the first county to come into being after the 1872-73 revision of the state constitution; this was why the point in question had never come under trial before.) The judges took Chase's suit under consideration—and did nothing. From there, his request was appealed to the state supreme court. On October 16, the State Supreme Court issued a peremptory *mandamus* (an absolute command from a higher court to a lower court) to Judges Harding, Handley, and Stanton to meet and organize the several courts of Lackawanna County. The Supreme Court judges had decided that the state constitution was meant to be interpreted as creating a new judicial district every ten years, based on a census count.

On October 24, acting under the state Supreme Court decision, the judges of the Eleventh Judicial District journeyed to Scranton and opened court (Judge Bentley resigning). It would now seem that Lackawanna County, and A.H., would have to wait until after the 1880 Census had been tabulated to be in their own Forty-fifth Judicial District—a matter of two or more years.

But the men of Lackawanna were among the most astute and agile legal minds in the state, and by March of 1879, Bill #5 had been signed into law by the newly elected Governor Hoyt. Bill #5, simply stated, defined which census the constitution referred to—which census was to be used in setting up a judicial district—namely, the *last preceding* decennial. At this moment, using the 1870 population figures, the Forty-fifth Judicial District was a fact; the northern end of the valley was at last free of Luzerne County.

(It is interesting to note, that while on their campaign to clarify the constitution, the legislature in Harrisburg, in June of 1879, passed a supplementary bill, #146, which covered such a situation as had existed while the judges of the 11th (Wilkes-Barre) District had failed to act, before the *mandamus* had been issued. This bill gave the governor the power to create a judicial district, if need be. The legislature also approved payment of Judge Bentley's salary for the time he had served as president judge.)

Simultaneously with all the fuss connected with the interpretation of the state constitution, the gentlemen of Scranton were also showing that they were not happy with Judge William Stanton; they were as anxious as the gentlemen of Wilkes-Barre had been to get rid of Labor Judge Stanton. When W.W. Scranton had gone before him in August of the preceding year, on the eve of the New County election, demanding Aaron Chase's arrest for libel, Judge Stanton had wisely tabled the case, stating that the case would be better tried in Lackawanna County; this was done in the last week of January, 1879. At the end, Aaron

Chase was found guilty of libel for the article he had published against W.W. Scranton.

But at the trial, evidence was introduced showing that Judge Stanton had been present in the newspaper office on the night the libelous article had been written, and in fact had even helped to write portions of it. This was all that was needed by those who had been trying to remove Judge Stanton. They seized on it to show him as biased and incompetent as a judge. On February 18, two weeks after the Scranton-Chase trial had found in favor of plaintiff W.W. Scranton, Scranton petitioned the state Legislature at Harrisburg to impeach Judge Stanton. He cited eight other counts of incompetency, in addition to his description of Stanton's participation in the libel. Scranton's bill was accompanied by another, additional petition, this one from 339 prominent men, bearing the signatures of Arthur Dean, Robert McKune, Dr. Throop, and other important men from both Lackawanna and Luzerne Counties, requesting that an investigation be made into Judge Stanton. W.W. and A.H. were conspicuous by the absence of their names on the list.

Before the bill had its first reading at Harrisburg, Greenback-Labor Judge William Stanton, the pioneer of Labor in government, who had been elected into office at a time, 1877, when labor counted for nothing, resigned. By resigning, he removed himself from the investigation and from possible impeachment. The "gentlemen" had won in their battle against Labor; they might allow a Labor politician as a mayor, but they weren't having Labor on the judicial bench, especially when supplanting old-family descendant Judge Edmund Dana.

A.H. and W.W. were known for their highly moralistic attitude towards life. That they had not signed the petitions was of great interest to many in the valley. Those who were the most interested, however, were not the labor leaders, who already knew they had a staunch friend and supporter in the Wintons. The ones who were most conscious of the missing Winton signatures—particularly W.W.'s, as he had been foreman of the grand jury at the time of the fussing with Judge Stanton in court (in the last week of January), and therefore an observer of what had really taken place—were the anti-labor people. And in 1879, upper-class management was automatically anti-labor, for they were busy playing out their roles in the robber-baron image. They were suspicious of labor; they feared labor. They feared, more than anything else, a rich, educated gentleman, one of their own ranks, who had the friendship of labor—particularly a rich, educated, gentleman who had just reached forty years of age: one who was still young enough and healthy enough, who could be expected to live another twenty-five years, because he had time to accumulate great power; one who was an attorney and had an understanding of governmental processes; who was intelligent, and who was a friend to labor. Such a person was to be feared more than any other political up-and-comer in the country, because of that potential. There was nothing that couldn't be in that person's future. For, if handled right, there was nothing that a man in A.H.'s position couldn't do. To take away A.H.'s possible power, the Second National Bank had been an effective weapon before; why not use it again?

Attacks on the Second National Bank had ceased while Lackawanna County came into being. Besides, A.H. and W.W. had been blocked successfully from important, in fact any, positions in the new county, so there was really no need to do any more to them now. All knew they had money; the depositors would not lose.

But after failing to see Winton signatures supporting the removal of Labor Judge Stanton, it occurred to the anti-labor men that for all the excitement at the time of the closing of the Winton banks, never a word was said against W.W.—especially by the laboring class. If the accounts in W.W.'s banks were deposits by small wage-earners and represented life-savings, then there certainly should have been some angry protests.

The depositors, however, had said nothing; they had trust and confidence in the Wintons. W.W. was well liked by everybody. He never antagonized anyone with whom he came in contact or with whom he had dealings. He had always paid a good and more than fair interest rate on his savings accounts, and should a customer of the bank be short the day a note came due, W.W. was not above discounting the note for the exact amount the customer could pay. In addition, it was known among the valley workers that, in all the years the colliery at Winton had been in operation, not one life had been lost at the mine. This was saying a great deal; mine accidents, cave-ins, and explosions were daily occurrences at the other collieries.

As far as exploiting labor went, the Wintons had always avoided that label. As for the hiring of young boys and long hours of work, the Wintons lived the same way themselves. They rose early in the morning and worked all through the day; it was the kind of existence that was the farmers'. Electric lights had yet to flood the streets and factories; man toiled throughout all the daylight hours—they couldn't see to work after dark.

This was also the age when school attendance was mandatory to the sixth grade only—not to age sixteen, as it is today. An alert child could finish the sixth grade as early as at age eleven and, therefore, be eligible for work. If his family was poor, his labor was needed to lighten the burden. For many, to be hired as a breaker boy at a coal mine was the start of a bright economic future; the joy on their faces was equal to that of today's school lad on his first day working at a supermarket. It was what the boy did afterwards that made the difference.

With this in mind, W.W. was famous for handing out little printed homilies encouraging the young lads and their older brothers to aim for economic advancement. This may sound like a sugar-coated, fairy tale version, completely out of touch with the reality of the industrial revolution of the late nineteenth century; but from W.W.'s point of view, this was reality. There was nothing harder nor more humbling than the life of the pioneer. Many might die in slums, but many, many were the ones who died on the frontier. If a frontier pioneer survived, he was counted among the lucky few. The slums of an industrial city might produce death, but many, many expected to survive.

For those who were born into the industrial age, life was desperately in need of radical revision. But to those who had experienced life on the frontier, such as

W.W. and Catherine Heermans Winton, Henry Heermans and the older valley residents, the industrial age was a civilized improvement over the terrifying fears of the pioneers who handled miscarriages, births, illnesses, war-party attacks, who always buried their dead themselves (and the dead were always ones close to them), who had no grocery store when they weren't able to cook, no grocery store full of ready food in cans or loaves of bread already baked waiting for the buyer. For the pioneer was daily in the position of having nothing to eat unless he went out and lay in wait for hours to shoot an unwary deer, or planted a seed and then similarly lay in wait over the summer months to harvest and store in the fall, hopefully without losing the crop. To people who came from the background of the pioneer, the industrial age was not to be despised. The pioneer existence was familiar to W.W. when he joined Henry Heermans at Razorville. For others, to be born in the age of steam and coal was an injustice against humanity. But for W.W. and his family, to travel from the pioneer to the industrial life in one generation was an improvement; it was progress, not exploitation.

So, as an employer, W.W. was well liked. He himself had been brought up on hard work, and whether the work was in the field on a pioneer farm or in a hole harvesting black diamonds, it still entailed long hours of hard work. The pioneer always cooperated with his neighbor; he had to, for it was a matter of survival. The neighbor in a frontier settlement was always an ally, regardless of background or income, provided he was cooperating to open up the community. Opening up and mining the coal lands, and shipping out the other products of the frontier valley, both for delivery all over the world, on the whole united the inhabitants of the Wyoming Valley into a working relationship. The management class that came into the valley on the wave of immigrant workers, who were not born from pioneer settlers, did not have this outlook and did not understand it in others. It was this rapport with labor, natural to W.W. and his family, instilled in A.H. as a family philosophy, that was feared by many of the money and political power aspirants. But for this fear, the Wintons might have regained their financial prominence.

After the Wintons failed to sign the petition calling for Judge Stanton's removal, agitation suddenly increased over the state of affairs at the Second National Bank. The bank's affairs had more or less fallen into limbo during the period of concentration while everyone's attention was directed to the establishment of Lackawanna County; during this time, the rest of the mortgage loan promised to W.W. had failed to appear. Without the added money, things had come to a standstill. Someone complained to the Department in Washington, and on March 15 George Goodale arrived from New York to take over as receiver of the Second National Bank.

Bank Examiner Drew had been replaced a short while earlier by another examiner, and it was on the authority of the new examiner that the receiver was brought in. At Goodale's arrival, A.H. grew fearful; administration and control of the assets now passed out of the hands of W.W. and his staff, and into Goodale's. As receiver, Goodale could order the sale or liquidation of whatever he wished, under the guise of trying to raise the necessary funds to pay off creditors. In this case, the creditors were the depositors, who complained only when organized into citizen groups by lawyers.

A.H. and W.W. discussed the new problem created by Goodale's arrival.

"You will soon be able to tell, Father, whether Goodale is going to be friendly towards us or not. If you suspect that he isn't, we will have to move to protect ourselves immediately. Whatever happens, we want to avoid bankruptcy."

"Because of the rest of the property?"

"Precisely. Technically, there can be no question of bankruptcy with us. To be bankrupt, the debts of the bank would have to exceed the total amount of all the assets. In that condition, everything you owned could be sold to provide, or to try to equal, the total sum of the debts.

"But in the case of the Second National Bank, the bank's assets—the bonds, the few pieces of real estate, the Treasury notes, the mortgages, plus the bank building itself—are all worth more than what is due the depositors. Thank God, the Second National has no other debts—just what is due depositors.

"What I worry about is that somehow, if the receiver can devalue the bank's assets to the point where they are evaluated as worth only a few dollars instead of their true value, or if somehow he can find a way to make the bank debt seem larger, then it would be possible to slip us from liquidation into bankruptcy. In that case, when bankruptcy is declared it would be possible for the stockholders—you, Uncle Isaac and the others—to have your personal funds caught up in the mess."

W.W. understood the drift of A.H.'s thinking thoroughly. As a result, three weeks later he had another conversation with A.H.

"Goodale is starting to make some very unusual sounds, A.H. He's talking about the stockholders of the bank being liable for three times the amount of the bank's indebtedness."

"I don't understand, Father."

"I'm not too clear myself. But he keeps mentioning to me a ruling that, in order to liquidate, the stockholders must have a capital reserve that is three times greater than the amount of the debt."

A.H. roughly estimated the amount of the deposits in the accounts. "He's saying that to keep the liquidation going he wants to have almost half a million to draw from?"

"That's about what it amounts to."

"And we both know that the cash on hand, the notes and bonds, and the real property that the bank owns won't total that much."

"Falls just slightly short."

"In which case you and the rest of the stockholders would be put in the position of filing for bankruptcy as the only course of action open to you."

There was silence while the two men thought it over.

"Well, Father, I know this much. We're going to have to do something, and we're going to have to do it quickly."

"What?"

"I'm not sure, yet. Let me think about it for a while. But of one thing I'm sure. Just as the bank closing was a squeeze and not crookedness or stupidity on our part, the people involved aren't going to stop until they get everything away from us—every single piece of property we own."

"I know, A.H. I'm well aware of that fact."

The seriousness of their predicament was emphasized a little over a week later. Without warning and for no apparent reason, a small news item in one of the newspapers called readers' attention to W.W.'s statue, which Catherine had had Starkey, the artist, install over the public drinking fountain in Providence's town square. The article called for the "removal of the bust of the busted bank president."

Providence Square as it appeared in 1906. Little has changed since 1879; large building at left is the Bristol House, with barbershop far left. Water trough (center) is still minus bust of W. W. Winton.

A.H. was as sharp and as shrewd as those around him. With the shift in bank examiners, Receiver Goodale's arrival, the conversations the receiver had been having with W.W., and now the lone, isolated article in the newspaper, A.H. felt certain that it was only a question of time before bankruptcy was declared. A.H. fumed and fretted for several days, trying to think what to do.

If he attempted to transfer W.W.'s personal property, not bank property, to another name—that is W.W.'s own personal riches, which normally would have no tie-in with the Second National Bank, since the bank had enough of its own assets to cover its outstanding debts—at this late date when it was public knowledge that the Second National Bank was insolvent, he, W.W., and everyone else involved could be convicted for criminal fraud. A.H.'s only interest was to protect the rest of the family's private assets. But *how* was his big question.

Shortly afterwards, A.H. sent W.W. back to the bank to have a talk with Receiver Goodale, the gist of which went something like this:

"Good morning, Mr. Goodale."

"Good morning, Mr. Winton; how are you today?"

"I'm very well, thank you. But all this bank upsetment is very hard on my wife and family. I do worry about them."

"I'm sorry to hear that. Of course you would be worried about your wife. I understand perfectly. I would be, too, if I were in your place."

"Yes, I worry that I may not be able to take care of her."

"Oh, you should take care of your wife, Mr. Winton."

"You really think so?"

"Oh, absolutely, Mr. Winton. It is very important to take care of your wife."

"Thank you, Mr. Goodale."

With this conversation behind them, W.W., with A.H. accompanying him, returned to Providence and the Winton family home. They were looking for Catherine, A.H.'s mother and W.W.'s wife.

When father and son found her, A.H., after greeting his mother with a salutation on the cheek, said, "Mother, I want you to take a judgment against Father."

Poor Catherine! It took a while, but eventually A.H. and W.W. got it across to Catherine, that by obtaining judgment against W.W., even though he was her husband, she, Catherine, would have first claim on all of W.W.'s personal property, in order to satisfy the judgment. To satisfy the judgment, W.W.'s holdings would have to be put up for sheriff's sale unless he could produce the cash. With her son A.H. guiding, a call was sent out for Thomas Livey, Elnorah's husband. And with her son-in-law, Thomas Livey, representing her, Catherine obtained that day, April 25, judgment against her husband for $78,583.

Catherine now had first claim on everything that W.W. owned. If he were forced into bankruptcy, Catherine would be sitting there with her judgment, waiting ready to claim his assets first before anybody else could get at them. A.H. was pleased; he felt they were now in a strong, protective position. As for Catherine's judgment being a dodge to "hide" property, A.H. was not worried about an accusation of that sort. He had only to cite the many instances, going back to 1850, when W.W. had acquired property, recording the deed in both his and Catherine's names. Because some of her money, from her father Henry Heermans, and from her earnings as a teacher, had gone into the purchase of the property, every time that W.W. sold property and bought more property he was trading partially with his wife's capital investment. In this sense, Catherine's judgment was legal, ethically and technically.

At this point, matters temporarily came to rest. Summer was approaching. For the year 1879, there were no great plans for the Fourth of July as in the past two years—no triumphal parade through Forty Fort to the Wyoming monument, not even a parade from Providence's Temperance Hall. Instead, incited by two stirring articles that had appeared in newspapers on the eve of the Fourth of July, 1879, unknown persons removed W.W.'s marble statue from atop the Providence fountain and hung it in effigy before the defunct Miners' Savings Bank of Providence. On this note, A.H. and his family—Elsie a little over a year old—departed for the summer.

For the first time since the A.H. Wintons began spending their summers outside the Wyoming Valley, they did not go to Nantucket Island. They traveled, instead, in a southeasterly direction from Scranton until they came to the Atlantic Ocean; their destination was Ocean Grove, New Jersey. Why A.H. decided to leave Nantucket for the New Jersey shore, nobody ever knew. It couldn't have been because he was through being a Blue Ribbon wearer and feared having to speak on temperance when he returned to Nantucket, because for one who had run for public office on the Prohibition ticket, summering at Ocean Grove certainly attested to the sincerity of his temperance ideals.

Ocean Grove is the most unique of New Jersey's shore resort areas. It was ten years old when A.H. and his family first visited there. The beach-front community is immediately south of Asbury Park. It was developed under the aegis of the Methodist Church, and is still controlled today by the Methodists' Ocean Grove Camp Meeting Association. Methodism at its strictest was practiced there in A.H.'s day, and it is still pretty much the same now. Generally, automobiles are banned, all traffic limited to pedestrians; the general rule was and is plenty of sun and ocean, plenty of hymn-singing and good fellowship, and plenty of preaching and revival shouting. With A.H.'s visit to Ocean Grove, his religious involvements can be traced from his Presbyterian youth to his association with the Episcopalians as a married man, and now he was hobnobbing with the Methodists while his daughter attended a convent school. But whatever his religious convictions, A.H. and his family found the environment and the other visitors at Ocean Grove very much to their liking, and returned year after year to this spot on the New Jersey shore.

In the fall, at a subtle, hardly detectable pace, the Second National Bank marched inexorably towards bankruptcy. To counteract—for now A.H. realized that Uncle Isaac, as the other owner of the largest number of shares of bank stock, was going to be caught in the tortuous turns as the Wintons were brought to financial ruin—to counteract this, on the first of November he had judgment entered against Isaac Dean for $54,310 and against W.W. for $5,849, both by Thomas Livey, this time representing Isaac's wife's estate—Polly Heermans Dean, Catherine's sister—and his family. Both of these were confessed judgments; the debtor openly admitted the debts to exist and for the amounts stated.

December 3, 1879 was the day the judgments had to be satisfied; that is, the defendants had to settle their debts. If they could not, the sheriff would seize their property and sell it at sheriff's sale, turning the proceeds over to the judgment holders—in this case, Catherine Winton and Polly Dean's estate, etc. Word leaked out about the judgments held by Catherine and Polly's estate; they had had to be recorded to be valid, and at the end of November, an attempt was made to serve W.W. with arrest papers. Very fortunately, at this time he and Catherine were visiting Mrs. Asa Hollister at Hollisterville in adjoining Wayne County.

On December 3, W.W. and Isaac Dean admitted that they could not produce the money to satisfy their creditors, Catherine Winton and Polly Dean's estate, represented by Thomas Livey. A.H., as Thomas Livey's attorney, moved to have the property of the debtors sold and visited the sheriff's office to arrange for a sheriff's sale.

Sheriff's sales were held yearly in February, but it was the custom among the lawyers and in the courts of the valley that when a debtor needed money to satisfy claims against him, his lawyer could request an early sheriff's sale instead of being forced to wait as much as a year for the next stated sale. This procedure was accepted as legal by everyone, provided the sheriff's sale was well advertised. With this in mind, A.H. prepared a list of all the pieces to be sold by both W.W. and Isaac Dean to satisfy their debts to the holders of the confessed judgment notes. A.H. saw that the lists were published in the newspapers, including a translation that appeared in a German-language valley newspaper.

At this, it was apparent that A.H. and his family were about to slip through the trap so carefully prepared for them. Before the properties could be sold to Catherine Winton and Polly Dean's estate—that is, before the wives would instead take delivery of the titles on all the properties and consider their judgment notes satisfied—Receiver Goodale, with lawyers Francis Silkman and William Kennedy, charged the four, W.W., A.H., Isaac Dean, and Thomas Livey, with conspiracy to defraud the Second National Bank, and had them arrested.

The four were brought before Alderman Fuller and posted bail in the amount of $10,000. At the hearing on December 15 to determine if there was enough evidence to bind them over for trial, it was felt that there was, and so the charge was held to be prima facie that the four had indeed conspired to defraud the Second National Bank. The charge was supported by such evidence as the mortgage note W.W. had made in order to borrow money to clear the debts of the Second National Bank, under Bank Examiner Drew's direction. Those pressing charges against the Wintons cited the mortgage, which they voluntarily brought forth, as proof of the Wintons' intent to defraud.

They claimed that they had heard, but had not bothered to get an appraisal, that the lands listed on the mortgage were condemned and worthless. On testimony such as this, hearsay of the worst kind, W.W., A.H., Isaac Dean and Thomas Livey were felt to be guilty of conspiring to defraud and so were ordered held for trial. At the same time, the sheriff attached the part of W.W.'s property that was in the hands of the D & H, the D L & W and in the First National Bank, although how he knew it was there and belonged to W.W. remained a mystery.

On December 19, four days after the hearing, another discordant note was injected—this time from an outside source. The editor of a local Providence newspaper called the *Echo* described the activities of the Wintons in an article in his paper: "Their work was the same as that of the lowest thief, and they should suffer just as much." To this, A.H. took exception, and prepared to silence Mr. U.L. Hopewell, the editor of the newspaper and the author of the article.

For all of Receiver Goodale's activities and collaboration with others, he and his friends were able to do nothing to stop the sheriff's judgment sales on December 27, as advertised. It would appear that A.H.'s maneuver had been successful, after all.

But the opposition was not giving up; in January of 1880, they got an injunction from Judge Handley, who had at last come over to the Lackawanna Courts from the Luzerne County courthouse, which stayed the sheriff's sale of the properties to satisfy the judgments. This again brought things to a standstill.

With things locked in a standstill, and hoping to break Kennedy and Silkman's injunction stopping the sheriff's sale of the property, A.H. decided to press for the advantage. Instead of defending against attack, he would do the attacking. On February 13, 1880, two weeks after the injunction staying the sale of the property to Catherine and Isaac Dean's family, he had Thomas Livey sue Kennedy, charging perjury committed on the instruction of his attorney, Francis Silkman. The charge was that Kennedy had lied when he had claimed that W.W., A.H., Isaac Dean, and Thomas Livey had maliciously conspired to cheat and defraud the Second National Bank by means of confessed judgments and sheriff's sales. When the case came before the courts, Kennedy's attorney asked for a continuance—so everybody was again held at a standoff.

Next, it was Receiver Goodale's turn to try to break the tied knot. A week after Thomas Livey charged Kennedy, Goodale charged W.W. with embezzling funds from the Second National Bank; he claimed that W.W. had taken coal royalties for his own use which had been due the Second National Bank.

In return, A.H. sent W.W. into court to sue U.L. Hopewell for libel, citing the article in the *Echo* in which Hopewell had called the Wintons the "lowest of thieves."

There were now seven cases going through the Lackawanna and other courts: (a) Receiver Goodale claiming that W.W. was an embezzler; (b) Thomas Livey asking confirmation of the Sheriff's sales to satisfy the confessed judgments; (c) Goodale, Kennedy, and Silkman claiming that W.W., A.H., Isaac Dean, and Thomas Livey had conspired to defraud; (d) W.W. suing the *Echo* editor for libel; (e) Thomas Livey suing Kennedy for perjury; (f) Goodale and associates' injunction to stop satisfaction on the judgment notes; and (g) an appeal to have the injunction stopping the sheriff's sales removed. Every time one of these cases came up for consideration in the courts, it was either continued to another date, or the presiding judge received all the papers in the case and announced that he was reserving decision. Essentially, things were at a standstill again. Meanwhile, every time one or the other of the participants went into court, it was duly recorded in the newspapers, not as news but as entertainment; with all the Winton in-laws and all the charges before the courts, Scranton had never seen the likes of such legal activity. Somewhere along the line, Filer & Livey announced that a new breaker was to be built at Winton and that the coal would be shipped by the D & H. And Aaron Chase and W.W. Scranton were appealing and reappealing their fight through the courts, too, frequently getting hung juries. Often one of W.W.'s cases and the Chase-Scranton affair would be scheduled for the same day on the court calender, and at one time W.W. was on jury duty for the Scranton-Chase case when one of his own cases was being called.

In all, everyone was having a lively time.

Before any of the court cases had been determined or concluded, Julia Collings came up from Wilkes-Barre and asked her sister Alice Winton whether she and Lt. Steever, the math instructor at West Point, could be married in the Wintons' home. The couple had great sentimental regard for Alice and A.H., and for the house on Wyoming Avenue. It had been the scene of their first meeting after the August 1 riot and of their first declaration of love, at the time of the Wintons' Christmas Masquerade Ball. All the family, including the bride's mother Elizabeth Beaumont Collings, gathered on September 15 for the wedding on Wyoming Avenue, and wished the couple a happy journey as they saw them off on their journey to Ft. Saunders in the Wyoming Territory.

The wedding attracted a good deal of attention as a social event, and afterwards A.H. began to worry about the house which he and Alice had as their home. It was conceivable that, in the tangled legal situation that existed, they could lose it. On October 16—a month later—the house was sold at sheriff's sale, for unpaid taxes. The sale was well advertised; it was one of a dozen to take place throughout the city. John Collings bought the Winton property for a little over $6,000. A.H. heaved a sigh of relief; a home for Alice and his chicks was now out of the reach of the predators.

The posting of the house as a sheriff's sale property unfortunately had an effect that A.H. and Alice never anticipated. Katie, now a bright girl of nine, was just old enough to understand such things, but not everything. She had been aware that things were not as they once had been for her father and grandfather. The pride which she had felt, when she had marched beside A.H. through Providence at the time of the Fourth of July celebration in 1877, was deliberately being forced into the background. Of late, the once shining memory had become tarnished.

Kate, still a child, had the child's sensitivity to adults, and she sensed, rather than heard or was told, that for some reason her father and grandfather were something to be ashamed of. What she was picking up was the reaction of the Wintons' neighbors and her schoolmates, as the story of the Second National Bank closing and the various court cases were paraded across the pages of the Scranton newspapers.

When Kate overheard talk about the sheriff's sale of the very house she lived in and called home, she took fright, magnifying the unknown in her imagination. If Kate had only spoken to her parents and told them her fears, she could have so easily been given peace and assurance. Unfortunately, she did not; instead, she threw her father down from his treasured idol's pedestal. Ever afterward, even when married and a mother, the feeling, that her father had done something terrible and had disgraced the family, stayed with her, preventing her from remembering with pride, or remembering at all, the many things he had been and done. The one who should have loved him the most, for the hero he was, was ashamed of the nearness of her relationship to him, even long after his death.

John Runk, A.H.'s law student, was admitted to the bar shortly after A.H. had made possession of his home secure. Then the festivities ceased, and it was back to the tangled web of the Winton finances and court cases. George Goodale, as receiver, ordered the sale of the Second National Bank building on November 5, 1880. It was a sad day for W.W.; he had been so proud of his bank. But there was hope, because A.H. and W.W. realized that they were the objects of a robber-baron raid, typical of the last quarter of the nineteenth century; as moneyed men they tried to have alternatives left open to them. To have Edward Fuller, the husband of Helen Silkman, buy the bank building gave W.W. and A.H. the possibility that, perhaps someday, they would be able to effect the return of the bank building. Edward Fuller was Byron Winton's brother-in-law.

The first break in the standoff of charges and countercharges came on December 15. Goodale's charge—that W.W. had embezzled bank funds—was finally called before the United States Commissioner at Wilkes-Barre. Judge Garrick Harding removed his judge's robe and went before the commissioner as W.W.'s defense counsel: a high tribute to the Wintons by the area's most respected judge. At the conclusion of the testimony, the commissioner said: "I have listened very carefully and attentively to all the testimony in this case and to the argument of counsel on both sides, and am satisfied there is nothing in the testimony to warrant me in holding to bail. Mr. Winton is therefore discharged."

In the first instance that one of the cases against W.W. was brought to a conclusion, W.W. was pronounced blameless.

A.H. and W.W. returned to Scranton jubilant. At the moment of the confrontation, the Wintons had carried the day beautifully. A.H. saw that all the newspapers in Scranton carried a report of the commissioner's decision. A wave of sympathy surged around the Wintons, and W.W. was congratulated by all, apologies being heard for the unfair accusations against the man who had done so much for the creation of Lackawanna County. There—it was out at last—the Wintons were tied to the erection of Lackawanna County. During the many hearings and delays, no support had ever been asked for the public-minded men who had given everything for the new county. Now that the predators saw that they were losing, it was all right to acknowledge publicly that the Wintons had indeed been the prime movers in creating the new county.

There were still six other court cases to be resolved, but A.H. had hopes of winning through. Christmas of 1880, then, was brighter than the preceding two. The Christmas mail brought an interesting advertisement. A.H., while studying law, had learned shorthand in the form of phonography; this system was based on sound, using straight and curved lines for consonant sounds, dots and dashes representing vowels. Special pens were manufactured for phonographers. In the Christmas mail, an envelope was addressed personally to Attorney A.H. Winton.

It was an advertisement for the Livermore Stylographic Pen from the manufacturer's agent, Mr. Winthrop, at 169 Broadway, in New York.

A.H. was relaxed enough, after the favorable decision by the U.S. Commissioner, to be in a mood of general good humor and geniality. The pen appealed to him, and he had the time to study the advertisement closely. A glimmer of an idea entered his head, and he lost himself in thought. He couldn't decide what to do. At the family gathering on Christmas Day, A.H. asked his mother whether she had heard from Ella, the wife Walter had deserted. Because of the grandchildren, he knew his mother kept in touch with her daughter-in-law. Catherine told A.H. that Ella was living in New York City, with her cousin's family on Broadway. Hearing the address, A.H. decided to let nature take its course.

The first four months of the new year, 1881, saw the new county complain about the super-solvency of the Providence Poor Board and point out why it was so rich: by collecting taxes for welfare and then shipping all eligible welfare recipients to other boroughs and townships, so that it had no one to spend its tax money on. In a wink, a petition was filed, and the Providence Poor Board, that in 1862 had started A.H. in his interest in area government, was no more; county-managed welfare homes were established in its place.

The first four months of the new year saw the first step taken toward A.H.'s other greatest desire, after creation of Lackawanna County, the only one yet to be fulfilled; on March 20, bids from contractors interested in building Lackawanna County's permanent courthouse were opened. After some deliberation, the construction work was awarded to John Snaith of Ithaca, New York. He had submitted three estimates: for $138,000 plus, he would build the design of I.G. Perry, the architect from Binghamton, New York, out of Ohio stone; if the courthouse was to be of Syracuse limestone (West Mountain stone), the cost would be a little over $139,000; and it would be more than $141,000 for Vermont marble. This beautiful building, sitting in its lovely, quiet repose, in a park of shaded trees like no other courthouse, was chosen to be of limestone, from the west mountain wall of the valley. Excavation was begun immediately on the courthouse, designed to give the feeling that it embraced the citizens it served as a protective home, where love for the law promised justice and fairness to all who had to enter. The men behind Lackawanna County had not wanted to erect a mausoleum to justice, cold and intimidating, whose architecture struck fear with each approaching step. In Scranton, this courthouse was to be the address of the area's most prominent resident—Lackawanna County. And so excavation was begun immediately, because the county was now almost three years old. There had been a reason for the delay in erecting a permanent building, however; a law required that a grand jury sit for two consecutive, full sessions before it could be claimed that there was a need for a courthouse building.

There had been very little debate over where to place the courthouse in Scranton. Lackawanna Avenue was not considered desirable because it was surrounded by trains and railway depots on three sides; train whistles and the puffing of engines were never ceasing sounds. A square city block, bounded by Spruce, Adams, and Linden Streets, and the famous Washington Avenue, was open ground, far removed from the noise of the trains. The Lackawanna Iron and Coal Company and the Susquehanna and Wyoming Valley Rail and Coal Company were its owners, and, in the kindliest of spirit, presented the city block to the county.

The first four months of the new year, 1881, at the end of March to be precise, also saw A.H. and his cousin Arthur Dean in Philadelphia at the Federal District Court, for their appeal asking that the injunction stopping the sheriff's sales be set aside. Instead of ruling on the injunction, the court dismissed the appeal on technicalities. The significance of the dismissal was that it gave some indication of how the district court regarded the whole question.

The inference by the District Supreme Court being that the fuss over the sheriff's sale was a local, county matter, it would not rule on the injunction at all because it was ridiculous in the first place. Then on April 15, all those properties belonging to Isaac Dean which had been sold at sheriff's sale were assigned to Thomas Livey, as trustee for Polly Heermans Dean and children. For Uncle Isaac, it had been a long battle, but A.H. had indeed been able to protect his personal property from being legally stolen away. However for W.W., no such concessions were to be made yet. The battle had always been between W.W. and A.H. and those who feared that they would have too much power; Isaac Dean had been caught up in the web almost accidentally, as an innocent bystander.

In June, the New York, Susquehanna, and Western Railroad, a new railway formed out of the consolidation of many bits and pieces of track, decided to extend its line from Stroudsburg into Scranton, for the purpose of carrying coal. John Jermyn was the line's general manager, and under him various coal lands were bought up. Seven hundred acres at Winton were leased, and plans for a new breaker were made.

A.H. had been right when he had decided to let nature take its course; stylographic pen agent Mr. Winthrop of #169 Broadway was indeed the long-missing Walter Winton. Ella, living almost across the street from him, finally caught a glimpse of her long-erring husband, and in August—on August 20, to be exact—had him arrested for abandonment. The Wintons were notified, and Thomas Livey was dispatched to New York to watch over Walter. In Walter's seven years of wandering, he had gone from Detroit to Illyria, Ohio, to Wisconsin, and from Wisconsin over into Canada. The detectives, always arriving just as Walter was leaving, lost him completely in Toronto. But now, after seven years and a divorce he said he had gotten in Wisconsin, Walter was found—or perhaps it would be more accurate to say that Walter had surfaced.

Stephen Tunstall arrived in New York and pressed suit for reimbursement of monetary support which he had given to the abandoned wife; after that he was no longer interested. All parties concerned preferred the role of ex-son-in-law—with emphasis on the "ex"—for Walter.

September 21 was another important day in the Wintons' journal of events. On September 21, enough bonds and notes having been sold, the first payment of twenty-five percent of the total debt was paid to the creditors of the Second National Bank. Goodale, knowing that the scales were tipping in favor of W.W. and A.H., was suddenly bragging about his financial wisdom in waiting to dispose of the securities until they had risen to a point where a more favorable return was realized. He expansively proclaimed that it could be as much as four years longer before all the bank's assets would be liquidated, that way assuring their sale at the best prices possible.

The end of A.H.'s public life was approaching; as the new county became more and better established, the professional politicians began to forget their fears of the Wintons. They had found that they were not faring too well when they came up against A.H. in a direct challenge; if he would be no problem to them, they would create no more for him. Alice's uncle John Colt Beaumont, who had been called back to active duty in the Navy, was now the commandant of the Portsmouth, New Hampshire, Naval Base. In November he was named admiral, and A.H. took pleasure in speaking of his wife's uncle "the Admiral" around Scranton. The Wintons were all reconciled to the loss of their banks. Receiver Goodate was left alone; he seemed to be showing some sense in liquidating the assets of the bank.

The Second National Bank building came back from Edward Fuller, to be under Receiver Goodale's control, and was sold again, this time to a group: John and Frank Jermyn, S. Nash, J. Gunster, Victor Koch, and Edward Merrifield. Alworth House on Franklin Street, which W.W. and the bank owned, was also sold, and another twenty-five percent payment was made to the creditors of the bank. Fifty percent of all money owed had now been settled.

21

A.H. now looked forward to one thing: the Lackawanna County Courthouse. It was but a block away from his home, and every day he unofficially inspected the building and the progress the contractor was making. Because of it, he and his father almost lay in ruin. But when the sun shone down on the mud hole dug for the foundation, he forgot what was and thought only about what would be.

He was looking forward to the cornerstone-laying ceremony. The procedure would be similar to that for the Armory cornerstone, followed in the evening by a celebration banquet. Based on the rate at which the building was progressing, the contractor had named Thursday, May 25, 1882, as the day when the building could be ready to receive its cornerstone. As had been true of the armory, it would be the Masons who would ceremoniously perform the ritual of placing the first stone for the new building.

When Thursday arrived, the weather was cold and rainy, although the summer month of June was only a few days away. Following their usual custom on foul weather days, the Scranton City Guard decided not to march. But the Masons arrived at the courthouse grounds, flanked by the Knights Templar in their eye-catching uniforms and plumed hats. In spite of the cold and drizzle, the square was filled with spectators who had come to watch a large crane hoist over two tons of marble block into place, for the Masons to declare plumb, level, and true. Hermetically sealed, in a copper box in the center of the stone, were: a copy of the Holy Bible; a copy of the Revised New Testament; a list of all churches in Scranton with the names of their pastors for 1882; an 1882 U.S. silver coin; a copy of every newspaper published in the county; a copy of the specifications of the courthouse; an engraving of the D & H's first locomotive in the United States, the "Stourbridge Lion"; a history of Scranton; a history of the erection of Lackawanna County, written by Edward Merrifield; an album of photographs of the County Judges, the County Officers, members of the Bar, the Architect, and the Builder; photographs of items manufactured by the Dickson Manufacturing Company; a history of the Delaware, Lackawanna and Western Railroad; a copy of the May 22, 1879, *New York Graphic*; a Scranton City Directory for 1881; a history of the Scranton Board of Trade; an American Almanac; the roster of the Thirteenth Regiment-Scranton City Guard; a May 1882 copy of the Pennsylvania School Register; and an autographed copy of the Program of the Ceremonies.

Lackawanna County Courthouse, seen from Adams Avenue, nears completion, 1882.
—courtesy The Lackawanna Historical Society

In the evening, over a hundred guests sat down to a banquet at the Wyoming House. It was a joint celebration: the creation of Lackawanna County and the laying of the Courthouse cornerstone. Bauer's Band provided the music, and afterwards, when the cloth was removed, A.H., as toastmaster for the evening's program, rose. Temperance man and Blue Ribbon wearer that he was, he took his champagne glass in hand. Bright lights shining from his eyes, he raised his glass:

"Lackawanna County!"

It was the simplest of toasts, but it said all that need be said. A.H. spoke in dignity and reverence, but also with passion. With two words, he had described his life.

The men around A.H. drank with equal solemnity, to match the tone set by their master of ceremonies. For this one evening, at least, all would acknowledge and yield to A.H.; the hero had been allowed to return.

A.H. first called on Edward Merrifield, who more or less repeated verbally the history of Lackawanna County which he had written for inclusion in the cornerstone. George Sanderson, Dr. Throop, Judges Stanley Woodward and Rice from Wilkes-Barre, Judge Jessup from Montrose County, ex-Mayor McKune, and Col. Boies, all spoke in rapid succession. A.B. Dunning—A.H.'s Uncle Abram—responded when A.H. proposed the toast, "Our constitution—the stepping stone to our new county"; and to "Old Counties—Farewell," John Beaumont Collings rose to speak briefly. Frank Collins was there, too, and had his moment in the spotlight when A.H. called for "The Judiciary." Of the Winton confraternity present, W.W. was the only one not asked to respond to a toast.

44 *Lackawanna County Memorial.*

At a subsequent meeting the following persons were chosen to act on the several committees:

COMMITTEE OF ARRANGEMENTS.

R. H. McKUNE, J. H. CAMPBELL, R. W. ARCHBALD, W. T. SMITH, GEORGE FISHER.

COMMITTEE ON ORGANIZATION.

DR. B. H. THROOP, E. N. WILLARD, H. A. KNAPP.

COMMITTEE ON TOASTS.

F. W. GUNSTER, DR. B. H. THROOP, A. H. WINTON, F. D. COLLINS, U. G. SCHOONMAKER.

COMMITTEE ON INVITATIONS.

LEWIS PUGHE, H. M. EDWARDS, J. F. CONNOLLY, T. V. POWDERLY, C. SMITH.

COMMITTEE ON RECEPTION.

H. S. PIERCE, W. W. WINTON, D. W. CONNOLLY, E. B. STURGES, J. B. COLLINGS.

COMMITTEE ON TICKETS.

E. C. FULLER, THOMAS BARROWMAN, G. S. HORN, J. ALTON DAVIS, VICTOR KOCH, THOMAS F. WELLS, JOHN F. SCRAGG.

The following invitation was issued to persons residing out of the city:

You are respectfully invited to a
Grand Banquet,
given under the auspices of the
Scranton Bar Association, and Citizens,
in honor of the erection of the County of Lackawanna, and the Laying of the Corner-Stone of the New Court-House,
to be held on the evening of May 25th,
at the Wyoming House.

Scranton, Pa., May 18, 1882.

Near the end, to A.H.'s toast "Our manufacturing interests—by industry we thrive," W.W. Scranton rose and struck a somber note. Prophetically, he said that he could not agree with the views of those who felt that Scranton would continue to grow forever. He insisted that the city would have to depend on something other than mining if it was to continue to progress, and progress would best be served by lower taxes and good government.

The Banquet. 45

The following is the programme of toasts:

President of the Evening, ... Dr. B. H. Throop.
Toast-Master, ... A. H. Winton.

1. LACKAWANNA COUNTY. - - - - - - - - - Labor omnia vincit
Edward Merrifield, Esq.
2. OUR INVITED FRIENDS AND GUESTS. - - - We welcome them
Hon. G. M. Harding.
3. OUR COUNTRY. - - - - - - - - - One and indivisible
Hon. J. A. Scranton.
4. OUR COMMONWEALTH. - - - - - The Keystone of the arch
His Excellency Henry M. Hoyt.
5. THE PULPIT. - - - - - - - - - - The light of the world
Rev. Dr. J. E. Smith.
6. OUR MILITARY. - The pride of our State—May we never need their prowess
Col. H. M. Boies.
7. THE JUDICIARY. - - - - - - - - - The purer the better
Hon. F. D. Collins.
8. THE SENIOR BAR. - - - - - - - - Old men for counsel
Hon. George Sanderson.
9. THE JUNIOR BAR. - - - - - - - - - - Lis sub judice
John F. Connolly, Esq.
10. OUR CONSTITUTION. - - - - The stepping-stone to our new county
Hon. A. B. Dunning.
11. OUR MANUFACTURING INTERESTS. - - - By industry we thrive
W. W. Scranton.
12. THE PRESS. - - - - - - - - - The lever that moves the world
Hon. J. E. Barrett.
13. OUR CITY. - - - - - - - - - The third in the Commonwealth
E. P. Kingsbury.
14. OUR COMMERCIAL INTERESTS. - - - - Made prosperous by energy
Thomas H. Dale.
15. OUR FIRE-DEPARTMENT. - - - - - - - Nunquam non paratus
Hon. Robert H. McKune.
16. OLD COUNTIES, FAREWELL. - - - - - - The transplanted oak
John Beaumont Collings.
17. OUR ABSENT FRIENDS. - - - - - Though absent, to memory dear
Col. J. A. Price.
18. THE LADIES. - - - - - - - - - - Omnia vincit amor
F. J. Fitzsimmons.

Former Mayor Robert H. McKune ordered a transcript be made of the festivities associated with the laying of the courthouse cornerstone, which he then had made into a book, "...and thus, on the 25th day of May, 1882, in the city of Scranton, were things done and words uttered that gave to me an excuse for compiling and publishing this work." McKune explained, "The only apology I have for offering this compilation to the public is that the events and incidents that are here narrated I believe are worthy to be gathered together; so that those who shall come after us may have some appreciation of how joyous we were when...it was our fortune to see our fondest wishes realized, and we were made happy, on the evening of August 13th, 1878."

It was well after midnight when A.H. bid goodnight to W.W. and the others at the celebration, and returned home. The worries and fears he had had in past years, that he would fail in his struggles, had fallen from him now as if they had never existed. He took with him a half-empty bottle of the Moet from the banquet. Reaching home, he stopped off in the pantry, picking up two glasses before going upstairs. Alice was waiting for him; she relaxed as soon as A.H. entered the room and she saw the beatific expression on his face. He came over to her, and kissed her by way of greeting.

A.H. prepared for bed, but stopped to light a small fire in the bedroom fireplace to warm the room from the cold rain outside. He drew the lounge chair before the fire and, seating himself in it, invited Alice to join him.

He poured the bubbling wine into the glasses and handed one to Alice.

"For the one last toast while I am still toastmaster. No one gave this tonight, and it is the most important.

"To you, my dear. Because of you, I have everything, I am everything."

Their glasses tinkled slightly, and then they sipped in silence.

Intermittently, A.H. talked, rambling from describing something at the banquet to voicing a thought which he had held within himself over the years when the battle had been the hardest.

A.H. kissed Alice—a kiss without passion; instead, it was a kiss of love, of the deepest and strongest love that a man could ever experience for anyone or anything. They were a beautiful couple. They had survived the most chilling fear of all: uncertainty. Hammered by experiences, their marriage bond was now so tempered that their nearness alone could weld them together, making them one; companionably, they sat for some time, caressed by an aura of love that had seen every desire fulfilled.

22

Life did not end at the banquet. Just as one does not stop breathing after the grand ball is over, there were still many days and nights of living for A.H., Alice, and all the Wintons. Arthur Dean was the first to fill the days with activity; he brought all the giant Heermans clan together for his wedding to Nettie Sisson of La Plume, a small town northwest of Scranton but still in the valley. Next, W.W. was again to fill the days with activity.

Throughout all the fussing and charges and countercharges, W.W. had remained a director of the People's Street Railway Company, a position he had held for many years. At his suggestion, the Bell Punch System had been installed on all the streetcars; this system involved a fare box which accepted exact change only as payment for a ride. An auxiliary box was also installed, its purpose being to make change if a passenger did not have the exact amount.

One warm Thursday in June, shortly after the memorable banquet celebrating Lackawanna's new Courthouse, a recent immigrant to Scranton from Germany had occasion to ride the streetcar over to Providence. He was unfamiliar with the exact change system, and, when the bell rang repeatedly, looked confused and wonderingly at the rest of the passengers. Finally, one rider took it upon himself to help the man out, and pointed to the automatic pay arrangement, at which point it developed that the German fellow had no change. The change box was next pointed to, which he obligingly used; everybody then settled back, assuming the situation was now under control.

But the fellow soon showed that his ability to comprehend had been overestimated, for on receiving his change from the auxiliary change-making box in an envelope, he proceeded to stuff and squeeze the envelope with its contents into the Bell Punch Box. It was now the driver's turn to try and get things back into order; slowing the horse, he turned his head and worked with the German until the fare was finally paid in the proper manner. Going back to take up the slack on the horse's reins, for lost time had to be made up to keep on schedule, the driver found that he no longer had any reins to take up.

Somehow, the horse had come unhitched, and could be seen hurrying back to the car barn. Left on a downgrade, the streetcar kept on rolling, and driver and passengers now found themselves in the predicament of being at the bottom of the hill to Providence with no way of getting up it. Everything came to a halt; the driver then ran off in pursuit of the horse, while in the summer heat the poor passengers huffed and puffed themselves up to Providence on foot. Thereafter, several letters were sent to W.W., suggesting what he should do with his Bell Punch suggestion.

The time was now the end of October, 1882, and the Second National Bank had paid the third twenty-five percent segment of the debt to its creditors. While computing the amounts due at the end of the summer, Receiver Goodale had fallen ill and died. Officially, the situation at the bank then came to a standstill, because the suits brought against W.W. had been entered in George Goodale's name and not in the name of a corporate or municipal body. For a while, it looked as if there might be a temporary halt to the raid on the Winton wealth. A.H. hoped that if he and his family were quiet, things might in time possibly pass into oblivion and they would have peace at last. But life is never peaceful, life is never sure; while W.W., in Goodale's absence, handled the administration of the third payment, he suddenly found himself in worse trouble than any he had yet been in—courtesy of A.B. Dunning, his brother-in-law and former partner in the days when he had had a general store.

Some years before 1882, Abram Dunning had borrowed money from a New York insurance company; W.W. had cosigned the note, guaranteeing the loan. The situation was very similar to that of Lewis Watres and his uncle in Philadelphia in the 1860s. Pressing for payment in the last months of '82, the insurance company finally seized some of A.B. Dunning's property as compensation. That should have been the end of it; but instead, the insurance company then went after W.W., demanding $140,000 from him—the amount he had backed for his brother-in-law.

As soon as the insurance company made its first overture to W.W., suggesting that he pay the money as promised on the note, A.H. grew very apprehensive. For some reason, A.H. had an unreasonable fear that things would go badly, this time. He hurried first to put his father in a protected position—always his first move. To accomplish this, he instructed his father not to pay the taxes due on 1,200 acres of coal land; thus on October 18, the acreage went to Lackawanna County for back taxes. By the county having first claim to the ground through the taxes, A.H. had safeguarded the land against any outsider also laying claim. He was not worried about losing the 1,200 acres permanently, because of the law allowing return of real property to the owner, provided the back taxes were paid within a stated number of months.

As it turned out, A.H.'s fears were realized; the insurance company carried their claim against W.W. into the U.S. District Court at Pittsburgh. W.W. cited the sheriff's sale to Catherine Winton, and also insisted that the insurance cornpany's claim had been satisfied when it had taken possession of A.B. Dunning's property, but to no avail. The court decided against W.W., also refusing to recognize Catherine's ownership; it ordered W.W. to sell his property to pay the insurance company. The sale was listed for the first of January, 1883.

A.H. had been wise, as subsequent events showed, to put the most valuable segment of W.W.'s property out of the reach of the insurance company. However, he was hesitant to let any of it go, and worked literally to the last minute to save everything. Just half an hour before the sale was scheduled to start—at 12 noon on January 1—he was finally able to convince the court that there was justifiable reason for delay, and thereby was able to postpone the sale for several months.

Immediately afterwards, on January 4, the claim of the insurance company faded into second place with A.H. Results of Frank Collins' labors in Congress, back in May of '78, were finally being made known. A formal invitation was sent out for that day, calling all members of the Lackawanna County Bar to a special meeting at the courthouse, to discuss and make plans for the arrival of a U.S. District Court. With its coming, the judiciary system of this country would have full representation at Lackawanna County's Court House.

But the road to establishing a U.S. court at Scranton was almost as long and tortuous as the one for Lackawanna County. It took from 1883 to 1886, three years, just to have Scranton designated as another stop on the U.S. District Court circuit in the Western District. It wasn't until 1901 that Pennsylvania was finally redistricted; at this time, the state was redivided into three areas: the Eastern District, still centered at Philadelphia; the Western District, still at Pittsburgh; but thirty-two counties in between were established as the Middle District, and Scranton was named as its headquarters.

W.W. was now sixty-eight years old. He was rich, still very, very rich; but the fire and the drive were no longer there as they once had been. George Filer had always been the one to carry the work at Winton, but he was no longer taking an active part. Without him, things were not the same. In February, W.W. sold part of his holdings at Winton to some of his Scranton neighbors. These men, backed by Buffalo, New York, financiers, had formed the Grassey Island Coal Company, a name taken from the first tract of land that Maurice Wurts had acquired when, before starting the D & H Canal Company, he had opened the first coal mine at the northern end of the valley. On the day the new company took possession, the boiler, which produced the steam necessary to operate the hoisting engine of the model breaker, went dry and exploded, sending fragments of the breaker over half a mile around Winton. Today, the twisted iron and timbers of the wrecked breaker rise in shaggy juttings into the sky, as they first did on that day in 1883 when the boiler burst.

Later, Byron, with more enthusiasm—he was nine years younger than A.H.—went out to Winton and worked with John Jermyn, as the New York, Susquehanna, and Western R.R. Company drove another heading on the portion of the coal land it was leasing at Winton. This vein turned out to be as fine as any that had preceded it, running approximately seven by ten feet thick.

And in this fashion was A.H., for his family, able to bring to conclusion the final attempts to totally destroy the Wintons financially and by humiliating them, drive them from public life.

Many of those who worked with A.H. and helped him in his devotion to Scranton had a share of the spotlight for themselves. Mont Flanigan, who had been so crucial to A.H.'s success, went on to a success of his own: he was elected Mayor of Wilkes-Barre to fill out a deceased mayor's unexpired term, and was very popular and well liked in the office.

Terence Powderly served three different terms as mayor of Scranton, although he was forced to skip an election one November because somebody suddenly claimed that he was ineligible to run, since he had not paid his taxes for three years. But Scranton was only a beginning for Terence Powderly; he became the head of the first labor union in the United States that was national in its scope—the Knights of Labor. It grew to a membership of 700,000 in 1886—although it was eventually to lose out to the A.F. of L.

Many times, as Powderly led his fellow workers, he was accused of not being violent enough, of dressing too much like a gentleman, and of having too much the idealism of the 1840s and not the aggressive realism of the 1880s; but Terence Powderly had been forever scarred. He had seen how things could be, and the memory of erecting Lackawanna County would never leave him. By 1894, he had studied enough law, and that year was admitted to the Lackawanna County Bar—a silent salute to the quality and kind of men he had joined to work with as Mayor-elect Powderly, even though they were supposedly the antithesis and oppressors of everything relating to labor.

A.H. was satisfied to live out his role as one of Scranton's attorneys. He spent more and more time with his family, and when his two daughters got older, he took great delight in escorting the ladies of his life about town. It was not unusual to see him at the theatre on three successive evenings. He and Kate saw a stage version of *Around the World in Eighty Days* at the Academy of Music, where he had spoken so well that memorable Memorial Day before W.W. closed the Second National Bank. When A.H. visited the Academy of Music the next evening, it was with Alice, to see Mrs. Scott-Siddons in *As You Like It.* However, it was Lawyer Winton who arrived at the train station another evening to delay actress Fanny Davenport and her troupe until unpaid accounts had been settled.

In 1884, the beautiful new courthouse that A.H. had waited so long to have in Scranton was ready at last, and from then on he had the pleasure and honor of attending court there. And that was what fulfillment of his dream was to him: a pleasure and an honor. Afterwards, he became court stenographer and maintained his only office at the courthouse; that is, he did very little private law practice.

A.H. lived to see Kate, in 1892, marry Canadian-born Gilbert Donald Murray, who had gone to Philadelphia to study medicine at the University of Pennsylvania and had then answered a call to begin his ophthalmology work at Scranton. And he lived to see his first grandchild, Alice Winton Murray, born in June of 1894.

The year 1894 was also the year W.W. died. Catherine Heermans Winton followed her husband a year later, in 1895. And then the ring was closed; A.H. joined them in February 1896, to leave Alice a widow for almost a quarter century.

After A.H. died, the Lackawanna County Bar drew up a set of resolutions and caused them to be published in all the daily newspapers in Scranton, to remind those in the valley that they had lost a friend, to whom the welfare of Scranton and of the Wyoming Valley had been a ruling passion:

> He was a man of rare intellectual attainments, a close student, a cheery, genial nature that commands deep friendship and effects close ties between man and man.
>
> As a public servant in behalf of poor, Mr. Winton showed goodness of heart; as a political speaker he had few equals, and in his social relationships he stood preeminent as one of the most amiable, genial and hospitable of men.

Elsbeth, or Elsie as her father had called her, did not marry for many years; she and her mother, the widowed Alice, and her uncle John Collings left Scranton shortly after A.H.'s death. The beautiful speaking timbre of A.H.'s voice had passed into Elsie as a love for music, and what was left of A.H.'s family at Wyoming and Mulberry Avenues spent several years traveling throughout Europe while Elsie studied for a musical career and performed as a violinist.

In 1898, to Alice's uncle, Lt. Col. Eugene Beauharnais Beaumont, went the honor of being awarded the Congressional Medal of Honor, Beaumont receiving it for his bravery at Harper's Ferry, Virginia and at Selma, Alabama, during the Civil War.

As time passed without A.H., the summers at the New Jersey shore were moved a few miles south to another beach-front community: Spring Lake, New Jersey. Here, Kate, her doctor-husband, and their family bought a summer home. Later, after Elsbeth had married William McKeever, whose family had lived in Philadelphia since the 17th century, they too came to Spring Lake and bought a summer home.

For all his wanderings, Walter Winton was a Scranton boy at heart. He returned and, of all things, amazed everyone by opening a wholesale diamond and jewelry store. The years while detectives had lost him in Canada, he had passed in a voyage to South Africa, and at Cape Town had visited the Kimberly Diamond Mine. He put his newly acquired knowledge to work and brought into Scranton, to the benefit of his customers, some of the most beautiful and unusual diamonds known in the world.

But Walter was Walter, who had always resented standing in his brother's shadow. After A.H. had passed away, Walter lost no time in describing himself as W.W.'s son, in such a fashion as to imply that he was the eldest, the only son, the only son who mattered.

On the twenty-first of October in 1922, at the First Presbyterian Church in Scranton, Alice Winton Murray, the grandchild A.H. had lived to see, was married. She married Edgar Wells Freeman, a lawyer from Plainfield, New Jersey. After the wedding reception at her parents Kate and Gilbert's home, next to the church on Madison Avenue, Alice and Edgar left Scranton to spend the first night of their life together at the Plaza Hotel in New York City. Following their honeymoon, Alice would go directly to Washington, D.C., where Edgar would take up his duties as a lawyer with the Federal Reserve Bank System, thus to depart from Scranton forever.

It would seem that this Alice, with Beaumont blood, would be the Alice going to Washington with her lawyer husband.

Books by Aileen Sallom Freeman

A. H. WINTON

ANTHRACITE TRUST

CANADENSIS

THERE'S a FOX in PINCHOT'S FOREST

About the Author

Aileen Sallom Freeman received her B.A. from the University of Pennsylvania, and afterwards studied at The Pennsylvania Academy of the Fine Arts. Her first foray into creative writing was at the age of eleven, when *The Grade Teacher* magazine published her play, *The Star Spangled Banner*. Now a professional artist, the author is married and has a son.